OSKAR
KOKOSCHKA
LETTERS

1905-1976

OSKAR KOKOSCHKA LETTERS

1905-1976

Selected by Olda Kokoschka
and Alfred Marnau
Foreword by E.H. Gombrich

with 33 illustrations

THAMES AND HUDSON

Translated from the German by MARY WHITTALL

Frontispiece: Oskar Kokoschka, *Self-portrait* from the
Bach Cantata 'O Ewigkeit, du Donnerwort' published in
1916, lithograph, 1914.

Abridged and adapted from *Oskar Kokoschka Briefe*,
edited by Olda Kokoschka and Heinz Spielmann,
published by Claassen Verlag, Düsseldorf,
in four volumes:
I. 1905–1919 (1984); II. 1919–1934 (1985);
III. 1934–1953 (1986); IV. 1953–1976 (1988).

First published in the United States in 1992 by
Thames and Hudson Inc., 500 Fifth Avenue,
New York, New York 10110

Library of Congress Catalog Card Number 91–67304

Printed and bound in Yugoslavia

CONTENTS

FOREWORD

by E. H. Gombrich

Those of our contemporaries who like to identify artistic creation with 'self-expression' have rarely been able to avoid the trap of circularity. They fashion the image of the artist out of what they know of his work and interpret the work in terms of their image of the artist's personality. No wonder that they are often disappointed when the documents contradict this imaginary equation.

It so happens that Oskar Kokoschka belonged to the generation of artists who launched this idea. Looking back on his beginnings from a distance of sixty years, he described how he had come to experience 'the drama of being, becoming and ceasing to be'. He continued: 'I became conscious of being actively one with life, which meant, in my case, seeking an artistic expression for my existence. I suppose that's what the term 'Expressionism' means...' (to Heinz Spielmann, 10 March 1968; p. 248). It is clear that for his generation self-expression was a postulate rather than an empirical observation. Indeed, the selection of the artist's letters that is in the reader's hand testifies to his constant striving to make his life and his views conform to his art and his art to his life and his views. His art, in this context, meant not only painting but also his manifold literary activities as a playwright and pamphleteer. Not that Kokoschka was ever inclined to simplify the elusive notion of the 'self'. In a moving confessional letter to Anna Kallin (September 1921; p. 78) we find him pleading: 'Child, accuse me, my transient part, but do not besmirch my works too, which are myself: if you cannot grasp me, my many other selves will give you one thread each. Together they live, and I am all of them.'

This selection from a voluminous correspondence will help the reader to grasp some of these threads. It is true that the artist might have been reluctant to grant the privilege he accorded his lover to the prying eyes of posterity. He violently protested when his faithful biographer Hans Wingler attempted to interpret his œuvre in psychological terms (letter of December 1971; p. 252), and one can sympathize with him; but he surely never wanted to conceal the place his own family occupied in his heart and in his thoughts throughout his life. Though this selection does not include his actual family correspondence, the letters here printed suffice to document one of his most lovable traits, his unswerving loyalty to his parental home. It is true that having passed his twenty-first birthday he burst out that he would either kill his parents or buy his freedom (letter to

Erwin Lang, February/March 1908; p. 17), but naturally he could do neither. His reaction to his father's illness and death, his concern for his mother, the financial sacrifices he made and his incessant worry about his brother Bohuslav and his sister Berta when they were in danger or distress reveal the warmth of his personality. Indeed, if there is one key to his character it is this human warmth, a warmth of which he had such an urgent need and which he found so cruelly lacking in the people and situations he was to encounter outside his home. In another early letter to Erwin Lang (winter 1907–8; p. 16) we find Kokoschka dismissing his acquaintances as 'marionettes', and even his faithful companions and mentors Karl Kraus and Adolf Loos struck him as 'cold' (to Alma Mahler, 3 January 1913; p. 33). Characteristically, he made this charge in one of his passionate love letters to Alma Mahler in which he revealed his longing for 'warmth, the protection of love, motherhood . . .' (p. 34).

Naturally the incomparable series of letters that tell of his passion for that *femme fatale* fill many pages of this volume. In sharing the artist's joys and despairs, the reader may feel that the recipient made a mistake in asking for her own letters back and destroying them, for we can now see this tragedy only through the eyes of the disappointed artist who may indeed have expected and demanded more than she was able to give. Not surprisingly, he vented his anger on the circle of musicians and intellectuals Alma Mahler frequented and whom he accused of having betrayed the spirit. He was undergoing rigorous cavalry training at the time, and wrote 'Technology, science and military training provide all our daily wants . . .' (5 March 1915; p. 64), but strangely his condemnation did not extend to the war as such. Maybe his attachment to his homeland excluded such a sentiment at that time. In any case, he had joined an élite corps of the Imperial Cavalry and was soon wounded in action and invalided out.

To judge by his letters, political events of his time only concerned him when they impinged on our cultural heritage. When, early in March 1920, political clashes in Dresden endangered the city's art gallery, he addressed the population in his capacity as 'Professor at the Academy of Fine Arts', declaring in an open letter that 'in due course the people of Germany will discover more happiness and sense in the contemplation of the pictures, if we save them, than from all the opinions of the politicking Germans of the present day' (p. 75). 'How I hate these politicians, who chase after the masses, and deny all the glory, majesty, magnificence, exaltation and divinity of the human spirit!', he was to write thirty-three years later to J. P. Hodin (10 October 1953; p. 211).

As the years went by, he felt increasingly the need to defend the world of the spirit against the crimes of heartless politicians. When the Nazi menace grew and he was outlawed as a 'degenerate artist', he responded with exemplary dignity and refused to become the pawn of political factions (letters to Kurt von Schuschnigg of 3 August 1937 and to Carl Moll in the summer of 1938). Instead of engaging in a hopeless fight, he meditated on schemes to rid mankind of the nightmare of chauvinism. When he was painting the portrait of Thomas Masaryk in 1935, he tried to win the Czech President over to the idea of a 'federation of elementary schools on a humanitarian basis' (letter to Albert Ehrenstein; p. 140), which he also attempted to propagate through the British Press, hoping against hope to 'breed a new snobbery, a new fashion of philanthropical hue, so that the bourgeoisie, sweating over its share portfolios, might turn its attention to the elementary school as the key social issue, and perhaps forget warmongering . . .' (to Anna Kallin, 11 July 1935; p. 141). He increasingly felt like Cassandra, who saw the disaster approaching without being able to divert it, blaming the impending fall of mankind on 'our hypocritical, bloodthirsty, murderous, white civilization' (to Alma Mahler-Werfel, summer 1937; p. 145). As his hatred of his time increased, so did his nostalgia for an imaginary past. 'In the 15th century human society still had a right to be called both 'human' and 'society', but today these values have been lost . . .' (to Paul Westheim, early 1942; p. 162). Remembering the Wars of the Roses and the suppression of the Hussites in that century, the historian may well feel tempted here to put in a word for our own age which has, after all, eradicated so many of the diseases that haunted the past and which, for all the hideous crimes it has witnessed, has been the first in history to organize official aid when disasters struck anywhere on the globe.

But despite these necessary reservations, we cannot but admire the courage and compassion with which Kokoschka denounced inhumanity during and after the Second World War, castigating the adoption of the racial myth in the propaganda against Germany (to Joseph Lauwerys, 27 June 1943; p. 165) and raising his lonely voice against the barbaric expulsion of whole populations from Bohemia on no other grounds than that their language was German (to Herbert Read, 6 September 1945; p. 171). 'I cannot live in such a world! I feel individually responsible for the crimes of a society of which I am a member.' (to Alfred Neumeyer, 1 March 1946; p. 177). His words sound more prophetic than ever when he blames the 'criminal chauvinism' on the idea of the 'National State' (to Jack Carney, 7 September 1946; p. 182). For him the ultimate cause of all these evils was the alienation of man from his spiritual nature, which he increasingly blamed on science. 'The masses believe the doctrine of man's descent from apes, but they overrate themselves: animals have instincts, but progressive man, modern man has nothing of that kind . . .' (to Henriette von Motesiczky, 2 May 1954; p. 213).

What he saw as a mechanistic world-view that had expelled the soul from the Universe struck him as a betrayal of all the values Europe had inherited from the Graeco-Roman civilization. Two hundred years before, the German poet Friedrich Schiller had given vent to that feeling in his beautiful poem on the *Gods of Greece* in which he laments the replacement of poetic myth by Newtonian science. The sentiment is more familiar to English readers from the writings of William Blake, who saw in Newton the arch-enemy of life. But where Blake became the visionary of the supernatural, Oskar Kokoschka turned to the vision of Nature in all her warmth and variety. He firmly believed in the healing power of seeing the world with eyes unclouded by theories. That is why he founded his 'School of Seeing' at Salzburg, which had for him a moral as well as an artistic mission (letter to Hodin, 10 October 1953; p. 211). Ten years later he wrote, 'as soon as people learn to see what we are doing, then it simply becomes imposssible to commit mass crimes.' (to Mariana Frenk-Westheim, 22 December 1963; p. 241).

What he hoped to achieve in his teaching was to make his students cultivate, or rather recover, a childlike immediacy of response to the sights of the world that had been smothered by second-hand reasoning. He sought the same immediacy in his own reactions to all the arts. In one of his earliest letters he speaks of his 'terrifying capacity for reaction' when watching the dancer Grete Wiesenthal (to Erwin Lang, February/March 1908; p. 17). Poetry was to him 'the most elementary of our playful urges' (to Alfred Marnau, December 1958; p. 227). We find him enthralled by the performances of Donald Wolfit in Shakespearean roles (4 May 1944; p. 167), but his later correspondence testifies most of all to his love of music.

It was this love that inspired his tributes to Arnold Schoenberg and Anton Webern and to such interpreters of the classics as Otto Klemperer, Wilhelm Furtwängler (to whom he devoted a moving obituary (28 January 1955; p. 217), and the pianist Wilhelm Kempff. Thanking him for his performance, he writes 'only the art of the demigods – Beethoven, Bach, Mozart, Michelangelo, Titian, the Greeks and Shakespeare – these transform even our span of life into an eternity, often in the twinkling of an eye. When it happens to me it's as if angels have appeared, a gentle draught from beating wings sends a shiver down my spine.' (23 September 1960; p. 231). He made no distinction, as we see, between the 'demigods' of music, of literature and of art. It is in the same vein of grateful admiration that he speaks of the masters of the past, Dürer, Grünewald, Titian (12 May 1958; p. 226), the Dutch Masters of the seventeenth century (28 March 1955; p. 220) and the Austrian painters of the Baroque with whom he felt linked by tradition and his childhood faith (24 November 1949; p. 204).

Uncompromising dualist as he was, he could see in most twentieth-century movements nothing but the manifestation of everything he shrank from, cold theorizing and soulless manipulation. He expected the visitors to his exhibition to be puzzled 'to find that in my work there is none of the experimenting with all the different phases, from impressionism, pointillism, cubism to non-objective art . . . The explanation is simple enough: I never intended to entertain my contemporaries with the tricks of a juggler, in the hope of being recognized as an original. I simply wanted to create around me a world of my own in which I could survive the progressive disruption going on all over the world.' (to J. S. Plaut, 13 May 1948; p. 193). He certainly had no use for the idea that an artist should express his age.

Maybe a reader who takes up this book in search of a commentary on the artist's individual paintings, such as we find in Van Gogh's correspondence, will be disappointed. True, there are some precious remarks scattered among the letters which will be found rewarding, on his portrait of Lotte Franzos (28 January 1910; p. 18), on the *Windsbraut* (April 1913; p. 37), on the Seilern ceiling (15 July 1950; p. 205) and on *The Power of Music* (12 May 1958; p. 226), but what this selection really offers is the record of a spiritual Odyssey that led a lonely rebellious painter to that exalted conception of the artist's mission we find in Kokoschka's memorable letter to an unknown German prisoner-of-war: 'The new world can only be given shape if we love our neighbour. If we are warmed by love, the sight of our neighbour, other people, a foreign nation, another race, will enable us to shape a new image of the world, in the contemplation of which the isolation of the individual and his nameless torment in a ruined world will give way to the splendour in which the embrace of love will illumine the choice, form and shape of a new order of humanity. All art . . . is rooted in this soil . . .' (July 1946; p. 181).

Contemplating Oskar Kokoschka's œuvre and reading his letters, we become convinced that this defiantly unfashionable praise of human warmth as the wellspring of art came from the very centre of his being – his authentic self.

LETTERS
1905 -1976

Publisher's note

The letters featured in this selection, which does not include any family correspondence, are printed in chronological order. When Kokoschka did not date a letter, or gave only a partial date, the missing details were derived from the postmark, if it survives, or deduced from other evidence. Square brackets have been used to indicate additions of dates and addresses not forming part of the original letters.

Kokoschka was a prolific correspondent, especially in his early years, and many of his letters have survived in the original or in copies. With only a few exceptions, written as open letters or with possible publication in mind, all the correspondence included here is of an essentially personal kind, intended for the eyes of the recipient only. The translation attempts to preserve the flavour of the spontaneous style of the German, not always polished or grammatically perfect. For the most part the text of each letter is printed in its entirety, but without any indication of the tiny sketches and drawings which Kokoschka frequently inserted. The relatively small number of cuts and omissions are indicated thus: '[. . .]'. Where no specific reason is given in the notes for an omission, the passage in question either repeated a statement already made or was of limited interest for the reader in terms of the artist's life and work.

The selection includes a number of letters written by Kokoschka in English, which he did occasionally from the late 1920s onwards and especially in the 1940s while he was living in England. These letters, identified in context, have been printed verbatim, hence the sometimes idiosyncratic use of English. Kokoschka also sometimes used English (and French) words and phrases in letters written in German, and these are distinguished from the translated text by the use of italics.

To Leon Kellner

                                                  [Vienna, December 1905]

Dear Professor Kellner,
Your letter does me great honour: in response, I beg you to select whatever you like from the drawings, as well as the portrait you ask for. The only things I should prefer to keep are the sketches representing the attack on the bathing girl, because I want to use them in a large painting in the spring.
You very kindly offered to draw the attention of the Viennese critics to me, but it would not be right for me to take you up on it just yet, because I don't feel ready, I'm still too unsure of my own wishes, to enter the public arena.
However, with your permission, I will reserve the right to request you to do so at a later date.
An area for which I believe I am already fitted would be decorative book illustration. And I should be very grateful to you for commissions, whether from yourself personally or from a publisher of your acquaintance.
With the greatest respect, yours most sincerely   O Kokoschka

To Erwin Lang

                                                      [Vienna, late 1907]

Dear E. Lang,
I damn' well miss you, I'm really looking forward to seeing you soon.
If I could only get away somewhere from the lost souls here at the School, to Africa, or England or anywhere, it might save my life. Here, you use up all your energy creating resistance and friction for yourself, just so as not to be forced to do the same idiotic things as everybody else. I hardly ever see Lilith Lang and Grete Wiesenthal, because I still haven't got a dinner-jacket or any manners. La Lang, anyway, will certainly be a Kunstgewerbeschule graduate in a year and a half's time, if she doesn't join me in Löffler's crammer.
Delward, the old rattlebag, is still singing the old Songs of the 'Orrible Murders of Children, the Werkstätte are still handmaking the same old culture, my old friend Carl 'Ollitzer ('Refined Artist') is doing his own programme and design, oh those songs of the good old student days, sung meltingly by three Jews. Fackel-Kraus has bitten the Fledermaus's lavatory attendant in the leg, because she isn't dressed by Hoffmann.
Dear God, I'd so much like to be happy and go away somewhere with a hundred Negroes, with hurdy-gurdies, drums and trumpets. As my book of fairy tales reveals, not eating is making my psyche more efficient and complex by the day, to the joy of the people at the Werkstätte.

                                                                       15

Janke strains like a chicken. Why does Vienna make you dreamy? Don't they iron your shirts with the same dedication in Berlin? I would like to get away at once.   Servus, Oskar Kokoschka

To Erwin Lang

[Vienna, winter 1907–8]

Dear Erwin,
I can't stand it here any longer, it's all as ossified as if the screaming had never been heard. Relationships all run such a dead, pre-ordained course, and the people are all such eerie consequences of their type, like marionettes, that it is possible to pick things from this person or that, and be sure of producing specific torments. And Lilith Lang, who would not necessarily be like that, had she not come here, roams about among these things, as if she was in a large, foul-smelling bird-cage, and can't be true any more, and takes a cruel delight in renouncing the little things about herself, which only mean something to me. I never speak to her, because I would be forced into an intimacy with the others which I would find unnatural and detestable. And I've forced myself back into my shell again, and am as secretive as I used to be. It's not hard for me to envy Isepp, who is in sight of the sun-drenched lands of the south.
Now I shall never escape from the stubborn, oppressive tension, I'm often so stale that I squeeze my bedclothes together and scream into them, just so as to do something real.
175–186 cm above the ground, hats go for walks, and clothes 15 cm lower, falling in folds as if they were alive, and everywhere all the folds are governed by the same monotonous theatrical law, and I shall buy myself a false red beard to put between hat and clothes, so as to disrupt this theatrical pageant of folds.
When she is alone, I see her pathetic smile again, and then I have to turn back; the classy thing about her sport is that no more strength is expended than necessary, and then without outward emphasis. It is a shamefaced sport. And she wants one to feel like a hero in front of spectators all the time, while I have to do exactly the opposite, and be even more furtive. I can't come to see you yet, because my people still need me too much. Is Grete Wiesenthal truly overflowing and childish? I have your cold expanses of mountain forests in my blood by descent, we could be quite cheerful. I will definitely come, if only for a few days. Oh, please, remain my friends, I would like a red letter   O Kokoschka

16

To Erwin Lang

Dear Lang,

I feel like howling at Wiesenthal's leaving. It is not pleasant to know a pubescent boy with his tragedies still undigested, but today, after dinner, I suddenly saw that I am one.

Intellectually already an old man, and still such a child in the sensory area, I shuffle on my bottom between the two.

Wiesenthal has five or six moments in every dance which I am always waiting for, almost with my whole body. I think she ought to refrain from the conscious attempt to express materiality – that turns it into something like Strauss programme music – and do more and more to seek out those dance figures, like the dulled prowling in the white Beethoven, which reminds me of a dumb animal, or the way she unfolds her limbs, her fingers, in the Blue Danube, or the quivering of her thighs when she is listening, or in the Beethoven that dreadful trouble with her bent body, the muffling of a note with a lowered hand etc.

Those passages get to me with a dark warmth that comes from my sensitivity's terrifying capacity for reaction. I have always had to take care to direct my entire inner self only at such things as couldn't answer back and restored my equilibrium.

In my earliest childhood, by a ghastly chance my mother gave birth very near to me, the blood made me faint. After that I cannot consort properly with other people. I shall either kill my parents after that, or buy my freedom. All these years my inner self has been building up, and now I must prowl about with it like a rodent, burdened with all that inbreeding. When I feel like stretching out my feelers, the old man in me rises and pounces viciously on the impulse.

If I send you my book of dreaming boys, you must be frightfully sure to adore it, because I am as sensitive as a hunchback to the smallest unkindness, and I would tear you to pieces.

If possible, give me that head you once drew of Wiesenthal.

Can you go with me to Java, Persia and Norway in three years' time? Do write   OK

To Max Mell

[Vienna, March 1908]

Dear Herr Mell,

In response to your kind request, I send the proofs herewith. The marked passage, which requires no prior knowledge, might serve as the best illustration for your article. I hope to be able to speak to you again before long.   Yours sincerely, OK

P.S. The title of the book is *Die Träumenden Knaben*, and it will be publicly unveiled by the Werkstätte on the 23rd of this month in the Kunstschau House.

To Arnold Schoenberg

[Vienna, September? 1909]

Herr Schoenberg, please don't start on the play on Monday as well! The man must be somewhere between turning softer and turning savage. Can you already do by heart the inner, unstoppable screams and breaking-up, and secret upward flights, and slight physical structural alterations?
                                                                          OK

To Arnold Schoenberg

[Vienna, 13 October 1909]

Write and tell me when I am to meet you, and then I'll bring all my bits of paper with what I've started. Write to me in any case, to tell me how much you've got down on paper!   Yours, OK

To Lotte Franzos

Leysin, Sanatorium Montblanc, 28. 1. 10

Dear Frau Franzos,

Many thanks for your letter and the beautiful photograph, which gave me much pleasure, less so your doubt as to whether I take truth to nature seriously enough. The anatomy-still-life painters and the cosmopolitan-stylists, in my view, do not even take it amusingly.

Oh, please, really, do not allow yourself to be misguided by those unkind people who disdain humankind, and never marvel, never open up, at a strange face, because they do not have humility in their bones.

Your portrait shocked you, I saw that. Do you think that the human being stops at the neck in the effect it has on me? Hair, hands, dress, movements, are all at least equally important.

Please take what I say really seriously, especially in this case, or else the

18

picture is marred by blots that will devour it. I do not paint anatomical preparations, otherwise I take it back and burn it.

With my best thanks to you, and to your husband for his kind regards,

O Kokoschka

Truly, you should not imagine that there is any other dog who remembers what you are like better than I do. I am very angry.

To Richard Dehmel

[Berlin, 10 October 1910]

Dear Herr R. Dehmel,

Thank you for your kind wishes. It will be difficult to draw you in the lecture room, because I'm shortsighted and shy. It might be all right if I have friends sitting to left and right to shield me. Can you do that? Otherwise, in any case, I'm modest, as you know. In January I've another exhibition at Cassirer's, and I'd like to have done your portrait by then, because I am better than Liebermann.

Cordial regards,   yours, O Kokoschka

Might it perhaps be possible in a restaurant?

To Adolf Loos

[Berlin, 23 December 1910]

Dear Loos,

Alas, I can't get away from Berlin. Schlieper paid the rent and one week's expenses. I did not get paid for a second portrait, because it did not find favour.

I've done four pictures in the last few days, and now grinning human heads well-nigh dog my heels, and I feel heartily sick of the whole business of portrait-painting.

My most cordial, friendly regards to you and K.K.

Yours, O Kokoschka

To Lotte Franzos

[Berlin,] 24. XII. 10

Dear Frau Franzos,

The card that I sent you quite a long time ago from Düsseldorf was returned to me a few days ago, and you must take me for a forgetful and feckless person, undeserving of your concern and tactful kindness. I have always needed the guidance of good people, and have been driven by chance in a direction in which – I mean, with regard to my most personal affairs, the things I invariably neglect – I have to squander all my willpower and ability, and in which I always inevitably suffer a fiasco, because I have never been used to answering altogether seriously for the most personal things. I even find it painful to abuse the shaky state of my health and peace by working on my soul, and deepening it, in the search for goals outside myself and for other beings that I can love.

I am now so weak that I cannot pretend any longer. Will you – and your husband – be in Vienna in the spring? I am very homesick for Vienna, although my connections have imperceptibly slipped out of my grasp, and I shall feel almost like a stranger, if I go back for a few days – but I'm afraid it will be unsatisfactory and only make my homesickness worse.

It was never my wish to distress you with the enumeration of the torments and unreasonable ruthlessness which have marred and darkened my existence from the first day in Berlin to the end. My whole life is a hell. I was an open, good, young man at first, and now I'm a malicious weakling, at the mercy of whatever sympathy happens to be offered. Please write me a few words sometime. The most cordial and friendly good wishes to you and your husband, from

> yours sincerely, O Kokoschka
> Berlin, Pfalzburgerstraße 33a

To Alma Mahler

> Vienna, 15. IV. 1912

My dear friend,

Please believe this resolution, as I believed you.

I know I am lost if I continue in my present unclear way of life, I know it is the way to lose my gifts, which I ought to direct towards a goal outside myself, the goal sacred to you and to me.

If you can respect me, and are willing to be as pure as you were yesterday, when I recognized you as higher and better than all other women, who only made a savage of me, then make a real sacrifice for my sake and become my wife, in secret, for so long as I am poor. When I no longer have to conceal myself, I shall thank you for being my consolation. You shall keep your joyousness and purity for me as a source of strength, so that I do not fall into the savagery that threatens me. You shall preserve me until I can be the man who raises you up instead of dragging you down. Since yesterday, when you asked me to be that man, I have believed in you as I have never believed in anyone except myself.

If you will be the woman who gives me strength, and will thus help me out of my spiritual confusion, the beauty we honour, which is beyond our understanding, will bless us both with happiness. Write and tell me that I may come to you, and I will take it for your consent.

I remain in reverence   yours, Oskar Kokoschka

20

Frau Lotte Franzos, drawing, 1910/11.

To Alma Mahler

[Vienna, second half of] IV. 12

Dear Alma, ·

You speak remarkably clearly and purely to that part of me which I was as a child and which I have remained, in spite of the many years of hypocrisy and coarseness that I had to live through until I rediscovered in you the good human being who draws me to her as into heaven. It is agony for me to see you in the midst of crowds of the frenetic or the moribund, and I would much prefer to see you only in places where you are alone, dear Alma, with me. Don't forget that you want to go to the opera with me, alone.

Dear wife, as you want to be, make of me the only man you love, as I do with love and faith in myself. Do not forgive me if my loving is less than the most that you can imagine. Anything less is a sin against you, because every thought of me must give you bliss, if the good in the human being is immeasurable and true. Forgive me for coming to you tomorrow, but only if you can see that I have become better, thanks to you, than I was yesterday and before that.

I am already weak with longing for you, dear helpmate　　　　Oskar

To Alma Mahler

[probably 25 April 1912]

My one and only Almerl,

Do not forget me, Almi. I had to control myself today, so as not to spoil the treat that you need so badly, but I am awfully sad. Enjoy yourself, my little sweetheart, and see to it that it really does you good, so that you reap some benefit from these bad days. I love you infinitely, I am grateful to you for your love and for your unkindnesses, because you are still a little girl in spite of all your gifts, and you don't know what you are doing. I shall see to it that our little Guckerl is not sad. Stay away for only as long as you enjoy it, and don't let politeness or friendship for others prolong our separation for a single hour.

I am writing to you immediately after your departure, so that you have something from the three of us as soon as you arrive. I want you to sense, and to hold on to, the fact that we with our entire love belong to you, and you can make us happy or unhappy wholly depending on your mood.

My Almi, forever yours,　　　　Oskar

To Alma Mahler

[Vienna] 26. IV. 12

Alma,

Your going away is not good for me. I did not want to ask you to stay here, because you ought to have all the pleasure possible. Yesterday I was still relatively calm out of thankfulness that you were with me. But today I am already driven to searching like a beggar in every nook and cranny of my damned life for the traces that remain of you, my love. You are so alive that I cannot comprehend the reality that separates me from you. Every word in French now strikes me as something remarkable. I've looked at Paris newspapers, to find out if the sun's shining, what's on in the theatre, and what perhaps, of all the random possibilities, you may actually be doing at a given moment, so that among the many choices there is one at least that you and I share at the same time, if only for a moment.

Please enjoy yourself, but equally do not allow the distance to come between us in your feelings for any external cause. What you are, I am: if you turn from me, I am once again like no one and have no world. I live in you, and I only live truly and really for as long as you believe in me.

If you can wish what I wish, then my gaze will reach to you across the whole of creation, Alma,   Oskar Kokoschka

To Alma Mahler

[Vienna,] 29. IV. 12

Dear Alma,

I am so much with you at night that I think I can smell you and hold you, and in the morning my poor family suffers because I shout much too loudly and am too short and sharp with them. It takes me too long to transform myself into the old, compliant son and brother, with his sympathy for the pangs of others. My poor mother is suffering very much at present from my electricity, which needs to be discharged if I am to keep lucid control of my nerves during the day. I am painting that Frau Sanders who has a dog that looks like a wolf and which I am training a little bit. It calls for physical exertion, handling a beast like that.

My angel, you probably know full well that you are watching over me, even if you only miss me at certain times, when everything else fails you. How much everything else is, compared to me!

Not as much trouble as I need!

I am beginning to relate all my earlier stores of ideas to you, and you will provide the solution, when once my long dream-life awakens to full human reality through you, Alma, who are my soul and my conscience. You will remove my chains one day, because you will have saved me, and will go away with me. I am one with you, Alma,   Oskar Kokoschka

To Alma Mahler

[Vienna, 1 or 2 May 1912]

Alma,

I cannot grasp the fact that I can't see you for weeks on end, I'm not used to being thwarted by an external difficulty. I think the longing for you may wear me out if I don't find a quicker way of distancing myself from the self which is now confused and rebellious, being obliged to bow to a necessity that is nothing to do with me. You were still palpable to my senses when I was annoyed at something in you and had lost you, because then I could grasp and repel the alien element in your head and your impulsive emotional reactions. Now you smile at me, the most beautiful smile, from an unreal world, and yet your gentleness does not warm me, because an alien medium comes between us, and thus you do not help to make me better when a deadly fear reaches out of the old suppressed consciousness and grips me. I want you with me on my bad days. I want to sleep through them, not seeing or hearing anything of all the things which prevent me, in my fear of the world, from growing towards my destiny. I have very often been unworthy of your love, because I have inveighed against something I thought was not beautiful in you, but what was still not me, because I am in love with beauty but not hostile to ugliness.

My better self believes that you are the same as me, and that's also how I am in love with you, and with the beauty that awaits me.

My good self does not blaspheme or freeze in the face of heaven, but wants to speak well to you, not express something destructive and disturbing which is not born in us.

When we see each other again, in better health, our wisdom will let us recognize the experiences of the living body, and our thankfulness will breathe an inextinguishable and continuing life into the elements of happiness, to form a figure in which we two will merge into one another, Alma, dear wife,   Oskar

To Alma Mahler

[Vienna, 3 May 1912]

My Dearest Love,

When you and I have walked a long way down the path of this human life, we will both acknowledge the grace which is in nature, such as you know it to be, and such as I sense it may be. Spiritual affinity and sensory clarity save us from sterile disillusion and nervous exhaustion. The stranger on earth, full of grace, must not suffer and must also not ossify in the analysis of his relationships to living things.

Alma, always be for me a woman who will not remain quiescent, but rises up again to watch life as it comes and encircles her, and I will be for you a man who does not cast you down in order to make himself stronger, but unites in you the light which illuminates higher nature beyond thought, beyond myself if I am isolated – the light which is unattainable by me alone, which I alone can guess at.

Alma, do not weaken because your goodness grows weary, do not weaken because you are fulfilled by motherhood, but remain over and above all the things my second-born double. Though I cannot see you, I rejoice with you, Alma.   Oskar Kokoschka

To Alma Mahler

[Vienna,] 8. v. 1912

Dear Alma,

I now believe that you must be joined to me, more strongly than any other person on earth, so positively do I feel your nature today. I can sense it as an emotion allowing me to sense myself, and as an idea and a desire for clear reality, setting my outward limits to the world.

Before, when I was with you, when I could happily and intimately feel the assurance of your nearness, it was my will that let me conceive of union with you as the ordinance of a higher morality. On my own, lacking faith in what had grown alien to me in the visible life, and therefore also lacking faith in everything I had created, I feared that everything belonging to me was in danger of being lost or spoilt. My will demanded palpable proofs for my zealous desire to remain pure from contact with what was alien: my own body, my imagination, and the people close to me. I had to see you and hear you speak, I had to come to you, Alma, noble Alma, in order that some fact of that alien life which you sanctified should stifle this sickly sensitivity etched on my emotions by lack of faith and by self-consciousness.

Now, I do not know where you are, but I believe that you have wholly entered into me, into my emotions, into my imagination, and therefore you probably work in me physically too, as my living second self, one being with me, present for my salvation and for your perfection.

Previously, I believed in the sanctity to come, and distrusted the present. I was cynical about people, and trusted in a conception of God from my childhood, of which I was aware as a glorification of myself, yet far away in the distance like a dream, seeming too pure to make other people think me good.

Now, I believe in you, and am as one resurrected to myself and found among men. The inner virtue that I recognized in you has conquered my distrust and disarmed my cruelty, which always lay in wait like a dog, ready to part me from my closest friend, whenever I ventured out of my isolation. Now the cruelty has been transformed into a great loving-kindness towards all those on whom, in one way or another, I have any influence.

Believe every article in a confession that will become plain to you later in many and ever more powerful instances, when we two no longer live in the loneliness of the heart.

I know only one emotion, and it takes the form of a prayer to enjoy blessedness, Alma, with you.   Oskar

To Alma Mahler

[Vienna, May 1912]

Alma,

I passed your house at 10 o'clock, by chance, and could have wept with rage because you can endure to surround yourself with satellites, while I retreat into some dirty corner. And if I had to take a knife and use it to scrape every single one of the antipathetic ideas others have about me out of your brain, I would do it before sharing a redeeming joy with you: I would sooner starve – and see you starve too. I will not tolerate any other gods before me. My love, you must force yourself to suppress every thought of a witness from your past, any adviser besides me, before it ever enters your head. I don't want anyone watching me when I share myself with you. I don't want a ring to fasten me on a chain that I won't allow to be put on me. I steer my life in one direction and I won't be diverted, you are of one mind with me and will live with me until I have pulled out by the roots everything in you that bewilders me, chills me and makes me unhappy. I am a strong and happy person, and I will perfect you when once you find your support, your only repose, your bodily peace in my being. If you can withdraw, my dear, good woman, if you are impatient with the delay, a time of torment will ensue for you that I would not wish or want for you, and so I warn you now to make up your mind whether you want to leave me or have me. I would have loved you with uncommon strength, Alma,   Oskar Kokoschka

Send me a telegram: if you will come of your own choice tomorrow, come at 5 o'clock, and please bring me the text and the picture without looking at it, because it would disturb me.

To Alma Mahler

[Vienna, June 1912] [I]

Alma,

I can't come to you in peace, so long as I know that another man, dead or alive, inhabits you. Why did you invite me to a dance of death and expect me to stay dumb for hours on end, watching your spiritual enslavement as you obeyed the rhythm of a man who was and must be alien to you and to me, knowing that every syllable of the work drained you, spiritually and bodily? His fame and liberation never signified a redemption he could have generated from himself.

I owe it to myself not to see you on any of the days which you devote to the memory of that man, because I shall never be able to accommodate myself to this ossified complex of emotions in you, which is the most alien thing of all for me, so that I sense it too exactly, however slightly it stirs. Everything that I have fought against in you came from there, whether it bore that name or another. You must begin a fundamentally new life with me, a new girlhood, if we want to be happy and forever united, Alma,   Oskar Kokoschka

To Alma Mahler

[Vienna,] VI. 12 [II]

Alma, my good angel,

I'm writing to you again because it would be a sin to do you an injury such as the violence of my first letter perhaps inflicted. You are so intimately related to the good spirit in me, and I want to protect us both with my passionate love from everything that would lead us to lose our purity and clarity: that's the only reason why I am impatient and want to burn everything in the past which is no longer muted through secrecy, and would be bound to make our union wretched. I say the same things to myself as I say to you, and so you mustn't take it for invective, if in my love I can't wait for it to age or fade. Our circle is closing ever more rapidly, and then we shall be at peace in the face of what is good in human nature, Alma   Oskar

To Alma Mahler

[Vienna,] 12. VII. 1912

Alma, dear love,

Do you feel that you are gaining strength where you are, o you, my beautiful heart's desire? You are still going to need so much vitality and strength when you live with me, but with each day that passes everything in me which was against your inner natural beauty is vanishing without trace. It was begotten violently by my distrust, which also distorted my vision, but now I don't understand how I could offend against you so, because I have loved you from the very first. Perhaps the present separation is good, because I can recognize my own feelings towards you, whereas when I have been with you I was only aware of you, and believed only in you, and forgot myself, lost in you.

You must be sensible, Alma, and wise. Your nature must become ever more beautiful, so that I too grow purer, and we are bound ever closer to each other in realization of ourselves. I rejoice in you infinitely, I never imagined such good fortune for myself, I only enjoyed the company of other people when they were happy or at least contented, so that they didn't depress me by their helplessness. Now I am to come to life myself, through you, and I'm not in the least ready for it yet. You will have to be patient with me even in our happiness.

Give Gucki a kiss from me, and talk to her about the beautiful imaginings that move you, so that she shares something of you. She is the only person who should be allowed to see the strength of your soul, if she is to remain natural for me, and free of all misfortune. It is through observing her, purely and objectively, that I can also grasp and comprehend you in relation to other people. Your child unites you to me, a sympathetic, autonomous entity with the outer reality which is you in another form. If what you and I have wished is not to be, then let your child be it. Dear Alma, my wife, I send you greetings with all my love,

Oskar Kokoschka

To Alma Mahler

[Vienna,] 14. VII. 1912

Almi,

I am in despair because you won't tell me anything about your daily activities – what excitement did you mean? You must not get excited! You haven't the time, you know it takes you weeks to recover. Avoid such occasions as far as possible. You know I'm miserable since you've been away, and that I would be very glad if this torment would at least restore your health. Please do not write to other people, do not think of others, write much more to me. Every line from you (you've got plenty of time) gives me tangible hope and endless joy. Do not get involved with other people for the sake of diversion, stay as you were when you went away from me. Take that seriously, I implore you to tell me about every thought that you have of me.

My thanks to Frau Lieser for her kind letter about you. Will she please write to me about you more often, facts, all the little things? Who are all those people you know? Give her my warm best wishes. I am so miserable.

28

I'm finishing off a lot of portraits of children [. . .]. Kraus is always coming up to see me, and I'm doing a lithograph for him, which will be for sale. Kammerer has published a silly article about the heredity of musicians, typical of modern doctors who sink into journalism instead of curing the sick. He says the long hair of musicians and painters is a sign of degeneracy, when it's every bit as likely that artists, as former lackeys, preserve certain characteristics of dress longest, or, if you want to be scientific, that harder intellectual labour results in better-nourished scalps (and hair). Lichtenberg writes of Lavater, who was the first of these medical idiots, that 'he finds more on the noses of his contemporaries than the whole generation finds in their writings'. But Kraus tried to tempt me with a Malayan snake-dancer: I gave her to the porter to look after. If you do not love me, I will have her learn how to swallow glowing coals.

I should so like to be in your flat, but I mustn't rob the maids of the sense of being unsupervised, so that they will be rested and the more willing to obey you when you come home. I haven't been able to see your mother, because I was frightfully sad when you left, and didn't want to see anyone, not even her, although she might perhaps have told me about your earlier life, in the well-meant intention of pleasing me. Write to me much more, dear Almi, I am so lonely. Almi,   Oskar

To Alma Mahler

[Vienna,] 15 July 1912

You must conduct your life nobly in order to remain an emblem for me, beware of trying to live a double life, all your energies must serve this one end. I want to draw all of nature from you, and have all my emotions fired by you. I passionately detest my present life, which lets me advance only one step at a time, and places ridiculous difficulties in my way everywhere. I do not want to paint any more of these mediocrities, I have discovered you, but you must be great of character and never show me a weakness such as ordinary women have.

Every assertion of your self from another side, every attempt to show off your beauty, hurts my pride and damages the trust that I have placed in you as my emblem. If you try to assert yourself impulsively with other people, it shows that you lack faith in yourself, and you regard an insignificant moment when you have forgotten me as important enough to justify offending against your emotions, my worth, the beauty I see in you, and my potential, as well as my true standing, despite my youth.

Act as if you believed that I am the only person to whom you have no relationship or living importance, and that you must not waver if you want to take upon yourself the danger of losing yourself in me, and then

29

there will be no danger at all if you are always absolutely serious about it. If you use the strength of your soul and the beauty of your body, which means so much to me, in order to make them an everlastingly living and effective sacrifice, then you are my emblem, you make me great, and will be one with me. Read this letter every day, Alma   Oskar Kokoschka

To Alma Mahler

[Vienna, *c.*17/18] VII. 12

My poor dear Almi,

Your letters are so sad, I can scarcely believe that you are getting any better there, or are you worried about me? If you knew how much I love you, and how I do everything for you alone now, and think only of you, you might muster the inner peace necessary to make your little body well. Go out for walks with Frau Lieser – who is a good friend to you, and who I beg through you to keep frightfully good watch on your health and spare you all excitement – two hours every evening, so that you get the exercise and project your mood more clearly and confidently on to the impressions of nature, instead of brooding on the same thoughts all the time. When you're suffering, it's torture to stay indoors, but nature reflects your mood, whatever it's like, and encourages you with the rediscovery in a recognizable shape of something uncertain which has been oppressing you.

I was really delighted by your revised ideas about retreat from society, which now sound as if they really come from you. Inner peace; giving up the struggle to shine and impress other people. We'll be so happy in just a short time, when I've overcome the difficulties arising from my age, inexperience in practical matters and former indifference to my own needs. I can already see now that it will be easy for me to live with you, in seclusion but not poverty, and create the conditions for our real, beautiful and harmonious life together. For the hundredth time, the old demons keep coming back again, a lack of trust in your real seriousness, terrible jealousy of every moment of your past and present life, and the devil that destroys all peaceful, spiritual needs. And with true heroism, Almi (because it's very hard for me to become wholly one with another person, having passionately refused all ties in the past), I suppress all temptations of that sort and believe in you, the only person for me, and make myself ready for you, so that you shan't find anything bad in me, and so that I learn all the tenderness you need, dear Alma.

I must go and spend a few days on the Semmering now, to do a small portrait for 200 fl., which I've already banked in my calculations. I don't like it in the least, but I'm doing everything that will enable me to come to you, including things I would otherwise have refused. Please write to me

30

more, every word from you strengthens me for the days of separation, which I find very disagreeable. I didn't get a letter on Sunday, and was distraught and in turmoil for the whole twenty-four hours. You know how everything bad rises up in me and swamps my brain, when you haven't loved me enough sometimes. You remember the ugly meanness aroused by a small lack of consideration for my feelings. But it never strikes me so violently any more, because I put all my willpower in steadfast belief in you.

Alma, write to me at the Vienna address as always, I will have everything forwarded for me to pick up directly at the Semmering post office, so that nobody finds anything out. I leave you now, but really I'm always with you, my love, Alma   Oskar

To Alma Mahler

[Vienna,] 25. VII. 12

My beloved Almi,

You could have spared me terrible anxiety if you had sent a telegram yesterday, Tuesday, as I asked you to. I came in not feeling very well, as a result of the really enormous disturbance and pressure, and spent the whole night in the studio, waiting for a telegram, and again yesterday, Tuesday, all in vain. And you sent an ordinary letter. Didn't you have the time? Or at least use express. Your last letters from Scheveningen, which I only got yesterday (three), were so sweet, and today's from Munich so icy. Is snobbish, sottish Munich, which has always disgusted me, such a thrill for you that you now write to me only as a duty? If you knew the terrible agitation it causes me, every time a letter from you is late! Don't fall back into your old failing of surrounding yourself with all that rabble who celebrate you as the heiress. I am also very hurt that you don't put first the thought that our reunion depends on my finishing my work and the financial freedom it will give me, rather than on the obligingness of a friend of yours and when she will leave you, while I am supposed to hold myself in readiness to fill the gap when one occurs. Almi, forgive me for thinking of myself again, but I have had only the best side of you in my sights for so long that you too must put a little thought into not unintentionally torturing me through thoughtlessness. I'd rather not meet you in Munich, because your recollections of musical vanities and my own very unpleasant experiences there upset me, and because I want to travel third class when you have found a place where I can rest with you for a time.   Forever your husband, Oskar.

I want to travel alone, because you must travel in comfort, so as to stay in good health for me, and I am not rich enough to afford it for myself.

31

To Alma Mahler

[Vienna,] 27 July 1912

Almi, sweetheart,

I feel as if all my blood might ebb out of me, silently and imperceptibly, from a wound in my heart, and flow slowly into you, for I lean more and more on you, Alma. Should you have a darling child by me, great, good nature is merciful and will extinguish all terrors and never tear us apart again, because we rely and rest upon one another. Now you will be restored to health in me, and I have found my peace in you, my darling. Now we will find the sanctity of the family, you will be a mother. I have long looked on your name as a benediction, a shield for your nature, in plain language a preservation of goodness out of nature's confusion. To mankind, the unknown in nature is like confusion until it reproduces itself in a child and takes shape. I couldn't explain if I wanted to why my life is so strangely governed. When I was oppressed and not free, a Jewish word for a succubus ruled me for years, not because I sought it but because it took the shape of a person who I imagined was a world. In those days I was in turmoil and sick in body and soul.

Alma, you were always waiting for me, but I was blind and full of yearning. Now I understand and experience you, you quiet happiness. Neither I nor even you shall be the significant thing for the human race – I have grown humble, my love – but the significant thing, nature, which we sentient human beings are permitted to experience and express as form: that will be eternal.

Almi, you husband sends you his love,   Oskar

To Erwin Lang and Grete Wiesenthal

[Vienna, 28. x. 1912]

Dear Erwin,

I'm a distrustful scoundrel. I only got as far as your street-door the other day, and then I got cold feet. I know we'd made a date, but don't be angry, because not keeping it was hard enough for me.

Please tell Gretel that I worship her photographs as much as I do her glory, and that I shall certainly see her and you sometime before you go away again.

Best wishes   your friend, O Kokoschka

Loyal and sincere greetings to my little friend Georg Michael.

O dear Gretel Wiesenthal (don't be cross)

(Gracious Lady!)

I saw you dance yesterday, you are even more beautiful than ever, and, if it would not make you angry, I would really pray to you like St Agnes or

32

another saint, as I used to secretly in the days when I was first privileged to meet you.

Saint Gretel Wiesenthal, who art hallowed in Heaven and on earth, do not be cross, and take us to be with thee in Heaven.

Hail Gretel, for ever and ever, Amen.

To Alma Mahler

[Vienna, middle of] XI. 12

My own Almi,

I am strangely taken by you, you really do represent a whole world for me, I love you as if it was the first time, like a child, like a mistress, like my wife and sister and mother – all grow together to form you, you are like a crystal of hands, all drawing me to you, seizing me and holding me, and I also sense a great order and structure arching over everything, you give me a new order with a single word, you, eternally childlike, eternally newborn. I will have so much strength that your whole life will be like a rebirth, and I will be your regenerator for as long as we both shall live. Your essence is actually the only thing I propagate, and you generate me. Our marriage will be a realization of my theory of ghosts, we shall exchange bodies. This is the first time that it is possible.

Forever, sweet Almili, I always feel your little head on my breast,

Your Oskar

To Alma Mahler

[Vienna,] 3. 1. 13

My dear, sweet darling,

Do you know why we are always so unhappy? Before I knew you I had a great knowledge of humankind because of my intuitive gift for creating people. But I had always been cold and detached from people from my childhood on, because, although really I wish well and potentially can be good, the development of my nature was upset by a disastrous discovery. As a result I experienced everything as insecure, alien to me, and absorbed by impulses that were alien to me. It's true that I became hard and interesting through my angles of vision, which were turned in on myself, and thus away from a natural course, and maybe I was able to give a lot of people remarkable insights into others and their effect on one another (as if they were ghosts). But I myself suppressed the best in me, bit by bit, and I became inwardly isolated as a result of having stepped out of line (my way of life brought me the society of none but cold people: Kraus, Loos...), and I no longer gave a damn about anything any more. I was ruthless, because I lacked something that I could not create out of

33

myself, something that can only be created through contact with others: warmth, the protection of love, motherhood, loving the nature of others by entering it and forgetting one's self. Then, by immeasurable good luck I found you, and it made me trusting and young. When I was a child I was as enthralled by nature as you are, and made myself at one with the wind and open country, often crying and shouting my praises aloud, and it made me stronger than I ever was again. Your inner music, too, I believe, cannot be notated, but lies in landscapes with their natural motion, the motion of water, wind and decay and growth and sunlight and night. I believe music for you is never more than the recollection of that, and like every cipher it is poorer than nature, because it needs rules that become all the more sterile as their formulation becomes more modern (that is, more attention-seeking). Then, all of a sudden, I was knocked violently off my feet when I heard you say things that gave me the impression that you were also changeable, and a self-willed ghost, and would appear to this person one way, and then to that person another way, entirely according to whether you had given yourself to one person or another. It probably upset me so much because I had never experienced physical happiness before, and just when the contact was made after great exertion by both of us, I discovered other people in your memory, who had been happy with you before me. Like any other young man I was selfishly disappointed, because my angle of vision was narrow from being too close to the object – our physical happiness – and I lost my inner trust. But in spite of that I loved you so powerfully that I simply became accustomed to ejecting the people who were before me, and I made the mistake of mixing up rudimentary memories and facts about other people with your living being, and I turned the facts, which had come about from speaking and feeling and doing, into ghosts, even real people – which of course only a creative person can do, but only a foolish one would. Another more down-to-earth, unartistic person would have concentrated on the ideas and opinions of the people in you, and would always have kept in mind the importance of separating you, your essence, you as a doing and feeling being, from facts in your life, or ideas and assertions that had accrued to you, or been learned by you, but were not yours. My creative gift left its natural habitat – the dead regularity of optics, logic etc., materials – and put on your skin, and haunted you, and had you speak with many voices, and divided you up into many ghosts, which were raised on the word of command (the reminder of some fact) and began to fight with me for my living light, Almi my beautiful eye, and for my living space, Almi my beautiful body, and for my living food, Almi my new love. Goddamn' dog and childish idiot that I am, I struck out at these imaginary ghosts and hit you, again and again, without seeing that I was hurting you, and without knowing that the ideas that may have

34

been drummed into you are quite irrelevant, because they are not what makes a person happy or enriches the world! Hot air! You gave birth to new life in me, in living interaction with me, and that was lived experience, and it was not until long after it had died in its own warmth, like dried flowers, that the thought dawned on me. I ruined our summer and ruined the immeasurable good luck that I had of being close to the most beautiful and dearest of creatures, day and night, without worries, in complete trust, and of being her only friend in life.

Almi, my ruining all that was so wrong, and so terrible a misfortune, that the only excuse for it was my really enormous lack of experience of good luck, and my childishness, but it's still unforgivable. The fact that you were able to forgive me is a sign of your truly great character. When the little things in life get too close they sometimes make the same hateful impression on me as they used to; but it's only right that you should be afraid of my clumsiness, and all the beautiful moods and emotions in the world will not make a scrap of difference to it. Perhaps, when you are really well, you will go away with me again, and then I shall be able to show you that I don't cling irredeemably to my stupid habits, but have changed a great deal and am perhaps more capable than you think.

I must have another chance to live with you again. Now that it's winter everything is compressed into a few hours and I could die of envy every day because other, less important people than me have the great good fortune of being near you, which I wasted so stupidly. Alma, if you have the stomach for it again, just think that I am quite certainly the right person – not to understand you, because you can have that from anyone civilized enough to adapt himself to another person – but to look at you and take pleasure in the way you live, and the way you express yourself as a feeling person, and also provide, physically and by emotion and culture, the equilibrium you need to stimulate you. You need someone young to take by the hand and go with into the landscape you knew as a child, then lost, then dreamed of, and which you will find again with me, until you have found the will and the courage to be well again. I have caused you great harm, I know, but I also know for certain that a person is only harmed or fails to be fulfilled if his goal has gone and he gives up the will to live.

Almili, my dear second self, it will all be so easy, you will only need people when you have been made whole by us or by the ups and downs of nature, and we two shall take pleasure in other people when they understand us, and we shall enjoy music in winter, like a necessity, when it reminds us of the secret natural forces which we saw in nature and worshipped as children.

I wish you a wonderful day, so that you get really strong, my only love. May creation's divine heart grant that you stand up really well to everything, that we shall be together again very soon, and I can turn my wrong to happiness.   Forever your Oskar

To Alma Mahler
                                            [Vienna, early February 1913]
Dear Almi,
I'm so tired, I'd give anything to have this picture finished. As soon as I've got the money I shall go away. I simply ignored the influenza in the summer, when I couldn't let up, and now I'm in such turmoil that I don't know an hour's peace. Maybe that's why I've sometimes written irritably, without meaning to. You know that I never stop loving you, and in a damned weakness such as I've never known before I simply reacted as if life itself had ended whenever you said anything that seemed unconcerned. I can only be any good to you when I'm well, and that's what I now intend to be. I starved and overworked during the time when I should have been storing up strength, and now I'm paying for it. I want to get on top of things again, and enjoy life, and not feel so helpless in the face of every unpleasant thing that comes my way. It doesn't suit me at all.
The picture will certainly make an impression on you when you see it on your return. I'm so glad your health is making progress, and you are beginning to feel again at last how wonderful everything is when one is well. You poor, poor, little dear have been ill all winter because of me. I am a cur. It's good if I am going to get better now too, so that we can keep in step. And then it will all be very wonderful.
If you would like something else to read, please write and tell me, Almi, if it's anything specific. Rowohlt have asked me to illustrate Kraus's *Chinesische Mauer*, in a de luxe edition (I have asked for 1,500 marks, await reply). Someone has written from Hanover, asking for drawings. Piper (Munich) want a print for a portfolio. Austrian Artists' League want me to participate in Budapest. That's the latest business news, and my dear little book-keeper is not in the office. Nothing important up to now.
Please write to me, Almi, and always say how you are and what you are doing and thinking. I'm delighted by your serenity and confidence in the last few days.   Forever your Oskar

To Alma Mahler

[Vienna, March 1913]

Dear Alma,

What an extraordinary woman you are. Everything is possible if we have faith in one another. I feel that you have purified me, and that I am leading you on to the path that should always have been yours, though you did not know it. I'm glad you've been through so many transformations, because it means our life together is spared all the calamities that condition the maturing of young people. It hasn't been very long yet, Alma, only a year for me, a dreadful lot of experiencing, purifying, and sheer willing. I've suffered as much as you, perhaps worse, because nothing affected me closely before you. Help me: make a first, serious resolve to give your life to me entirely, in the way that I've made myself wholly over to you, and our united strengths will create a work that you couldn't ever do by yourself, because you haven't seen it, and I couldn't, because I'm too weak by myself. I need your soul's strength, I need your love. On the very first day, I already saw you as an inalienable part of myself, don't let's tug in opposite directions any more, wasting our best energy fruitlessly and pigheadedly.

Alma, you must try, once more in your life, to have faith in something beyond the commonplace and the fascinating (seductive). Alma, everything depends on you, through you I can work miracles, and through you I can come down to earth.

Alma, I rely on the purity in you to help you to cultivate the goodness in me.   Your husband, Oskar Kokoschka

To Alma Mahler

[Vienna, April 1913]

My dear, dear Almi

Your two letters today are manna for me, a taste of heaven. Yesterday, I had nothing, alas, and I was inconsolable, because I've been plagued for some time with continual palpitations of the heart. It damn' well hurts too, when it goes on for so long, all day the day before yesterday, and yesterday, and no rest at night either. I had to walk out on my class. I'm really longing for some rest, too, and I won't learn to love life until I'm united with you. Gibraltar is my dearest wish, I should have been sent there from Berlin once, a childhood impression I'd never have dared to realize. The picture is moving towards its completion, slowly but getting better all the time.

The two of us with a very strong, peaceful expression, hand in hand, on the edge within a semicircle, sea lit by Bengal fire, water-tower, mountains, lightning and moon – until the details of the individual

Alma Mahler, lithograph, 1913.

features recrystallized in my idea for expressing the mood that I wanted at the first, and have now lived through again – a solemn vow! In the midst of the confusions of nature one person trusting eternally in another, and making himself and the other secure through faith. All that's left now is purely poetic work, putting more life into individual places, as I've made so sure of the fundamental mood and dimension of expression that it won't leave me groping around in uncertainty any more.

In the book, I've now got twelve of the drawings ready, but not yet traced.

I've done none of the text yet. I haven't been mobile enough. All the same, you can see that in spite of a serious debility which lasted all winter, and in a period in which I'm receiving stimulus and vital strength from no one, I am working and not dropping. And only now am I coming back to moods which are essentially personal to me, and which I experienced too painfully and subjectively at the time of all those portraits. I can now separate my involuntary, exterior life, it takes such an undemanding course; and even my relationship to the people I see is so remote that I'm really inoffensive and relaxed. I used to be too subjective, and I was always tempted to find my inner self in the exterior and dissipate my imagination on other people and on life. That's why my work is now more powerful and less arbitrary, as if seen by another person, and illuminated from outside. The most fundamental in me is coming uppermost, and the transient, the sensational, is dispersing, because it can't adversely influence what is essential to me. If I live with you for a few years, in health and happiness and mutual confidence, you will be able to have great joy from my work, too.

Almi, I wasn't implying anything by the word 'unworthy', it was a response to what you said about that bad night. I meant that if things you regret torment you, you have no cause for it now that you love me and things like that ought to be impossible. You ought to be proud that you understand yourself now and live in a way which is worthy of you. I meant well and had no intention of hurting you, it goes without saying. Almi, believe me when I say that I love you all the time and it would never have entered my head to hurt you. If I ever did so in the past, it wasn't from malice, but you made me confused about you as a result of all you told me and your originally unsure attitude towards me, and then you must have taken my desperate attempts to find you again as acts of violence. That must have hurt you very much, because in my immense love I put you in the place of the whole world, in one vehement movement, and I will not give you up. I was too young and irrational then to trust in time and natural remedies – like your superior wisdom, behaviour, etc. I think you must be able to see that I have changed a lot in not too great a space of time.

Almi, I am happy with your life, your calm, your serene seriousness, as it is now developing. We will be the closest of friends and the most loving of married couples. I rejoice in your frankness. Almi, I'm very sorry that you haven't got my self-portrait with you, you always said that you wouldn't go anywhere without it. You didn't get Maud to bring it. Don't you find anything in it any more?

I don't want to send you the text, much sooner surprise you with the whole book. Or shall I send it up, and you mark what I should use?

All my love is yours, my Alma   your Oskar

To Alma Mahler   [Vienna, May 1913] [1]
                                                            14. V. 1913

My Almi,

What is life without you! Only a passing show of torments, worries and sadness, so that a man just curses everything to hurry up and be over. I simply do not know how I can love you so much, such physical unrest, spurts of energy, and at once again you, you, you, Almi, and then tired again, and gasping for breath. And if you too feel even a little bit as your poor telegram describes, then it's really ridiculous that we are both pining away in order to recuperate from each other.

Dear Almi, take my advice and try to find some distraction, look at pictures, music, go and visit people, for God's sake, so that you forget, otherwise this journey, which you did not undertake lightly, will have been pointless.

Gucki has been at Mama's since yesterday, I wanted to go out there, but I telephoned Mama first and went in the evening; she looks well and is sweet and lively. I told your household quite clearly that they ought to send you a telegram every day, and I heard from Mama that you have no news about Gucki and are worried. Until the day before yesterday I was with her all the time, and now Mama is very jealous for her well-being. There is no need for you to worry at all, Almi.

Do you really like me, Almi? I shall never let you go away again except riding on my back, so that no one can take you away from me. I sleep in your coat, so that at least I have your smell. I would so much like you to be at least cross with me, but here and hitting me with your dear, beautiful little hands! I shall never stop weeping with happiness when you are with me again.   Forever your Oskar

To Alma Mahler

[Vienna, May 1913] [II]

My beloved Almili,
I'm very distressed to hear that you're not enjoying anything. I've told you over and over again that I want you to see and hear what's on. Go and see the Russians in the Debussy 'Nocturnes', which is on at the moment, look at some pictures, go on excursions with other people, if you know any who will cheer you up. You know my fear of losing you makes me an old tyrant, because the time you spend with other people is such torture for me that I constantly feel that I'm only an incidental element in your life, when I sense that you are interested in something else. But today I also have the sense of responsibility for you which is the thing which primarily makes me worthy of your love. It means that I can see which is the more important, your leading an untroubled life or the pathetic fantasies of my childish way of loving you. Your life is irreplaceable and every day on which you do not have some joy (regardless of whether it comes from me or other people) is my fault, because you have now blessed me with the gift of your love, and therefore it is my duty to think always of what is best for you, even to the point of self-denial now and then, which a real man must be able to bear. My dearest, radiant creature, light of my life, do not spoil the present time with longing, leave such sad things to me, I will be compensated for it, one way or another, by the wider vision and clarity which I get from suffering and which makes me better, so that you can be pleased with me. Be happy, you are the only love of my life, I wish you luck in everything you do, and my only part in it shall be the pure joy of seeing you natural, lively and serene, even if you are never with me again. I love you like a heathen praying to his star. My Almi, I am dedicated to you entirely,   your Oskar

Gucki's cheeks are already round and rosy, and she is very kind to me, as if she wanted to play your part, since you are away from me.

To Alma Mahler

[Vienna, mid-May 1913] [III]
Monday, V 1913

My darling Almi,
I didn't understand your telegram about the School. I didn't go in today, because I was expecting further news, but it didn't come. I'm scarcely aware of it (the School) at present, because I go to bed early every evening – if that was what worried you, I think it's probably wiser to carry on with it to the end of the year (June). It doesn't take away any of my strength, because it leaves me cold, I do not exert myself in the slightest.

41

Two more editors from Paris were here today. The exhibition at the Salon d'Automne this autumn is definitely on, with a room to myself. I am delighted, because it means I shall no longer be wholly unknown in the city which has such a magnetic attraction for you, and I shall have the chance to go there myself.

Alma, I'm not happy about your persistent tiredness. You were well here, the doctor said you were better than you had been for a long time. I'm convinced that the kind of recuperation you think is necessary for you is not quite right. In the end the external situation is not as important as the readiness to be content with life, wherever you happen to be living, when you are as much of a person as you are. In Naples you were happy and healthy, in spite of its being winter, but in Paris, on your own, you are constantly ill, even though you have, or could have, everything anyone can get in the way of the accredited pleasures of life. But I've learned not to refuse you anything, and I would only rejoice if you would get better in spite of everything. If you think that will happen, then don't let the thought of me stop you from staying there. Guckili is well and receiving the best care we can devise for her. You must do everything you please. If you are not guided by your own desires, you neglect yourself and do little for me, because behind every sacrifice there is indeed the lure of the secret wish and the longing to have had something better through doing it differently.

I have patience and love enough to wait for you until you come to me of your own free will, without any sense of sacrifice, but because your own happiness bids you – until you believe that you are best off with me, and that you can recover your health with me. It won't be so sensational then, your happiness in life, but it will be more sincere. Sadly, you do violence to your wishes, exactly as you did to your poor sacred body for so long, because you are inwardly so modest that you have absolutely no trust in any possible way of life which you have thought of for yourself, and which is appropriate to your glorious, simple and imaginative nature. Instead, you always listen and look elsewhere, in directions from which your contentment and therefore your health can never come. The satisfactory overcoming of ourselves can only come from within ourselves. Being too careful of oneself for the sake of things that aren't worthwhile, so that one yields to people for whom one has a secret aversion, doesn't lead to happiness, however satisfactory the resolution of external difficulties, and however abundant the means at one's disposal. At best one is temporarily stimulated, but then the flight from oneself – tiredness, that is – returns. Once it used to be regarded as a crime if a person was promiscuous, because he was expected to be able, with his faith, to make his All from what he had – even if the choice had been made in error. People wanted to know a person by his firmness of faith and his fidelity. Nowadays a weak era excuses experimentation on the bodies of others, and above all, unhappily, on one's own too: on your poor, sweet body. But I shall not feel entirely sure of you until you, who have experienced everything, come round to doing what is really necessary and good for you and for your life, in accordance with your experience, consciously and entirely willingly. All gifts and all culture must have at least the ability, which the simple person derives from faith, of feeling and doing what is right for him in the circumstances. That makes a person happy, even if suffering the greatest physical torments, because he trusts himself.

I would so much like to be with you, my Almi, and do everything for you that would please you. I have a little surprise ready for you when you come back. Please, Almili, don't spend any money on me, but buy everything you want for yourself in Paris. You should arrange with the shops to send them your orders from here, in the case of goods where it is important to you that they come from Paris. In that way you won't be forced to make the journey for shopping, when you only ought to make it when you need a change of scene, or when you have to convince yourself of whether or not you have chosen badly, and want to exchange me for all of that.

Please don't be sad. I love you as one who serves you must love you. Your beauty inspires me, and I am forever conjuring up pictures of it. If you are already thinking of going to the Semmering, and you think that an arsenic cure will do you good, then do it. There is just one favour I beg of you, and that is have the injection in the arm. Sooner sacrifice a little beauty than modesty, because I need this strong sense of you, if you are to be the means of my forgetting the unpleasant experiences which I had to go through as a child, when my feelings of that nature were hurt, and then later when I first experienced love. I shall never find anything more beautiful or more tender than your body as long as I live, because I will always glorify you in my work. You must sense something of what I suffer so violently, and prevent it, not as happened recently with Dr Fleischmann. Full of love, your Oskar

To Alma Mahler [Vienna, May 1913] [IV]
[21?] V. 13

My darling Almi,
No letter today, I was on tenterhooks all day – this one missing sheet of paper is a world when it comes from you – I miss you so much. Do you feel the separation as much as I do, Almi? I don't know what to do, I know no rest all day long, I'm defenceless, at your mercy, my dear, sweet goddess. I am in love with the destiny you make for me, whether it brings sorrow or joy, but can't you imagine what a person like me, used to enduring and

respecting only what originated in his own initiatives, must feel when I suddenly become aware of an influence on me and my life which comes from people I don't want to have anything to do with?

That's why, my darling Almi, if you love me enough, you must be careful not to give in to other people more than you yourself want to, so that we, and our love, are not at the mercy of strangers. We shouldn't let them get nearer to us than a particular limit, up to which they do not impinge on our togetherness and our trust in each other. You must be clear about what is valuable enough to you to be worth a disruption in our relationship. As long as all is well with you, I am the happiest man on earth, because I know that my anxiety and my longing for you are at least counterbalanced by your happiness.

But when you yourself insist, then I curse my poverty for not allowing me to give you what you need to be well, and I suffer all the more under the meaningless power of money, which takes away so much of our happiness and causes us so much worry, because it makes us desire things which we can only enjoy at the cost of what is best in us.

I'm going to visit Guckerl now, and will write and tell you how she is. I am working, and am alone all day, because even Reinhold rarely calls on account of the rehearsals, which I don't want to go to without you. Enjoy yourself, Almi, do what you need to, but not what might hurt us, and take care of my sweet, sacred, little body. And spare me a thought now and then, write to me again, if it gives you pleasure. I am not very happy, my dear, sweet Almili,   your Oskar

Almi, you sent me a telegram yesterday evening, 'Be good to me'. I really exist only for you, I think of nothing else but you. If I am not cheerful, you must not think that I would not be glad to be so, but just remember how hard it was for you to leave me. I still feel it very acutely even now, because I neither seek nor desire anything that will distracts me from you.

To Alma Mahler

[Vienna, June 1913]

My darling Almili,

I'll stay here in town after all. I'm so tired now that I'm going to lie down for an hour, because I had scarcely four hours' sleep. The trams have stopped running. I also believe it won't be so hot today. Your home without you is torture. I don't want comfort, only you, my Almi. Don't be cross with me, think of me with love. I'll start working as early as possible and come out to you between 6 and 6.30. Please, dear Almi, don't drive yourself too hard again today, then you won't be tired and unloving in

44

the evening. All day long I look forward to the few hours I spend with you in the evening. But if you wear yourself out on unimportant things, you get irritable and nervy, and I suffer for it. Yesterday you were indescribably good to me – if only it could be like that more often. When you are rested you are wonderful with me, in harmony, and you're secure in your love. And I can work, inspired by the thought of how dear you are.

Dear Almilizi, be my darling, and remember that you love me, even in the daytime. I'm thinking of you, and in a minute I will do some more to your picture, until I've made up a little of what I lost overnight. Adieu, my Almi, I am all yours. Your empty home tortures me, I couldn't do anything there.   Forever your Oskar.

To Alma Mahler

[Vienna, July 1913] [1]
Sunday

My darling, lovely Almi

I took your letter with me to your Mama today, and she too was really delighted that you have the same rooms as you had as a child. Your letter was delivered very late, and I had already started to cry because I didn't think you loved me any more. I would so much like to be with you, but I think you get more rest without me, and you really need it for the good of your poor, dear, loveliest little body. Write to me, Almi, if there's a book you want, or anything else; I'm very sorry that you can't enjoy yourself because of the importunate crowd around you, all wanting peace and quiet but not letting anyone else have it. But if this place is not good, in your own house you will really come to your true self, and you'll be able to express everything of what you are, and of what ought to be everlasting. I can't believe that one day I shall really be lucky enough to live with you and be able to think 'she's near me' without anxiety. Your love and the certainty of not losing you will wake me up and make me the beloved husband you have wanted. I am working, and for your sake I will forget that I'm alone. Just so long as you come back stronger! Then Almili, please, never leave me again, you are everything to me, if you are not there then nothing has any purpose. I love you so much. You will be very tired after bathing. Please don't write as much as usual, because you need your rest. I know you're thinking of me, without your using up all your spare time. Almili, I implore you, don't love anyone but me, and don't allow tiredness to come between us. Almili, my darling bride, always be frank with me, as I am with you at all times, and never again hurt me for the sake of some other person, so that I lose faith in you. That was what made saying goodbye so difficult for me this time. Keep tight hold of me with your wonderful love, and think how lovely it will be when we are completely united.

Give our Guckerl a kiss from me, Almi, and give yourself one on your darling little hand

To Alma Mahler

[Vienna, July 1913] [11]

My one and only, dearest Almi

Today's letter from you is another hailstorm of abuse, and I love you so much, and I don't know why you are angry with me. If Justi's breaking off her friendship with you is the dire consequence of that evening recently, then I think it's safe to assume that she will be seeking to renew it within the next three days. But I wish you would't lump me together with your women friends: 'It's very easy to be a strong character where other people are concerned, and a ditherer in one's own affairs, like you and Justi.' I've a better opinion of myself than that. You know that I don't ask for any acquaintances, but if you nevertheless make them for me, I shall still turn them down when they get on my nerves. As I have no need whatsoever to see Justi or anyone else, you have no reason to fear that a single hair on the head of your old gossipmonger will be harmed by me. Don't get worked up about such nonsense, it's simply sinful to let these inanities ruin 'two whole days of your life'. You ought to be glad that you have the chance to lead a healthy life, and enjoy books and nature! If you're ill you have the means to look after yourself, but your temperament, which is something you can't endure in me, plays tricks on you too, my darling little girl. Sooner be happy that you love me than sorry that I won't love anything else. I implore you, Almi, live quietly, and stay away from excitement, otherwise I really don't know what the point is of my not seeing you for such a long time, if it's not for the good of your health. I will take care not to let you be aware of any of my worries, and I will endure your coldness patiently, but only if you intend to get well, and if you keep in mind that we don't want to have the kind of relationship that some people have, living in constant dread that they have put their lives in the hands of someone who is not in earnest about it. It makes me very uncomfortable, for instance, to think that a scoundrel like that doctor touches you, that you pass your time with all manner of human flotsam, or that a waiter may see you before you've finished dressing, or even when you're in bed, and so on. But I don't give in to my natural jealousy, and I prefer to sacrifice my own peace of mind, so as not to harm you by loving you too much. But if chambermaids, relations or bosom friends are jealous, it's unnatural and in very bad taste. If Justi goes on pestering you, she will be struck off my list of permissible people.

46

You shall not be hurt by anyone, my dearest, onlyest, most beautiful and most noble Almi. Please be good to me, even if I can't see it! Every good thought and every good deed makes you more beautiful, while every harsh feeling or indifference towards the beloved makes us unbearable to ourselves. Fare ye well, you and my little scamp Gucki, write and tell me sometime what the little monkey gets up to, whether she's happy, and if she likes it up there.

My deep love for you fills all my days, love me too, my Almi,

Your Oskar

To Alma Mahler

Vienna, 21 VIII 1913
Wednesday evening

My dear Almi,

At long last, your first letter. I didn't know you were so far away. I'm happy to hear all is well with you and that it's so lovely. Unfortunately my letter will take three days to reach you, by which time it will have become supererogatory for me to beg you to take really good care of your health during the critical days. I'm really pleased that you've met someone, so that you're not entirely alone, but I can imagine that it would be a stern test for your courage if I came and joined you, and we lived together in full view of witnesses. What do you think?

It might perhaps have been very pleasant, however, if you had become my wife, then we wouldn't need to be furtive about something that has long been ours. But all that is unimportant so long as you are at peace, and content with not having been in too much of a hurry to undertake something which you ought to do of your own accord and with complete conviction, and not before you are fully convinced. I wish you a truly happy and pleasant rest, don't forget your Oski, my darling Almi,

Oskar

To Alma Mahler

[Vienna, autumn] 1913

My dear, sweet, most beloved Alma,

I spent the whole of yesterday in dreadful anxiety, because I was expecting to hear from you, from first thing until night, and I knew what was stopping you from writing to me. Of course it was impossible for me to work in such a state.

You are right to say that this musical chit-chat, which is so often confused with a real love of art, no longer has any charms for you. The only thing that surprises me is that you can still get so agitated about the opinion other people might have of you. There's absolutely no more necessity

47

now for all this soul-searching and hunting for motives, because you are now set on the finest possible course, and you have lived worthily ever since you really fell in love. You have an inner satisfaction from that, and a growing inwardness that lets you be at peace with yourself, and helps you find yourself again, after having lost yourself and everything beautiful that was in you. Those things carry far greater conviction than all the acclamation that you can get from people who take advantage of sensuality, ambition, career-seeking, favours done, or faults of personality, or frivolity, and confuse you because they deceive you concerning yourself. Since you resolved to do better, there is no justification for any repentance about the past, Alma. I only say it because I know that much ado about nothing only stultifies, and can't generate anything enduring or satisfying. If I avoid these temptations now, already, while I am still young, and have advised you to do the same – perhaps not in the most successful way, because I myself was still too discordant – it's a sign that it doesn't require very much acumen to separate the valuable from the valueless. There's only one thing really necessary and really valuable for you and me, and that is the love of a person who has been through the refiner's fire. It's what makes us capable of not only recognizing values but also experiencing them, and hence making them last.

I am entirely yours, help me not to live uselessly, Alma.   Your Oskar
Write and tell me how you are.

To Herwarth Walden

[Vienna, December 1913]

Dear Herwarth Walden,

I should be in the position to send you a good picture on 15 January. Can you wire me 500 marks advance for it on 1 January? I would like to have the remaining 500 marks towards the end of January, when the picture is in your hands. I haven't finished it yet, but am far enough advanced to be able to promise it for the 15th. If you are keen to buy something by me (it depicts: sad child, cat chasing mouse, burnt-out building, faint signs of spring), help me one more time, and once again you will see that I shan't disappoint you, but do more than I promise. Wire me, please, if I can reckon on your remittance (but I must have it before 1 January, if possible).

The contribution to the book by Herr Neitzel (Alsace, Saverne) should be something substantial, tell him, without letting on that it's from me. Of their drawings (*Sturm*), I want above all the one with the boy pointing towards the sky and holding a girl in his arms (me, with the head of *that* girl).

In my studio I have a large canvas, which I've been working on since last

January: *Tristan and Isolde*, $2\frac{1}{2} \times 3\frac{1}{2}$ metres, 10,000 kr. I finished it a few days ago. I need to raise 10,000 kr. on it before 1 January because my sister is engaged – to a commissar – and is getting married in February. That means a bond! I shall then have only half as much family left. The picture will cause a stir when it's made public, my greatest and most powerful work, the masterpiece of all Expressionist strivings.

Are you coming to Vienna before New Year? Buy it for yourself, and, with your ability to make the most of modern painting, you could have an international success. Once again I shall have to bury it somewhere private, because I must have the security before New Year, if I want to avoid a row with my sister, whose fiancé has made a promise to pay the sum at the Ministry as her dowry.

If you think you have the stomach for the affair, we could set up another alliance, as in the early *Sturm* days; I am already working on something else on the same scale, and one day I shall violently break the silence that I've spread around myself at present. The security has to be placed with a Viennese bank, Kompass, Ist district, Wipplingerstraße, manager Prager, and the sum can be paid in monthly instalments of 300 kr. But the guarantor must be good.

So, as you see, I would very much like to do business with you again, but it must be worth something. Let the dealers peddle in pictures, you are too magnanimous and out of the ordinary for that. The picture ought to go to America, where my name is slowly filtering through!

So: yes or no, wire or visit!! Please, at all events, 500 marks advance on the next oil painting, to   yours, O Kokoschka

To Herwarth Walden

[Vienna,] 3. 1. 14

Dear Herwarth Walden,
Thank you for the advance of 500 kr. The picture will definitely be finished by 15 January, and you will certainly like it. I raised the 10,000 kr. for the big picture in the following way. I needed to have it before the New Year, if I was to succeed in taking care of my sister and disburdening myself later. I raised a bond for 5,000 kr., and 5,000 in cash, with the big picture as security for both. I shall repay the bond in monthly instalments of 200 kr. to the bank, but I must repay the cash before the end of January, because it was advanced by a friend who has no resources. So you see that the picture is the only chance I have of drumming up this (for my circumstances) enormous sum. You will understand from the above how difficult it is to send the picture away in the uncertain situation (besides, the paint isn't dry enough yet), because I may get an opening and prove myself in Vienna. Do come to Vienna and look at the thing.

Then perhaps you may find you can buy it for yourself, which would be the best thing from my point of view.

With warmest regards, yours, O Kokoschka

To Herwarth Walden

[Vienna, 27. 1. 14]

Dear Herwarth Walden,

Due to influenza contracted during this damnable winter, I haven't been able to work for a time, with the result that I didn't get on with the picture I promised you. Now, however, I have started a characterful portrait of an old man, which I will send you as soon as it's ready.

Please don't be angry, and forgive my unpunctuality. These everlasting worries make my existence damned sour.

Best wishes, yours, O Kokoschka

The drawing is on tracing paper, ready to be transferred to the stone for printing.

To Alma Mahler

[Vienna,] 3 March 1914

Dear Alma,

There is nothing I want from you, as long as every fibre in you stays alive for me. There is nothing I can ask of you; as long as you love me you will know where I connect with you. If you do nothing which excludes me, we do not suffer and we are not separated. Full of love, forever, your Oskar

To Alma Mahler

Vienna, 7. III. 1914

Dear Alma.

It is not my intention to extort reparations. Since your weathercock nature makes the respect and love which would be enough for me contingent on every imaginable kind of condition and chance, and continually leads to humiliation and cruelty, I am alone. I hate lies! That is why I am frank.

It is not in my nature to suffer perpetually under things that mean nothing to me, or to complain about them. If you cannot govern the inclinations of your love for me in such a way as to be just to me, then we must try to manage without a closer union. Your Oskar

To Alma Mahler

Vienna, 11. III. 1914 / Wednesday

My darling Almi,

I went to see Gucki yesterday. She is very well and cheerful, but at first she struck me as reticent (in front of Maud). Later I saw her again, alone, when she was in bed, and she told me that she had just had a letter from you, and it was about 'Wolfi'.

You ought to bear in mind that she's only just learned to read, so it's an important event, because the child expects something that is alive and speaks to her from the lines, because deciphering them is still hard work, Almi, and she believes everything. When we write letters to children we need to think about how to conjure up a personal presence – which is lost in writing to grown-ups about 'important, day-to-day matters'.

I'm not reproaching you, Almi, but I happen to have noticed and confirmed that children are like the rest of existence, they can believe, and they want to have their belief aroused. Gucki kept on asking me what you are doing: details. I told her you had sent me to see her, which pleased her. Mama is perky, and the children give her great joy.

Your Oskar

To Herwarth Walden

[Vienna,] 28. IV. 14

Dear Herwarth Walden,

As you requested, I have now sent you twelve drawings of nudes (ten in colour), in addition to the *Still Life* which was sent on the 24th inst. I absolutely must have 1,200 kr. on 1 or 2 May. If you can get me rather more than 500 kr. for the *Still Life*, the total, including the drawings, would provide me with what I need.

Please, dear Walden, try to sell the portrait of a man now in your hands as quickly as possible. I shall be satisfied with a modest price, 600 kr., if I can have it by the beginning of May. My oppressive debts and the personal misery in which I have been living in Vienna for two years, quite alone and without a friend, have made me an outsider, forced to beg for money, but I cannot bring myself to make deals with rabble. Dear Walden, I also sent you the photograph of the large painting, *Windsbraut*, which measures exactly $1\frac{3}{4} \times 2\frac{1}{4}$ metres. Sell it to a gallery: Halle? Stettin? Couldn't you get me a commission painting frescoes in America? I am ripe to do what is my proper work, and find myself forced to go on daubing little pictures, which do not give me any satisfaction.

Best wishes,

yours, O Kokoschka

To Alma Mahler

Vienna, 10. v. 1914 / Saturday

My dear Alma,

I waited a long time at your place before you left, and then at home, without seeing my brother. You had Frau Lieser with you in *my* time, and my inconsolable misery drove me away.

If you had been serious about wanting to see me, you would have found me. Your address did not reach me until Friday, so I already felt dejected. Instead of yourself, you sent me 'something', which is the reason why I am always left behind to worry about you. I have a quality that nobody else has, and nobody really knows about. It has made me take three ferocious devils on myself: complete isolation, tormenting jealousy (of everything you leave me for), and voluntary, severe poverty. When I am fully mature, they will be three angels who will have given me strength, but for the present they are the bitterest anguish, because I am easily hurt, being inexperienced, and often lose hope in my powers. And where is my dear wife the while? What life does she exert herself to seek, in all seriousness? Is she doing something for 'her happiness', which lies in the inadequate, the unsatisfactory, the old? Or is she at the side of him who cannot have enough help, support and assistance, because he is only now becoming something?

Will my dear wife give up the 'sensual' happiness of enjoying life and the ennui it brings, which she has experienced a thousand times? Because she is wiser than those who surround her, and will not allow anything unfruitful in her life to feed on her heart. How much strength and love she will gain from giving birth to something valuable, and caring for it tenderly. I saw you, and believed you were 'my maternal genius', because I have no ancestry. And you were surprised that I did not want to find a place for myself in *your fully finished world*. You need a new heart for me. I didn't know that a woman of rank in the world will no longer descend, will not take any trouble, not venture to exchange it for my inner rank, because it would require an effort to find out what I am worth. And the danger is that I shall be lost entirely, if you do not possess the patience of love.

Can the woman who seeks fully finished examples in the world carry me under her heart? How much you were going to love me! (Messrs X and Y in music alone!) Where there is criticism there can be no beautiful works of art, no beautiful people, no love!

And even if I turned out to be the most misbegotten monster imaginable, you would have to stand by me! For it may be that you have more right to be confident than all those who do not come near me, because you can see more clearly the difference between me and all other people, works of art, births. Divination is an act of genius, and it is also female! *If you really love me*! But if it is not your destiny for me to be enough for you, then you are the poorest creature on earth besides me.

If just *one* wish remains, there is divided attention, and nothing is left of love but sensual hatred. Every time you regard your physical well-being as more important than your love, every time you withhold yourself from me, imagining that something other than your love will restore you, and ascribing to something outside yourself the power to raise you, when it can only be done by your own innermost efforts, every time you 'enjoy life' at the level of people with lower minds – each time you come back disappointed and poorer, having made our love weaker, and driven me back down the steps that I climbed so laboriously, because I have to start again at the beginning, *without* you.

Almi, we cannot choose at will to be foolish sometimes and wise at other times. Otherwise we lose both possibilities for happiness. And you will become a sphinx, who can neither live nor die, but slays the man who loves her and is too moral to take back his love or betray it for his own good. As yet I do not know the man I can become. You are visible to all, and know yourself and your potential. And you want *me* to concur in your motives, and adapt myself to your habits. Watch! *I* must communicate with a human being!! That is what I shall do! And you shall entice *me* out, and make me safe. Oskar

To Alma Mahler [Vienna, late July 1914] [1]
Monday

My darling,

I myself was sadder than you can be. I also believe you don't love me very much. Now, and over perhaps the next one or two years, which will be the most arduous of my life, I shall have to change. I have learned enough, at the cost of much happiness. Those who do not abandon me now will share in my eventual triumph. Have faith in me, Almi, be brave and stick it out. Otherwise, for all eternity, you will have warmed only old men, and the Ochses and the Berliners will finally take to their graves the things that I needed to give me eternal life: your faith and your youth! Oskar

To Alma Mahler

[Late July 1914] [II]

My darling Almi,

You know you can wheedle everything you want out of me. Make up your mind to a proper life with me, and come to a decision about what will give you greater joy: me, you, or other people. I must be sure of you, if I am not to wear out my imagination with evil, ugly fantasies. It is a sin in

53

the spirit. I can do everything, and you ought not to want anything else. Your rare personality gives you the power to create something, and you are distracted, and enjoy the familiar feel of lovely, happy secrets. It's high time that you believed that you still have a chance to know yourself entirely, and stopped looking at your earlier experiments in living as something permanent, because you acquired something that doesn't make you rich. Otherwise you wouldn't love me, of all people. Your earlier life provided the possibilities that you can now experience to the full. Don't waste our entire youth, don't take years to join yourself to me in the way that we must be joined in the end. I still don't want anything less whole or less serious. Preserve your seriousness and candour for me, it's the only way our life can bring the happiness that we both hope for. We shouldn't live for our bodies alone, or for the hours that vanish without fruit to prolong our lives, those wonderfully happy months of our mutual understanding. Don't eat up my brain without its doing you any good. In your earlier resignation you lost your seriousness: not the one that furrows your brow, but the one that recognizes that dedication must be exclusive. Like me, you should not have any other attachments, or else my creative strength, which is kindled by you, will be inhibited where they apply, and I shall never be fully mature, and I shall be untrue to you, and to that which is higher than sensuality, because I shall have become untrue to myself. Take the creative love of a young man seriously, and give up, once and for all, the frivolous common sense of old men, in which there is no extravagance, because it is general and objective.
Almi, have faith, Almi   Oskar

To Alma Mahler
                                                          [Vienna,] 30. VIII. 14
My darling Almi,
As I said before, be glad that you're not here to feast your eyes on the sights to be seen. You would be ashamed, even of being better dressed than the poor, dear, touching, ordinary people. I can't sleep for distress and shame that things are better for me, while these simple, starving, bewildered lads and men, who have had nothing but misery all their lives, are being driven to their deaths, or crippled, and nobody gives a tuppenny damn about it afterwards. The streets are filling with pitiful women, who are already pale and ill, but still have the strength of soul not to let their menfolk see how it affects them. Today, in my street, there was a woman who fell on her husband's neck like one demented, because he was having to leave, carrying his few worldly goods in a piece of sacking. Yet the recruits are docile, and grateful for a friendly look. The people we know are not human, but egotistical, inflated pillars of civilization.

To Albert Ehrenstein

[Vienna, October 1914]

Dear Ehrenstein

I've already found the natural means of showing God that I am not to be led astray by His temptations. I will give the dear woman the picture, without her knowledge, I will have it smuggled into her house in Breitenstein. Because it represents her, I've always sworn not to let it go to greasy private paws, only to a gallery. And although it is not hard to predict, after this sequence of miracles, that the Princess will certainly make an offer, I am not going to let her change my mind!

It is all the more appropriate that our first disharmonious emotion occurred when I could not make any contribution to the house built for the two of us, I couldn't even pay the cost of my upstairs room in the builders' estimate.

I can't afford a house, not even a room. But I can paint one!

And the boat, in which the two of us are being tossed about on the ocean, is a house, big enough for the whole world of sorrows that we have lived through together, and no house in the world is more solidly built. And I'm going to the war, secretly. After the red picture I really had to. I am curious, and have made my peace with God.   Yours, O Kokoschka

To Ludwig von Ficker

[Vienna,] 17. 11. 1914

Dear Herr von Ficker,

I am still waiting to hear from you, because I do not want to believe that this unhappy news is really true. But now I suppose that there is no chance that it's a mistake, since in the meantime you will probably have heard a complete account of the event? I reproach myself bitterly for not having written to our friend more often. I know that often a small encouragement will serve to brace someone who has reached the limit of his spiritual strength, and tip the balance to help the body hold out longer.

Do you know if it was illness or by his own hand that he met his end?

I should like to do everything I can to keep his work alive.

I shall see to it that people set his beautiful songs to music, and I myself, to the best of my ability, will illustrate some of the poems in colour.

Perhaps enough donations can be collected to allow us to arrange a ceremony to commemorate our friend worthily.

Allow me to express my warmest regards,

yours very sincerely, O Kokoschka

To Ludwig von Ficker

[Vienna,] 6. Dec. 14

Dear Herr von Ficker,

I cannot refrain from thanking you very sincerely, in spite of your disclaimers.

You can scarcely imagine what this generous assistance does to relieve me of worry – something I have been labouring to achieve for years, and never could, but now it has come to pass.

It will enable me to work without wasting my energies in the struggle for existence.

Even if I am conscripted now, I shall have brought my plans a good step further forwards.

Although I do not know this good man, I will endeavour to do something to please him.

I will try to do a different kind of service to our mutual friend Trakl. I am very sorry that your loyal efforts have had no real success as yet.

With my warmest regards, and the wish that you will be able to think of publishing *Der Brenner* again very soon,

sincerely yours, Oskar Kokoschka

To Alma Mahler

[Wiener Neustadt, 3 January 1915]
1st day of exile

My Almi, my beloved,

I am in an alien world, longing for you dreadfully, and would gladly escape from my imprisonment if I could. The first day has been waiting, waiting, with heavy new clothes and a helmet, until I got a headache and made my escape; I came home to pour out my heart to you. Everyone uses a comradely 'Du' from the first, but for all their friendliness they are eternally separate from me, because they are aristocrats, and I have more sense than to want to bridge the gap, which would be to misunderstand this fictive equality. I can't forget what I was, and I have what I shall be one day to look forward to. Whatever the raw elements in me that you have pursued with such concern, here I behold human genealogy wonderfully worked, supple nature retaining its command of the inner fire that burns in us, where it suffocates someone like me who comes from nowhere, and leaves me smoke-blackened. But when I cease to be a single jet of flame and become a glorious fire lighting up the future, then I shall prefer to be the being that I am, because I have a longer and deeper reach, and my breath will give life to a little world – with Adam and Eve in Paradise. But what a lot of fruitless longing, and how many years of chaos will have to flood over us, before the dove brings the first green olive branch to the altar of sacrifice, without having grown weary flying in

56

darkness over the barren waters. My sweetest Almi, you are a light woven into my fibre, fare well and make me stronger with your love. Your Oskar

To Alma Mahler [Wiener Neustadt, 6 January 1915]
4th day in exile

Dear Goddess from last night's dream!
I was being chased by an enraged little man, and I fled to you across extraordinary Italian landscapes which were illuminated by a fire; and you were not like a person, however, but like a word that I heard all the time inside me, while the other inhabitants of this nocturnal planet conducted loud conversations without any warmth. I awoke strengthened, and heard again your soft, darling admonitions in your darling letters. I telephoned you today, in order to hear your angelic voice once more, and as a result I shall be very good for the rest of the day.
The enraged little man was the major, who screamed a shrill 'No!' at me yesterday, when I asked for permission to go and see you. It's quite funny: the officers here have heard some rumours about me and take me for a Futurist, and I benignly try to persuade them otherwise, hoping, by my words and my looks, to arouse their curiosity about the significance of true art, although it is highly unlikely that these pitiable scions of great families will ever attain to the enjoyment of it. But they show great respect, which in turn does not have the presumptuous desire for self-improvement of the circles I have just left.
Don't go away too early with Guckerl, it is all snow and ice here, and my two little darlings would be unhappy.
I belong to you, Oskar

To Alma Mahler

[Wiener Neustadt, mid-January 1915]

My Almi,
I had a glorious morning today. Although I heard first thing that I shall have to lay out my entire capital for my future horse, the news did not devastate me. I, together with all my uncertain existence, which is just beginning to take shape, was set upon a horse, and at 7 o'clock I rode out of the stables as an actual dragoon, just like the ones in the pictures in history books. The sheet-ice was like a skating rink, and horses were skidding at the rate of one a minute. One went down, with its rider, and our whole file was in danger of bolting, but I, with my proud, stoical indifference, surveyed the icy landscape with the sun just burning through, otherwise I would probably have lost either my nose or my horse, because they bolt at the slightest thing.

And then drill on four alien legs in a gigantic snowfield, with bushes and mountains as markers. Buglers chasing around, and captains bellowing, who will not accommodate themselves to the fact that the state of one's mind conditions the majesty of a beautiful landscape. Then down into a ditch, and over waves of tossing, frozen furrows, countless riders at the trot, and the glaring snow giving you the devil's own headache afterwards, one obstacle after another, then on through the long forests, where we wind a sinuous course to prevent the snow falling down our collars, and then away at a gallop till our minds are blank. And still I'm up there. Suddenly: 'Trarah!', we shoot off the horses head first, some of them bolt, we are never to break ranks! Smoking permitted. Dismount unaided, although my feet dangle frozen on either side like two peaceful Arctic explorers. Resaddle (unaided) in the clearing, shown how by my two friends, who always shouted to warn me when there was a danger of falling. Then we all stand steaming, we with cigarettes, the horses with their own warmth. The captain, sporting mutton-chops anno 48 and gauntlets, divests himself of his military virtues and stops screaming, which calms the ravens who were often driven off their perches. And then we all trot into the stables and into the coffee-house at 11.30. I would never have thought that I could stick it out for so long, on a wooden saddle, with aching head and eyes.

Yet another rider and his horse went down on the sheet-ice outside the barracks because of one of those damned motor-cars.

Now every inch of me aches abominably, and furthermore my boots are much too tight, because the bootmaker ruined the ones I ordered, and I had to take a pair he had made for somebody else, rather than have none at all. Then from 12 till 7 a.m. there was the same ghastly prattle – nothing about art and the World War, thank God, those two subjects are unknown here – and my hole in this hotel, with bankruptcy staring me in the face. Another ghastly thing is that I must pay social calls on the families of all the officers in my regiment, and soon at that, and there are very many of them, because the aristocracy, whose leading regiment this is, do not wish to know about the war, and are gathering in droves for the training of the 15th Dragoons.

If you pay me back, Almi, I shall avenge myself 3,000 times more drastically, because I have all the time in the world to reflect on it. You have less time, because you must attend to the Bittners, Pfitzners, Karpaths, Wieners, Budapesters!!!! And the Ochses, Berliners, Schlesingers and Liesingers.   Your Oskar

To Alma Mahler

[Wiener Neustadt, late January 1915]

My darling Almi,

At last you send me a few affectionate words for a change, which cheered me up and increased my pleasure in life a little. You've been sending me such a thorough scolding every day that I can scarcely credit the richness of your store of curses. What is it in fact, my dear woman, that has made you so incensed with me? Surely not the fact that I was jealous of Wagner, who was filling you with such rapture on the evenings when I was trying to telephone you. At all events, so far as I'm concerned there is only one all-highest un-will, and that is yours. My 'occupation' here ought not to give you any cause. I'm probably the most helpless of the recruits, and I sink wide-eyed into the abyss at every moment that passes, when I make a botch of what everyone here accepts is the only correct object in life, namely to become a good soldier, with a good seat in every saddle. I wash my hands in innocence, I didn't start the war, and, left to myself, I wouldn't have been courageous enough to aspire to becoming anything useful in this profession. Since I'm on duty all day, in the snow, on horseback, on foot, in the stables etc., I've abandoned my hope of being able to work and earn something to live on. However, I'm so used to living from hand to mouth that it doesn't scare me, it's simply the temptation to give up that devours my courage – only a little worse, because I can't console myself with the thought that it's for my work.

I beg you, when you go to Berlin – I feel very bitter that those useless blighters still haven't been able to help you, for all their fashionable nonsense – please don't put yourself in the hands of another fashionable ape, but take a good look at his face first, and ask yourself if you really trust him, and then listen to what he will tell you about his brand-new methods. If he's very busy and sees you as a favour, just keep in mind that that is part of the charlatanism, and ask him if and when he will heal you. Will you, please? Of course you must seek out your friends and enjoy yourself with them, although it's you I want to have the pleasure and happiness, not them. But don't forget to keep some love and friendship in reserve for me! Especially when you are in pain.

Adieu darling,   your Oskar

To Ludwig von Ficker

[Wiener Neustadt,] 6 Febr. 15

Dear Herr von Ficker,

Thank you for sending the money, which means that I can buy the horse. But now I see that my calculations were wrong. I have to get up at 5.30, and am busy till 6 in the evening, squadron and infantry drill, digging trenches, and similar pleasant activities, and often night-duty in the stables. I have not the foggiest idea of how I shall keep it up in the long run, with a body that is no longer as supple as those of young bucks of twenty, thanks to all the worry and stress I have had. The really pressing calamity is that I have no time for painting, and thus am unable to earn enough for my keep or the multifarious expenses that a one-year volunteer like me cannot avoid.

Thanks to the money which you got your friend to lay out for me, I am relieved of worry about my parents for probably a year, but I could not think for one moment of living on it myself, because the time would come when I would be at my wits' end. Unhappily, I did not take up one part of it, which exceeded the sum needed for my parents, because I did not foresee that I would join the army so soon, or that I might find myself in such dire straits now.

If you think that you could reawaken our patron's interest in me without giving him too rude a shock, it would cheer me with the hope of coming out of these exertions with some profit, in that I am in better physical shape now, and shall be able to resume the pursuit of my old goals with more energy, because I may not need to undermine my energy any more with worry about how to earn money: such a stupid thing, but we can't do without it! There is another way in which this interlude here may help me: there are a lot of old families in the regiment, the Prince of Parma is my second lieutenant, so it's possible that I may find a circle of influence in Austria itself at a later date, if I am not forced by poverty to drop out humiliatingly.

If you can see your way to look on this outline of my position and the proposed intervention as a necessary effect of the war upon my finances, you will not be surprised that I need help, whereas previously I always took pride in standing on my own two feet. If you think the time is not ripe for any intervention, please, my dear friend, do not breathe a word about it and forget this unpleasant business.

I hope your call-up will not be too irksome, and that you are well? We, after a decidedly frenetic training, are about to go to the front.
Best wishes,   yours, Oskar Kokoschka

To Alma Mahler   Wr. Neustadt, Hotel Central
                                          [first half of February] 1915.

My darling,
If you saw me on horseback, you might not be so cross with me. I feel quite confident now, and today I brought the squadron home. I rode at the head and never ceased bawling "Shun!' and 'Eyes right!', even when a regular officer was passing. On the Heinrichsplatz the Colonel

suddenly called me and sent me to take command of a bunch of men, so I galloped at full tilt across open country to the troop in question, always under the critical eye of the captain, and there all of a sudden I plucked up the courage to be so bold all at once, even though I still haven't learned to ride. Then, with my little troop (eight men), we splashed through the forest at the trot, with our heads down on the saddle, lest a branch should seize us, like Absalom, by the hair.

Many, many greetings, It's time I went to the barracks. This evening you will get another letter with a detailed drawing. I wish Pfitzerich a donkey to ride on, and Professor Ochs a cow.

I am a dragoon, and anticipated as much on the last fan, where I am charging three dragons. If only I had a commission, but it will take another six weeks at least. Oh dear, what a shame! Forever, your Oskar

To Ludwig von Ficker

[Wiener Neustadt,] 21. [2. 1915]

Dear Herr von Ficker,

I received your kind wire recently, saying you could send me another 700 kr. from the Foundation. I wired back at once that I would be very grateful for it, and Loos also wrote to you at my request, asking you to send the money by wire, if possible, because I am in very dire need. I myself have been incapable of writing to you for a week, because I am run off my feet, and so tired that I can't wait for my few hours of sleep. In one period of 77 hours I slept once from 8 till 4.30 a.m., the rest was sentry duty (48 hours – 2 × 24), drill and riding. On Sunday I have stable duty from 1 p.m. to 1 a.m., and then have to get up again at 4.30 a.m. – and that's a considerable blessing! On top of that, I have no money, for although the entire officer corps pours its scorn and bad temper on the head of a new one-year volunteer, he still has to cough up in all directions, pay for hay and oats, tip non-commissioned officers etc. I beg you, my dear friend, if you still have half a mind to help me, if you yourself are not so hard-pressed as to have no further desire to concern yourself with other matters, please send me the money soon, and explain my position to the donor. I shall of course gladly repay it all, just as soon as I can get back to my work, but there is no question of that at the moment.

If only I was already a corporal, even with the infantry for all I care, and could go to the front, and get wounded, and then I could go back to my studio, which I yearn for like a distant homeland (going to Vienna incurs 40 days' C.B., no leave).   Yours sincerely, O Kokoschka

To Alma Mahler   Wiener Neustadt, Hotel Central
                                                        [late February 1915]

My beloved,

How are you now? I hope your little face is better and the Berlin quack
did not fall too deeply in love with it. How did my queen receive the
homage of the brilliant gathering that assembled for the Mahler
performance, after being deprived and yearning for her freedom for so
long? You tell me nothing about yourself, nothing about all the things
you must have seen in Berlin, or who travelled with you, and I have no
news about you from Vienna, either. Do your friends occupy you so
completely that you don't miss me at all? Is the power of music so great
that it can drive me from your mind after years of living together, without
your even noticing it, or feeling an unquenched need for me? And who
was it told you that I am deliberately treated badly here, do you know
someone from the regiment?

I see I have to tell you for the umpteenth time that I was not led here by
the desire to force myself into a class of people who do not want to know
anything about me. It is in fact precisely the bourgeois elements, being a
common lot, and better off in the army (I have absolutely no idea what
their civilian existences are like), who give themselves airs in uniform. I
am objective enough to be able to distinguish between what importance
this world, and the world as a whole, has for me, if it doesn't suit me, and
what I have to blame myself for. The service only affects me superficially.
The one thing that really troubles me is that I don't get as many hours off
as a soldier is entitled to, and which my constitution needs. Giving me a
hard time physically is the only truly wicked deed of these parade-ground
pashas. But I can imagine far worse, and I know my poor brother is far,
far worse off, and his life today, even in comparison with mine, is one of
undeserved ill-treatment. For that reason alone it would be ridiculous for
me to complain. Besides, I have what I really did join up for: a handsome
horse, on which I already cut a fine figure. The artillery is not for me.
Do you still love me? Write and tell me so at great length.   Oski

To Alma Mahler
                                                Wiener Neustadt, 2. III. 1915

My darling, Wagner-crazy Almi,

You don't live through me, because that's the way you want it. Only the
company you keep knows whether you live at all. As one whom it does not
concern, it's very hard for me to guess where your path is leading you. It's
now very likely that you yourself know nothing at all because you are
confused. You must be sad because you are alone, the victim of your own
freedom! I have no wish to pour you into a new mould: even if I could,

62

you would be sure to think you had lost something of substance. There are enough pairs of hands as it is, ready to catch a butterfly or tie down a restless woman. All I own of you is a little of the dust from your wings, and I want to see it in the light, not on my ten fingers. I've learned not to be greedy when I'm promised the earth. Time is on my side, because I give life, I do not destroy it, I have a purpose and a meaning, I am not something evil, I understand qualities without flattering them, and I do not betray secrets even after they have come to the knowledge of strangers. But I have a fire which I would dearly like to communicate to you, for it burns the impudent fingers of strangers who try to place their hands where mine have once lain. Oskar

To Alma Mahler

Wr. Neustadt, 5. III. 15

Darling Almi,

We got back from Bruck very late last night. The whole time we were there, we were marching ankle-deep in mud, digging trenches, slithering to the bottom of them to shoot, and lying in the mud in open order. My nights were spent with about 120 men in one hut – in great fear of lice, which were to be expected in view of the constant turnover of numerous and dubious occupants. It's bad enough not taking off one's wet boots and clothes by day or night for three whole days. There are a vast number of huts there, in amongst trees and bottomless mud. Prisoners are kept erecting new ones all the time, and there are hussars, dragoons, lancers and infantry firing rifles on all sides. The inspector of cavalry was there and very pleased with our squadron of recruits. But the journey back was frightful, in an unheated lorry from 7 to 11.30 at night, in sodden clothes. In spite of that, we were up again early as usual for riding drill in the rain. Either I shall go down with pneumonia, or there is nothing in the world that can harm me now.

And now you have Ochs in Vienna too. It must be wonderful for you. Prophets to right of you, prophets to left of you! It made me angry to see how much store you set by your protégé taking you a little seriously as a musician. Your boundless gratitude for being taken that little bit seriously by a musician, and your indifference towards my seeking to make you the centre of my world, are out of all proportion, and I cannot understand it. I am a totally different person from your followers of Bach, or Brahms, or Wagner. The only one who had a personality of his own, even if no creative originality, was Mahler, and he towered above all these so-so musicians, with their softly-softly tread, by reason of his elemental vigour. Today Schoenberg is the only one who is at least at home in his blind alley. How did you solve your prize puzzle? Taking the

by-road via Bittner to the Salon-Tirolean, or Schoenberg, who reaches the portals of art, even if he doesn't pass through them? You say you observed a great movement in Berlin society. I only pray that it doesn't end by flattening the few shaky prospects which the spirit has of sustaining itself in the world it created, and that they don't all finally come to the conclusion that they must eradicate the spirit, because there are so many of them standing shoulder to shoulder that they take themselves for a world in which the spirit is superfluous because the world no longer needs to be created. Technology, science and military training provide all our daily wants, and on Sundays, why, there's a roast goose, ready when we come out of the Music à la mode Café! If there is some fool, somewhere, beating a hole with his head in the Great Wall of China which separates us from the true Paradise, then the least we can do is beat the dust out of his backside which can't follow: his head has broken through and gazes on the wonders of Paradise!
Farewell, dear Almi,   Oskar

To Albert Ehrenstein
                                        [Wiener Neustadt, *c.* 8 March 1915]
Dear Dr Ehrenstein,
First of all, thank you for your generous eulogy, which for all its exaggeration caught exactly the right measure of praise that I am now wholly deprived of.

Every day I get up at 4 a.m., ride with my squadron from 7 till 12, till my knee-caps are ready to drop off, across ditches and dirt and sheet-ice, as if I had been born on horseback. The NCOs scrounge so much from me that I end up with hardly enough to eat! From 12 till 1 we have midday break, then from 2 till 6 what we call 'Tarot on foot', i.e. skirmishing, target-practice, and similar indoor sports, under the command of an over-zealous major, mixed with appalling effing and blinding from two reserve officers of common backgrounds, who, knowing when they're well off, behave as if the entire world since its creation has been waiting for the filth that pours from their lips. In addition to them there is a swarm of captains and colonels, whose time hangs heavy on their hands, and so we have to pay social calls on them, though I take little pleasure in it.

Last week I twice did two 24-hour shifts of sentry-duty outside an empty shed in Arctic weather, as a punishment, and one 24-hour stint as acting corporal on stable duty, which involves alerting the stablemen to the horses' droppings, and rattling off a report on said horse-droppings to every military busybody who pops up at whatever hour of the night he chooses; on the reliability and speed of such reports depends the satisfaction of higher authority. At this very moment the decision is being taken as to whether I go to the front in marching order as a private, or to Holič on 15 March as a volunteer cadet. I am so short of sleep that the only thought I can hold in my head is how am I going to get my hands on some more money. Give little Tschopp a grandfatherly salutation from me. From Saturday till Sunday or Monday I again have 24 hours on barracks inspection, supervising the cleaning of the latrines; apart from that I'm free from 6.30, so if you have the time, please come out here. I get forty days if I absent myself without leave, and leave is simply not given. How I hope I get sent to Holič, and you too! There were a few occasions when the insults reduced me to tears, but now I've grown a thick skin. With warmest regards,   yours, O Kokoschka

The article for the *Reichspost* ought to be nice and long and overstated, and appear soon!!!! The one good thing about being here is that nobody ever mentions the World War.

To Alma Mahler   Wr Neustadt, Hotel Central
                                                          16. III. 15
My dear Almi,
I've had no letter from you for several days, and readily confess to the error of using my imagination to put the reason for it in the rosiest light possible. The emotional need is less painful when filtered through the resonance of the past than when it is immediate, but it is still so strong that against my will, if you will not write, the magical threads of memory tangle and render me helpless.
I await in hope the conclusion of your protégé's theatrical activities, as it may again allow you the time to favour me with a few, mostly reproachful words.
I am always devotedly yours,   Oskar

To Alma Mahler
                                    [Wiener Neustadt, *c.* 18] March 1915
My dear Almi,
I had no letter from you today. It's your own fault if I want to root out the Pfitzners etc.; if they have you to themselves for the whole day, as they do, there ought to be five minutes for me, when you could at least write a letter. Today has been the most splendid and most contented day that I've had for a long time. It was sunny, not cold, and I rode out at 8.30 a.m. with one of my 'friends', a corporal, and didn't get back to barracks until 6 p.m. The people in the villages goggled at the two dashing

cavalrymen, going in the direction of your house as far as Schneeberg-dörfl. We could only do it because the rest were in Bruck, on firing practice. In the evening, incidentally, a platoon-leader wanting to cadge something from me put me on report. I don't care, no one can deprive me of my beautiful day.

Adieu, adieu, I'm tired, adieu Almi, be good to me.

To Alma Mahler

[Wiener Neustadt, early April 1915]

My dear Almi,

I'm leaving here tomorrow and going to Holič for four weeks. Today I got my first pips, of which I am very proud, because I got them without patronage, and against the wish of my superior officers. You may think I have not been showing enough interest in your musical activities, but surely you can imagine how remote everything to do with audiences, public performance and the world of art is for me, especially now. It's harder for me to summon up interest in a successful result, when it's a matter of reproduction, conducting and so forth, that goes against the grain of the work [. . .]. In my opinion, if you must contribute – and the magic of an association with your glorious self has had an effect on old money-bags L. L. – don't make poor Schoenberg earn his money by jittering on the podium like an ape, trying to anticipate and recreate the emotions in things he had neither learned nor created. Simply make him a gift of it, as is right and proper for an artist. But the whole wide world, and especially the world of art, is so different from the world I'm in, that perhaps you are right and I am wrong.

My visit to you is a very pleasant memory, which will help me survive the new posting, where life will be very irksome indeed.

To Alma Mahler

[Wiener Neustadt, May or early June 1915]

My darling Almi,

No letter from you today. I write to you every day, and if one letter fails to arrive, it isn't my fault.

I'm so tired now, Almi, with the work and the heat, and with worrying about whether you love me at all. The landscape around you is safe, familiar and beautiful. You're in good health and have a right to drift pleasantly along in your life. If you concern yourself with me, you come face to face with something quite different which you can't bring to a satisfactory conclusion. I must stay on the road, in order not to go under like the many who want wife, children and success, as well as wanting to be true to themselves at the same time. My joy in life is much more powerful and exacting than other people's, just as my agonies and fantasies were worse when I reached for pleasure and it proved fickle. Your house would have become mine through a confidence trick, and my wrongfulness would have distanced you from me – though you would never have known the true reason for it.

We dig pits for ourselves and are then surprised if life doesn't keep its promises. For that reason, I now wholeheartedly think it good that, in all innocence, you spoiled my sensual pleasure before I was mature enough to do it myself; that you didn't become my wife and didn't bear me a child; and that you are now giving up the house before we have even seen it. Society, money, obligations are only excuses, the decisive reason lies in ourselves. We can create pleasures, but we can't satisfy our appetites. And the only admissible service that we can do for other people, who don't understand how to seize the world for themselves, is to leave enjoyment to them, because we renounce it for ourselves when we've created it. A mother doesn't eat her own child unless she is a useless, worthless beast.

To Alma Mahler

[Wiener Neustadt, late June] 1915 [1]

My Almi,

You hurt me more with your letter today than you have ever done before. I wept because I see now that I have no refuge anywhere, and you take pleasure in my inability to fit into this world, and when I cry out you will sooner pour scorn on me than draw me to your heart. May you continue to be courted by gentlemen who have been in the trenches, and those who are in sunken orchestra pits. I know what I am doing. When I can't endure life any longer I shall throw it away. Accusing me of seeking out a particular class of men in order to give myself airs is the most idiotic thing imaginable, and it shows me how alien your judgment of me is, and how low an estimation of myself I must have had. The root cause of all my difficulties here is precisely the fact that I do not seek any good connections, and therefore I have no one to cherish and instruct me. That is also the reason why they will haul me out of the cavalry before very long, because they're bound to think I don't belong here. In fact what attracted me was the belief that I would not need to associate with anybody, and the hardest thing about military life is that I am suddenly presumed to have a talent for social life, like a woman. I hoped that the gulf of rank and money would set me apart here.

Farewell, my love, you will never understand me,   Oskar

To Alma Mahler

[Wiener Neustadt, late June 1915] [II]

My darling Almili,

I'm losing my mind from distress and pain. I can't forget how happy I was for a short time – too short, alas! I've just been weeping again. I think I shall kill myself because I need you so much. They wrote and told me that they won't take the picture. I've no desire to paint anything else. I admit defeat. I cannot and will not go on living without the cheerful song of my little bird.

Thank you for the money. I have to accept it, alas, because of these people. Not for long, my Almi. Don't think that I was a bad man. I loved you more than anything and my love was pure. Now I am exiled from all living beings and I am alone.

Forgive me, my own, forgive   Oskar

To Alma Mahler

[Wiener Neustadt, late June 1915] [III]

My dear Alma.

Your last letter makes it sound as though the cause of our separation was something other than it is. Don't be anxious on my account, and don't write to me except to tell me how you are, my greatest concern is not knowing how things are with you. That's all that remains of the riches I had when I was beginning to love you: a beggar's mite. Don't worry about me if I can't muster sufficient calm and confidence to balance your experience and the qualities you have acquired in a fully rounded life, but take care of your health, so that you can go on to enjoy many new experiences on your own. The only thing I want is for you to know peace, and I shall be the last person on earth to disturb you, my love. The first letter, with your decision not to see me again, frightened me so badly because your mirror had been broken just a short time before, and one is always a little superstitious. Don't be cross with me for babbling all that nonsense about 'protection', that was what I had always done, what was expected of me. Because of it I'd forgotten that I too want to live, until it was almost too late. I snatched you away for a short time from the life you believe to be right for you, but I realized what I'd done, and gave you back your complete freedom to decide for yourself what you wanted, and what kind of life pleased you. Admittedly, I didn't do so at a time when common sense should have told me to, but I did it when I saw that you were suffering, and that it would destroy you. Write to me, please, only about how you are and only when you feel love towards me, so that it ceases to be a burden to you. I hope that you will soon be completely recovered, with every trace of what I've done to you wiped out. True, it

68

will endure in me, because at bottom I too, like you, cannot change myself.

I kiss you, truly believing that I never wanted to drag you down, and never meant any harm.   Oskar

To Adolf Loos

[Lemberg,] 22. 7. 15

Dear Loos,

Arrived in Lemberg today, after eight days. Off to join the regiment tomorrow morning – three days' journey. It's now part of a German cavalry force ordered to Russia! No trenches, but reconnaissance, thank God, and – the wonderful thing about Russia – the chance of an Iron Cross. Along the way, many villages destroyed by gunfire, cemeteries, all the famous battlefields, cholera, tinned food, lack of money for the last five days.

Best wishes,   yours, OK

To Adolf Loos

[Galicia,] 6. 8. 1915

Dear Loos,

I was really lucky to escape with my life yesterday, because the Cossacks show no mercy if they catch you! I and a patrol were ambushed in the endless forest and swamp hereabouts. We lost more than half our men. Hand-to-hand fighting, with all of us thinking our last hour had come. It was pure chance that two or three of us got away, me last because my horse is weak and, to crown it all, went lame!!! Then a life-or-death chase, with the first of the brutes only ten paces behind me, firing all the time and shrieking 'Urrah-Urrah'. I kept feeling his lance in my liver. I used my sabre to flog my horse to its limits and just made it back to my unit. You should see how they respect me!

All good wishes,   yours, OK

Don't say anything at home! I'm so glad to be alive.

To Herwarth Walden

[Galicia,] 12. 8. 1915

Dear Walden,

Please despatch the following *as soon as possible* at my expense, my parents will repay by return if you send them the bill. Send the parcel directly to

69

me at the front, because nothing is reaching the regiment via the military post office in Austria.
6 prs thick brown socks, not wool
300 good cigarettes (strong)
1 set silk underwear or similar
1 bottle brandy or whisky (and glass)
1 large tin Köstens' wafers
5 tins sardines
1 good flashlight and 5 spare batteries
6 jars assorted savouries
3 jars preserves
1 clothes brush
1 tin dubbin
1 box Sarotti bonbons.
If they won't all fit into one standard parcel, please make two or three. I need everything. Again, please be as quick as you can.
Yours, with all good wishes, O Kokoschka

To Albert Ehrenstein

[Galicia,] 24. 8. 15

Dear Dr Ehrenstein,
I'm sorry not to hear anything from you any more. How is your brother? Things have been very hectic for us here, and very dangerous. Especially riding patrols in swamps and forests. Unhappily, our orders are to move on to yet more of the same. Last night I slept in a room for the first time in weeks, because we took a sizable Russian town and set up quarters there, as happens all too seldom, alas. Today we press on again. Let's hope things get no worse. Best wishes, yours, OK

To Herwarth Walden

[Vienna,] 27. 10. 15

Dear Walden-Doctor,
My wounds proved more decorative than lethal. A bullet in the head and a hole in the chest. My engagement is broken, my studio resolved, and a big silver medal in exchange. I am a pensioner!!!!!! Many thanks for sending the goodies, which were returned, alas. I wonder if my number will be up next time. Please send the *Sturm* to yours truly, 2nd Lieutenant O Kokoschka, Vienna I, Palffyspital, Josefsplatz 1.

Warmest regards, Albert Ehrenstein.
Best wishes, Loos.

To Albert Ehrenstein

[Vienna,] 25. III. 16

Dear Dr Ehrenstein,

Don't be angry but I'm so much on tenterhooks that I take no pleasure in anything. That includes writing. My sick-leave runs out at the end of April, I don't yet know what will happen then, and no one will take it to heart. Loos is running after the Hentschel woman like a schoolboy and apart from that . . .

I see a lot of Rilke, who speaks of you very warmly. I have an enormous desire to paint, and would not lack offers, and would like to do it for my family's sake, but it's not easy to sing with a sword dangling over one's head.

Please send me your new book. And paper for my brother, who is always writing for more things. I hope your malady is better by now, it must be frightful, and make you feel very depressed.

I've revised quite a lot of [the] one act of the 'Drama' – dreaming youths. Would also like to print the 'Zeitecho' poem with corrections. Would hope to get a huge fee. Will send you everything soon. Hope you manage to stay there until things come to a happy end, and I wish myself the same with knobs on.   Your faithful old friend, O Kokoschka

Poor Franz Marc has fallen too, do write something good in his memory!

To Albert Ehrenstein

31. V. 16 [Bennoplatz 8,] Vienna

My dearest Ehrentafelstein,

– whereon your own name shall be engraved to all eternity for the services you have done me. I've been in charge of three hospitals for several weeks, and have had no chance to do any work of my own. Today I received a new posting, to the Military Press Quarters, and must leave the day after tomorrow. Please drum it in to Gutbier with the utmost urgency that he must send the 500 marks with all possible despatch to my parents, G. Kokoschka, [Vienna] 8, Bennoplatz 8. If I had a commission from the state, perhaps via Gutbier, I could say what I really want to as a War Artist, which is the imminent possibility, but I would not be left in peace to do so unless I had a permit to wave at people. I couldn't get hold of Rilke, he didn't reply to two letters, doesn't appear to be anywhere in Austria-Hungary.

All best wishes, I think I'm developing T.B., I ache all the time – and I'm to start exerting myself again now?

Yours, old and haggard, O Kokoschka

71

To Albert Ehrenstein

[Vienna,] 10. 7. 16

My dear, thoughtful friend,
Your friendly letters and the outcome of your exertions reached me today – very many thanks. I hope things in Berlin are at least halfway tolerable for you. I can just imagine Kurt Wolff's troubles. K.K. has publicly acknowledged the great impression your book of poems made on him. He is not here now. I shall be here for five days only, and must set out with those painters on the 14th. I'm dreading the journey and it will certainly cost me my head before very long. Through Kestenberg (please give him my regards), I have tried to wangle a commission from the German High Command, by way of a recommendation from Bode, and am curious to know the outcome. Or professor at an academy – that would be the most bearable. But the chances are thin. My sister is looking forward to receiving a visit from your sister soon. My mother sends her warmest regards. I am already tired to death of life and await the end of the world, when I hope the earth will open for me and let me take my rest. yours, OK

To Ludwig von Ficker

[The Isonzo Front,] 21. 8. 16

Dear friend,
I wonder how things are with you and where the war has landed you. I don't know your military P.O. no., or even your regiment, and would so much like to know if you are well. I hope this card will at least reach your wife so that you know I'm wishing for your speedy and safe return to your real work. I've been back at the front six weeks and remain

yours very sincerely, Oskar Kokoschka

I wish you everything that we all want.
Have been spared a few times, by good luck.

To Adolf Loos

[Dresden,] 25. IV. 18

Dear Loos,
At last, after all this time, in the midst of your eternally unhappy love-life, you spare me a thought! Aren't you ashamed of yourself, forgetting me like that, you Lothario? Have you read my *Hiob*? The Court Library bought it, or the University Library, or one of those places, or Heller will lend you a copy.
Dirsztay ordered it, but the publisher tells me he sent it straight back, together with the invoice, otherwise he'd be able to bring it with him.
My new book, now, *Orpheus und Eurydike*, really is a great play, I'm sure,

Adolf Loos (top) and Karl
Kraus, drawings reproduced in
Der Sturm, 1910.

in the same class as *Penthesilea*. Either that, or I'm altogether wrong and ready for the scrapheap, with rust where my self-criticism should be. Please recommend me to the Jesuits, Fathers Kolb and Audlan, and ask them to build a big church or monastery for me to decorate with murals, so that the Austrians have a chance to enjoy my work.

When are you going to Switzerland? I wouldn't mind going with you, but I'm as lethargic as I used to be in Berlin in the old days, and I think you'd have to fetch me and carry me there!

Reaching thirty was such a terrible business for me that I've completely lost all my self-confidence and initiative. What is my idol doing in her bourgeois married bliss? Have you any news of her? Does K.K. still think I shouldn't write? It's a torment to me that modern plays are such drivel, because I like going to the theatre. I shall have to write my own plays, if I want to see anything that holds my interest. I beg K.K.'s forgiveness!

To Alma Mahler-Gropius

[telegram: Weißer Hirsch, Dresden, probably 1919]

Revered friend,

I see from two letters awaiting me here that you already know my *Orpheus*. Your joy is mine.   Oskar

To Alma Mahler-Gropius

[undated telegram: probably after 1918]

What we experienced, whatever it may be, as we comprehended it, is all that really belongs to us. It survives inside us. If you still triumph and exult as you once did, my dear friend, then it has been the same for you as for me. Wherefore the years will not grow grey for us, and we shall not hesitate for a moment to give thanks for everything which was our own desire.   Oskar

To Alma Mahler-Gropius

[Weißer Hirsch, Dresden,] 20. 6. 19

Revered friend,

I return your letters, in accordance with your wish. I could not believe that you seriously wanted something from me. I hope that you have so ordered your life that it makes you happy. I would so much like to be fair to you, and if I came face to face with you and saw that I could not be, I would despair.

But it was far from being my wish to hurt you. Better that I should stop breathing first.   Farewell, Oskar.

74

To Ludwig von Ficker

[Berlin,] 8. 12. 19

Dear Herr von Ficker,
Please can you write and tell me if Trakl is buried in Innsbruck, and if not, where he is and what obstacles there might be to getting him brought home? I heard today the sad story of his sister, to my sorrow, and feel as though I suddenly heard the voice of that dear dead man, reproaching me for having forgotten him for so long. I'm glad you are back in Innsbruck, and are well, my friend, and I look forward to hearing from you again.
With the warmest regards and with many thanks, I am, as ever,

yours sincerely, O Kokoschka
Dresden Academy, Brühl'sche Terrasse.

Open Letter to the Inhabitants of Dresden

[Dresden, late March 1920]

I address this appeal to all those who intend to argue the case for their political theories at gunpoint in the foreseeable future, whether of the radical left, the radical right or the radical centre. I implore them not to hold their proposed military exercises outside the Zwinger Art Gallery but in some other place, such as the firing ranges on the heath, where human civilization is not put at risk. On Monday 15 March a masterwork by Rubens was damaged by a bullet. Pictures cannot run away from places where human protection fails them, and the Entente might make the argument that we do not appreciate pictures the excuse for raiding our gallery. Dresden's artistic community is no less alarmed than I am: we are conscious that we could not create such masterworks ourselves, should those entrusted to us be destroyed. It is we who would be answerable if we failed to employ all imaginable means in good time to prevent the impoverishment that the robbery of their most sacred possessions would mean for future generations. There can be no doubt that in due course the people of Germany will discover more happiness and sense in the contemplation of the pictures, if we save them, than from all the opinions of the politicking Germans of the present day. I dare not hope that my alternative suggestion will be adopted, but it is this: in the German republic, as in classical times, feuds should in future be settled by the leaders of political parties in single combat, perhaps in the circus, and enhanced by the Homeric abuse of their followers. It would at least be less dangerous and less confused than the methods currently employed.

Oskar Kokoschka
Professor at the Academy of Fine Arts in Dresden

To Alice Graf

[Vienna, 18 August 1920]

Dearest and most honoured Colibri,

Has Alice not seen my sweet Edwarda anywhere? I would never say it to
her face, but your ears, my little Colibri, may hear that I shall die if I do
not see her again soon. She must read my books, I myself – and the stories
of all my loves – are to be found therein, word for word. And how I wish I
had been with her in the reindeer sleigh, where I should have kissed her
knees.

Write soon, a nice long letter, most tenderly, OK. Lieutenant

To Lotte Mandl

[Vienna, October 1920]

There is someone behind the windows, observing and sketching the
world outside. You were ten years old, and you ran past and were seen.
And five years later perhaps you will go past those windows again, and
think to yourself that you will take a look inside. But they are not windows
at all, they are the eyes of Herr Oskar Kokoschka. What a lot of other
things my little friend Lotte will see even better as she grows older!

Most sincerely, the subject of this little book.

To Lotte Mandl

[Vienna, January 1921?]

My dear little friend Lotte,

If you do not mind this picture of me being so crumpled, I would like to
leave it here in your room for you to have as a memento, because I have
no more recent photos in Vienna. A picture is nothing if it is not looked at
kindly. But it can be a whole world, and all the more wonderful in
proportion as our imaginings are benign.

Good morning, dear Baby, OK

To Alma Mahler-Gropius

[Dresden, 27 May 1921]

Alma,

I have in front of me the picture that I once painted of the two of us, in
which we both look so exhausted, and you are giving me back the ring. It
came into my hands by chance, because there's going to be an exhibition
here of my most important works, a kind of survey of my life to date, and
the owner did not want to entrust it to a stranger before the opening. Now
it's in my green pavilion, and I look at you, drink your health in Spanish

76

red wine, and do not believe that you betrayed me, or that, when I was wounded, you forgot the things that mysteriously link us to each other. We are both to blame for being so foolish as to give up so great a love in favour of an even greater, abstract love.

Life rolls on so insanely fast. I gave everything away, your ring, your red necklace, your coat, even my memory, in as much as I put our experiences on the stage. But today I am alone again, and I feel as if you were thinking of me, and as if everything I gave away was nothing in comparison with the secret power that goes from one heart to another, forever giving birth to itself anew, until one of us is dead.

If you were as brave as I am, now would be the time when we would first begin to live and love each other.

I'm leaving for Spain very soon.

Ever the happiness of the one in the other.

To Anna Kallin

[Dresden, first half of September 1921]

Malina,

I sent you the flowers I love because they are simply my idea of you. But you have accused me of saying you are my only child. You shall have the right to know about me and understand me. Very well, so that I can really be called your friend, I will explain what happened to me when I was – as you must always be – unscarred by life.

I loved a woman, from the moment I first set eyes on her, with my whole existence, even unto death for love's sake. She said: The fairy story of your life, grown man as you are, is Bluebeard. And mine is Lohengrin's wife. He tests one woman after another, hoping that purity will conquer him one day, and she needs to be forced, again and again, to have faith, the deepest faith. And I was as I shall remain, and I did what I still do today. I tried to awaken faith, I let myself be stabbed, literally, deep in the lung. I was distressed, but persisted when in wartime this woman took a husband, who abstained from the war for her sake, while I committed myself for the sake of love as I saw it. For my part, I was justified, because neither the war nor my wound was an accident, but was foretold in my work, which is nothing but pictures speaking of my actions. And I made my pact in the eyes of the whole world, in which I have since become an influence, one of the real leaders; I must still prove my woman is right! And therefore I seek her, and put her to every test I can think of, try every path that will lead to her heart, to the uttermost from the innermost in me, and of course it's often remote – I seem to shimmer, if you look at me from the outside. I don't ponder, I have pondered once and for all – I shall do what I must, until I have succeeded in my task of proving my world of love justified: a woman is pure, sublime above all doubt, she can love, can keep faith, even the deepest faith, without allowing herself to be made unfaithful by others or by herself. Faith is set above herself, above her own being.

And a man exceeds his own strength in trying to create this faith, because they must both be of one mind, on which not only their need but also their fate can depend.

You look upon everything as hypocrisy and vanity for the present, and you know for your part what was better in your heart, before you met me. Why are you so touchingly obstinate, Niuta? Child, accuse me, my transient part, but do not besmirch my works too, which are myself; if you cannot grasp me, my many other selves will give you one thread each. Together they live, and I am all of them. But personally, from me to you, Malina, do you honestly believe that it was vanity that made me not defend myself in the night of a rainy Russian autumn, alone – because not even a friendly thought visited me – although the earlier shot had not paralysed me on the right side, and I could have drawn my revolver? There was no woman with me then, to induce me to play a part, was there? I allowed my side to be pierced, in order to convince myself of the purity of my belief that love and the imagination are stronger than death. And death is everything in bondage, everything which will not fulfil its purpose. Theseus is always there.

Malina, I stroke your hair, I will come and see you soon, and I love you whether you love me for a few seconds or with all your faith, like simple Edith, until my mountain buries me, when my world caves in [. . .]

votre Flèche

I've burned my right hand so badly that I have to stay in bed, because I can't dress myself. So Hulda will have to address the envelope.

To Anna Kallin

[Dresden, mid-September 1921]

Niuta, my little singing-bird,

I suppose you have your Mama with you now, and have warmed up a bit, my darling little girl. Before I go to Vienna I will come and see you again too, and kiss your busy little playing fingers in gratitude for all the dear kind words and letters. I will speak encouragingly to Colibri, and hope to be of some use to her, and even do her some good. I've been dreadfully worried all week about the rioting in Vienna, I'm never easy about my guileless little parents, and then Hulda has both hands bandaged because of some blood-poisoning which is moving around inside her, so that when I get home exhausted in the evening it's both unwelcoming and weepy at the same time. What with the daily grind and the foul cold weather, I am constantly on edge, and there's really nowhere I can relax except in a large cinema here, in the balcony, but there must be some door at the back, because there's always a small, uncomfortable draught down my back. I think I shall have to stop going there because I shall catch cold, don't you agree? – the first seat on the left of the screen, which I don't watch, because I've been to the same programme about six times now, and I sit there looking at the dark house, without anyone near me, and think how warm the Egyptian sun is, and how far away I am from worry, inhospitality and the cold in Dresden. I wish I could work magic. Perhaps one day I shall be able to, all of a sudden, but I think it requires much, much more love than one person can stand.

Malina, I give you a quick kiss on the lips before you notice it. Au revoir, my two little flower-sisters,   your Flèche d'Orient.

To Anna Kallin

[Dresden, late September 1921] [1]

Niuta must come back, if possible, I would be very hurt if she rejected me altogether. I am secretly in love with Niuta, and perhaps I should have confessed it long ago, but I thought: will she be able to do anything about it, would I not do much better to stand by, and be ready to jump up if she wants to play with me? I'm afraid that she really will go to Italy, I know what she's like when she's made up her mind, perhaps she will vanish from my sight, won't spare me another thought, won't have any further use for me, won't have any more interest in me, not even the slightest. She will become a thrilling transatlantic coloratura soprano, may even get engaged to that * * * Italian, who I hate from the bottom of my heart, especially since I noticed that she plots with his family about my affairs, and keeps it from me.

I often write till 3 at night, then I can't get up, and have to miss the dancing-master. By doing that I doubtless plunge Hilde Goldschmidt into philosophical reflections on the unsatisfactoriness of human aspi-rations, which I don't like, because it will make her inordinately sceptical and unfeeling, and it will be my fault, when she ought to be learning how to have faith and thus become a nice person. I hope and pray that I am a really unimportant person for her, and therefore have little influence on her opinions – preferably none at all.

I shall have finished in another four or five days, and shall then be wanting to know from you, my dear good Malina, what is going to happen, and who is going to be leader, governor, prime minister. I beseech you, my beloved, do not think of honouring me with the distinction, which ought to go to a more worthy man. The office is too difficult for me and, once torn from the simple milieu of my profession, I would find it hard to adapt to the role of a master of the art of living. In case you have no one to hand just at the moment, please send me a wire in good time, so that I can have my vital functions medically adjusted, until you have the time, during a rest from coloratura, to take charge again. However, I wish you would think of some way to praise and reward Hilde Goldschmidt, perhaps by awarding her the Mary Wigman Medal. I think she loves dancing best, she's right, it's more rewarding than painting, where years pass before one experiences a few seconds of joy. Colibri is totally wrapped up in her family and no longer gives me a thought. Please give her my warmest good wishes.

I haven't written, because I'm writing a play and my fingers are so stiff from the pen, which is useless. Your unhappy Flèche.

Quick, Malina, and of your own free will, give me your hand to kiss.

To Anna Kallin

[Dresden, late September 1921] [II]

Malina Niuta, my love,

You don't look after me well enough, although you know I am not excessively long for this life. My ambition, as a *Fareweller* from life, is to stand on the high wire in the circus and fall from there into your arms, and then break my neck, so that all is beautifully over and there is nothing left for me to do or long for. But you, first of all, with the utmost fecklessness, undertook a European tour in order to test the tensile strength of your principles, and then spent several weeks waiting for that conceited Italian. Those weeks should have been devoted to the instruction under your very stern and beautiful eyes that is vitally necessary to me! I detest that Italian, and I'm perfectly convinced that you will offer him your heart and your hand, unless I succeed, secretly, by means of silent prayer, in moving Colibri to recall you to your duty of persuading me to wear my sequined costume of violet and orange silk. I hate that Italian and I wish he was dead, because he is a constant threat to my life.

Imagine me performing my death-defying feats on the high wire, and suddenly being surprised up there by the thought that you, down below, are perhaps thinking of him. * * *

You may be very, very stern with me, and rebellious enough to poison me, but you must be faithful!!! Because I must learn it!!! Fidelity, that is. I have heard that if one is to be an artist one must first be insanely beaten as a child, and I have never been beaten in my life, except by my first teacher in elementary school. But she wore a green snake bracelet – more precisely, a bracelet of tula metal with green eyes – on the right upper arm which she bared to wield the rod, and a black low-cut satin dress (she

80

called it a 'robe', and I thought I was a *robber*). Anyway, one of the glass eyes fell out, and I stole the gem, and due to its talismanic power I fell in love with the girl who was top of the class, who sat across the gangway, because we still had *co-education* then. Thus it came to pass that I missed out on the real school of life, but if I had graduated from that I might be a marvellous tightrope-walker by now, dancing high above my fellow citizens. Instead I am still in love with the girls who are top of the class, and have more need than ever of the stern-eyed teacher, who chastised me out of love because she wanted to make something of me. I must not hang about much longer, my life no longer stretches out before me at such excessive length as it did, my days are numbered, and you won't have your full share of them. My brother went back to Vienna today. We both cried because we are very fond of each other, I shall go and see him again in November. Now I shall sit on your bed until you go to sleep, then I shall steal your smile and a kiss, because you are not stern when you are asleep.

My swetheart, sincerely yours,
toujours fidèle à sa Maîtresse M.   votre flèche humaine

I love to receive very, very long letters. Please? I implore you.

To Anna Kallin

                          [Dresden, late September 1921] [III]
Malina,
I won't go to Paris, you know, because I've been waging a kind of battle with the French since before the war. So I've never been tempted to go there. I want to deprive them of all the things they boast about; it's a masculine matter, in which I not only think I can stand my ground, because I don't have to allow for anyone except myself, but I also anticipate final victory. In the last analysis it's the antithesis of personality and style, the latter representing a communal spirit which I always enjoy vanquishing, because it is contrary to my unchained imagination. I am a true adventurer, and if I sense resistance in any ancient country it draws me there, in order to make a place for my will to live. Perhaps my entire manner of seduction, which is so repugnant to you as a woman, is only an elementary school, appropriate to my inner, relative youth, and it will look harmless when compared to the tasks that I have set myself. In years to come, when I am well established in enjoyment of the life of a new kind of statesman (you must not overlook the fact that almost as long ago as 1907!!! I invented, and am the leader of, a movement in the intellectual and spiritual dimension which is called Expressionism and now has the upper hand in a specific stratum of

European society), I shall probably be some woman's very devoted and grateful lover, in proportion to how far she has surrendered to my wishes. I was very touched by your sending me the letter from Edith. I can't write to her, because I love her nervous disposition but not her circle of interests. Her fate, but not her circumstances. The thought that she is coming here soon is agreeably stimulating. If you knew me, Malina, the three of us would go to Egypt, and I could create an empire to be my arena.

With the utmost tenderness,   your Flèche

To Anna Kallin

[Vienna, January 1922] [1]

My poor dear Niuta Malina

I haven't been able to write for such a long time, and your letters are so touching, because you don't know how to be cross. Today is the first chance I've had to get my breath. I discovered when I got home that my father, who is of a great age, had had a cancerous growth on his face for months, and had been seen by an incompetent doctor. I had a dickens of a job to persuade him to go with me to a sanatorium and have radiation treatment. But it is years since he last spoke to a stranger, and also it was important that he shouldn't realize how dangerous it is, so you can imagine I had my work cut out. At the same time my parents' servant had decamped, so that we were simply cut off from the town and vice versa. Everything conspired to make me a nervous wreck. We live on the outskirts of Vienna, and all forms of transport have become antediluvian, so that I simply give up, reduced to 'nichevo' à la Soviet Russia. Malina understood all that, and for that reason she remained my dear, faithful little singing-bird, but Niuta may have thought some bad thoughts. My father is out of danger now, thank God, and we've brought him home, but if I hadn't acted so energetically and so quickly, who knows what the outcome might have been.

I have a suggestion, Niuta. I shall be mourning my birthday on 1 March, postpone yours until then, and we can console each other together. It would give me really enormous pleasure if you would, and it might be some compensation for the anxiety and muddle here.

I shall return to Dresden very soon after 1 February (at most plus or minus a few days!) Please come to me then without any delay and help me – only I shall help you, to get back on the rails. And sing to do my heart good. Let the Reys of this world for Christ's sake make their proposals to somebody else, who hasn't learned to sing for me. Don't catch 'flu. I left my fountain pen in Dresden, and the only way into the city is by car, which must first be fetched from there.

Niuta, Malina, I kiss both of you on your hands, cheeks, brows and mouths, too, if you will forgive me, and I am eternally glad that I have you. Always, your Flèche.

To Anna Kallin

[Vienna, January 1922] [II]

Niuta, Malina,

It makes me so happy when your letters arrive, because I cannot escape from the misery here. I've got a bad cold now, and need to stay in bed, after having valiantly endured every ill for weeks on end. Furthermore it would be easier to despatch letters from Turkey than from here, which is the reason why I must go to Lake Tiberias or Cairo this year without fail. And you must go with me, so that I can place directly in your hands the letters that I feel like writing you whenever I am in low spirits. Pure egoism on my part, because what I want is your replies equally fast.

We can expect a thaw here at any moment, because there has been impenetrable fog since yesterday. At the same time it's still very cold. Can you come with me, Niuta, or follow me, to Venice in April (end of)? There's an exhibition opening there that I'm in charge of. But I don't trust myself to go without you, because you take care of me so cleverly and understand me like a sister, and because you are so tender and have lovely red hair, and you won't lose me. And because you sing to me and comfort me, and if I'm unfaithful to you, you are hurt, which I need to know so as to be justified in doing it, because I only do it in order to know if you would miss me more than anything in the world. You must describe what poor wedded Edith left with you for me. I'm very curious to know if it's the chain-mail tunic with glass spangles that I once ordered from Paris. You must speak and write French to me, to give me the chance to get away from Dresden at last. Will you? You must be very cheerful and laugh a lot with me, will you? I shall be with you on 1 March, and six or seven weeks before that. Your Flèche

To Adolf Loos

[Vienna, January? 1922]

Dear Loos,

I've taken to my bed again, I caught a cold last night. Next time you go to Zagreb I shall go with you, because I'm very interested in Croatian women. Now, pay attention. It's vitally important that I get an invitation from Zagreb or Belgrade, official, from a museum, to hold an exhibition there. In case no one there has heard of me, give them this pamphlet and the monograph. I want to paint the king and queen of

Yugoslavia. We'll go there together. Talk to all the journalists, so that they fill the papers with gossip, anecdotes and reviews.

Meanwhile, the big Venice exhibition is opening (April), and I shall be there. I told you I was going to be the major attraction, with the support of the German government. Apart from me, there'll be only Liebermann, Slevogt and Corinth, making a more modest showing. Therefore I must get back [to Dresden] as soon as my cold is better and put the finishing touches to my big paintings. Then from Venice I will go to Belgrade and Bucharest, and make drawings of beautiful expensive women, and more importantly make love to them, and recover from all my worries – which were necessary, after all. Mind you sing my praises in Milan, and everywhere else.

Have a good journey, and good luck.   Phthisically yours, Oskar

To Alice Lahmann

[Vienna, second half of January 1922]

Dear Colibri,

My very warmest congratulations on your good news, and I hope you are quite well. I am only sorry that now there will be no more room for me in your heart, I wish I could be your little Dage myself. You had no business to grow up so fast. All my girls are outgrowing me, and I'm left all alone, and nobody hears me howling.

I've had a lot of worries here, now I've got a stinking cold, and I hope to be back in Dresden in a week's time. Dear Colibri, please tell your Dage I bid him welcome as a new earthling, but if you overdo your praising and loving and cosseting of him, I shall silently withdraw, and never let myself be seen again. I may go to India and woo a coolie girl.

Most affectionately, Lieutenant Glahn

To Anna Kallin

[Venice, *c.* 5 May 1922]

Niuta,

Now I know that you don't love me (not even my work), and that I can't entertain any more hopes, unless I want to turn into a Don Quixote, embracing the air. I sweated blood to get here, and you knew – your intuition told you so as well – that I am waiting for my luck to turn here, because I've struggled for years for my work and nothing else, and at last it's all on show here. And I've been left dangling, wretched and unloved, and after three weeks of waiting I feel as cold as a corpse.

Edith passed through, and spent a few days with me, she did not begrudge the effort to find me, although I didn't write to her, but she too

has obligations, a yardstick, and limits that I don't fit in to, and therefore I have stayed out. Why is everyone so eminently practical? How is it they understand how to adapt their feelings to the given circumstances of the day, and why haven't I learned it? All around me I see people blessed with nothing but good fortune, who miaow from time to time, so as not to provoke the gods, but so far as the essentials are concerned they always know exactly where to shelter their heads and their hearts when tragedy threatens. There is something I didn't realize before, and discovered only today in the exhibition: you are now nothing more than a picture for me.
Farewell, Malina, Niuta, Noisette   Flèche is frozen

To Alice Lahmann

[Venice, Hotel Bauer-Grünwald, early May 1922]

Dear Colibri,

Your legs *et surtout tes genoux sont exquises*, and if I was your husband I would place you on an altar and and make my morning prayers to you, and once a month I would make a human sacrifice to you.

Tell me, sweetheart, why is Niuta so silent, and why is she not here? I came here on my own, and could have got lost a thousand times in this damned, nookshotten, crumbling, bourgeois rabbit-warren, because I can never manage to find my way. I would so much have liked to take Niuta somewhere in the country – Tuscany or somewhere.

There is talk of taking me to London from here. Why is Niuta not here, when she's the only one left unmarried, and still free to adopt an orphan who sighs for a Mama? I have grown quite handsome here, erect in carriage and almost gaunt.

I kiss your knees, Edwarda, *in devotion*   Your Lieutenant Glahn.

To Alice Lahmann

[Florence, 10 May 1922]

Colibri,

There is no one here either, I am on the verge of tears, why does happiness evade me so obstinately, Colibri, Colibri?   Your Lieutenant Glahn

To Alma Mahler-Gropius

[Dresden, 9 October 1922]

Alma,

Your little face was so sad in Venice, let me make you smile with an opera story, because it's about you. Cast your mind back: once when we were in Munich I began to get upset because you stood longingly outside the

Anna Kallin, drawing, 1921.

locked doors of the opera house, straining to hear if there was any sound from inside. I felt ashamed because I didn't have the power to open the doors for you. And now I have that power – but where are you?

Here, on 12 December, Busch is going to conduct *Mörder Hoffnung der Frauen* by Kokoschka (and Hindemith), *Arlequino* by Busoni, and *Petrushka* by Stravinsky. Designed and produced by me, of course. And it will surely blow away some cobwebs. But I shall not rest on my laurels. I foresee *Orpheus*, by a man like Scriabin or some such maestro in New York, and the masterpiece I shall present at the Metropolitan Opera will make you rejoice in me again. Send forth your commands to the world for which you yearn – still, probably – in your heart, where you remain a child; in America, where once you were really swept off your feet, you shall be overwhelmed again. I invite you there so that I can show you how strong I am.

At present I have absolutely no grounds for my prophecy, but with me everything happens as I wish it to, sooner or later! Unhappily, life does not run on parallel lines. But it ought to do so, just once, for you, so that I can see that I did have the power to make the shades give me what is mine by right. Do not let this wish of mine, to thrill you in the Metropolitan Opera one day, slip from your mind, promise?   Oskar

To Anna Kallin

[Dresden, October 1922] [1]

Dear Benin,

No letter today, but yesterday, Sunday, I had two. Perhaps this evening, when I get back to the house (which is so empty) there will be one after all. It's made me feel cold all day. On 12 December my *Mörder Hoffnung der Frauen* is being performed here, in the opera house under Busch. I am in charge of production and design, and can do exactly as I please. I shall, what's more. I'm dreadfully sorry that you aren't here already. I do so, so wish you could be with me when I have all the ideas that I must start having from today forwards, in order to make the production a grand spectacle. I could have let my imagination run free on the work with you here. It would have made it an exploit of love, and all stirrings of the imagination are sad if they are not the exploits of love. The stage would have been the temple, and what I imagined while you lay in my arms would have reappeared there as a *tableau vivant* before our eyes, like a higher form of souvenir postcard, because a large number of other people would have witnessed it too. Isn't it a shame, Benin mine, that you are not at my side at important moments? But you are here, Benin, close beside me, I can feel your breath on my cheek, I love you, my girl-god

Your Flèche

To Anna Kallin

[Dresden, October 1922] [II]

Benin,

I'm furious, I shall go to Serbia and get killed with the gipsies in the struggle against the authorities over the abduction of a Balkan village maiden, if you dare go so far as to torment me with trips to America on 5 January, although you know perfectly well that I shall be flying to London by airship on 6 January.

Don't tug at my heartstrings with filial love, which is as strongly developed in me as it is in you, you will only be unhappy in America, I swear it! You will undoubtedly marry some bicycle salesman there, and at the very moment when you say 'Yes' to his wooing you will feel a stitch in your side, because you will hear by clairvoyance my dying gasp, exhaled at that very moment, as I fall for the Romanian cause. That won't be very nice for you, and I feel sorry for you and for me, because we could have gone to lots more museums and, in general, we could have known a happiness rarely granted to an unbourgeois couple in operatic tragedy. As it is, you will suffer stitches in your side, and I will suffer stabbing in mine, as once before in my life in similar circumstances. I'm sure you are no more willing to conjure up the parallel than I am, so do not allow things to go so far (as to America or Serbia respectively) but let us meet in the middle chez NOUS. As soon as you can. Will you? Why didn't you write yesterday? Colibri is a traitress! I will not kiss you, Benin, in case you are laughing too hard, until a moment when you have no tears in your eyes, evermore   Flèche

To Anna Kallin

[Dresden, October 1922] [III]

Neither flirted nor tempted!!

Dear Benin,

I come straight from the theatre, where I was up on the grid. I have no idea what opera they were playing, I think it was Korngold, it was so post-Wagnerian. Listen my dear, you must at once, AT ONCE, go for a three-hour walk, and, if at all possible, uphill. I have heard talk of naturopathy in the past, but I imagined it was something like one of Lahmann's potions. Today I was supposed to go to Wachwitz or somewhere like that for a concert, no, you are quite wrong, not for amorous dalliance. When I reached the door with Posse, I broke loose and, when he shouted, I put a spurt on and got lost in the mountains. Darkness fell, but I went on climbing, undaunted, exhilarated by the altitude, so that I paused for only a moment outside Colibri's door, thinking of the pageboy costume (Thou shalt have no other goddesses beside me, First Commandment), and then sought the way downhill, across bogs, following will-o'-the-wisps, and through forests and ravines. And I felt so well, for the first time for weeks, that I shall in future make a point of accepting invitations to go to musical events. That's why I went to the opera. They had just lowered the set for the first act of Wagner or whatever it was into the depths, and I almost fainted in the arms of a man in a canary-yellow wig, known as the Intendant, for there at my feet yawned an abyss 20 metres deep, into which the superfluous acts of the opera disappear.

Benin, you ought to like me a lot, because I love you very faithfully and thought of you all the time on my walk.

Kissing my Benin, her Flèche

To Anna Kallin

[Dresden, October 1922] [IV]

Benin,

You never write more than half a page now, and you fill them with accusations. You are a wicked, badly brought-up nomad girl, and I insist that you start to behave more decorously forthwith, and stop hating so much, otherwise your face will turn yellow instead of brown! I admit, I have a confession to make. Every day, ever since you started believing that I missed writing to you one morning because of a woman, I have been seeing seven very charming young ladies, who are white all over. Porcelain, you jealous tigress! The Bustelli figurines have arrived. One has lost a finger. I had my first idea for the opera yesterday. If you were already here it would be a very pleasant game for us, as it is it's really a stupid devotion of serious attention to the superfluous. What do I care about the theatre – let alone the audiences! The day before yesterday, Benin, you did not write a single word, yesterday you wrote only one page. I write to you every day. If the letter does not arrive it's the fault of the post. My darling, darling Benin, I want you to be very happy

your Flèche

To Anna Kallin

[Dresden, October 1922] [V]

Benin,

You are expected with all my heart, at last it's no longer such a dreadfully long time until you return. Come, Benin, my beautiful Fräulein Benin, come to me quickly, do not forget to be exuberantly happy, do not crease your brow in thought but open your mouth wide and show lots of teeth, ready to bite down hard and hold tight. You shall eat me all up, oh yes,

89

making love is a war which has slain every one of the exotic and homebred concubines in a bitter battle to the death.

Be sure to bring the sort of Mesopotamian dress which suits you, with bare legs and little slippers to wear in the tent. And a scarf round your head and bangles on your feet, so that I don't have to waste time thinking my way through your European clothes, and don't get dazzled by the exotic costumes of your defeated rivals, who are all only shadows. Your place is the tent. You alone, my favourite wife, nomadic Benin, Rhamnis, are my beloved, such is my longing for you that I curse the days, the life without you which I have to live. Until you are here. Look here, young lady, you shouldn't always send me these short, half-written letters. They won't do. I don't believe that you think they are enough as a substitute for yourself.   Flèche

To Anna Kallin

[Dresden, early March 1923]

My Mirli,

I'm longing to hear your news from London, how you are getting on at home, and if you can make yourself understood, and above all if the journey didn't make you ill. If I had known that it was going to be such a rush, I would have gone with you as far as the frontier. Please, Mirli – you won't do it because you do not love me enough in practical terms, but I beg you just the same – do everything you should to be really well and fit, and avoid everything which tires you, because that's the sign that it's not good for you. Watch your way of life in that respect, you must not let yourself get tired, I know all too well what it's like. Look at me, my girl, at the shadowy existence I lead for the better part of the year, because I've allowed myself to be deceived about my nature and my right to live, during the eighteen-year battle for imagined illusions, honour, fame and other will-o'-the-wisps. If I was not so tough I would probably be an invalid. As it is, I am divided and doubtful, overflowing and then again like nothing on earth *vis à vis du rien*; and if, in spite of that, you want something from me, you can only expect to get it if you are as relaxed about my mortality as you are prepared to come out with me at a moment's notice and have a good time without being afraid that you yourself may be going through a bad patch. You must remain unbroken: it's easy for you, because you've never had any accidents at all, and you are constitutionally healthy. So, at this stage of your life, while you've got your wits about you, you should already avoid doing anything at all that's bad for you – you are my nature, my shelter, my joy, my senses, my beloved and my helpmate, friend and child. Everything else you should touch with caution – if it helps, take it, if it gnaws you, get rid of it.

90

Don't·stay up late, Mirli, don't worry needlessly about me, don't be afraid. My Mirli, your Un wants his Ben sitting on his lap.

I shall probably go away at Easter, but only for about two weeks, the painting was good to begin with, but now it's got dangerously stuck. Perhaps there's no more to be done with it.

To Anna Kallin

[Dresden, late March 1923]

Mirli, my darling,

Why on earth do you torment yourself with such obviously sick thoughts that something might happen to me? I beg you, my little, darling, silly girl, for my sake, do what would really please me and look after yourself, when I've had to let you go for this long age, and don't know how you are, whether they're leaning on you, or if you will come back safe and sound to me at all. You know perfectly well that if you aren't more healthy, lively and innocent than I am then you don't get the best out of me, and you're unhappy, as you were last week, and I'm embarrassed, ashamed and have no idea whether you want me, or whether you have really let me talk you into it. So, Benin, daughter of Lady Rhamnis, I wish you by day and by night, waking and sleeping, a truly joyful heart and a smile on your face which I would so much like to kiss. I don't even know where I shall lay my head. I see no reason why you shouldn't accept the frou-frou: firstly you deserve to have everything of the prettiest – who does, if you don't? – and secondly I don't think your parents will worry about it as if you were a disobedient little girl, and take your Sunday hair-ribbons away. Besides, it's not important, if you don't get it I'll give you a nicer one. The first three days were easy, Mirli, because I imagined I would have to work hard, but now I'm already getting under Reserl's feet simply because of you, as I recognize, because I miss you at every moment. I rejoice in you Mirli, as much as if I was a boy.   Your Un [. . .] Should I write to your parents? I will come and meet you at the frontier when you come back, my sweetheart.

To Anna Kallin

[Dresden,] 26. 3. [1923]

Mirli, Ben, Malina, Noisette, Niuta,

You sent me an express letter, which showed me in a flash a great misfortune that you are determined to tumble into, unless I follow you alone, and do what you, without knowing it, expect me to do. Instinctively, from your foxhole, you bombard me with cunning, illness, appeals to my emotions, your helplessness against your parents, all because you know how weak I am in unimportant matters. And you went to London to prove to me that you love me less than your father – me, who makes no objection to your loving whatever you do love, or do not love – but you only think of asserting your will against mine. Because you are using the means listed above – not that you are aware of it, but the symptoms reveal themselves inexorably one after the other – to force me to make a pact in some form or other with bourgeois existence; what you are so eager to bring about is my dependence on other people, namely, in this case, your good (or bad) parents; you want me chasing discounts instead of writing, so that I earn some money, if I don't watch (which I can't) while you, capricious and elegant woman that you are, demonstrate that you are poor, look ill and behave badly. Poverty depraves a person who lives alone, but for two, or three, or five, or thirteen (ghastly thought), to live like that is a ghetto, and is none the better for being a bourgeois ghetto with or without the blessing of the social authorities. You know that well enough at a glance where other people are concerned.

If you loved me, Mirli, it would make you want something, and when someone wants something they do it, and ensure that others don't stop them. But you have not won your parents over, you haven't made them waver in their principles with regard to you, the most drastic expression of which is that they believe in the omnipotence of a bank account. My principle is that I shall not lose the foundation of my desire to work, which is my independence and responsibility for myself alone – my fate or my downfall. You know that I exhaust myself in quite a different way from a businessman, who doesn't need to exploit himself but operates with the labour of others. Since he is a saver as a matter of principle, he can have a well-ordered family, but I can be a spendthrift, because my whole life is nothing else, and the most I can have is parents. My work contains everything that will die with me, and nothing that will reach beyond me or outlive me. The only right an artist has in a materialistic age is that when he has no more illusions left – that is, when he is exhausted – he has the freedom to take his own life. And a woman who sets about loving an artist as you do robs him of his clear vision of his position. Mirli, you are still free of something very moving: you are free of the instinct which develops into a hardness in women, especially women of your sort, and makes you move in the way it directs (think of harmless Hulda!). You needed to be told this truth about me and yourself, show your Papa, so that he doesn't only hear bad things about me from other people: this is the sum total of my badness.

Kissing Mirli in the eyes of the whole world,   Un

To Anna Kallin

Mirli,

I'm tormented now by the thought that you will have been upset by my letter about your helplessness, and the distance is too great to cut short the torment for you, until this letter arrives. This whole business of writing is a bloody nuisance! You were in a bad mood with me when you were here, and made no allowances for my being overworked. When you left I threw myself into my work, consuming vast amounts of cola and coffee the while, and the result was that I thought I smelt disaster, uncertainty and catastrophe on all sides, and that on the other hand I ought not to deceive people I love, and who rely on me, about my true situation, and how I'm exploited. It was all overwork! And anger with the cruelty of the bourgeois world.

But now that I've almost finished my painting – tomorrow, Friday, from 7 a.m. to 7 p.m. will be the last day I shall spend (ever in my life, I hope) abusing my health and my nervous energy so violently, and in the evening Fritsche will put the painting on the train to Berlin – now I see all of a sudden that in the end, instead of showing your parents how narrow-minded they are, with an example of the absurdity of the opposite position, you will opt for being offended at me. That's not what I wanted and it didn't occur to me when I wrote. Now I realize it, but you will probably already have the letter by now. So, my darling Mirli, listen to me, and if you like me take the following to heart and do it: of course you can come here, and you ought to at once, and stay with me. We will be adventurers, but we will love each other and stick together. If you want to, you can rub me up the wrong way when I'm tired and exhausted, but afterwards you must feel sorry for me and make it up to me by healing the wounds. Let your people carry out their threats, you won't need them, I shall not fall ill, and I shall care for you always, and when it's no longer possible we'll put an end to it together.

I'm going to Vienna on Monday, and to Berlin on Saturday, to put the exhibition together. I shall be in Vienna until the 20th, and then hope to find you in the Großer Garten, unless you come to Vienna. I have to go on working until the end of July, to pay off some debts, and then we will go away and won't come back. Mirli, don't be unhappy about your Un, Ben is and will always be his beloved.

To Anna Kallin

[Dresden, end of March 1923]

My Mirli,

I didn't write to you yesterday, I was absolutely whacked from slogging at the painting without a break from 9.30 to 6.30, because I knew that, if I don't finish it, it will be yet another chore when I get back from Vienna. I hate all pictures, I hate my whole profession, I hate Europe, the whole of my existence is just a semblance, a nonsense, which is so maddening that you might as well give the same respect to a machine which stamps and shudders and lets off steam as much as I do.

I hate my life, and I know full well that I shall go on leading exactly the same life as long as I stay here in Europe, regardless of whether I am famous, regardless of all the advantages as well as the disadvantages of this self-destruction. What's the outcome? I sit in an empty studio with a kind of hangover, not knowing why I've put myself through such torture. Listen, girl, you can put these letters I write about my troubles on the fire without a second thought, they only get written in the belief that it can't go on like this forever, and that I won't endure this kind of life indefinitely. But if you prefer – and you are grown-up enough to know what you are getting into with me – do just whatever you want and what I want too. Because I like you. Tell your people what to do with their security, and come here and be ruined with me.

Do you know what would be a proper existence, Mirli? Africa! But it would take a miracle to transport us from here to there. I would like to be an African king, and I would drive out all the European shopkeepers and commercial travellers, and arouse my black people. That would be worthwhile and exciting enough for me to go on living, confining those awful bourgeois to Europe, where they would have to go on bartering feathers and postage-stamps and flimsy little pictures until they are carted to the cemetery. The world of the Europeans is appalling! To hell with it! Enquire in London, Mirli, about African books (language).

I kiss the top of my Mirli's head. There's no need for you to earn a living, you silly *syolnushka*, do you think I shall let you be poisoned the way I've been?

Your Un

To Alice Lahmann

[Zurich,] 25. 8. 23

Colibri,

We made it! We're going on to Lucerne and Montreux, and will either stay here or go on to Italy. What do you think? When will you get here? Write c/o Herr Böhler, Haldenstr. 12, Lucerne, my dear little humming-bird,

Yours, Reindeer-Lieutenant Glahn

[Vienna, early November 1923]

Mirli,

Now I know how well off we were, and I was, in Switzerland. I hope you will never receive or need a lesson like this in your life: to be grateful for the relative harmlessness life can have for someone before he's up against it, when it is irrevocably at an end, and irreparable. If you had seen only a little of what happened here, the unhappiness, the helplessness and the heart-wrenching end, and the need to practise deceit all the time so as to stop my mother seeing anything, or else she would have gone mad, and then the god-damned grisly business with a dead body on one's hands, hiding it for a day and a night until society has performed its hyena functions in all piety. You smell so bad to yourself that you want to run away from everyone else, and from yourself. The cemetery where I have laid my father to rest for a week in a temporary vault is right beside our house. My mother senses it and behaves like a three-year-old child who puts on a brave face because she's afraid of the teacher, but when she looks behind her she can see something horrible under the bench. I shall have my father cremated next week. I couldn't do it straightaway, because people in the neighbourhood would talk. Mother mustn't hear anything, and must be carefully brought round to not want to know anything. When once you know what being dead means you are no longer wholly alive yourself.

My brother sat up with my father every night for three weeks; you can imagine the state he's in. You know, a little bit of talent, such as I've got, exacts a heavy price from the parents, a very heavy price, in the form of a life which is neither entirely normal nor entirely insane. That's the source of all the hopelessness, complications and tragedy in our family. What need have I to go poking my nose into the psyche of a South Sea savage who has survived the death of his race? It's all there in my own house. And in my own skull!

That's enough of that. I shall try to air the house, let in fresh ideas, and carefully rearrange the furniture and the memories. You mustn't forget that my mother was married for nearly forty years and is over-alert, instead of being blunted, and doesn't like to go out in search of distraction like other people. She won't agree to any of the suggestions I make, but imperceptibly draws us children to join her on her desert island. (I am now 'the eldest'!! – to hell with that, my wits are going: it will be my turn next, and perhaps I won't have been able to raise myself out of the prison of my flesh into an idea that will outlive me!)

Mirli, my dear, if you are a real human being and not a stranger in my heart, you won't be counting the days now, you will be loving me as a woman should. And however long you may have to wait, you mustn't get blunted, and you mustn't be rational and scold what is not altogether sound in me, but be sympathetic and encourage me. [. . .]

And Mirli, you mustn't say heartless things ever again [. . .], even when you've lost control of yourself, because I don't know what comes out then, and I don't want to believe any of it. When a bad odour comes from the mouth, a person washes in secret, when something bad comes from the heart, he makes himself good in secret. The lesson I have been learning throughout my life is: act according to nature, not morals. That's why most people take me for a good-natured fool, and fail to notice that I know what to do – and that I have to be proper even though others aren't! And you too must be proper because of what you are, and mustn't be any less so because others aren't. The fire must burn, even if the putrefaction beside it reeks to high heaven. Only by this means can one person find the way out of himself towards another who is also lonely and would dearly like to have a friend to embrace and live with. Haven't you met enough people who make you wonder how they can run around so dead, existing and not realizing that this kind of mentality is without rhyme or reason? Oh, Mirli, I'm longing for such a time, and even more for love, and I've never yet in all my life until now seen any proof that this sun exists, that warmth will enter me from without, and not just constantly leak out of me. Have you enough time, Mirli? If your parents go to Paris now, don't be cross with them (with your father). Write to Colibri, who has lost your address. One other thing, write to the hotel in Switzerland and ask them to let me have the painting I sent for as soon as possible. If I have any more time now, I must find something neutral to divert me for the good of my health. I am full of sorrow, and my little Ben must kiss me until I can emerge.   Your Un

1–3 Oskar Kokoschka in 1905/6 and (left) in 1909, and Alma Mahler, to whom he wrote many passionate letters during their three-year love-affair, 1912–15.

4 Relaxing on the terrace of the Hotel Panhans, Semmering, Kokoschka is seen with the writers Egon Friedell and Peter Altenberg, July 1912.

The First World War

After volunteering for service in the Imperial Austrian Army, Kokoschka became an officer cadet in the 15th Regiment of Dragoons in January 1915.

5, 6 Kokoschka in full dress uniform as a dragoon, 1915, and (below) in field dress in Galicia after his posting to the Russian front.

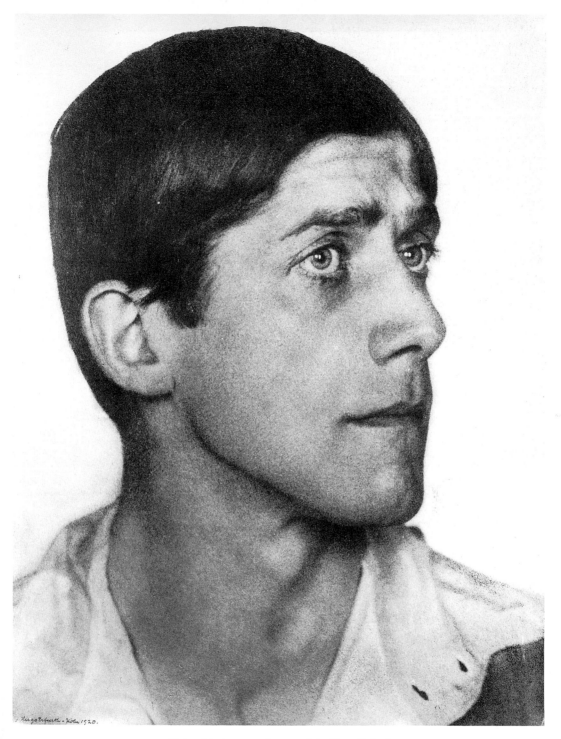

7 Kokoschka in 1920, photograph by Hugo Erfurth.

8 In conversation with Herwarth Walden, editor of the journal *Der Sturm*, Berlin 1916; Walden, who also had his own gallery in Berlin, gave Kokoschka active support by publishing his drawings and exhibiting his paintings.

9 In the spring of 1928 Kokoschka travelled extensively in North Africa, accompanied by Helmuth Lütjens, a colleague of the Berlin art dealer Paul Cassirer; the artist is seen in the Algerian desert with Bedouin tribesmen.

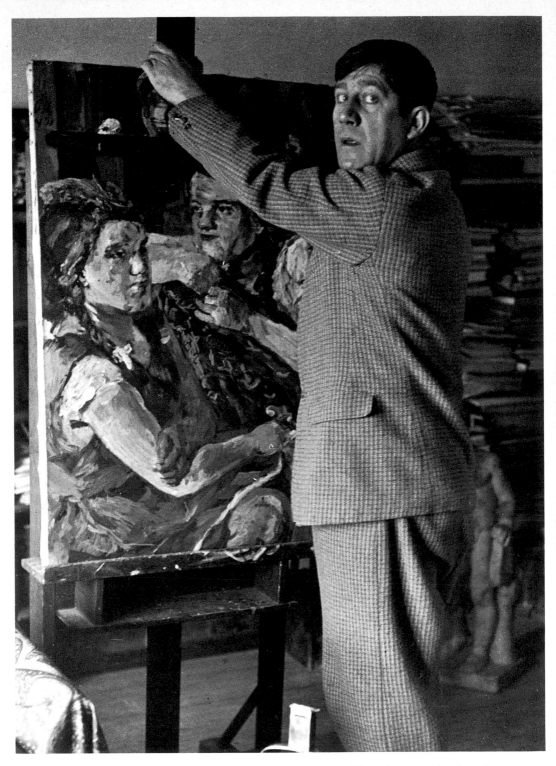

10, 11 The artist in his studio: (above) with his *Double Portrait of Trudl* (the teenage daughter of a local chimneysweep), Vienna 1931; and in Paris, 1933, beside *Jacob, Rachel and Leah*.

12 Teatime in Paris, *c.* 1930; on the right is Kokoschka's model Daisy Spies, who often posed for him in the years up to 1931 when Paris served as his home base.

13 Kokoschka on the balcony of his studio in Prague, with a wide view of the River Vltava and the city centre, 1936/7.

[Paris, early November 1924]

Dearest Colibri,

Are you perhaps a shade less the only love of my youth, because I've not been able to write before now?

I needed you so dreadfully badly for my whole life, not just as someone I can write to (which strikes me as a bit of a tease). That's nothing. Often I want you so painfully that I could howl like a wolf. You are the only woman I have really lost over the years. How I wish I could have that time over again! And you are the only woman who gave me a notion that I am not omnipotent, which is what I always believe otherwise. Because I wasted the only chance I had, that time in the Großer Garten. I should have sculpted you in marble then. And I was too clumsy! Dear Colibri, please live, don't die, don't become so heart-wrenchingly mild and transparent, I'm crying over you for the first time – because I'm getting soft. Please, please, my dear angel, send me by express post a photograph of yourself, or lots of them, showing your hallowed knees. What use is letter-writing at all! I sign myself   your Lieutenant Glahn

To Alice Lahmann

[Restaurant Foyot, Paris, mid-November 1924]

Dear little Colibri,

Why are you cross with me, and refuse to answer me? It is clear enough that Niuta only stuck to me for as long as I was in her sight, and then she again succumbed to her own bad taste. She never really cared for me, only I for her. That's why she took the first occasion which was to my detriment to return to her equilibrium. But what about you?

I have been in the City of Light for a whole week! . . .

I went into a bad, cheap restaurant behind the Sorbonne and invited a sixteen-year-old girl, who was sitting all alone in a corner, to eat with me. The other *filles de joie* had each secured a gallant. Of course I saw at once what sort of place it was. I saw every possible symptom of illness, [. . .] undernourished, feverish. A slip of a thing, a child of sixteen, with no talent for whoring. Went again the next day, she had blood on her handkerchief. Next I went to look for her in her digs, because on the third day she hadn't come to eat at the café. The little shrimp was in bed, running a temperature. Got her milk and Parma violets. On the fourth day a hullabaloo from the concierge, who threatened to throw the young lady out of her seedy hotel, even though all her bills had just been paid, because she'd spent most of the last three months in bed, covering everything with blood. (In fact, I had cleaned and tidied the room the day before, which wasn't easy.) Today the girl is dead. Yesterday I took her to a hospital with great difficulty, because she couldn't walk any more. A friend helped me carry her down from the sixth floor, and all the time the little creature, with whom I could hardly exchange a word, was resisting going to hospital. Wanted to conceal it all and get better. My money had run out, so my friend went and bought all the little necessities of life for her – powder, rouge, etc. – but by the time he got back she had been cleared away. To make room for another one. T.B.! And every single person she knew was a medical student. They can keep their precious Paris!

Dear Colibri, since my father died I've been endlessly sad, and have had no pleasures of any kind. Only *dégoûts*! Write to me, please, a really long letter.

Tender regards, from your   Lt. Glahn.

To Alexandrine, Countess Khuenburg

Avenida Palace Hotel, Lisbon,
18. iv. [1925]

Dear Countess,
Your letter made me extraordinarily happy, you are so considerate. Just imagine, I have a consuming passion to travel, I adore every new impression as if I had rediscovered this or that, and yet I am troubled by a feeling of utter sadness, as if I was bidding farewell. If I could show my love and joy in everything, draw attention to a beauty that I have noticed and another person might perhaps overlook, then I would be in good trim. I am travelling with a German who is very attached to me, but he's a sober fellow and I am forced to bottle up all my excitement. I can't travel alone because I lack sufficient energy to tear myself away. I always feel as though the great Finis will be waiting for me at the next place I reach. I don't trust life any more. Certainly not since the death of my father. In Biarritz I told my travelling companion that there was going to be a putsch here. Sure enough, the very next day they started to fight a regular war here, as if they were hell-bent on reducing this attractive city to a heap of rubble before the night was out. I wanted to finish my picture in the Castle, notwithstanding, but they politely showed me the door because it struck them as highly suspicious. Grenades exploded around my hotel during the night. This morning I went to see the other party, the monarchists, but got nowhere with them, because I don't speak the language. It is said that there will be peace tomorrow, and the train to Madrid will run.

Dear Sister Aline, how I wish you could see the sea here! The air stretches towards South America, the vegetation is amazing, the country, at least the southern half, is as green as it is at home in May, when the birch trees come into bud. The Tagus is pink, and the light is so overpowering that you imagine you can hear it or smell it. And herds of horses, and rich earth, and people, farmers and fishermen, like real people born from women's bodies, not manufactured in the world's factory. There is a park called Los Angelos. Ladies' maids are often black. The houses, the new ones built since the earthquake, are covered in coloured tiles, blue and red.

The Braganza Chapel costs 1 escudo, for which the custodian turns on the electric light, and you see a musty corpse, killed in 1911.

I look forward to seeing you again, dear Countess, and will assuredly meet you in Vienna between the dates you mentioned.

Yours sincerely, O Kokoschka

To Alice Lahmann

Palace Hotel, Madrid, 23. IV. [1925]

Colibri, my darling,

I've escaped from a genuine Portuguese revolution in one piece by the skin of my teeth. Lisbon is smaller than Dresden. And afterwards it was swarming with informers of the winning party, and I was on the other side, funnily enough, because I happened to be painting in the Castle. Now they're holding trials there! Not very nice! Brrr. I wonder if a letter from you will reach me here. Velázquez in the Prado here makes one feel small!

Tenderly, mindful of your strictures,   your OK

To Alice Lahmann

[Palace Hotel, Madrid,] 24. IV. [1925]

Dear Colibri, with the gently flapping wings –

yet you are lively enough to pursue me here? You are not too tired, little woman, to take in hand the affairs of your friends, as if your own were not undoubtedly tangled enough, and give them an imperceptible but decisive nudge? Please let me be your friend, not one of your friends, because you know how jealously my character seeks exclusive rights for itself. I am only a victim of myself. In the huge sombre mansion, where I walk along corridor after corridor, go up one flight of stairs and down the next, there is a very small room. Cruel as I must be, I believe nothing of the beautiful world of the living, which I observe through all the windows. Nothing, neither love nor pleasure nor permanence. That is, because nothing is permanent. I went to the Escorial today, on my own as usual, and I saw someone else, the shadow of someone else, who had his very small deathbed here in his desolate palace. From the bed a window giving on to the high altar of a monstrous church of his faith, and on the other side of his bed – the throne room. These two powerful consolations – for a sceptic who gives superstition no credence, yet is superstitious enough to chain these two to his bed, and cruel enough – to himself – to believe from time to time. Directed towards others, this trait is nothing but a superficial pleasure. Oh, I forgot, beneath the floor of his bedroom is the vault for all his descendants, with an empty coffin for the living king.

Colibri, I am as afraid of people as that man was. Not of you! Because beneath your paper-thin, frivolous skull you conceal, asleep, the mind of a philosopher. Why are you so vehemently concerned about the fate of Niuta? If she wants to stand by me in my last hours (and all the hours of my life are my last ones, unless I'm drunk) – why hasn't she been at her post all this while, for God's sake? Have I got to have a long palaver with her first, like Hebrews and South Sea islanders? Back then, when I was aghast at my father's death, because I had become the head of the family overnight, and had recognized our mortality for the first time, and so I didn't write, didn't say anything, played dead in my despair – she was swanning around The Hague with all manner of idiots, and with my friend P.C. Am I the one who has got to 'be understanding' about all that, and take an interest in the trivia of a social primrose path? I don't have the organs that would let me do that, I have to seek my salvation, I have to be about my own business, I can't learn to 'be understanding', and all those other fine phrases. I have enough to do, facing up to the fact that in thirty years' time – if that long – I shall have as mouldy a face as those cadavers, or even some of the kings I saw in Lisbon, in the burial vault of the Braganzas, entrance fee 1 escudo, paid into the coffers of the Portuguese Republic, in return for which they put the electric light on for you. And I might have been shot there on top of that, during the revolution. Then it would be only three to five years before mould was growing on my nose.

Colibri, dear lonely woman, give me a reindeer too, don't divide the world up according to people's birth certificates and the ups and downs of their nervous systems, into white and black, into Finns with brown skins and white eyes, and such as I, with wide-open eyes and no skin, who therefore will get no reindeer from you? Niuta betrayed me, that's clear enough without any words, I need neither telegrams nor eyewitnesses to confirm it. In her soul! If she loves me in spite of it, she ought to sacrifice herself for me! I need two women, one on the right of my bed and the other on the left. Both clasped to my breast, so closely that for a moment I can chase away the ghosts I believe in with all the strength of my brain and my knowing, so that I can embrace the two consolations as superstitiously as that shadow in the Escorial – at once, without wasting time in debate! I must outstrip myself, multiply myself a hundredfold, then there will be dust enough. And – listen, my dear, dear Colibri – I do not want to perish like everyone else without having given my name at least to a concept of rapture, rapture for the – others, the survivors, so that this new preconception, this new superstition of its time, will make young people happy, so long as they know nothing of down there. It would be better still if a few virgins would play musical instruments for me. I would so much like to paint. But my time will not come until my thunderstorm is over, and some god or other sends me comradeship.

Tenderly contemplating your unique knees, your OK

P.S. Naturally, I have brought a little sweetheart with me from Biarritz, but one human being is no better than none at all, because I know that a mind can die like a market-place under a cannonade, like a marriage during five o'clock tea, like a child the first time it —. Twelve apostles kept watch around Christ in the night and when he grew afraid all twelve were fast asleep. Of course I have a higher opinion of women than of the most zealous apostles, and regard Martha and the Magdalene in the New Testament as a fine thought, of decisive importance for the success of this art-loving religion.

Please don't send me cards, write me nice long letters!

Fare very well, dear, tender humming-bird heart!

To Marguerite Loeb (original English)

[Savoy Hotel, Paris, 11/12 May 1925]
Saturday, 3 o'clock

My darling,

you are a little dear deer covered with 'fur'. I depend on you because you are like a mother to her child. I would prefer to get in a rush through all the odd struggles, to meet you for ever, awaiting to be awakened [in the] morning by your voice and hasty angry fingers. Because I am *tellement* lazy, odd, odious, impossible, unreal, ugly, silly, tricky a boy and beating each record in *méchanceté*. But you are the only good, only one real Tamariske, I ever met in life. I trust you, yours longing Kokoschka

To Marguerite Loeb

[Savoy Hotel, Paris, late May or early June 1925]

Margrit,

Just think, I've had the chance to start exercising my brain again these evenings, after having had you throw it into some confusion. And I'm ashamed to discover that we are both hypocrites and liars to ourselves, persuading ourselves that we did it, that nature united us, whereas what brought us together was only curiosity – something that is always alive in me, and will be in you while you are still young. Sympathy and mistrust on your side – mistrust and sympathy on mine, provisionally, until distance and habit satisfy the inquisitiveness in some other way, and a sense of estrangement calms me. I calm down because I perceive, yet again, that I can never reach a fundamental understanding with people from the world of the middle class, much as I have wished it all my life, and much as it hurts me every time when my lovely visitors, after a long or a short stay, go back to their fathers' houses (or move next door).

What is all my talent, if I foresee and comprehend from the outset everything that other people only know after their experiments have gone wrong? What stupidity to believe in all seriousness that you are frightened because your father has forbidden you to live with me, or go without a chaperone, to express it more grotesquely, that is, more socially acceptably! What frightened you was my wish to spend the watches of the night with other people, arm in arm! With a chaperone!

I don't set any store by such minor variations, it's enough to me that you perhaps prefer kissing me, but you're nibbling at a secret, just like me, and your nature warns you to make yourself scarce.

It would be egging you on to be dishonourable towards yourself, if I helped you to evade that telegram from your Papa. He thinks you ought not to see me even in the morning unless you spend the whole night with me, spend your whole life with me. He thinks you ought not to become a lady, half a warm human being and half a cold cocotte, but preserve yourself, so that you can be a woman, when at last you find a man you really love! One can learn a lot from experimentation, but not how to remain a human being.

You haven't had enough opportunity yet to ruin yourself, which is why today you perhaps take too lightly the 'Perhaps' that I offer up to you, like an honest man, as a tribute to a young girl with a whole life in front of her. I make the offering to the gods of life, a beautiful life that I dream about, like the floor of the church in ? (I can't remember where). And, in turn, I see pictures of life shining in on me. Accept the flowers like a little god, as a sign of my gratitude, and farewell, beloved,   your OK

To Anna Kallin
                    [Savoy Hotel, Paris, late May or early June 1925]
My one and only friend, dear Ben, dear, sad, good, silly Niuta,
Do you imagine my state is much different from yours? Working, working, taking everything the human race gives us in the way of new courage, new disappointment, new determination and new faith, and

110

pushing it into a hole from which – in my case, at least – nothing emerges. Nothing of vital importance, because the recognition I get from other people leaves me cold now. I've just heard from Berlin that their Excellencies Bode and Friedländer are softening, and are looking at my new landscapes every day. Perhaps it's to my advantage that other people – increasingly circumspect and cool-headed individuals – derive pleasure from my travels, which entail enormous exertions on my part, and which I undertook in order to numb my own pain. What I got from it all is pocket money, while next day the middleman bought himself a car from the share he got for sitting tight in Germany. For my part, even today, at my age, I've still not been able to provide enough security for my family to satisfy my conscience. I have to pull up suddenly again, as always, whenever my heart is ready to be deceived once more into thinking. Now I will be able to fulfil myself, that is, be what I already am – and I have to summon up the cunning and the mistrust to engage again in the everlasting tumult, and I'm sick to death of it. And I have to run away, can't do what I would like to do, can't even, just once, be really close to one particular individual, because I don't know when or where the next punch-up will start, which means that I'm none too good-tempered, and none too optimistic. Once again, I've hurt somebody who wanted my whole heart, and I know it, and I also know that it needn't have gone as far as it did! But aren't I human too? Don't I need love too? A clenched fist alone won't fill anyone's stomach.

You see, dear Ben, you are a fool. The other birds fly hither and take a little nibble, and they let me stroke them and goggle at them like exotic animals, let a fuss be made of them, and then some more important business calls them away. You alone are still wet enough behind the ears to imagine that I am any different from a Negro in a circus, who has a black skin while others are white, and who laughs when he sticks a hairpin into himself. Other people don't do that, because instead of hairpins and photographs and fetishes they have wives and children, bank accounts, houses, cars and servants. And they have the promise of paradise to come, should they wish to rise up again on the Day of Judgment.

You think you need to protect me, stop me hurting myself. But, silly Ben, that's my job, that's why I have an audience, hurting myself is what I make my living from. If I stopped, then I'd be white like the rest, and maybe I'd also have a wife and a child and a kitchen sink. But it simply wouldn't be proper for me.

That is what justifies my life. Letting the rest see how well off they are. That's art!

But it simply wouldn't be proper for me. I haven't learned how, and they would set the police on me the very first day, and forbid me to be a

111

repentant sheep, grazing and living with the rest, and dying and going to paradise with them.

I must be a hero, and give off just a whiff of the odour of a criminal. Do not believe that I really seriously intend to live another thirty years. Rather, believe that I shall very soon, with one bound, be with you and spend a night in your arms. Please, dear Niuta, always, always, be good to me, because I am   your Un

To Marguerite Loeb

[Savoy Hotel, Paris,
late June or early July 1925] [1]

Dear, dear Tamarisk,

Thank you for your long, wonderful letter which did me more good than the nurse, who I kept with me until this evening, to give me my gargles, steam and tinctures, or the 6 (six) specialists, who are robbing me of all my money with quartz lamps, X-rays (I have a marvellous, life-size photo of my skull now, cost a mere 400 francs from the X-ray doctor!), and the devil knows what quackery besides, until I got better of my own accord. My nose, on the other hand, is every bit as swollen as it was at first, but it was neither that, nor this illness, nor that illness, but a bit of everything, and essentially all I had done was – break my nose!! What have you got to say to that! I am really proud of all that I've managed to do to my body. And I ran a temperature, for days, like a sheep. Now I've got scars on every limb of my carcass. The doctors were very funny. The nurse herself had killed an elderly man just the day before, and you can guess that at first I was a bit aghast. But I was too helpless to make it without help, and the six doctors prescribed too many phials and drops and pills and such like. It was more than I could cope with, with my temperature. Sometimes there were three of them around my bed at a time, and none of them saw that my nose was broken. Admittedly, I also had a small infection in each tooth, from Schwabecher, be sure to get the tooth he fixed for you looked at at once! Your tongue has been sensitive ever since.

Tamarisk, I was very, very moved by what you wrote about the letter with the photograph, you are so good to me, and even though you aren't here, you still find a way to reward me. And I deserved it this time. My nose – broken! Isn't that darned clever? The Tirol isn't important for the time being, put it off for a little while and go when it's possible. Because it'll be a few days before I can leave my room, and I must spend at least two weeks in England, if I am to paint enough to make the journey worthwhile. Oh, how I wish I was with you, Margrit. Darling. Kissing you, all of you,   your Kokoschka

112

I'm supposed to spend some time in Holland, too. It might be four weeks before I see you, if you're going to the Tirol. Perhaps one of us will come up with another idea of how we can get together sooner, before I go to England. Because I cannot last a whole month without you, you dear, tender, wonderfully beautiful, only real Mooress (moresque), you only bestower of rewards, to whom I look for the proper, glorious and perfect reward for all my boasts, and you my only playmate, who knows everything about Wei and Tang and Henri II and Catherine de Médicis pottery, and now knows everything about me that is printed in the heavy tome. We can now have a good laugh about me together: See overleaf!

[Sketch by Kokoschka from his letter to Marguerite Loeb]

To Marguerite Loeb

Savoy Hotel
[Paris, late June or early July 1925] [11]

Damn it all, Tamarisk,
I've had no letters for two whole days, and you know that on the third day – today – I start moving on. Do you think I broke my nose for nothing, for the express purpose of not even being comforted by anyone!!! I am perfectly capable of going down to the street with my sickbed, to which I am no longer confined, and despatching Jakob to solicit on my behalf. I must see that someone likes me. Margaret, pay attention, I miss you dreadfully! Everything strikes me as entirely cerebral again. Everything around me. I started to paint again yesterday. I can't travel for another two–three days yet, until all my open wounds have closed. I cured myself, and threw out all the doctors and nurses. The nurse had killed an 'elderly'

Jewish gentleman two days before me. I told each of the doctors a different story, including the radiologist, and each of them gave me different powders and lotions for a different ailment. It didn't take long to get what I wanted, a mountain of pills, tinctures, drugs, gargles etc., and I swallowed, rubbed in, gargled, painted on the lot, at three times the normal dose! The only thing I didn't do was make compresses, because I found it too boring, but I think all six *corbeaux* were in agreement on that. The result: my nose is returning to its previous noble shape (you know what a wonderful Grecian nose I used to have!), but everything is raw, especially my throat, and my nose because all the strong stuff I've taken has made it sore – that will take another two–three days to heal. Do you think I ought to capitalize even more on the situation by putting red paint on my nose, or building protective scaffolding round it? I'm still bursting with entrepreneurial spirit!

Margrit, my sweetest, don't goggle enchantedly at all the Heidelbergers with their boulevardiers' noddles. Don't lift your skirt so high always, when someone's sitting opposite you, so that they can see everything (*don't show your privates!*).

Do you think we shall ever see each other again in this life? Are you still even half fond of me? Do you have even the slightest recollection of what I look like? How many months have you been gone, without going into a decline? It was very, very sweet of you to tear up the photograph, and as a reward I am sending you some of me. Please come a little closer, Tamarisk – look at me, heroically remaining all alone with a broken nose, with no one to nurse me, or comfort me or reward me, and I don't even get a letter – for two days on end.

Why? Should I start to suspect something? I shall wait half a day more, and then I shall go! Smothering you with kisses,

your Kokoschka, Tamarisk.

To Marguerite Loeb

The Abbotsford Hotel [London, 19 July 1925]

My dear, real Tamarisk,

You are the only one who really loves me through and through, and all this while, although you were thrown back on your own resources, heard nothing from me, not a letter, and although you knew that I wanted to meet someone here with whom I had to set things straight, you have behaved in a wonderfully brave and upright way. You haven't despaired, and you didn't feel any mistrust, you simply loved me innocently and completely. Do you know, my darling, that that is a miracle unparalleled in my experience, and that I don't know of any word strong enough to tell you what a wonderful, dear, sweet girl you are? And yet it is such a short time since you met me, and you still don't really know me at all well.

Margrit, this is not the way to thank you, on a sheet of paper! I'm counting the days, like you, until I can see you and be alone with you. And watch and listen, as you enjoy everything, and find beauty in everything, because you carry the sense of beauty inside you, and introduce it into everything you experience – you are a real, natural, innocent human soul, as straight as a tree and as healthy as everything natural, for me. Living with you offers something that I look forward to immeasurably, and I am certain that with your tenderness for me I shall be protected against everything that makes me ill. And that I shall one day be able to grow as straight as I must be, if I have understood my gifts aright. Margrit, my one and only beloved, sweet human being, you must remain horribly healthy and be dreadfully happy with me.

On Wednesday I leave here for Amsterdam, to do a few paintings in Holland, and then, on around 31 July, I shall come and meet you, wherever you are by then. I've almost finished my second painting here. The first impression this country has made on me has been very powerful, because it's the first time I've been among Anglo-Saxons, and it took me a few days to overcome a very strong sense of alienation. And because I shall have to do business with these people before long, and establish a reputation here, I've made a more serious effort than in Paris or Madrid, Rome etc., and I think I will be successful in time. The first thing I must do, however, is learn to speak and think fluently in English – you can make that so much easier for me, if you will speak only English to me, and be patient with a child who is slow to learn how to answer and understand. I want to learn from you how to talk to other people, as a child learns from its mother. Please, dear, kind Tamarisk, make this sacrifice for me, and forget the German language as far as I am concerned. I must, I must, let the world broaden and fill me. The world is too big, and I still have far too little in me. How shall I fulfil my task, if I don't know the basic elements – which are the peoples of the world! I will learn from you, and I'm not embarrassed in front of you, because I love you, and it is all right if I seem weak and a beginner in your sight. Please, Margrit, do you agree? A thousand pleases, will you do it? Understanding you will be easy, by your eyes, from your lips, and in your arms. And when it gets really impossible, you will only need to kiss me, my angel. I'm so glad you are well and doing all the things that are good for you. I hope that we shall not be forced to lose as many days in the future as we do now. I'm going to write to you very often now, so that you have no need to worry about me. I am with you and I embrace you – till we meet again, my bride. My warmest regards to your mother and brother. Good night Tamarisk, let us dream to each other.

To Marguerite Loeb

Pontresina, Grand Hotel Kronenhof-Bellavista, August 25

My dearest Margrit,

By now we've asked ourselves a thousand times what we can do to let something good come out of our love, and to make ourselves certain in our own sight and that of the friends who give us advice. And to ensure that no one suffers because we perhaps took too little care, or acted without enough thought.

I love you so completely that I want to make you my wife, gladly and whenever you please. I have such complete confidence in you that I will voluntarily let you go away from me again, as dreadfully far and for as long a time as your parents think is necessary, so that they can be convinced that you have not made a mistake, and that you want to be united with me. Your parents, who are now able to watch you and judge for themselves, will find out when the time is ripe to end this imperfect situation. And then I shall learn by the quickest possible means whether you have remained the same or if life was stronger. After this third separation, the last in our lives, I want to be absolutely certain, without vacillation on your parents' part, and without further postponement, that you have made your choice, and that our question has been answered in your heart once and for all. I will not come to see you, therefore, or call you, or even write to you, so as not to influence you. I will wait for you, if you want to live with me, and I will come to you wherever you decide you want to meet me. And take you, with the clothes you stand up in, as all the happiness and riches I shall ever need in my life. It depends entirely on you now, if you will come, and when we shall meet. I am staking so much, and I wish the prize was already won. Remember all our moments of happiness, and I will pray to our good spirit to love us – you, my Tamarisk, and me,   your Kokoschka

To Anna Kallin

[Vienna,] 19. 11. 25

My dear Ben,

You bang on the wall, like a nun immured, and I – I don't know if I've pitch in my eyes, mud in my ears, or my boots stuck fast in clay – I don't stir, don't hear, don't see you, like Tom Thumb, bawling fit to burst your diaphragm. My heart skips a beat, it's true, now and again, when I start thinking about Dukes, or whatever his name is, or when I hear a record of Melba and think it's your voice in Dresden, or buy the 'Hymn to the Sun' on impulse, just when I ought to be writing to you, and I remember you wearing a yellow dress that made you look like a bee, and being so happy with me, and singing the 'Indra' song. And I know I shall definitely be in

116

Paris on the 8th: I would have to be, for who should know better than me what lingerie you ought to wear? I won't give any answer to the news about the Wartmann exhibition, who cares if the exhibition reveals my weakest spot, apart from me, and I don't expect to live forever – and so I can't bestir myself on behalf of my own success, either. But it's clear that Dr Wartmann has a son, and you've been making eyes at him. Why shouldn't you be as romantic as me? I always have a correspondence on the go with someone who is going to marry me, and who annoys you dreadfully. I should be delighted if it was all going to go on like this for ever, with the sun shining. But then another winter comes, all of a sudden, after another wasted year in which I've done nothing but chirp like the grasshoppers, and it's cold, and once again I'm conscious that at some not impossibly distant date I shall have gone, blown away as if I had never been. And that no one needs me, and that my trouser legs won't even throw a shadow. When it's like that, who, in God's name, is supposed to have the stomach for self-importance? You know, Mirli, I get on with everyone who rubs against me like a friendly cat, and then again I get on with no one, because I'm never up on the roof at the right time, when the moon's up. I simply don't believe that I'm your misfortune; I wrote that particular play once before, and it's been set to music by the Bohemian maestro Křenek, the divorced son-in-law of the victim and principal character in the opera at the time. And the world première is to take place in Kassel in October 1927. A town, that is, which has enough art-loving inhabitants to fill the theatre five times, perhaps, if it goes well, but the world will not be changed, for all that.

I dug over our entire garden while my mother was in Brioni – I've been at home for more than two months now – and was crowing over my little brother because I had 'created' a park, in my opinion, with a pond (cemented, bricked and tiled), pergolas (carpentered, varnished and planted), paths (gravelled and smoothed), a little spinney, and all from a jungle with my own two hands! And in six weeks, whereas he, in the space of three years, had raised nothing more than a few fat grubs on rotten wood in a preserving jar. Then on the day before they came home, our dear, beautiful, red-brown dog Patschi fell ill, and because I am never anything but unloving and vain, instead of nursing him myself, I let one vet after another treat him, until he was driven mad by a stupid injection and lay paralysed the whole of one night, snapping if anyone went near him. And, being too lazy to get up, I persuaded myself that I was too cowardly, and was afraid of getting rabies. Next day, the fourth vet and I put down this really decent, noble and lovable dog. Thereupon we cried for three days on end. And my brother has a bad conscience, because he always used to slip out in the evenings, without taking the dog with him. And I don't try very hard to talk him out of it, because it suits me to see

117

him like that, although I'm sorry for him at the same time. But always crafty, as you see!

The upshot is that my horticultural creation looks suspiciously pale now, and nobody mentions it. But you know from history and literature that a man who is destined to ruin whatever he touches will not rest until he has tempted fate to the limit. I've persuaded my folks that they are tired of the house in Vienna, and now plan to establish a bigger and better-fated one in Locarno (perhaps because I've read it so often in newspaper headlines). Today, using most of the money that I amassed this year to provide an income for my folks, I bought two gigantic Aubusson tapestries, more than 80,000 square metres [*sic*]. And must build a life's happiness around them. To prevent myself setting up yet another expensive façade, behind which, as usual, lie rubble and broken glass, I have started something somewhere else, far away from here, but I'm sure it won't come to any good. In America, in point of fact, so that the lightning, which is bound to be drawn back again, will get diverted and lose its way, instead of striking the house in Locarno, which is meant to make my folks forget the dog. I'm its real target! To tell you the truth, Mirli, I'm completely, totally indifferent, truthfully, if everything of mine, after a glorious beginning and brilliant rise, ends up embedded in the mud like a rocket. I'm used to finding my own hands empty. But the others' hands! The poor old others!!!

That's the reason why I'm letting myself drift towards America. Really, it's more a matter of being steered by chance and a sort of evil genius in me that makes itself known whenever a disaster is ready to be wrought. It's against my still over-watchful reason to voluntarily push myself in that direction, however. A time will come when I shall no longer possess even that inhibition.

My mother is going to Locarno in a few days' time with my brother, to see if she likes it there. I can leave when she comes back. That may turn out to be 8 December. In any case, whether on that day or another, you can count on me coming to Paris. And for no other reason, I swear to you by our dearest memories, than because you will be buying or will have bought lingerie there! What other business would a man like me have in Paris? But if I find you still there, shall I travel to America with you? (I have a visa already.) It will all depend on the wind, chance, disaster, sexual temptation, financial inducements, the effect of a whisky and soda, a love-letter, a charming conversation with your respected father, a Canadian postage-stamp, a book about Easter Island. (Mirli, please buy me that English book by a lady anthropologist, I think, as soon as possible, will you? I believe it really is my dream and my Eden!)

Ben, Mirli, how many pretty serving-maids would you actually give me, if you were rich and had a house where you would wait for me if we were united one day? And would you really insist on these maids (and, please, will they include a red-head, smelling of nettles? And a fat one? And a fifteen-year-old English country girl? And would they be made to wear lots of undies? And would very short skirts arouse your wrath? You know how I adore idylls!) being very nice to me, subject to your toleration and indulgence? Even more important, would you lose your temper with a silly goose, a *wench* from the country, who starts to squeal in the night as if it had never happened to a woman before, since we respectable ladies of good society . . . You know Mirli, I want from you all the understanding denied me at home with respect to my erring ways. I won't raise a hullabaloo about it for all the world to hear, certainly not. I know better than to put my feet on the dining table, I won't disgrace your house-to-be, by God, not I, I don't even like being taken for a hero and an erotic tenor. But I've had enough of scenes, and secrets, and bad conscience. I'm sick of all that! Of flowers one should preserve the scent, of girls the scent of the memory, not the anger of discovery or the shame of the inevitable betrayal, but the rosy confusion of what may come to pass at the next favourable opportunity. (Never be told any more lies!) Mirli, I am yours tenderly,   Un

Ben, you should be as kind as Empress Maria Theresia, who instituted the Rose of Chastity, in order to declare the reputation of ladies known by her beloved Emperor Franz I officially spotless. Instead of raising Cain.

To Anna Kallin   [Vienna, turn of the year 1925–6]
                                                              Happy New Year to us both
Dearest Mirli,
If I come to London in the spring, will you still be ticklish? I've always received all your little attentions with great affection, and have slowly come up out of the darkness; there remains a desire to have my revenge one day for the lesson fate has taught me. Will you be my comrade for ever, through thick and thin, and in spite of my cussedness? It would be such a comfort to me to be able to warm myself thoroughly for once on you, against your fur, so that I could get strong and well again! Be mine, and I will come and join you in March, and we'll make a pact, not as your respected parents and the virtuous world would wish, but like someone who's been locked up and wants to escape with his beloved, who smuggles a file in, instead of running off with some canary from the opera house, who seduces her by riffling his bankbook under her nose.
Mirli, I want you to apply your red-headed girlish brain to thinking up all the possible ways you could help me, and then help me again, however desperate they might be. As you know, I'd make a good souteneur if I

119

didn't have this half-baked profession, which obliges me to wear a mask of decorum with a professorial beard attached to it. That's why I have perpetual bronchitis, because I can't stretch myself to the full. If you love me exclusively at the risk of your soul, at any price, you will eventually succeed in steering me into my proper channel, the gutter all my fibres yearn for. You must attract people who are fools, empty their pockets of lovely shiny things, and pass on to me all the gifts they shower upon you, so that I can be proud of how you love me more than all other women love their men, and preen myself with the thought!

But in the end, Mirli, you will have convinced yourself that I can squeeze you much more tightly and hold you much closer than any of the fancy men in well-pressed trousers you may meet. Don't be unhappy if yet again I can't bring myself to write to you for rather a long time, because I'm too low and too depressed. It should make you all the more willing to take a swipe at my nose and – let's say – my teeth. Get yourself fighting fit, and nice and brown, and fierce and naughty for me,   Un

---

To Anna Kallin

[Berlin,] 11.1.27

Mirli,

I've been in Berlin for an hour, and am using up the stamps I still had in my wallet, as there were none in Vienna. I don't believe you've really suffered, it will be the same for you as for me, everything is on the point of collapse at home, and there is so much to do from morn till night that one simply can't manage anything else, not even get out to send a telegram. I went into town once, to buy cooking utensils and gramophone records – the Westminster Abbey Choir in the Matthew Passion. I shall be here a month or six weeks, then I shall have to go back to Vienna, to check if there's no 'flu there, and then I must buckle down to something substantial and do myself some good. I won't think about that just yet, however.

I combed my hair with your comb first thing this morning, as soon as I got here, and I shall probably use the velvet myself too, in my toilette. Some stupid person painted the head from Dresden, which arrived in Vienna on the same day as your letter about it, you can wash it off with bookbinder's paste, when it's dry it flakes off but always leaves a few little bits behind. That will make it look better, more like the original, but the caster ought to have left the joins. We'll talk to him again. He's going to send me the Athene of Antenor, too. Darling Mirli, please don't go down with 'flu, the *Wiener Journal* says every household is so badly affected where you are, that the doctors are letting themselves in with skeleton keys.

I'm already looking forward to my weekend of kisses with you, Mirli. It would suit me down to the ground if it was the weekend now. I'm painting the old turtle tomorrow. I don't know of any portraits of women, perhaps you and Colibri will find something. When I came to tot it up, I found that I had debts of 15,000 marks this year, not counting the ring, and that could help me to bring my folks slowly round to the idea of moving to England with me. In any case, you could make enquiries there about exactly what the climate is like – fog, sun, temperature – on the side of England where Wales is. Is that the English Riviera? And is there a Gulf Stream there? And what does a country seat cost there, with room for my sister and brother-in-law as well? It would take the load off my brother's shoulders, it would relieve my conscience a little bit, and I could also spend more time at home. A seat with around twenty rooms and park to match, woods, seashore, WCs, garage and stables. And the upkeep? And then I shall paint it all. In ten years' time I'll be Lord Something, and will die out if you don't have a daughter.
I'm envious of Marek, and would love to have a picture-postcard from him. Planting a kiss on your beautiful bum, my darling Mirli,

your Un

I'm staying at Cassirer's again.

To Anna Kallin

[Courmayeur, *c.*19/20 October 1927]

Mirli,

I'm stuck fast in the ice, but every day I climb ten or twelve hundred metres further than the day before, and paint pictures with frozen fingers. Shall be crossing to France in the next few days, via the Little St Bernard. Will write. Send me a long letter and photos.   All my love, Un

To Anna Kallin

[Annecy, mid-November 1927]

Dear Mirli,

It's shockingly cold here, and I'm pinned to the spot by incessant drizzle, in November, in the French provinces. *C'est le comble de malheur*. Write and tell me the important news, archaeological and other. Please ask at my house in Ovington Gardens if I left the ms. of my *Saul* there.

All my love   Your Un

Hôtel des Négociants, Annecy (Everything's shut!!)

To Anna Kallin

[Tunis, 15 January 1928] Sunday

My poor dear Mirli

I'm appalled to hear that you were so ill. I was hoping, actually, that your nerves would have recovered by the next day. I'm so blind, and treat you abominably, otherwise it couldn't go as far as it always does. Twice this year a misfortune because of me. Even if it's called 'flu or something else this time.

What am I to do? You know I have to work, for a variety of reasons, and you don't want it to be true, even if you consent to it with your mouth, you resist it with your neck, your heart and everything else, and you keep falling ill on me. Poor silly Mirli, do you think I'm any different from you? I'm torn in half, too. When I'm with you I think of going away, when I'm away I think of going back and helping you. There's no point in trying to find out why you wish I was different, and why you choose me nevertheless, or why I do the same. Each of us wants the whole world and its centre. There must be some ancient remnant of a way of looking at things that survives only in our feelings, without being able to show itself clearly. Probably something Gothic – the City of God on earth – or Punic, preferable to us specialists on any account.

My dear, there are two museums here, one in Carthage and one in the Alaoui (Tunis) – stones, stones, stones, nothing but stones, genuine Punic. I'm in the process of establishing a Punic monopoly with my petroleum-find (left-hand helix), but I can never get into the museum: from 1 till 6 I paint, in the evening I'm tired, go to bed at 9, and in the morning from 9 till 12 I have 'flu and stay in bed. Lütjens drove me mad with his misplaced energy, lack of imagination and slavish surrendering to fate. Furthermore, he now has a cold and sprays his microbes right and left, on to the food of elderly English ladies and parties of American tourists, into my handkerchief; and he speaks (stutters) at the top of his voice: 'u. u. une, e, e ggggrante booutttaillö de la vin rouxe-e-e . . .' and so on. Hell! But one thing that we can be sure of is that death will part us. I'm rapidly turning into an Arab fatalist – up a ladder above a tomato-seller, who keeps bringing me coffee from the café across the road under the dome of the mosque. I think that's what's giving me 'flu.

Your comb is wonderful, Mirli, and your comb-cleaner. You show me true devotion, although I don't show you any, and I'm quite sure that by now you're thin as a rake, and believe in your pride that it's rather grand to lie in bed, and say in a thread-like voice that you're not hungry. Please try and summon up a bit more zest for living, and see more people. I too find Halpern enormously likeable, and now I can admit that my real reason for staring was that I was glad to see that you can have the company of people like that. Write again soon, and don't be cross if I

122

don't get round to it so quickly. But Lütjens is ever at the door with your watch, and I could very easily spend a minute in bed, while he reckons on ten or twenty paintings from me.

Try to laugh again, Mirli, and don't get pneumonia, and don't take my flirtations to heart, I've already given it up because I must paint. Then I start fretting again about my family. I must have cried in the night, because my pillow was wet.

Your little face is sad now, and you will forgive me for nipping out through the door, Mirli,   your Un

To Anna Kallin

22. 1. 28 Tozeur, Hôtel Transatlantique

My poor Mirli,

Are you better now? The *Daily Mail* of the 16th, which I've just seen, says the sun is shining in England for the first time. I hope it carries on doing so. There is rather more sunshine here, but it's still cool. And I've damn' well caught a cold. Overnight journey from Sfax to here, with no blankets and a dirty pillow.

I've got a cold for the first time in my life, and of course I'm already painting. On the minaret above a mosque. Below me, chanting students of the Koran. An Algerian sheikh turned up yesterday evening, and we went to the tam-tam festival. One of his kinsmen, 2 metres tall, *7 feet linear*, danced at the end and I was moved, because he danced in exactly the way I did when I was young.

[. . .]

Thinking of you tenderly   your Un

The Berbers here are my kinsmen, and know me personally. The great sheikh gave me his hand.

To Anna Kallin

[Touggourt,] 3. 3. 28

My dear Mirli,

I'm in Touggourt and have made a friend in a public dance-house. In order to avoid such wicked temptations (when you're not with me) I've asked this friend to take me to an Arab monastery, and so I am working 20 kilometres from here, painting men.

They look more like falcons, however, and the further south I go the more at home I feel. My Col de Sfa landscape, incidentally, really was like a Rubens! In spite of a bad night (I composed an entire novella yesterday but I haven't written a word of it down yet), I'm very well. Very affectionately,   Un

Palace Hotel, Madrid, 17. IV. 28

My dear Mirli,

A bundle of letters that you sent me in Touggourt caught up with me today at last, and, rather like looking out of a window, they've cheered me up and my sometimes really alarming worries don't seem so dark. Even though you were ill when you wrote – but can we two really be ill? I've had the 'flu since Chamonix, and I've dragged myself the length of North Africa with it, and I can't shake it off, because for weeks on end I've had to sit on trains, alternating with bug-ridden hotel rooms, in order to travel from one mistake to another. I don't believe the Stone Age was any more comfortable than this; I found stone knives in Gabès, and discovered a rich petroleum deposit. Atlantis wasn't necessarily in one particular place: as you know, it's Abyssinia, from Kilimanjaro to the south, North Africa, (Tel) Atlas, from Majorca to Wales and southwards as far as Benin, Palestine, from Arabia (Mecca) to the Indian rock-temples, Altefina, Mexico – wherever, at different times, there have been Migrations of Peoples for the sake of petroleum, coal, Stonehenge, lunar decay. I don't like it when the *Berliner Tagblatt* pontificates, I'd rather they tried harder to predict the crash in rubber shares.

I got even more hysterical in Seville than in Algiers. It's a god-forsaken hole full of kitsch, and there I was, trapped for ten days in such a dusty hotel, without money, and Job's own postbag of news from home. My brother's had an X-ray, and there's a shadow on his lungs, my mother has pleurisy, my sister scribbles a short note and drags them both off to the French Riviera via Milan, where a hell of a storm is raging just now, no address for my folks, who don't know any languages, and are very easily confused and hurt, and will arrive more ill than when they left. I'm not even sure if my sister, in whom I have more confidence, as she has some worldly wisdom, went with them. And my own catarrh is so bad I can't stand up straight. Suffer the most appalling states in the hotel, because the longest that anyone could spend in a town like this is two days, and by the tenth day, what with fantasies, the feast of fools, my worries and my incarceration, I am ready to commit murder. Now I must find out as quickly as possible what's happened to my folks, once I get an address. With that journey in prospect I shall very shortly have clocked up 20,000 kilometres by train this year already, and my bank balance in Berlin has just arrived, o = o. I didn't see a single naked black girl; the kind you send me are available only to an envious god, either the Jewish one or our Catholic Christian one, to fondle in his harem. My friends in Morocco tried various arguments to persuade me to become a Muslim. Perhaps Allah will help me, since Jehovah and our god, created by Charles V (my personal emperor), do damn all for me. I've come across Charles V in every sphere my interests have taken me to date, really the last great man to be a monarch, as I imagine one. His mother was Joanna the Mad, who also fascinates me, because she shares my necrophilia and passion for dolls with her whole family, and passed it on to her heirs. Perhaps I inherited it from her, for I am, as you know, a Habsburg bastard like Don Juan d'Austria, through Franz I and my grandmother – things like that often crop up much later. Your Habsburg is a usurper in that case, and she would have to present stringent blood-tests in evidence in order to be more than dust in my eyes.

One day I'll go to Toledo, there's a house there where they used to whip themselves in the evenings as religious observance. The woman who says she's the Tsar's daughter, the Braganzas in their open leather coffins, the world needs that museum in London that was burned down. There's a pressing need for legitimacy.

The Chinese lady is my Chinese lady, Mirli, even if I should force you to the point of caressing all those women instead of me, and driving them mad. I was hoping to meet the Chinese lady in Berlin on the 15th of this month, she wanted to make a film with me, and I don't need to tell you that I wasn't interested in the film but in a part of the world (or body) that I hadn't touched before. But of course I have to get these Job's messages about my folks, which turn all, all, all pleasures to dust and ashes, and make me myself cowardly and stupid. I need my brother, and I need him healthy. If I had any money I would get out of that damned house in Vienna like a shot, and move my brother to a really healthy place of my own in Switzerland, in the mountains with his beloved fallow deer, birds, fish, all around him. But I've made no progress financially for years. In order not to lose courage altogether, since I simply couldn't think of any way out, I stayed in bed for whole days at a time, and took a sleeping powder, so as not to need to think. It wouldn't let me rest for whole nights on end. Of course I smoked, and was as lonesome as an old discarded tooth.

I enclose some photos of me taken in Tunis, Algeria and Morocco. I was snapped with the marabout in his monastery, too, but I shall have to write to him first, because he had them taken by a secretary.

I don't know when I shall be able to come and join you again, Mirli, I would very much like to have been a guest at the wedding, in disguise, and furthermore I desperately want to see the wonderful, creamy-complexioned *wenches* of Dartmoor, because you have the key to them. But for the time being I have to dance to a different tune. I'll write to you as soon as I know what I'll be doing. Meanwhile, go courting on my behalf: I'm superstitious and always believe that the more women (pretty ones, of course) interest themselves in a fellow, no matter how, or how many, the more good luck it brings him, for some mysterious reason. I believe firmly in the magic powers of breasts, bellies, eyes and bums, and thighs too!!!

With a big kiss, Mirli, from   your Un

To Anna Kallin

                                    Hotel Ritz, Barcelona, 4. 5. 28

My dear Mirli,

You sent me a letter recently that really amazed me. How good you are, and what self-control you have, and how willingly you stick by me. I don't have the weaknesses that you, as a woman, could at once lovingly reinterpret as strengths; I have needs, which are much more dour, and therefore you make a sign of me, so that you don't lose your way in your web of emotions.

But my darling Mirli, you must be aware that people like me, who know the promised land with their whole souls, don't, don't ever reach it. And yet my only escape from an unbearable distress all around me is that I still haven't wholly grasped it, it will have to come upon me from outside, and I shall have to let it in – although I struggle against it with all my strength, with deaf spots, consolations, distractions, physical aches and pains and imaginary excursions – and I myself will never, ever enter that promised land.

I saw such a wonderful, yearning and noble picture by Titian in Madrid, *Adam and Eve*. I spent whole days walking round it, without once standing still, and I almost forgot that it wasn't me who painted it. In Tunis I saw a mosaic, Orpheus, by a Greek master, which makes the tears rise from my heart like a warm spring, whenever I think of its serene beauty; I wish I could die wrapped in the blue cloak of that Orpheus. And the Athena by the potter Antenor, which grows like a tree out of the thirsty soil, full of sap, and an Eve I could lay my hands on, and prowl round and round! I live in perpetual terror that there will be an earthquake at the Greek museum where it is before I get there. I really meant to go there this time – but once again I didn't. All that is the promised land for me, Mirli, which I can only gaze at from my tower of debts. Anyone who looks at me thinks I'm a tall green tree, with a high crown on top, but an arboriculturist knows that all my green comes from ivy and mistletoe, which have grown up all over me and my dried-out, brown, withered skeleton from bottom to top, so thickly that credulous people like you who want to believe their eyes think that I'm a good green sign. As we say in Vienna, stuff it in your own hat!

Tomorrow, Mirli, I really must set off to see my folks, and the big ideas I dreamed of seeing materialize this year. Again, as they would say of me in Vienna: some hope!

126

I don't know what will happen in the next few days, I don't know what all my aches and pains are. Instead of all these hotel beds, I would like to have a bed of my own, so that I could say 'take up thy bed and walk'. But you took that away from me, Mirli. I only ask you not to give it back to me, but if you fall into such despair that you just want to close your eyes and shut out the future – I won't even speak of the present – try it! Take up my bed, and see! Try it.

I have one hand around your neck (what a shame that Pussy's is thicker than yours) and am   your Un

Auf Wiedersehen!

To Anna Kallin

Great Southern Railway Hotel, Killarney, Ireland
24. 6. 28

My dear Mirli,

This country is good for painting but bad for living in. *Ye olde* umbrellary and *Lamb* and *Mint Sauce* and *Custard*. And some very strange condiments! But needs must when the devil drives: I have to produce nineteen paintings!!!

Tomorrow we start two days of travel by every conceivable means – hackney carriage, boat, train, charabanc – until I've found a suitable place. The hotels are *ye olde* . . . Lütjens is dying for news of the tennis, and I am my usual anxious self.   Your, Un

To Alice Lahmann

[Zurich, 29 July 1929]

My dearest Colibri,

You understand me, I know. You are masterful, you are beloved, you are *noblesse oblige*, and you give of yourself without pausing to calculate what you are worth. I've made the detour – short enough, compared to my wanderings – to an ineffably Swiss manor house, in order to catch a glimpse of our tall Miss. She escaped from her entourage for an hour today, and we ate together. I hadn't been able to keep a morsel down for two days, and now I'm in bed running a temperature that makes everything dark before my eyes, and I'm as lonely as I was in Palmyra and Baalbek. And in Zurich there's a great congress of Jews: as everywhere else that I've ever been, they – the Jews – are not alone, but have a masterful wife or mistress in tow, and masterful children, who swear allegiance to their father's clan, business or art (by me, for the most part), and are divided only on the question of their dominion over us nomads, whether they exercise it over us as Jews who are Zionists, or as

Jews who are not Zionists. I do not say this as an anti-Semite, on the contrary: when a man has spent his whole life fighting his rivals every inch of the way to gain the advantage with the immortal beloved (who gives us immortal daughters, who become immortal beloveds in their turn), and perceives that he has lost honourably to superior numbers, has some substantial holes in his hide and won't be permitted to bear the last and best of them as a trophy to the grave – that man is quits with his opponents. I've stuffed my head full, not with resentment but with my tears for the bowl of strawberries that I had looked forward to so much and didn't get – although of course everyone else had some – and now I can see nothing, and won't until I get the chance to weep my heart out on your heavenly breast/bosom. All immortal beloveds, together with their immortal daughters, are one woman, who – in the contrary direction to the gentleman who pulled himself up to the moon on his own forelock – lowers herself to earth on, pardon me, her own afterbirth. You are still a beauty, Countess Colibri, like your grandmother, still the same flesh and blood, at least, as where our tall Miss comes from – I don't know if she's something else – and all Arab women and other bright-eyes, whether that all amounts to a swarm of bees is more than I can comprehend: I have no more time to comprehend it in. The only certain thing is that I begin and end as Herr Oskar Kokoschka, and the few nomads left will go to the devil as mangy as I, before they are kissed to sleep. Only the ones who are masters of the world, because they cleave to one another, will dance their goat-dance around the immortal beloved and drive in reindeer sleighs to celebrate the solstice – don't laugh at me! I shall be at home by tomorrow evening, where a tax prosecution awaits me, and a financier's complaint about some pictures, and before long Feilchenfeldt & Ringelnatter will discover that I've returned without any pictures, and will boot me out. A huntsman without game, a lover without a child, an ape without a tail . . . kissing your picture, yours, Oskar K.

To Anna Kallin

Hotel Flora, Rome, 22. 6. 30

My dear Mirli,
Do please give this cure a try, you must look after yourself or you will become consumptive. It's a very good idea, and I heard about something similar from crofters in Scotland, incidentally. The phenol business is an old Austrian remedy (garlic), hence Arabian – Asiatic – prehistoric. And in addition, since you are so fond of smearing stuff on your body, do try rubbing in the best olive oil every night, all over your skin, especially breasts. Africans who do it never get the 'flu, even when everyone else succumbs, they told me in Tunisia.

128

I too am in a pretty poor way, but there are too many different things for much to be done about them. The main problem seems to be something to do with the small of my back, and various subterranean twinges which come and then clear up again. My left eye is not quite kosher, either, and I've a roving neuralgia, moving around my whole nervous system, which is not at all pleasant in the important places, like my left eye, right hand, pelvis, heart. When I was in Djerba, I got a kind of irritation of the costal pleura, no doctor, so I bought and consumed a phial of grey ambergris, which upset my kidneys. I'm getting over it all again as usual, but time races by so fast that I always have the impression that a whole year has passed between one look at the clock and the next.

Thank you for the novella. I want to write a play in English, if I can muster the concentration, as a way of drawing breath. This eternal, aimless nomad existence, and getting so little work done, is driving me crazy. This eternal lusting after every girl of every hue, without ever being cured by one, or because of one, makes me even more ulcerated, so that compared to me Poor Heinrich is a king, a Rothschild, a *nemchik*. Nay, he is a Landgrave (I but a poor hanger-on in the art trade), he in the vanguard of a crusade (I in the guard's van from Gabès to Reval), he consorting with popes who can command a Michelangelo, a Titian or a Charles V to build or occupy tombs (I a mere sightseer, entering by the *ingresso gratuito*, and on speaking terms only with the corporal of the Swiss Guard on duty at the door). To be honest, although it's a marvellous sight when the Pope rides through the church on the shoulders of his grovelling parasites, with that huge triple crown on his head, I wouldn't want to be on speaking terms with him, because he can't make a saint of me. On the other hand, it's quite impressive how he can pronounce on somebody – a nun or some other person who's perhaps been dead a century – as if they were standing before him for him to judge, and declare them a saint and admit them to heaven. Even if it's only a show, it's of a different order from parliaments and politics and all the other dreary things we have nowadays. It's a memory of genuine magic-making.

I made a very good friend of a black magician, incidentally, in Hara Kebira on the island of Djerba. He was supposed to scatter sand outside the door of a Jewish maiden (a colony from the time of the destruction of Jerusalem?), whose Papa was dead set against me, and who I would have dearly loved to paint, abduct and make Queen Esther, if I'd been king in Babylon. He had green trousers, black turban and the most beautiful Jewish face with the most classical gestural language, and the whole village was against me as one man, when I crept through, because I could have brought bad luck by my peering at them. And the girl, Rachel Cohen!!! was like a lovely cloud sinking to its knees. If I don't make any impact with all the assistants and contacts I've set up and left behind (I stirred up the whole country from north to south as far as Tunis, the French Resident-General, the Controlleur Civil of the island, the Jewish sheikh of the village, the intended bridegroom, who is studying the Talmud, his father, who is her uncle, in the bazaar in Tunis) before I return in the autumn, there is a grave danger that, stuffed like a goose with noodles and sweetmeats, she will be married next year and become a stethophage, and she will lose the sheen of her tears, as gentle as that of pearls, if I cannot wear her like a pearl on my bad skin. Or does one need a pure skin? If not, she will bear repulsive brats, one after the other, and suckle them to the age of seven or eight, and they will piss on the mat she sleeps on; she is now thirteen, nubile that is – you must be twelve to marry in England, mustn't you?

Mirli, my darling, please don't be angry with me for persistently courting Damaris, but her being taller than me makes me cross, and then she is in the most convenient direction for me geographically, which makes my thinking simple, and my desire real, so long as I enjoy travelling south. If ever I get to India or even China, I hope to get letters from an Indian girl, a type of human being I have never seen. Incidentally, I have various little things for you in my bag, which I shall be loath to give you when I do actually meet you somewhere. I don't want to stay here, because foul air, noise and medal-bedecked officers make life harder. I only want to finish an iodine cure that I was talked into by a doctor who should have sent me to Anticoli, where they make all the naked female artists' models for the whole world. Instead I'm here, but it's all the same basically, and not important. Glands are glands.

Please send me a photo, two photos, lots and lots of nude photographs of yourself, but mind you look nice and plump, stick out your behind, as if you were proud of it. And be quick about it! And write 'to be forwarded' on the envelope in case I've moved on. And get better! What do you want to be ill for? If I ever finish with being ill, I shall be bankrupt too, because I've no savings, so then I might as well go pluck my harp, and where will my Mignon be then, if she can't dance on her own two feet??? Don't forget the photos, as quick as you can!!!

All my love,   your Un

To Alice Lahmann
                    11 June 31, 3 Villa des Camélias, Paris XIV
Darling Colibri,
Such is life: here I am, in exile again, all alone and friendless. It makes my third exile since leaving Austria, and now Germany. [. . .] The Germans are just impossible, they have no idea of what a person or a human being

is worth! I'm going to launch a great offensive against the whole Jewish-oriented world! I shall make drawings of the 'Holy Mass', extracting all the heathen motives to make something new. The Pope will excommunicate me, and all good bourgeois vermin with mercenary ideas. It will be published by Vollard, which is tantamount to a bestseller.

Why has everyone forsaken me? It is six months since I had an answer to my letters or my telegrams, which are sometimes a page long. I am now just as poor as the young woman whose breath alone can restore my life. There is hardly any furniture in this little house that I've rented in Paris, where I intend to live for several years. My bed is a *lit de camp*, so narrow, and so cold and hard that I wake up at least once an hour. But I deliberately acquired it because the one young woman whom I love in all the world told me that she sleeps in Helsingfors on a divan which is much too small and full of holes. Why should I have anything better? You must stay with me here, if and when you come to Paris, I have a yellow room, a green room and a blue room, and a big bathroom, just as you like it. A huge studio on the floor above, with a huge mirror, but not a stick of furniture apart from a drawing table, my camp bed and a few wicker stools. An enchanting maid, a lot of schnapps, a little garden the size of a bath-tub. If I now had a soul who loved me, needed me, understood me and knew how to break my stubborn spirit, I should probably be the only man in the world able to give a new direction to my poor sad fellow-men, reduced as they are to selling their old trousers. I shall stay in France for a few years now, and am very touched to find that, although I come from Germany where I fomented spiritual revolution, here they love me as a new face, and have faith that I have a future before me, perhaps even a great one!!!

My darling angel, I ask you once again to do what you think is best for me. Either tell the one and only young woman, by whom I wish to have a daughter, that she must come to me at once and believe in me, as a husband for life whom she will not leave again, even if I make her 'unhappy', or simply write and tell me that I should give up all ideas touching the superhuman. That means little enough nowadays, after all, just whatever has nothing to do with dealers, speculators and such-like dirty dogs. I am still young, self-confident, and full of good intentions, and with a pure young woman I could work wonders. Colibri, beloved bird, do not forsake me, lend me your aid. Kissing you upon your fragile skull,   your Oskar

[Paris,] 18. 1. 33

Dear Ehrenstein,

I must have 1,000 marks, no matter what it costs, or who it comes from, my life is in danger. My lungs are playing up, my temperature keeps soaring, and I must have abscesses in my bronchial tubes or some other damned place, because the fever always stops when I bring up some bloody pus, after which I have a few days' remission. I am undernourished and of course I haven't a doctor or any other person to tend me, and have to do everything for myself. Sometimes I'm too weak to crawl, and then I have to go without food for a few days, even if there happened to be any oats or potatoes in the kitchen.

They threatened to throw me out of the house on the 15th inst. and keep everything in it as security, and having been flat on my back with fever the day before, I was naturally too frightened to leave the building, where at least I had a roof over my head – it was snowing, too. So once again I took the risk of writing out a bank slip (I've still got a Crédit Lyonnais cheque-book) for 6,300 francs, dated 1 February. Not only do I have nothing there in the bank, but also less than 50 francs in my pockets. No pictures, because two were stolen en route by some damned Galician carriers, and nothing in the studio, because I can't work in such demoralizing circumstances.

Dear Ehrenstein, among my former friends there isn't a shit who will help or even answer. They all sit on their fundaments, as they did in the war. I'm in the gravest danger, and yet I've always waded in with a will whenever I've been asked for help. George Grosz, the well-known International Communist, has annexed himself to fatherlandish sentiments, and runs a drawing-school for American pork-butchers and the daughters of war profiteers to boot. I was the real revolutionary who got into trouble for it, and now they'll let me snuff it without lifting a finger. Someone must come and get me out of this hole. I need to be kept out of jail, I need something to eat, and I need to get away from this town where the dirt fouls up my lungs. I'll pay it back with interest within a year. No one shall suffer in his hallowed wallet on my account. I'll be able to repay it when I can work again. Please telegraph something. All the best from your OK,   who detests K.O.

Please help me, urgent!! I have no one else to turn to.

Paris, May 1933

'An earlier Liebermann drove the English from the Continent', was the proud boast an ancestor of Max Liebermann's could make to a gathering which had assembled at the invitation of the Crown Prince, later Emperor Friedrich.

That earlier Liebermann was credited with the production in Germany, on a new kind of loom, of fabrics which Europe had been obliged to buy from England until then.

The Old Master Max Liebermann, who has become a Berlin character by virtue of his mother wit, resembled his ancestor, in that he threw open a window in his profession at a time when painting in German studios was done in a fug, with only a small number of shining exceptions. It was then, around the 'eighties, that Liebermann got off the train at Lehrte Station with his pictures painted *en plein air* and in bright sunlight, and founded the Berlin Secession with Leistikow. His emperor, Wilhelm II, seems not to have thought much of this new Liebermann family enterprise, because he dismissed Liebermann's work with the expression 'gutter art'. His Majesty was more conversant with plastic art, as we know. Max Liebermann has always been obstinate, an obstinate Romantic, and one of the things that proves it is that this setback did not turn him into one of those court and society painters who adapt their convictions to the taste of their patrons. These were the Gründerjahre in Germany, when the speed of material advances went to people's heads, and they were prepared to accept that the possession even of a forged Florentine Madonna was a sign of *bon ton*. Max Liebermann, however, took stock even then, and declared his position with his now-famous statement that he preferred a well-painted carrot. An artist of spirit and imagination, one whose skills are matched by a sense of responsibility, must be successful in his profession by virtue of his superiority: such, we may suppose, was his reasoning. Are we going to reproach an artist for something that we know is inseparable from an artist's fate: that he races ahead of his time in the quest for the goddess of truth, and that, needing to understand himself and somehow find his proper place, he comes to regard himself as a minor Zeus? What is remarkable about that, when it is said that the great Zeus himself embraced a cloud instead of the goddess! Today, especially, when the state and the leaders of German society, along with the entire nation, have more pressing concerns, it is understandable that the individual artist is not of interest to the general public, but it is the duty of a fellow-artist to testify on behalf of Max Liebermann.

A short time ago Max Liebermann announced his resignation from the Prussian Academy of Arts, after that institution adopted the Aryan

Paragraph. He had been the Academy's president for many years. The association of the Berlin Secession, which has also added the Aryan Paragraph to its statutes, will in future likewise be deprived of its co-founder and former president.

It is with lively regret, increasing with time and absence from Germany, that I see no one in the ranks of his comrades, among those who have followed him for a lifetime, who feels – or, rather, who is ready to say – that this old man of eighty-six, even though artistic alliances and their interests can no longer concern him, could depart this life reflecting bitterly on human weakness.

I still have half my life to live, my work is not yet finished, and what I have achieved is perhaps to some extent problematically misunderstood, hounded and outcast: such has been the path I have trodden since my eighteenth year. A thorny path, like that of almost all artists. So let me be the one to speak out in the name of his German fellow-artists on behalf of Max Liebermann, whose work is done. It takes no special courage, I know, to stand up for Max Liebermann and say: if his decision is irrevocable, then let this parting be made in friendship, lest a tragic misunderstanding ensue which will divide teachers and pupils, and can only harm the development of new art in the new Germany.

We all know Max Liebermann as a leader; he led us into the open air, into daylight, into the German woods and out on to the German meadows. And furthermore we know that for all the ties that bind us together as a nation we must not allow the root to wither that sucks up nourishment and strength from the eternal-human, and thus determines our growth and our crown. Let us not forget that all Father-Lands are rooted in the womb of our common Mother Earth. Let the flames we kindle in honour of the Mother, the tutelary goddess of corn, of the vine and the rose, be the fires of celebration, not the bonfires of persecution.   Oskar Kokoschka

To Albert Ehrenstein

[Vienna,] 22 September 1934

Dear Tubutsch,

I have had your letters and your reproaches – have you not had either my telegram or my airmail letter? I've had another letter to M. go astray only recently, on account of the over-enthusiasm of certain patrons of the arts here. In sum, I would like to be in M. by 5–10 October, and spend a year, perhaps, painting everything important for a big travelling show, to go from New York to Shanghai in due course. A kind of New World Symphony, like the Czech composer Dvořák's. Heads of all the important people, the greatest possible variety of races and landscapes, and cities and human locales. (I leave for Prague on the 25th, and will

expect to hear from you there, and will then write to you airmail again.)
An epic of awakening reason, and simultaneously an instructive picture-
book for the old European sacerdotal kingdoms, something that will spur
them not to pin all their hopes of prosperity on the armaments industry,
while placing the care of the people in the hands of God – and the police
force, military courts, and political economy. I've had a good German
translation made of Robert Briffault's *The Mothers*, and written a preface
for it which will cost me my head if it's published. It must be translated
into Russian.

Dear Tubutsch, see to it that we get an incredibly competent and active
guide, because painting is unhappily inseparable from more mechanical
things, and I quake somewhat at the thought of packing and carrying
without speaking the language. We must get as far as the Chinese border
and do a great work together. Everything that I've been able to do in this
part of the world has lost its savour for me, and now I'm galvanized at the
thought of making people stare again. In America and England my name
is good, and my artistic credit hasn't yet been exhausted, hasn't even
been tapped. Send me the tickets, valid for 5–10 October, care of the
Russian Embassy in Prague, and make sure that we really will be assisted
with all means. In France, too, I could knock them out with a single show,
if I only had the right promotion, if they really wanted it, and understood
and needed it. I can do it! I'm very much looking forward to meeting
Gorky.

Up to today only a visa has come, no tickets yet!!! I will send your
medicines ahead, via the Russian Embassy in Prague. Everything is
impossible here, unless blessed by the archbishop. Please write at once to
the embassy. Sincere thanks,   your old friend OK

To Anna Kallin

[Prague, 5 October 1934]

Dear Mirli,
[. . .] I've got away from Vienna again, after a long year, and as yet I
don't know where I shall go next. For the time being I must stay here to
earn back a few of the bricks on our house in Vienna, which is mortgaged
up to the chimney-pots. I've done absolutely no work since Paris, and
have had to run up a lot of debts. I can well believe that you're glad to be
back in London after Europe as it is now. I almost went into politics while
I was in Vienna, on account of those blue-blooded gigolos, bellicose
liberals and toadying cardinals who lock up the entire population of
Austria in concentration camps in order to promote the tourist industry –
and what tourists! Government agents talk these young hotheads into
being now Nazis, now Communists, and then the old Imperial and Royal

soldiery (i.e. Hollywood uniforms draped on the backs of scarecrows) turn up, together with national guardsmen let out of jail for rum, and break the heads of the 'misguided elements' with rifle-butts! We don't need police-spies, or Cheka-Gauleiters, or God as head of state: we'd do better with matriarchy and workers' councils in the elementary schools (not in the factories, which profit in the scramble to re-arm, and dissolve the shop-floor councils because it's peace-time!). That was the theme of my lectures and essays. But no one took any notice of them, and the young, if they are not enrolled in volunteer formations to build (for nothing!) roads to facilitate tourism and – maybe – military strategy, are being educated by the priests to be illiterate, to the delight of Lord Basil Zaharoff (you know, the old Armenian thief, who is still at his game of financing armaments). The One God's will be done!

All best wishes, Un

To Albert Ehrenstein

[Prague, autumn 1934]

Dear Tubutsch,

Don't be angry, but I shan't be able to travel until December or January. Once again I'm up to my eyes in debt: to live in Vienna is to be cheated, fleeced and robbed in broad daylight – and always with a 'Grüß Gott!' Since I have no choice, unless I want to see my brother kicked out of our house, I tried to complete an old commission here. But no sooner had I started than a row blew up, thanks to the interference of a brother of the Vienna Nirenstein – God's arms are long – who is private secretary to my quasi-Maecenas, Federer of the Witkowitz works. Well, as I had already extracted all the money there was, and the famous Prague landscape was half-finished, in spite of my dragging my feet for the last two years, we are at daggers drawn. That is to say, I wrote my Maecenas a cheeky letter, saying that I was no longer prepared to go through gallstones or kidneystones, i.e. the art trade, but would be offering my paintings as an itinerant artist, like Dürer with his handcart. Consequently my venture foundered, and therefore I can't come and see you yet, or the lovely girls of Tartary and Little Russia and Great Russia, whose smiles would have made a few of my grey hairs drop out. I've got to stay here for the time being and paint a second picture, and perhaps a third, because other people can't raise the cash for anything – manufacturing guns just doesn't pay at present, now that gas is used on the battlefield – in order to earn the money I must have enough to settle my Viennese debts and leave a bit over for my brother. I can't leave him there without a kreuzer to bless himself with, praying to the saints to send him bread and water and a slice of salami. Did you know that they're seriously considering canonizing the

136

'Martyr-Chancellor'? Heaven is getting a mite too politicized, it's high time people started to lose interest in the world to come and made do with this world. All my letters were intercepted in Vienna, because I'm not in the Fatherland Party and I had a telegram from Moscow, from you. I forgot to bring your medical shopping-list with me from Vienna, and until it's been forwarded I will send you just the coffee and the other mixture, and I shall be coming myself in another six weeks or so. But I'd like to bring a good little girl with me, Edith Sachsl, a Czech Jewess, who would be done for if I left her here. Your friends ought to fix things at the Russian Embassy in Prague, so that she too gets a visa and tickets. She is a brilliant fashion artist, and will be able to make herself useful in Moscow. At all events I shall spend from spring until autumn painting everything in Soviet Russia that will excite the Americans, the English, the Dutch, the French, the Swedes, the Colonizers and the Colonized, and arouse them at least to visit the Union as tourists. And that could avert a world war, because the Holy Alliance, the Pope, Rothschild, and the various generals all glorious in cocks' plumes, having been soundly beaten in the Great War, are agreed that the salvation of the Western world lies in following the example of the erstwhile American war-production industry, and that the way to ensure *prosperity* by the new year is to speculate in war production. Priests, academics, journalists and politicians are fanning patriotism in readiness. So please write and reassure me that no one there will mind my postponing my journey, and that when I do arrive I must stay at least six months, painting everything on both sides of the Urals for the great travelling exhibition afterwards.

My lung is playing up, and Prague's dust, fog and pollution are not the best medicine for it. Write to me here, and let me know what your own arrangements are, and whether you can stay there a bit longer. Please don't hurt my feelings by accusing me of changing my mind like a prima donna. You have no idea, my dear Tubutsch, of the burden I have to bear, and the dog's life a painter leads when he's on his own, having incurred the wrath of Cassirer's heirs, Feilchenfeldt and Ring, by voluntarily dissolving his contract – in the middle of the Depression! I feel as if the curse of Orestes was on me. It really was a choice between bending and breaking, and sometimes even my poor mother, brave soul that she was, lost heart! Please write a few helpful lines to Rowohlt about my brother's novel. And don't send me telegrams, it's a waste of money – write me long and newsy letters instead.

Giving you a big hug, dear Tubutsch, your old friend,   OK

[Prague,] 8 February 35

My dear Helen,

I shall not waste your time with excuses and explanations, when all a connoisseur of human nature like you needs to hear is that as soon as I get over one attack of 'flu I go down with another, and have therefore done nothing for five weeks, and do not get any letters written either. I have a frightfully nice young lady on my back, but the lowering effect it has on me is equally frightful, because she is incapable of rousing me from my lethargy, and receives every word I utter as an ordinance of higher wisdom. What I need instead of that is some excitement, being as I am full of rust and lactic acid-amidogen (for my diet of goulash and smoked pork is not according to Gerson). Thus all my profound insights into the cosmic order are lost to the wider public, because a muddle of internal and external reasons holds me here, and I cannot tear myself away of my own free will. If bankruptcy sweeps me away on the tide, reasons beyond my ken will also wash me up somewhere where I can lay my head. If only I could travel with the energetic American women you want to send to visit their Tuareg sisters. When you make up the party, take especial care that the women are beautiful and not handicapped by the insane condescension most whites have for all other peoples.

Lévy-Brühl, who must still be in Vienna, knows all the Moroccan officials in Paris who could help you, and is very nice. Salomon Reinach is a sweet man still living in Paris, and he knows some decent officials in the colony. I have temporarily forgotten the name of the director of the museum of Islamic art in Algiers, but he keeps in touch with both of them, and is known for his special interest in researching the Tuareg and for his frequent travels among them. Laval's bone-headed democracy, among other acts designed to hasten the final mechanization of the entire planet, has driven out what were left of the Atlantides, in the name of the comité des forges and Thyssen and his cronies in the steel cartel, and such Queens of Sheba as still drag out a wretched existence there are obliged to sit beside the oil companies' road, making up poems in honour of the patriarchate for the edification of Cook's Tourists, so that honeymooning Gretchens learn some mores. They've been made beggars, as elsewhere. Incidentally, the Libyan language has been preserved as the women's language among some of the black tribes that have been driven out of the oil-producing areas. Of these, the Mandé in the south have the most beautiful women, and have preserved all the customs that used to mark cultic-celtic cultures, and the things you know about that sweet Egyptian flapper, Hatshepsut.

If only an American pork-butcher would give me the money I need to get away from here, I could avert the mortal danger I am in of having all my cells destroyed by a lack of oxygen, and then I could provide that mystic Schweitzer, who is now the Vatican's only liberal opponent, with the examples he needs to support his outlook. It makes thoroughly good sense, but unfortunately he bases it only on the rabbinical squabbles of Christendom, and for the time being, for all practical purposes, it amounts to an esoteric flight from the world, while his motto 'reverence for life', profoundly true as it is in itself, is a blind alley. The place to look for an example of repudiation of this so-called fascism is on a page of the book of human history that lies some 4–6,000 years back, in the chapter 'Monotheos versus Monotaurus'. The latest fashion in Spain at the moment is for American millionairesses to enter the ring as bull-fighters. Perhaps the woman who started this fashion could have her attention diverted to Crete, and be persuaded, firstly, to prevent Laval's *poilus* from undertaking any further missionary penetration of the Hoggar, either by commissioning a book about Hoggar culture, sure to be epoch-making in America, from Lyautey (or whatever the name of that aged field-marshal is, who sits sulking in a corner in Paris these days, and must surely have cultural interests just to spite his successor), or by founding a female order on the spot herself, which would start missionizing the Europeans by means of cinematic enlightenment and other propaganda. Think of that whole insane pestilence bred in Hollywood and at the Ufa Studios in Berlin, romanticizing the Foreign Legion, while the Riff Kabyles are the enemy, diabolically cruel, sinisterly lurking, swathed in blue veils. One such stupid concoction, *The Lost Patrol*, is running here at the moment. If only those swine in the Viennese film industry, which does not stint its efforts to boost the Blue Danubian war economy, would allow the crackling encasing their skulls to admit, for example, the idea of the smash hit it would be if they made a film from the standpoint of the downtrodden natives in some colony. Lacking the technology and capital of the white movie moguls, they have to put up with having all manner of beastliness attributed to them, while the audiences aren't fundamentally prejudiced at all, and only go to the cinema to escape from life in this damned Europe of ours, if only for an hour or so – exactly like Gauguin in his day, or better still Becker in the Dutch East Indies, or Stevenson in the South Seas. But rabbinical sclerosis has made the reflexes of our movie moguls hereditary, and it is clinically impossible for them to react in any other way than with the 'Hurrah-for-King-and-Country' mentality displayed in all films set in foreign parts.

Those are some of the bees currently buzzing in my bonnet, but the most important thing for the 'Encyclopedia of Women' is to get a book written about pre-Roman Mediterranean civilization, with the lion's share being devoted to African history, while it can still be studied in the field. My memory has gone to pot, and for the present I can't think of any more of

the kind of evidence and sources that you, my darling, vital, dauntless, combative, but immensely sympathetic Helen, would want. The American consul there is definitely a donkey! These are not personal asseverations, from which you have asked me to desist, but my strictly private opinions. In order to make you write to me again, because it makes me happy to get the kind of exciting letters you send, I will say nothing today about Orphism and Peasants' Revolts. Ask me about them again soon, and speak encouragingly to me, and in the meantime receive the heartfelt thanks of one squatting amid the laundry odours of Prague, when he might be in Shanghai with Sung women, or in Hoggar with the Queens of Sheba, yours,   OK
Give my love to Robert Briffault, the Homer of the Women's Wars.

To Albert Ehrenstein

[Prague, June or July 1935]

My dear old owlish friend,
I've finished the job, M treated me like an old friend, but there are too many other factors, family and entourage, to be able to entertain any hopes of him. I've made him look healthy, everyone agreed about that, but all I was thinking of was: 50 crowns a day in tips, and I didn't even earn a gong, Order of the Bohemian Lion, or anything like that. Up to a week ago I went up there every day, although I'd long since finished the painting, which is ready to be hung just as soon as a wall in the palace of the League of Nations has been found for it. They can hang me at the same time, because the taxman here wants 10,000 kr. from me. I've just delivered a landscape for which I got 20,000 kr. six weeks ago, which has melted like the dew, while Federer will probably sell it for 50,000, thus catering for his very last client in the Bohemian Forest.
Next Sunday's *Prager Tagblatt* will feature a little call to arms by me, alongside a reproduction of the Masaryk portrait. He showed an interest in my idea of a federation of elementary schools on a humanitarian basis, but they don't want him to lay himself open by following my suggestion and asking the people in Geneva to work out a constitution that all the members would have to endorse, as in a single state. The constitution would have to avoid *Realpolitik*, anyway, and be an ethical matter: the fundamental principle to be the recognition that morality is one and indivisible. But M's writings, where all that is already to be found (world revolution), can no longer be bought in this country. The Czechs, the Jews and the upper crust are dissolving in pity for the poor Habsburgers, and sympathy for Werfel, Schuschnigg, Starhemberg & Co., and getting themselves baptized, while the liberal Czech press and the liberal German press are striving to outdo each other in printing sermons,

because Catholicism is the *dernier cri*, and the word 'Soviet' can at last be mentioned, in much the tone of admitting to acquaintanceship with social inferiors and poor relations. So I can't pay off the 50,000 schillings I owe in Vienna, and the interest on the mortgage blights my brief earthly existence. Bohi has lived on dumplings for the past month, and will freeze next winter, because the cupboard is bare. The b—— publishers will only print Werfel, Emil Ludwig, Max Brod and Zweig and Wallace, God help us. I've just had an invitation from the Prussian Academy, beginning 'Heil Hitler'. Am I to be spared nothing? In future I shall show my work in Addis Ababa, and nowhere else.

With a warm hug from your old, decrepit   OK

When are you coming to Prague again, now that my debts won't allow me to leave?

To Anna Kallin

[Prague,] 11 July 1935

Dear Mirli,

The enclosed article was published yesterday, 10 July, in the *Prager Tagblatt*, with a few editorial cuts which, although short, had the effect of badly distorting it.

To popularize the idea of a federation of elementary schools, it absolutely must be printed in full in a respected English paper, like the *Labour Leader* or *Manchester Guardian*, so I turn trustingly to you and know that it will be done in a trice! It can appear under the sub-heading 'The Catholic Congress in Prague', to emphasize its newsworthiness, since Hitler's naval re-armament, Mussolini's Abyssinian war and the Habsburger putsch don't appear to provide enough material for England's apathy, whereas they are canonizing one saint after another there, and a eucharistic congress is about to be held in London.

I suspect that certain things are not supposed to be said as categorically as they are in this article, and that the suggested remedies are not such as the professional statesmen would recommend.

Darling Mirli, please see to it that it is published as soon as possible, in several papers simultaneously, if it can be arranged, and without cuts, as a manifesto and an appeal to the League of Nations. Perhaps we could breed a snobbery, a new fashion of philanthropical hue, so that the bourgeoisie, sweating over its share portfolios, might turn its attention to the elementary school as the key social issue, and perhaps forget warmongering, which would be good for all of us. All it would take would be gauging correctly the initial acceleration, the initial speed, preferably with a propaganda campaign starting with a bang. England ought to have a fellow-feeling for the Czechs, because there are parallels in the history of the Reformation in both countries, and because the Czechs are the nation most exposed to political danger here in the east: to the Reichswehr to the north, to the Habsburgers to the south. Talk to socialists, reformers, women at meetings in Hyde Park and above all one of the leading womens' rights organizations. Throw yourself into the battle like a new Joan of Arc = Mirli of Hampstead. I'd like to go to England again.

I'm painting the President, who is eighty-six, rather frail, but very patient. It's a history painting, with the Hradschin on the right, Comenius's *Orbis pictus* on the left, and Hus at the stake in the background, somewhat indistinct. I shall show the painting in London, it can be mentioned in connection with reprinting this article. Thank you very much for your letter, I'm already looking forward to the next. I also enjoyed very much the articles and pictures you enclosed, of cows and human curiosities.

I also want to thank you very warmly for releasing the little Czech girl from the Catholic house of correction in Austria. It's very sad that *Realpolitik* makes everyone here so nervous that I can't get anyone to burn their fingers with the matter. Getting my article published also took an entire week of struggle, first refusals, then the original castrated, then at last something about half readable. Yet no one at any point put their finger on the nub of this cultural-historical phenomenon: the Czech mission = the elementary school!

You'd better buy your own copy of the *Prager Tagblatt*. I won't enclose it with this letter after all, because it would attract the censor's attention. But read it for fun, for comparison's sake.

Send me new photographs of yourself, what you look like, colour of hair, colour of tongue, height in socks, weight in imperial and metric measures. And write and tell me how you are. How I am is, I'm waiting. I should like to be waiting to leave for Shanghai, to see the thousands of lovely girls on the flower-boats, before Edith Rosenheim and her society industrialize it all. Then there will be nothing but a war economy, and then just words of command, and gas.

I hope you're well, Mirli . . . With a loving kiss,   Your Un Oskar

To Anna Kallin

[Prague, February 1936]

My dear Mirli,

Thanks for your lovely warm letter, I was very moved too, I like the English as much as if they were my own kinfolk. The Balkan continent completely fails to understand them! They've accomplished something similar to what certain outstanding individuals achieved in the Middle

Ages and antiquity. St Theresa, who sublimated religious love as a physical love, in a pietà of poetic ecstasy overcoming misery. Voltaire, who so refined the famous courage of the male sex that he dared to *épater* God and *le bourgeois*. Marx, who looked at reason's endless despair over the present time, the lack of consonance between perceptions and actions, and the idealists' flight from reality into belief in an unending Beyond, and agnosticized it all as the bourgeois soul, and rejected it like a true stoic – at the same time cooking up a new version of the future, in which man remains always the same! A whole nation put that into practice in England, from the 18th century until the very recent past. They generated a peculiar virtue of their own, which derived from the civility of the 18th century (*'your most humble obedient servant'*), to produce the character of the civil servant which distinguishes the liberal 19th. I mean the official who performs his duties in the consciousness of his own responsibility, no longer serving robber barons or a priest-king, but the whole of barbarian humanity, which the English took it upon themselves to tend like a *nursery*. That *honesty* is out of date now, I suppose, since the whole world has decided to play the part, and the official is paid by the state, and rates his virtue according to his salary, just as the priest does his prayers, and the judge his morality. Only the English were *loyal* and *fair* and *honest*, and the late king was an average Englishman in that well-meaning sense.

The only blot on the funeral ceremony, and a sign of the times, was the fact that Starhemberg was allowed to be so close to the catafalque, legitimized as the representative of Austria – that gigolo who pays his gambling debts with the misery of a whole nation, which was too placid to put up any real resistance to his armed bands of gangsters. That ruffian learned from the Munich Bierkeller putsch how to go about it, and then threatened the Viennese Socialists: Asiatic skulls must bite the dust; then he got his debts settled repeatedly by the cartridge manufacturer Mandl and his wife, and Kohn the financier from Brünn, and since then he has officially carried the hallowed candle and is a militant Catholic by the grace of Mussolini. But the supply of money from Rome has dried up, and he's pondering whether to offer Austria to Hitler or to a European banking group, because he's run up the most horrifying debts again. A week ago he threatened a new terror in Vienna. Anyone who does not support his Austria First Party – i.e. doesn't pay a subscription – is a traitor to the country and as such may be eliminated! He got the idea from Streicher. Is that the sort of person the English court should allow to represent the people of Austria with the new king? Please – you must make a stink in the Socialist papers in England, at once.

That gigolo only represents the cut-throats, the priests and the usurers in Austria, everyone else wishes him in hell, but under their breath, alas,

because there are no authorities where they can lay charges against gangsters like that without getting strung up.
With a big kiss from   your Un

To Anna Kallin

My dear Mirli,
Many thanks for your beautiful pictures. I ought to have followed your example long ago, and opted for the happiness that takes no notice of the ant-heap called human society. Then I too would have a Voltairean forehead like yours, and verses would flow as sweetly from my pen as the thoughts that play beneath your crystal dome – which most people don't use for thinking at all, but merely as a hat-stand. But alas, instead of writing verses, all I ever do is worry, from the moment in the morning when I sit on the bed to put my socks on. I've had a headache for months now, and the bandage over my eyes hurts. I wear it because, like Cassandra, I don't need to look to see the catastrophe which everyone else is only just beginning to suspect may be coming. The second world war has already started! The shareholders, who make money from torn human bodies, are in the thick of it, but when it's over they look forward to buying aristocratic *vases de nuit*, and country houses with domestic chaplains and a papal blessing. Here, people are desperate to prove themselves more Catholic than the Pope. Here, they've banned the *Arbeiterzeitung*, while in Vienna anyone caught reading it gets five years. Yet the above-mentioned owners of stocks and shares are allowed to send Starhemberg and his gang Czech money and Skoda rifles, to enable them to set fire to Vienna. Furthermore, the *Prager Tagblatt* has been transformed into a Fascist paper, thanks to money from Goebbels (via Vienna), without a single word of protest from any of its Jewish subscribers. Within six months – the conventional period of mourning – it will be exactly the same anti-semitic rag as the *Wiener Journal*, which has 'gleichgeschaltet' itself with the *Völkischer Beobachter*, and prints nothing from Spain but the same filthy war reports as *Gringoire* and the *London News*. And the subscribers keep taking it because it still looks the same, and still prints the political ads and forthcoming marriages.
Mirli, do not kid yourself that you look like Dante. He was a Fascist of the clerical party, and developed logical theories of a unified world-state with the Pope and the Emperor as a two-headed Führer. He possessed too little common sense and too much of the mind of a chess-player, like most politicians; he was a madman with a strictly logical, mathematical mentality, and believed the rest of the human race were idiots who would rather chase skirts than pursue philosophies. If he hadn't happened to be

a few centuries too early with his political theories, he could have been Schuschnigg's protégé, like Werfel today. His ideal was the corporatist state – exactly what the priests, the Nazis and the armaments shareholders are setting up today; paradise for them and the inferno for the rest of us. I cannot endure existence any longer! I feel sorry for Olda, because she still regards life as something certain, as insurance against the void. Because she believes me, here, although I see the maggots and worms wriggling on the cadaver of humanity, yet do not trust myself to speak of it, and cannot do anything about it, lacking money, a voice, friends, or a future. For her generation there will be nothing but the lumpy, lime-bespattered straw mattresses used by victims of the plague. How I wish I was Pussy, and could be rocked to sleep in your arms; here's hoping sleep will come without benefit of gas-mask to your devoted Un

To Alma Mahler-Werfel

[Mährisch-Ostrau, summer 1937]

Alma, thank you for your letter, and for not forgetting. I'm never ill, you know, only enfeebled from time to time, due to the lack of oxygen, or the '*splendid isolation*' that people like us can still be proud of having landed ourselves in, intentionally and at an early date. Now it seems to be the inescapable fate of every thinking person, and before long it will be general: it seems to lie in the nature of our hypocritical, bloodthirsty, murderous white civilization. If there is something wrong with me, it can always be traced back to an external cause in the end: for thirty years I've eaten in restaurants and station buffets, lived in places that are not my home; when I'm tired I give myself a good pep talk, put my hand in my own pocket when I see that something's needed, without ever getting the chance to replace it or to build myself up again.

It's so long since I saw through the swindle of fame and vanity, avarice and ambition, that I have no idea any more of what they mean to other people. All I want to do is carry on with my game, and not be incessantly reminded that a mass grave lies gaping at the feet of every one of us. I've been discharged from the hospital: it hurt, but the people who have to do with me are generally all so kind and harmless that I end up feeling embarrassed at not being worse than I am, so as to make all the trouble I give them worthwhile. On the other hand, I leave with a slight feeling of relief that I can now forget that I haven't helped any of those who have far worse to put up with than I have. After all, what can happen to me? One day I'll die, but I've known that since the war, and I've had the occasional lesson since then in what it will be like. But these other poor souls want to live, and their right to exist is based on the fact that they've got to live, because they've got to stay in their fixed position in the social

145

order, while it's only by chance that the said social order still survives. It's only by chance that all these phantoms and ghosts in human guise don't attack each other this very day, with knives as dirty as madness can make them, man against man, nightmare against nightmare. What use is one of imagination's traffic cops (= an artist?) in a world like this, a manikin, one pitched against the rest? Be glad that you've escaped from that big house, many guests mean many parasites, and much muck to sweep out of doors. What happened to make it necessary? Or is something *going* to happen in Austria? Don't worry, it won't be worse than before, only each member of the human race is gradually growing tired of the monkeys and their eternal squealing, and is ready to go down into hell, because he no longer believes in the paradise he's been promised on earth. Or in heaven? Not to be found in the biology textbooks, perhaps in Vienna they have a censored edition of science!

Knowing that you think of me is like a tonic, I have forgotten nothing about you. Write to me. Read my *Orpheus*!

To Alma Mahler-Werfel

[Mährisch-Ostrau,] 30. 7. 37

Alma, your extraordinary letter arrived, by no less extraordinary a coincidence, at the same time as a letter of farewell from another woman, who for seven years has fulfilled her self-appointed task of keeping me alive with unrivalled loyalty and self-sacrifice. There were times recently when it was a dubious undertaking. She suffered unspeakably, because she was naive, and didn't understand that I *must* follow a constant inner voice, and put at risk again and again the life she was trying to preserve. Now at last I've succeeded in loosening her hold on me, as gently as I could, and she will be free to live her own life again. The chain of my mistakes remains to be unwound. Since my mother died, as the result of those infamous events in Vienna during what is now known as the Dollfuss era, I want nothing more for myself alone, but I've learned not to bear personal grudges! I know that we're all adrift, the prey of our own impulses, with a tiny lamp of reason, shedding a dim light in the greyness that will become blackness sooner or later for each and every one of us. I could have turned out differently, but I didn't. Instead, I went into the slaughterhouse, and got a bullet in my head and a bayonet through my lungs, only I was rejected by God and sent back to the life I would have been glad to lose. Since then I have not allowed myself to drift in quite the old way, but the light of my reason is still too little for me to be able to tell others about it. Perhaps you've already heard about my plan to wrest elementary education out of the hands of individual nation-states – that is, the political parties that run them – and put it under scientifically

146

organized international control. A large number of preparatory steps would be necessary. A person with the wit to make the best use of isolated chances can also realize this miracle, which will set up a self-evidently rational and life-affirming goal, in opposition to the suicidal urge that has gripped mankind ever since the end of the war. I want to have a shot at it, and you can help me. Help me in any event! Did you come into the world to serve only your own interests? What have you created to take the place of what you destroyed? That's the question you should ask yourself, instead of whether someone, who is as much dust as you are, can forgive you, or has forgiven you.

You can help me by exploiting your influence with Sch. Bring all your will-power to bear on him, not for any frivolous reasons, but in order to compel the man symbolically regarded as the voice of the German nation to apologize to me publicly for his attack on contemporary art (after I had conceived this plan of mine): that is, to make him publicly withdraw his denunciation of the helpless artists who remain in Germany. This is the first sign of a weak point in the mechanism that, ultimately, was the inevitable outcome of the mentality in which we were all reared. If a *rascal* who has been crowned king allows power to go to his head, and suddenly reveals that he is still a pleb in the way he acts and reacts, then it's not a comedy any longer. It shows up the weakness in a social structure which has been shaped haphazardly, according to the faulty wisdom of an elementary school primer. We must do something, and quickly. Thanks to this maniac, who has now given himself away, we can grab the society whose puppet he is by the short hairs, if we have the courage and determination not to let this moment, this chance, slip by until everything has been glued together again and glossed over with ideology and *Realpolitik*, and resumes its slouching towards the end of the world. Help me! Once Schuschnigg grasps the fact that I too have undertaken a cultural mission of crucial importance to the people of Austria, perhaps he will lend me a hand for the political reasons that are important to *him*. Go to Innitzer, go to every Tom, Dick and Harry who has ever been a guest in your house, seek them out, muster them all, and bellow in their ears that on the one hand there is a housepainter from Austria who intends to use the power apparatus he has seized from the Germans to have his supposed rivals, real painters, castrated! And then tell them that on the other hand there is a painter who wants the world to understand that when you are faced with a maniac who is given an official platform to make pathological speeches before an élite troop of cowards, the so-called upper ranks of society (which I despised as heartily in your time as I do now), the courage must be found to put him in the lunatic asylum, along with the 'upper' ranks who listen to him. The fact that this upper society (everywhere, not just in Germany) profits from these pathological assaults is no reason to regard the task as impossible. All anyone needs to do is look on it as his human, personal responsibility, then put his personal powers of reason to use, even if everybody seems to be acting like bits of driftwood with no reasoning power at this juncture! Help me, Alma, help me at once, and then I may be able to believe that it has all been a bad dream since I knew that you were alone in the nursing home, after they took away your child, my child. I've never wanted a child again, since then, and yet I'm so dreadfully fond of children. Alma, believe in me with everything that you still have it in you to be, and take the rainbow as a good sign! I still have faith in you!

My greetings to you   Oskar

To Kurt von Schuschnigg

Mährisch-Ostrau, 3 August 1937.

Your Excellency.

The undersigned, Professor Oskar Kokoschka, an Austrian citizen, requests the protection of the law in the following matter.

As reported widely in the international press, on the occasion of the opening of the House of German Art in Munich by the head of the German government on 19 July 1937, the crudest abuse and threats were heaped upon a large number of German artists whose names are spoken whenever present-day German art is discussed in the world at large. Simultaneously an 'Exhibition of Degenerate Art' was also opened in Munich, intended as a kind of Chamber of Horrors, an illustration of the antithesis of what is permitted and acknowledged as 'pure art' by the head of the German government.

The representative of the German Chancellor had the following to say about the artists (including the undersigned) whose works are pilloried in this exhibition: 'These ruffians, the lackeys and pacemakers of international Jewry, have committed crime after crime against German art.' The German Chancellor himself, in his speech, declared that the pilloried artists, 'in so far as they are not swindlers, who should therefore be brought to trial as such, suffer from defective vision', and called upon the Reich's Ministry of the Interior to establish 'whether this defective vision is congenital or acquired. If congenital, steps must be taken to ensure that it becomes impossible for them to pass on, and thus propagate, the defect.' In other words, the German Chancellor threatened to have these artists sterilized.

These remarks of the Chancellor were received with tumultuous applause by the select audience, despite the fact that every educated layman must be aware that the art of painting cannot be confined to the mere copying of an object imprinted on the retina. The very act of seeing is an act of the conscious mind and not merely the reflex reaction of the optic nerve to a stimulus, and hence there can be no fear of a defect of vision being passed on, as an infection is transmitted by a bacillus.

The suggestion that there is a causal relationship between the creative artist's inner vision and possible faults in his eyesight appears all the more absurd if one reflects that it would be consistent with the theory advanced by the German Chancellor to have, for example, Beethoven castrated by the agencies of his Ministry of the Interior, had the latter been unfortunate enough to live and work under the Chancellor's jurisdiction, for it is known that Beethoven suffered from an organic malady of the hearing, and, furthermore, that some of his compositions provoked the most violent disapproval on the part of some very influential contemporaries.

The reaction the German Chancellor's speech elicited from his audience, if only because of the propaganda effect it must have had on the masses, gives grounds for fear that the German authorities will follow it by whipping up a new iconoclasm, in order to effectuate the 'Cleansing Action' instigated by their leader. It conjures up the threat of the destruction of works by German artists – by no means a merely symbolic act, like the book-burning of 1933 – and it endangers the existence of a substantial proportion of the life's work of the undersigned, especially as those who have hitherto been entrusted with the protection of these works of art, responsible museum directors, are now in custody.

The undersigned has an exceptional interest in the Austrian government's taking appropriate diplomatic steps to ensure the protection of modern art, in view of the current atmosphere of a pogrom against it in Germany.

The undersigned believes he is correct in the assumption that the legal protection assured him by his government extends to his intellectual property.

At the present time, a relatively small number (unhappily) of the works of the undersigned are safe from the threat of the National Socialists' 'Cleansing Action': some in the official exhibition organized on the occasion of his fiftieth birthday by the Austrian Museum, and some in the exhibition of Austrian art organized by Dr Stix on behalf of the Austrian government, which was first shown in Paris and is currently in Berne. The undersigned requests that those of the paintings in question which are on loan from state museums in the German Reich should not be returned, without the prior provision of an official exculpation or a binding guarantee on the part of the appropriate authorities in the German Reich. He makes this request, not only because their continuing to remain under the jurisdiction of German authorities puts the very existence of his life's work at risk, but also because he can no longer regard

149

it as a mark of honour that his art should be a subject of interest in a country where a political regime reserves its attacks for the weakest of its opponents, because their opposition is 'only' intellectual and spiritual.

The undersigned ventures to suggest that, in the interests of protecting Austrian cultural assets – which description he believes he may with propriety apply to his work – in view of the encouragement and recognition recently granted him by the authorities charged with the duty of sustaining cultural activity, the government of Austria should make the strongest possible representations to the government of the German Reich for the release of the undersigned's artistic work, under the terms of the Cultural Convention agreed between the Austrian Federation and the German Reich in 1936.

The approach will assuredly be made easier by the fact that world opinion, conscious of its cultural obligations, will lend sympathetic support to the Austrian government in such action.

The undersigned wishes to express his most sincere thanks to Your Excellency for the legal assistance that he herewith requests from the government of his country.

Oskar Kokoschka

To Alma Mahler-Werfel

Hotel Juliš, Prague, 16 Dec. 37

Alma, why are you going away, and where to? Why do you write at all if you won't be clearer? I don't know if some personal reason lies behind this puzzling news, or if it has an external cause – it is so long since I saw you that I can no longer be sure.

I will certainly not be coming to Vienna, what would I want there, where everything is strange to me now, and my art has never won me friends, with the sole exception of dear old Carl. Is it true, what the papers now say about the political future there? If so, it's the end! It won't be long before what happened in Vienna will be done all over Europe, destroy and don't give a thought to the consequences. Arrogance and deficient humanity and the crassest materialism do not make for cheerful company. I don't want to lose my vision, it's a wonder that I've hung on to it in this accursed age. I'd like to see you too, Alma, and ask you what you think about life – what remains of it for the two of us. I don't rail at our poor country, on the contrary I have nothing but kind words for those poor unhappy devils. The fact that I've never been able to stand the cream of society, because I don't like the taste of it anywhere, but least of all in Austria, where it always had an exceptionally closed mind, blocked to all traffic – that has nothing whatever to do with the country or the people in it.

150

I love to hear from you, don't be anxious, think of all that I've survived in my life so far, it's unlikely to be any better in the future. It's the price I pay for being a *rara avis*.

All best wishes, yours,   Oskar

To Anna Kallin

My dear Mirli,

I combed your letter in vain for voluptuous photos of yourself, or any news of the big world outside the mousetrap. You're quite right, we are now in a state of war. Why don't Parliament and the papers in England protest against the way those unscrupulous barbarians open every letter from abroad, and nose through the contents in order to add to their economic intelligence and satisfy their passion for snooping? Those letters are posted by people who put their trust in international decency and the confidentiality of the postal service, while those same barbarians are mobilizing their military because there are foreign countries where the press is allegedly not yet 'gleichgeschaltet'. The only thing we can do now, if we want to prevent those madmen spying on the mail that passes through their land, is to use airmail, which is much dearer. They behave like ill-mannered domestic servants. Before long they really will constitute a 'special race' on the periphery of human society, and thus give substance to what is otherwise a vague concept. Your letter had of course been steamed open! Even though the leading Lords have such dainty tastes that they applaud barbarism and have therefore sold Austria, you people in England ought to form a society with the objective of enclosing a few succulent truths for the spies to read in every letter that passes through that godless land, to make them blush – if they still can. As usual everything's going wrong for me, on top of which I've been ill, and sometimes I lose my sense of humour. How did we come to live in an age where the savages have radio and military technology, while the civilized have to bear the burden of Christian missionaries, Nazi hucksters, and the international distillery and arms-trade speculators? [. . .]

Is it spring in England yet? Send me some photos and remain my darling. With a big hug from your disgruntled   Un

To Homer Saint Gaudens (original English)

[Prague,] 15. Apr. 1938

Dear Sir,

I can see from your cheerful letter that you are very well and I am glad about it. I wonder whether you will pass Prague on your Europe trip. I have to answer your very kind letter without knowing your German address which you forgot to put on the head of your missive.

I see that you had to postpone my engagement to Carnegie's Jury, which you promised me last year as absolutely sure that time. You must in your democratic U.S.A. have probably not enough independence and too much political difficulties to get the non-Fascist artists into the Jury, while I, alone struggling against 'Führer-Neid' and the 'Gleichschaltungs-Nudelwalker' engine of Fascism, still can afford to do whatever I like. For the moment I accepted the Presidentship of the 'Freie Deutsche Kulturbund' in Paris, where they chose me unsophistically to lead them. (I guess it would not be Mr. Dufy, the 'Modezeichner', whom they might select to give the answer of a cultured world to the Barbarians of München.)

I am a little freer in my movements (I got the Czechoslovakian citizenship after only one week diplomatic interference! A good example for your country!), so I need now only money! money! money! You see I am so broken down, that I even cannot afford to buy letter-paper and have to send you this epistle on a scrap of paper I found by chance! In June there will be the big show of 'German modern art' in London, I was asked to send 12 important pictures in order to play the first fiddle. I wonder where to get the pictures since Austrian Museums and private collections also fall under the subjugation of the Barbarians. I am half a fool because my fool brother sticks in Vienna still and the Gestapo paid him already in the first days of the occupation of Austria a visit in my house, where they sealed my belongings.

I must get out of Europe and I would only like to know whether I can have some help from your Carnegie Foundation this year 1938 or not! If not, I will arrange without it surely, as I lived 30 years now in eternal struggles and survived! But I like better to know exactly where my place is, instead of waiting for nice little promises to be realized. I lost my face last year in your country in accepting the last prize – 'Trostpreis' we call it in German, – and I cannot risk this danger in my weak position another time. So I would like to tell you frankly, my dear friend, that I would never more have any relations with dear Carnegie's Foundation in case you call me not, as you promised, this very year to America as head of your Jury. There is no [agreement?] between Hitler and La Guardia now and I am Czechoslovak.

Give my love to Mrs St. Gaudens and remember my word I pledged solemnly, which is never broken. Behave you well, with best regards
Sincerely yours   Oskar Kokoschka

152

17 May [1938], Hotel Juliš, Prague
Confidential!

Dear Mr Read,

I asked Miss Palkovská to write to you on my behalf some six weeks ago, to answer your kind letter about the '*Modern German Art*' exhibition, because I was ill and unable to write myself. She has not yet received an answer to her letter, although she herself is the owner of two of the pictures that are intended to be included in the exhibition. Furthermore, no invitations from your committee have yet reached the collectors whose names and addresses were enclosed by Miss Palkovská with her letter. I am perfectly sure that the omission is in no way your fault, but on the other hand you did mention the beginning of June as the deadline, and if that is still the case time is running out, so would you please be kind enough to tell me how matters now stand? I gather from the letters of our friend W. in Paris that the nature of the exhibition has taken on a different colouring each week, according to the way the political wind happens to blow. It's very sad that a project intended to defend intellectual creativity against iconoclasts and illiterates can be disrupted by day-to-day politics in a powerful country which does not yet glorify those anti-intellectual elements; but the good will and better understanding of the majority are sure to prevail in the end. That is why I set great store by the success of the exhibition, especially because an artist who does not possess an English, American or French passport these days is outside the protection of the law, together with his life's work. Incidentally, I would like to thank you for the laudable amount of space that you gave my work in your new book.

May I ask you to send me by return a list of the paintings by me that are available to you? And please use airmail, because almost every letter that travels by ordinary post is opened by Nazi spies. What is the World Postal Union doing about it? You would put me enormously in your debt if you could create the opportunity for me to paint Sir Hore-Belisha [*sic*] in England. I've already written to our friend Augustus John about it. I've got to start again at the beginning, and therefore I need powerful protection and if possible a work-permit in England. Otherwise I'm lost, because your Lords have generously made the Nazis a present of my homeland Austria.

I remain yours most sincerely,   with many thanks, O Kokoschka

[Prague,] 26. v. 38

Dear friend John,

You are an angel and you will excuse the delay of my answering your awfully nice letters with my waiting for the english visa. The Consul finally found the Fincham letter somewhere and expedited my required forms to London to-day. I hope they will avoid there to make inquiries about my person at the German Authorities, in order not to give those people a possible hint, how to hamper me to go.

Is there any possibility to portray Hore-Belisha? That would help me to safeguard my brother in Vienna for whom I have to care and who is in danger to be annoyed there on behalf of me. The Germans are cowards, you know. As soon as they see that their victims become dangerous to them, they sneak away and make innocent faces like unjustly offended children.

But the weak ones they slay down in a sadist way, see Ossietzky! My pictures are doomed to perish if the radical wing in Germany prevails finally. The more conservative wing instead tries to sell our pictures in the U.S.A. or somewhere else, that is the reason why the 'Pranger' Show in Munich was arranged (now in Berlin).

The Czechs are wonderful, good-nerved and good-humoured, only they know that the danger from a week before can be repeated any time and your government will possibly under different circumstances and in other situations not be able or willing to offer the same assistance as just now, in order to save them from the horrible fate of Austria.

In Vienna, there they are like prisoners, hunger revolts are suppressed and broadcast and newspapers are silenced alike as in Germany, everybody with a glimpse of truth suspected to be not a firm adherer of the invaders – is in prison. Nobody, except merchants in important matters of economy, gets a passport, so it would be stupid to ask for information about me there. Please do tell them in London that they must not utter a word about me. I am glad that you help me and will see that my turn comes to open my mouth or better to show them my fists. Hore-Belisha would be an enormous chance, you understand? – My kind man, many thanks and best wishes for peace's sake and for a happy life again. Yours sincerely   O Kokoschka

To Carl Moll

My dear Carl,

Forgive me, it has taken me an age to answer because I don't understand you. I am not playing politics. For example, a 'Degenerate Art' exhibition was planned in London. After pressure from Berlin, in accordance with arcane procedures of English politics, all of a sudden a number of other painters (from the Berlin Academy) were invited, and so I withdrew my permission to show my paintings (there should have been fourteen). I gave up a surefire success, because I would have triumphed a thousandfold over those banal daubers who have 'gleichgeschaltet' themselves. But I justified my refusal as follows: I am not playing politics, unlike the others: I am not trying to rehabilitate myself abroad by stealth, by showing in a foreign country with 'colleagues' who (against their better judgment and only under the orders of the authorities) outlaw me in the homeland for which I feel, and where my roots are in spite of everything; and I will not be a party to an evasion of the law that would lead to prosecution in the German Reich. In the Reich, all my paintings have been confiscated, and if they have not yet been destroyed it is because of the high prices I get: the reason is foreign currency, not moral scruples. In Vienna, an old portrait was cut in pieces by official order, on 5 May 1938, at 40 Reisnerstraße, by Gestapo Section II H: that was something new, a first. A victory to be proud of! The pieces are in Prague, as are the witnesses. The portrait is of a young man who I painted thirty years ago. So once again Vienna bears away the palm! A Renoir drawing was also destroyed or carried off.

You seem to take it for granted that it can be put down to 'pure wounded vanity' on my part, and it's of no significance if a few important and worthwhile people have their corns trodden on when, for good or ill, the fortunes of 75 million people are at stake. Leaving aside the fact that I don't see how the destruction of paintings – not just mine but also the French Impressionists, and even Rembrandt – will affect the fortunes of 75 million people, you know full well that the 150,000 painters you have there, working on commission, daubing exactly what they are told to, will create nothing of any worth or significance, either for the future or the present. According to your mechanistic principle, however, in which numbers count and provide moral justification, those people must contribute substantially more to the well-being and happiness of the 75 million than the few worthwhile painters whose corns have been trodden on. If they'd thought like that in France, the world today would have only the vast amount of stuff turned out by the French schools of kitsch and splash of that period, and no Manet, Renoir, Cézanne or Van Gogh. Extending the principle to art history in general – if you think of what the priests got up to in the Middle Ages – what we know as European art would simply not exist, there would only be the 'gleichgeschaltet' banality which has always been in the majority [. . .] and repugant to contemporaries as 'degenerate' and 'revolutionary', which is why iconoclasm and inquisition always persisted. No, my dear friend, I am too good a German for that: too good a European, too good a human being, and I love other human beings!

'The smears of the paid hacks in the gutter press' roll off me like water off a duck's back. Before long (in two months' time, when the 'Degenerate Exhibition' gets to Vienna!) you will have the chance to read the jubilant resurrection of the ghost of the late Moritz Seligmann in the *Neue Freie Presse*. All his great hits of thirty years ago will be brought out against me again: 'degenerate', 'nigger art', 'cultural Bolshevism', 'a menace to our young people and the lower orders'. And if I still had a place there, I would be denounced to the authorities, and hunted from pillar to post all over again. And if there had been concentration camps in Austria in those days, in the lifetime of the blessed Moritz, I would have been shoved in one then. Now they will deprive me of my Greater German citizenship; they are already cutting up my pictures in Vienna. No. I will have nothing to do with this bigotry and Moritz-Seligmannism, but not because, in your words, I 'yearn for the Kremlin'. On the contrary, as you know, I was officially invited there, but didn't go because I wanted to have nothing to do with any type of dictatorship. I do not want to put my art at the service of either politics or dealers! I want to be free! Free from foreign currency! Surely I proved that, when I voluntarily dissolved my contract with Cassirer in the middle of the inflation 'cycle', see the *Frankfurter Zeitung* leader, 1929. I would like to meet the 'gleichgeschaltet' artist of today who has sacrificed as much as I have for the purity of art, or gone hungry as often, in order to uphold the integrity of the German artist, and who would have found it so easy to make things more comfortable for himself and become a high-ranking lackey. If you consider that I've disowned your preface, in that I've officially 'allied myself to the worst enemies of the German people', then I'm very sorry that you think so. In my opinion the worst enemies of the German people are all those who will not allow them to think and feel and act for themselves, and want to turn them into performing poodles or military automata. That won't lead to greater well-being and happiness, but to boundless misery, not merely for your 75 million, but for the entire 2,000 million of the human race, and if we're being strictly mechanistic, the larger number is the one that counts. I have officially allied myself only to the good old painters, as ever, and to nobody else!!!

With a fond kiss to dear Mama and yourself,　　　　　　your lonely OK

To Ruth and Adolf Arndt

[London,] 20 Oct. [1938]

My very dear friends,

I just want to tell you quickly that I've arrived safely, and that I think I shall be able to stick it out here and perhaps even prosper. At the moment, of course, things are precarious, because of being allowed to bring in only £5, and a small painting, the 'Girls Bathing' which you saw when you visited me in Prague, as well as my painting things, are now in a pawnshop, where they raised £4. 4s. The cases stayed behind in Prague, and they may get here by Christmas. But after the first panic I've been able to open my eyes again to the joy of being alive; I shall have to tighten my belt for a while, but then things will look up.

The thing that worried me most was Passport Control, but Lord Cecil had put in a word for me, so I was given three months straightaway (as an exceptional case!), and yesterday Sir Kenneth Clark, director of the National Gallery, suggested that I should stay here for the duration, and he would see to everything. Today I have an invitation to tea with Rothenstein, director of the Tate Gallery, who has also taken up the cudgels on my behalf, and tomorrow I have been invited to the Courtauld Institute. Everything goes swimmingly with the help of people at the top; if I wanted, I could probably take up the position I deserve in a very short time (without any help from the French dealers' ring, which is imperative everywhere else, and just goes to show what those barbarians over there have missed). But I'd prefer to start work as soon as possible, without the attention and invitations of public figures, and above all to have someone here who I could rely on unreservedly to deal with the problem of existence for the immediate future. This eternal recurrence of primitive worries gets me down every time, because I always build houses of cards, which then fall down. Either it's my own fault, or that idiotic movement over there has been contributing to my troubles vigorously for years. My main worry, apart from Bohi (after the renewed reassurance you, my dear, dear friends, gave me about him), has been about what will happen to my paintings. Now Czechoslovakia too has turned about-face (it's incomprehensible, how quickly this spiritual sickness spreads), some of my collectors have taken flight, the museums are already being 'purged', and my work is left ownerless there, too. It makes me sad.

Please, should you see Bohi, it would be best if he doesn't know exactly where I am, or it will create problems for him. I would like him to write quite often to Holda (just enough to let me know he's alive!), addressing the letters to Mr Fincham, *Staff of the Tate Gallery*, Westminster, Millbank, London, and tell him to send my sister a postcard every week, because she always fears the worst. And may I really count on you for the time being (it won't be long) to see that he doesn't starve? I am so grateful

157

to you for that, I still don't know what I should have done about it, if you hadn't come to the rescue!

The big painting is with Kuoni, as I told you, and it's all paid for, I've had confirmation from the shipper in Prague. I don't want Herr Fleischmann to have anything more to do with it, I do not care for him one bit. It's a pity I didn't meet you, but things had got very uncomfortable for me in Prague, and every day could have been my last at liberty. Now I hope that you will both come to London before long, and that by then I shall have got on top of things well enough to have somewhere for you to stay with me as my very welcome guests, so that some cheer returns to our lives, and my head and my heart, too!

I am with you in Glion in spirit and in friendship, send me sonnets, I implore you!

To Albert Ehrenstein

London [September 1939]

Dear Ehrensteiner,

This will cheer you up: recently, in the course of my attempt to go to Chicago to teach in a university, the American Consul in London turned me down as an undesirable alien – in spite of the fact that the Dean of the college personally telephoned the Consul about the matter. As it happens, I don't care, because things are the same everywhere: uncertain, unpleasant, and liable to drive you to suicide. And you thought that I could help you get a visa for the land that raised the Statue of Liberty! If you were a gangster, maybe, then Chicago might still be on the cards. But a mere beast of intellect – forget it!

My hair is going grey, my sister is in Prague, where that totally barbarous and pointless bloodbath has been taking place, my brother is in Liebhartstal, unable to keep up his mortgage payments any longer, so he's going to have to let the sharks have his house, together with all our memories and all the things which are precious to us, and irreplaceable. He's going to work as a farm-labourer. I can't write to either my sister (if she's still alive) or my brother (if he's still alive) for fear of putting them in danger, because the Gestapo hordes will still be there, even if all Europe has already been driven voluntarily into Moscow's arms. This is what European wisdom and intelligence have come to in the end: the governments of our time are more stupid than the governments of every single previous generation. I cannot see any escape, this so-called war will last 30 years, not 3, and none of us will survive it. It makes no difference if we die in Europe or the back of beyond. Give poor Genia my dearest love. I can't write and tell her she should be glad that Hemme will be spared the horror that is to come. Happy is the man who is already dead. We have to brace ourselves for the fact that there will be no Last Supper for people with hearts, imagination, courage and humanity.

Yr humble and obdnt servant, yours ever, OK – KO

To Anna Kallin

[Polperro, Cornwall,] 1 Oct. 1939

Dear Mirli,

Thank you for your card. Unhappily we neither of us have any news of our relations. Olda's father joined the Polish army quite unnecessarily, and put his trust in England yet again. Not a single plane did they send, in another week it will have vanished from the papers, and only the poor devils who are dead or crippled will know that it ever happened. The same with this barbarous business (reported in just one edition) in Czechoslovakia, which has led to nothing but bloodbaths and was started completely witlessly! There was some agitation for similar action in Vienna six months ago, which I vigorously opposed, thank God. Chamberlain's circle needs the Hitler saga, and is too stupid to notice that meanwhile Moscow has hired the German army, just as in the Middle Ages. Moscow could turn Germany into another Soviet republic any day, but prefers to go on dangling this bogey in the window for the time being, to terrify the bourgeoisie and so serve its own purposes. Nazi Germany is part of history already, all there is now is this militarized and armed band of tramps, who look to Moscow for their daily bread. The people in the City and the reactionary Lords are to blame for all this, we are the only ones who believe it has something to do with war or peace or homeland and duty and justice. In fact, it's the naked intellectual and spiritual poverty of the so-called democracies, who fattened the forces of reaction for years, in order to build up the war industry, for fear of the *unemployed*. That question will get far, far worse, until this entire war will come to an end as the result of total European bankruptcy! Leave the *nursery* and come and join us here. I can't go to London, I have nothing to live on, now that all my collectors are dead or broke, and America is out of reach. [. . .] The day will come when I shall have to thank the English for their wise policies. And I suppose you you will scold me again for not removing myself from a country where I don't fulfil my duties as a guest. With a loving kiss, Un

To Joseph Needham (original English)

London, 4th November 1941

Dear Professor Needham,

I cannot thank you enough for the sacrifice of your precious time spent correcting my humble suggestions of a future peace plan. I feel deeply touched as you have been the only man, since the supporter of my idea, the late President Masaryk, died, to see the importance of a scientific reform of mass education. I hope you will continue in your benevolent interest as I do not think it spent on an unworthy idea, otherwise you would not have offered me so surprisingly to bring my contribution to the knowledge of such a distinguished assembly, as represented at the Tercentenary of Jan Amos Komensky in Cambridge.

I followed your instructions in accepting thankfully your very valuable corrections and your information about bibliography. You must know that I am neither a politician nor do I suffer from national prejudices. My desire is that of any honest and logically thinking man, to help as much as one can to steer out of the present mental and physical chaos under which mankind suffers. As you allowed me in your kind letter to make changes within certain limits, I made some discreet alterations in three places where I thought it would help to strengthen the argument or where a positive programme should be suggested. Please crown your friendly effort for our common sake in accepting them.

Concerning your question about Overton, I found the fact of Comenius' acquaintance with Overton mentioned in a German study on T. More's *Utopia* and his followers, of which Hartlib is one of the most interesting ones as he links up the English and German socialist movements. Unfortunately I cannot remember the author as I had to leave my books together with other essential things behind me when I left Prague.

May I hope that you will permit me to express my deep gratitude personally when I come to Cambridge?

Yours very sincerely

Oskar Kokoschka

To Anna Kallin (original English)

[London,] 5. Nov. 1941

Dearest Mirli,

I just returned from Scotland where I got soaked and bogged in the peat, but Olda managed to get me out anyway, packing all the shells, mutton skulls, fishing nets, glass balls (to fix the nets in the sea), feathers of pheasants, lambs wool and my oil colours of course and watercolours and several torn socks. But on my very day of arrival I see that these people wish to take Olda to do the war for them. Who should cook my breakfast, fill my old age water bottle, bring me to Professor Plesch where my kidneys get their weekly injection? I ask you, who should then type my thousand missives to the people who are in need of rational thinking, need badly my instruction in Comenius' education plan under international (you know!) scientific control? By the way, the Cambridge convenor of the 'Tercentenary of Comenius' congress, Professor Needham, accepted my very peppered lecture about the true!! meaning of Comenius' message, including my peace aims, and printed it in the Cambridge Commemoration among the speeches of Beneš, Masaryk and Ambassador Maisky and so on – although I never had been in Cambridge nor had anybody dreamt of inviting me on this occasion! Fine, what? But what kind of peace will it be if my voice fades out in future, if my right hand (the typing and correcting one) gets paralysed because the English do not like the war and shift all the filthy work on the bloody foreigners? I ask you? I got Olda a marriage certificate in order to avoid such interferences 'for the duration' but it seems it does not help much. Therefore I have to place her somewhere, where she will be at least among friends, and I thought it could be easily done, with your benevolent assistance, in the Czech BBC where the Czech Fascists of the government have nothing to say. With them Olda's father is battling; that is why they have called him as well as her up under the present regulations of Mr. Bevin. Will you help me, Mirli? You know that Olda is an outspoken leftist, that she is intelligent, industrious, speaks Czech, German, French, English and writes it, that she is Dr. of law and will be a reliable worker if it deals with honest politics. Only I need her here in London and she must get an intelligent job and some spare time to look after me, otherwise the English will not only have missed the bus but they will have bored to death the greatest living painter.

In love yours always   OK

Please come quickly! And do what you can with Mr. Griffith to convince him that an able assistant is better than a stupid one!

To Paul Westheim

London [early 1942?]

My very dear Paul Westheim,

Fred has just given me the good news that you escaped alive from the Fascists and have arrived safely in Mexico. I'm beginning to think miracles are possible, after all! Since intellect can achieve nothing in today's world (ours, unhappily). People today are greedy and out for profit, servility makes them ruthless, cowardice makes them cruel – excessively so, and in the end they lack all ability to find a meaning in their own actions. That's why the mob is crying out for a 'leader' everywhere. He does the thinking on behalf of the rest – as the outcome proves. It seems to me that this development, which reaches its culmination today, has been on the way for the past three or four hundred years. In the 15th century human society still had a right to be called both 'human' and 'society', but today those values have been lost and we have to make do with misunderstood Darwinism. I'm so glad that they let you into Mexico, because I think the people of that country must be prouder of their freedom than any other on earth. I was very sad indeed to hear that thanks to your imprisonment by the Fascists you lost an eye – but rejoice that your other eye is noticeably on the mend! I wish you the best of luck and every blessing for your future now, my dear, dear, unfortunate friend. Write to me at once – it's best if you use picture postcards (but not views of landscape or buildings), because the various censors' offices hold them up for the shortest time – and tell me if and what I can send you, and what I can do to help you. I tried over and over again to reach you in France, but by the time I'd traced your concentration camp, alas, the heroic Paris police had already handed you over to the Nazis. Such fine gentlemen! Such a civilized heritage! And such fitting thanks for the help given France by the Spanish volunteers and the thinkers and poets driven out of the Third Reich: a worthy acknowledgment of their great love of France. Who knows, if you had had any money, or even been a millionaire!! But as it was, your pockets were empty, and you were only one of the cultural proletariat, a sort of cultural Bolshevist, the lowest of the low for those who represent today's culture.

Write often, and write soon. Good health and even better luck!

In love,   your old friend, O Kokoschka

To Joseph Needham (original English)

[London, spring 1942]

My dearest Professor Needham,

I thank you for your great help and moral support that is most valuable for me in these days of insecurity and general apathy. I hope your book will now be published soon and will play its part in shaping the things to come in its way. Only a few items I wanted to lay before your eyes, whether you think that they could be still improved:

Page 65, 10th line from bottom: I want to omit Bismarck, otherwise all the robbers would be found amongst the German people. In any case $\frac{3}{4}$ of the world were bagged by the English government at that time, while Bismarck only swallowed the German countries Elsaß-Lothringen [Alsace-Lorraine], once sacked by Louis XIV, who would be worthier to be mentioned in this connection instead of Bismarck.

Page 68. 11th line from above: Nazi-Fascism? I cannot make that subtle

162

division. The Mussolini of Abyssinia and the Franco of Spain, the Mikado of the Chinese incident, Horthy's white guards in Hungary, Dollfuss in Vienna, who had the wounded Wallish hunted with bloodhounds and had him brought to the gallows, and so on. They are all representatives of the same reactionary forces whose militant expression is Fascism. Nazism is only more popular in England because Ribbentrop stayed too long in London.

15th line from bottom: it must be Committee's standard because there never existed an international educational committee's standard so far. For your fine coined word 'Winstanley's cooperative farming' I thank you very much as a very good improvement. I was very glad to see you today and to listen to your speech. I hope that you will help again in the transforming of this institute into a true Komensky university. Unfortunately the Czechs are much less interested in participating in our efforts to follow the advice given by this great educationalist.

It is always the self-contradiction with democracy that, what they preach, they do not want to have realized.

My sincerest gratitude and my very best wishes

Yours ever   Oskar Kokoschka

To the editors of several daily newspapers (original English)

[London, 1942?]

Dear Sir,

Will it be of any interest for English readers to know about the embarrassment I felt when recently asked by Austrian Refugee children to show them the frontiers of Austria on their cheap world atlas published since the war began?

Is it incidental that 'the first free country to fall a victim to Nazi aggression', according to the statement of the Moscow conference, should be the only one not marked out on the popular publications of this kind in England? Or is it by the same mistake which shows Estonia, Latvia and Lithuania, the 14th, 15th and 16th Constituent Republics of the USSR, as countries invaded, on these same maps? In view of the urgent task of re-education of the Nazi youth, will there be a special set of maps designed where a signal expression is given to the effect that the liberating powers consider themselves as in no way bound by any change effected in Austria since March 15th 1938? As a reminder for the designers of the above mentioned maps, it may be useful to know that 'the Anschluss' has its verbal origin in the dictionary of appeasement. How will in future English tourists find their way to the country, traditional here for its 'Gemütlichkeit', if Austria has been wiped out from the English globe?

Yours faithfully   Oskar Kokoschka

London, June 27th, 43

My dear Lauwerys,

I really do not know whether to thank you or Mayerowitz more for the happy moments when I met you and when I read your so very kind letters. I was already asking myself – and a bit worried too – whether I had done right to smuggle my essay (it was actually only a part of it) into your pocket before we parted. Now I am thoroughly ashamed in seeing that you spent so much precious time of yours on it, even in trying to improve my bad English. The missive discharged from my clumsy pen ought to have been better repressed. But what a relief to know of somebody thinking one's own attitude a sound one, when, due to the war mentality, reasonable behaviour seems to stand on the brink of extinction. With the exception of you and maybe an Irish friend of mine, all acquaintances of mine confirm my rather depressing view that they suffer more generally from Hitleritis than they happen to know themselves. But that these people, unfortunately, believe that Hitleritis is a racial disease, localized only in the confines of the III. Reich, or that it has something to do, in one or another mysterious way, with the bloodstream rolling in the veins of the Germans, that is obviously a quite unexpected result of a generally mis-directed mass-education. There seems to be today no country left, where all the problems are not thought to be with the others only; the same education everywhere makes people refrain from realizing that reforms have to start at home. All this makes one feel absolutely hopeless at times. It seems that man at present is everywhere deliberately rendered unable to perceive the development of forces that are instrumental in bringing about this misery, poverty, social evils and absurd institutions. This was the aim of the religious Sunday school, it still seems to be, in the main line, the national educational aim everywhere. Everywhere and equally, the ruler is considered to be inviolate. The oriental idea of charismatic leadership is accepted either in theory or in practice. England is no exception, whose Chamberlain was as omnipotent as Churchill is and he still would be, if he had not died, although he appeased with Fascism everywhere. It is a sign that it is beyond the power of the people to change. People are educated in the ideology of the chosen people, which makes men fight in a series of total world-wars till the total extermination of the enemy. At present it is the German people to be the sacrificial goat in our rite of purification.

I was ashamed more than I can say to see the theory of determinism embraced by the guardians of the working people, by the English Labour officials here, who are still free to think, to discuss and to act according to reason, without a Gestapo behind them. They must not yet fear to have their ashes sent in a casket to their relatives. Willingly, without being under compulsion, they have accepted the racial myth of blood and soil of Hitler-Loeb. Where in the world are those then to whom the victims of Hitleritis, in Germany first and in turn in the other affected continental concentration camps as well, can look for help when the allied armies shall land? The victory of the Holy Alliance of Metternich made it clear that military victories can be defeats in the spiritual sphere, where free will stands against determinism. It is the same policy of 'proskynesis' in the League of Nations Union here, where they succeeded to cast themselves down prostrate before the official voice and even to crawl backwards on their own into superstitions of the best puritan witch-burning, in the most hideous reactionary effort to infect the innocent with their own insanity (caused by fear for their endangered vested interests).

These hypocrites' chatter about healthy-mindedness of our own and amorality of the destitute ones simply stinks to heaven. Something is deeply wrong at least with the ruling classes everywhere; sometimes Labour officials in certain democracies belong to that class as well.

> News Chronicle June 16, 43: 'Quarantine urged to Nazi-ridden children of Germany. No contact with healthy-minded.'
> When the Re-education of Germany was discussed yesterday by the General Council of the League of Nations Union, Mrs Edgar Dugdale opposed a proposal that British and German youth should meet through a system of international education, saying: 'It might do a great deal of good to German youth to bring them into contact with British youth, but our first duty is to our own youth.
> 'No child who has been brought up for the last 10 years on the principles of Nazi amorality should be brought into contact with a healthy-minded child. I would as soon bring a child infected with plague as I would bring a German child into contact with a British child.' A resolution was passed urging the government to propose the immediate formation of a United Nations Bureau for educational reconstruction.

This bureau will not find much work to do because more or less all the continental children have been brought up on Nazi educational schemes, as they are needed as cannon-fodder like the others. Either you have to draw the mental cordon sanitaire all round the continent and live here in splendid mental isolation, like in a ghetto of the chosen people, or instead you must educate the grown-ups here accordingly, so that they must not think that a bunch of English-chosen Quislings on the continent will stop the revolution there, ripe since the days of Metternich & Co.

By the way, it might be interesting to know whether Lord Cecil's sister would mind the children of the German untouchables to sit with the little Indians? India belongs to the British Commonwealth, in a way at least? My dear Lauwerys, you must read my countryman's excellent book where honest thinking and finest policy is tracing a civilization in future which does not contradict culture. It is: *Need Germany survive?* (Gollancz 7s. 6d.), written by the Austrian Julius Braunthal. Propagate it everywhere, please, among progressive teachers. This book is the more brave as it is written by a man who happens to be a Jew as well, not only a Socialist, wherefore his life was doubly endangered by the evil policy of Hitleritis.

Please forgive my long badly written letter. I did it only as you asked me for it. And my effort is directed to try to convince you that education today is only a political problem and reforms cannot come through the ordinary channels as advocated by liberal democracy. You see what spiritual influence a good man like Lord Cecil enjoys even in his own family. Education is firstly a police regulation to keep the lower classes down, and only secondarily, today, is its aim to teach them the three Rs. War-factory workers and soldiers can really do without even that basic knowledge, if only they took it into their hearts that obedience is the ancestral inheritance of the little fellow.

As you do, I look forward with keen pleasure to our next meeting. Make it possible as soon as you can do. My wife and I send you all our best wishes.
Yours very sincerely, Oskar Kokoschka

To Ivan Maisky (original English)

168/55 Park Lane,
London W 1, 1st January 1944

My dear Mr Maisky,
This is to wish you and your countrymen all the best in the coming year. May victory come soon to bring your country and the suffering people all over the world the well deserved peace which everybody desires so much after all the terrible destruction. To think that this catastrophe could once have been easily avoided, that must worry some responsible people today, if they have any conscience at all.

I would like to have your opinion in a matter which might benefit the USSR propaganda in Great Britain and the USA. As you may remember, you met my friend Major Beddington-Behrens, who helped me with the Stalingrad Fund. He has an interest in a large English publishing firm of old standing. I suggested to him that it would be of importance to the English-speaking public to get better acquainted with Russian literature, old and new, for which there is today a great demand, entirely unsatisfied. He showed great interest and I am sure he would gladly accept your guidance on the starting of a series of cheap editions of good translations of works most valuable from the literary point of view, and of course from the propagandist one as well.

I hope you and Madame Maisky are both in good health and that you will be able to pay attention to the matter proposed here, as we should not lose valuable time. The start will be decisive concerning the whole character of the enterprise.

With the very best wishes from myself and my wife

Yours very sincerely   Oskar Kokoschka

To Donald Wolfit (original English)

Elrig, [Portwilliam, Wigtownshire,]

4th May 1944

Dear Mr Wolfit,

May I, as a foreigner in this country, express my greatest admiration and deepest gratitude for the unforgettable experience my many visits to the Scala during your exceptional Shakespearer Season had been.

I thought till then that the greatest playwright had been forgotten in this country, judging by the lipservice generally paid to art. I do not know much about the standard of taste in the past, for instance in the Edwardian theatre, but judging by what I read about the period of Garrick, I believe that the sober-minded people, who at that period ruled the world with coal and steam, must have felt themselves far too superior to their bear-baiting ancestors than to pay true homage to the sovereign of the stage.

Now, when by sheer luck during the raids I saw your Shakespeare on the icy evenings in the Scala theatre, I watched a stray auditory gradually changing into a devoted community of people, whose minds you had freed from the nonsensical grip of the mechanical world of the present. I saw you perform a miracle, enabling us, for longer than a few hours we listened to you, to shake off the universal frustration of man's present life. Your acting made us soar in a delirious spiritual atmosphere, as if we had been coming to Shoreditch to see Shakespeare himself. [. . .]

I was astonished when the critics now, at the end of your season, finally discovered you and, maybe, even the 'leading society' in time will be tempted to discover for themselves the difference between the message you are bringing them, and the trivial murder-plot of the average commercialized theatre.

Unfortunately I am unable to come back to London for your last performance as I hoped to do. Perhaps you will sometime play not too far from London and I shall be able to come to see King Lear. I think you know an old acquaintance of mine, the stage-designer Stern from the

Reinhardt Bühne from Berlin (both of the past), who could tell you of my own interest in the theatre, if it interests you.

Very grateful for the great work you are doing and very sincerely yours

Oskar Kokoschka

To Jack and Mina Carney (original English)

House of Elrig, Portwilliam, Aug. 18th, 44

My beloved Jack and Mina,

It is so long that I did not hear from you all through my fault because we left London and you stayed where you had to face all the dirty things. Don't blame us please. But we both needed some sleep. One simply could not sleep on the eighth floor and it made me nervous when Olda had to run for shopping to Hampstead, for Chinese to Tottenham Court Rd, for her Pan-Slavonic circle to Kensington, so that I never knew whether she will come back. Now we have had a really abnormally hot month together with the Stursas who have been simply sweet. Ullapool seems to be the only spot in the British Isles where they have sun, food, boats and sea, all together in a little place which is absolutely unspoiled. No traffic, no shops, only three pubs and four chapels. Unfortunately they give you a bill after a month, therefore we landed again at Korner's always hospitable house. It has the snag in it that it continually rains here. While I did many sketches at Ullapool, I could do nothing at all here so far. Therefore I took up my 'Comenius' play. I have to work on it as if it were an accordeon, I must reduce the 160 pages to 60 pages in order that it gets a normal shape. It is just the right job for a Flood with no Mount Ararat in view on the horizon, with no pigeon carrying the wand of peace in its beak. I fear that the fascists go now underground and on the continent they will corrupt the valiant Gurkhas, Negroes, Senegalese fighting for democracy there – therefore the mess will go on indefinitely. I only hope that the Soviet people will not mix with the respective national communists (refugees), once these people will be transferred to the Continent by Morrison & Bevin! Please do write me one of your comforting letters if you still remember me with love.

Here I enclose a curriculum vitae of the daughter of the house. You may have met her with Dr Palkovsky. She has been bombed out during the night in Hampstead, escaped by a sheer miracle and does not dare to return to her job. She has got a shock. Do you think that you may hear about a job in the country? She loves working for newspapers and needs something like that to protect her against Morrison & Bevin. If so, please help!

I read a book: *The Machiavellians*. – do you know it? It is very upsetting but there is some truth in it which cannot be ignored. You ought to have a

168

look at it for the sake of Stursa's peace of mind as well. Please write to us in any case.

The thing I am suffering from very much – and for that reason I daily regret we left London – is that the people where we stay, wherever it is, listen after meals to the broadcast. It is a part of a rite of digestion for them to hear the crackling voice recording: The damage we have done . . . 1,899 aircraft destroyed . . . panzer divisions smashed . . . pants kicked . . . Gurkhas, knives between their teeth . . . Huns on the run . . . Hitler . . . It is sooo booombshelling tiiiresome for a non-war-like brain to listen to the bubbling of the cabbage. And thereafter the sadistic emotions which such a religious cult involves. I simply cannot stand the Democrats, old grannies which ought to go to bed, young running noses which tell you what to think of our Führer Churchill, American officers with generous postwar projects how to standardize the cannibal civilization which I prefer to be left undisturbed in order that it can revolve into the jungle from where man is supposed to have come to make a mess of the world. I do not like sadists. I cannot bear revenge in cold blood before the photographer on women which cooperated with the Nazis. It will all end to make a monkey out of myself which I would regret for the sake of this innocent species of mammals. Is there no help from Democracy? It is tooo madening. I am against the cult of stoning the scape-goat and take immediately sides with the victims of religious persecution. I say this is no end of the war. This is going to be a thirty years religious war because there are no longer even the ideological subtleties in which Democracy differs from Fascism as Mr Churchill himself says. Nay. Both sects have pooled their contents together and produced a third one which seems to be so horrid, although its outline cannot yet be seen, that I wish to close my receptive organs in order to see no evil, speak no evil, hear no evil.
In Love Yours   Oskar

To Edith Hoffmann-Yapou

[London,] 24th Dec. 1944

My dear Edith,

I am delighted by your acceptance of most of my suggestions, which shows how much in earnest you are with this book, and how much you support my ideas. This book ought to outlive me, and a voice inside me tells me it will carry the truth beyond this appalling era to a later age, and a future generation will pay attention to the experiences, ideas and proposals of an incorruptible eyewitness. What more reliable eyewitness is there than the artist, who does not see merely the kaleidoscopic world of the average person, but searches the sensual world for meaning, for reasons that lie in both the foreground and the background!

I was hard on you, and I'm sure there must have been days when you despaired and cursed the heavy burden that you had voluntarily taken upon your weak shoulders. Especially when you were on the point of giving life to a new human being. And the war and the bombing on top of it all. But the sacrifices were not in vain.

You will derive very much joy from this book, and reap much honour from it in the future. I am as sure of that as I always am when I see my influence about to enter a new sphere. What has been done will be found to be right in due course, by the many unknown people who have heard me. The fact that you have understood enough to give my voice the background of love shows a praiseworthy selflessness.

Please come and see me as soon as possible, and together we will smooth a few more rough edges. If you look with my eyes, you will soon be convinced of what is at stake. As a whole, however, you can already be very proud of your book. And I shall do my part to see that your light does not remain hidden under the bushel. Come before the New Year!

I wish you, your baby, *husband* and Hans good health and everything else that is good, if this terrible time allows any of us to hope for anything better.

In love, yours   O Kokoschka

P.S. Just as soon as we have reached agreement on the few outstanding points, I will give you your manuscript, with my placet.

To Herbert Read (original English)

[London,] June 27th, 45

Dear friend,

[...] Whatever I say against the policy of this country is said for the sake of illustrating my arguments, that materialist conception of life is causing the onslaught on cultural values for the defence of which I, as an artist, must stand up. The creative artist must say it now and as frankly as possible, or he would fail in his moral duty. We have not yet Fascism in this country. We are only hampered by the phenomenon of voluntary 'Gleichschaltung'. In Germany it needed coercion to bring it about.

But as long as we dare to reason in a clear way, to state the case and face the truth as we can see it – so long there is democracy preserved in principle. We must not be afraid to wash our dirty laundry openly – by discussion. Not one voice, for instance, is against the annihilation of 80 millions of Japanese people, neither from the Left nor from the Right. But we accuse the Germans of not having opened their mouth and annihilate them for the same reason. My arguments are not 'topical'. They are symptomatic and ought not to be quickly forgotten. Mr Kennerley should not underrate the fact that all the possible risk goes to me, whereas

170

the merits of having scored something new are with him. I should love to discuss it with you, as I am convinced through and through of its importance. You were once so kind to ask us to come to see you, and this time I should love to have a whole evening or so of your precious time, it would be really to some purpose. Mr Kennerley, refusing it, says, he 'feels very strongly about it', and so do I in having it included!!

People never tire of pleading that art is the best ambassador but when an artist dares to say what he sees, placid censorship immediately stops his mouth. Concerning the clean hands, that also you will find in my essay, relating to last war. None of my ideas are new to me, or likely to change before the book comes out, as Mr Kennerley suggests.

Could you please try to get a committee meeting with you and Eliot and Mr Kennerley, where I could be invited to present my case myself, of course after you have read the article.

Love from us both to you and family,

yours sincerely

O Kokoschka

To Herbert Read (original English)

Elrig, Sept. 6th 45

My dear Herbert Read,

It would have been a joy to meet you and your family at Braemar. [. . .] We hope that your son could stay in England as just shortly afterwards the cease-fire in Japan closed a ghastly chapter with an argument that only true democracy-initiated Fight for Liberty could use. I liked Stalin's plaidoyer and statement of his own good case not less. London has the chance to listen to Dr Beneš's prime minister now who, for a fat loan, will not sell the heads of German-speaking citizens of his C.S. Republic. On the radio I heard already that, so far, only 300,000 emigrants to the C.S.R. from the Baltic had been driven out. These people seem to have been taken by a quite unreasonable fear when the Soviet Armies marched into these countries, says Dr Fierlinger. Whereas the 4 millions of Sudeten Germans shall get a 'humane' way of expulsion in accord with the Potsdam agreement. Not only that there seems no country ready to receive them, but the *Times* already published a sharp article yesterday against the refugees here in order to help in the housing problem. Many letters from the C.S.R., often from inhabitants of the Nazi concentration camps and Jews, implore us here to arrange for their escape because, as citizens of German language, they are automatically destined for expulsion. They have to wear the degrading badges of 'Germans' because Dr Beneš in his official declaration identifies language with race. This is the new version of Fascism that will (possibly) be supported by the Gentlemen of the City with the help of financial loans. It all seems to end

171

with a 'Völkerwanderung' into hell. We underrated the superstition of the so-called dark ages. There is no lunacy in the past to match the plans of the economic man, and no devilry of statesmen of the past who asked for a greater measure of loyalty from their contemporaries than the leaders of Democracy at present who had promised mankind to produce a freer, happier, more stable, wealthier society.

Fascism may soon become the general attitude towards the problem of civil liberties. I read, with great admiration, Huxley's *Time must have a stop*. He is a profound thinker. There is no escape for man from American hellish technocracy and Heil! to the White Man who progresses towards Ape-dom! Did you read it? I remember only Céline as a visionary who left an impression comparable to this seer's vision!

I wonder what the next future will bring. Everything that seems too horrid to be imagined today is left behind by reality tomorrow. Please do write to me what you expect from the Labour Government. I believe that they are not able to change the course of events. I knew it when I saw that the English, for the first time in history, had to fight for foreign interests. Lend-lease meant only food in payment for their services. Of course it had to be stopped once the services were no longer needed by Wall Street. Any government here would be impotent to produce a reasonable plan. It is not to be found on the economic lines. Society has annihilated an entire class of creative human beings and replaced them with dealers, merchants, brokers, wholesalers, and retailers who cannot produce anything – except the Atomic bomb. [. . .]

All the best wishes to you, love to Mrs Read and your kids from your

O Kokoschka

To Josef P. Hodin

[Elrig, September 1945]

Dear Hodinus,

You must read *Democracy today and tomorrow* by Edvard Beneš, Right Book Club (113 Charing Cross Road W.C.2) 1940, page 197: 'How is it possible that in this age of enlightenment there are governments in Europe which openly and cynically proclaim the domination of brute force, which refuse to accept the humanitarian and Christian conceptions of life, which destroy every idea of international morality and honesty and which respect no given word, no pledge, no agreement and no treaty?' The provisional government's programme, signed by the six state parties in Košice, contained a paragraph stating that there should be no persecution or punishment of political offenders on racist principles. 1942.

'I know that these are not the principles of the whole German nation. The

German nation itself is subjugated. For seventeen years democratic Germany and Czechoslovakia collaborated with each other in peace. It is the present German régime and the dictatorships in Europe that create this situation of utter confusion and disruption, hate and violence, war and revolution. Take what they have done to the Jews. Take what they have done to their political opponents. Take what they are doing today to their neighbours. All this must be considered as the complete disruption of modern human civilization, of every human moral and legal conception to which humanity has come through thousands of years of its evolution. That is war and revolution.' And that directly contradicts the summary in the government documents ordering the 'transfer' of 'Germans, Hungarians, traitors and collaborators'.

Is a person German because he first went to a school where he was taught in German, or is it in the blood? And in the soil as well, naturally. The first article in the Fundamental Law of the C.S.R. declares that every citizen is equal before the law. Even if the language he learned at his mother's knee was Latin, or German, or Yiddish. Did a legal decision of a legally constituted national government overthrow the constitution of the C.S.R.? If so, when did it happen? If not, is it not a flagrant *coup d'état* to expel German and Hungarian citizens of the C.S.R. from the soil where they have lived for generations? But this is how Dr Beneš concludes his survey (page 202): 'One must have also a right conception of democracy as theory and one must have the courage to put these theories into practice rightly, justly and courageously. Otherwise all these great words about democracy are but "vain" words, words, nothing but words, intended to cover the most vulgar, egoistic interests of ruling classes, parties and individuals.'

So what? As yet I have had no news from the C.S.R. of a resistance movement forming to oppose this new version of the race myth on the basis of language (and having to be suppressed as under the Hitler Reich). Is this a sign that the concentration camp is to last for ever, in the name of Nazi doctrine, after the fight 'for the Liberation of the peoples overrun by Fascism' has been brought to a victorious end? I take it that Dr Fierlinger will now receive a nice loan for allowing a few noble Aryans – I mean noble Czechs (honorary Germans) – to stay alive, who he can always kick out later when it suits him.

Dear Hodinus, it's my belief that democracy was superstition. There is only nationalism, and that's identical with fascism. Whichever way you look at it, the song ended with the Atomic bomb, and will do so however long we go on singing it, until the Third World War breaks out. When they asked old Solon what the best form of government was, he answered 'the one under which the least injustice is done to even the lowliest member of society'. What a long way we've advanced since then, with our mathematical happiness of the greatest number in our Darwinian struggle. Heil! to the white human ape! Salut! Nazdar! Živio!

I'm so sad not to see you! We're going to Ullapool, where I shall try to do some drawing, in the hope that my thoughts will brighten. Flowers, grasshoppers, grass, children, girls and sheep. For as long as the atomic bomb spares them. [. . .]

Congratulations on your 'Munch', I'm looking forward to it.

All best wishes to both of you   yours OK

To Hans Meyboden

[London,] Oct. 4th 45

My dear Meyboden,

I was very moved by your letters, and the only reason why I delayed answering is that I've been looking for ways of helping you, and wanted to have something encouraging to tell you. [. . .]

Continents will be left to pay the price, long after the disappearance of all of us who failed to prevent the catastrophe. The fact that during two world wars we were already arming for the third, which will exterminate the human race altogether, cannot be laid at the door of any one nation. All of us in our generation are to blame for not having managed to find something stronger, something more clearly right, with which to defy this crude, bestial materialism. Now the white man has involved the coloured races in his disaster, so the catastrophe cannot be countered from the Orient, as has happened a number of times in the past, when the West has seen a light shining in the East. I've become a complete and utter pessimist! I'm ashamed that I'm all right, while my brother's two-year-old son may perish in Vienna this winter, because I can't save even a child from starving or freezing to death! I live in a democratic country, where people will celebrate Christmas this year with pudding, brandy, turkey and guzzling. But I am not allowed to send anything over there to the one room, unlit and unheated, where my brother lives with his family. Where it's years since they set eyes on sugar, or fat, or soap. Where the Gestapo never gave up looking for me, and deprivation and fear wore my brother down to a skeleton. For the time being I may not even write to him directly, although Austria was the Nazis' first victim, although the powers who guaranteed the country's independence broke their word unanimously, and gave official recognition to the incorporation of my homeland into the Third Reich after the invasion! After the Liberation they systematically sacked it (of what the Nazis had left), and now the victors are squabbling amongst themselves, because unfortunately the Nazis exploited an oil-find in Austria, and none of the Allies want any of the others to have it. That's why little children will have to freeze and

174

starve this winter, while democracy celebrates Christmas! And a happy New Year, as well! More or less the same thing is going on in Europe, Asia and Africa. New concentration camps are being added to the old ones, until the whole world will be a 'ghetto', where 'human' society is kept behind barbed wire. This war was nothing more than the expression of a totalitarian state of mind which has become universal. There are different external conditions to account for differences in the wickedness and violence of the manifestation, but the process is a universal one: a process of bestialization, for which there is no hope of a cure.

My poor, dear Meyboden, I have no new world to tell you about this time, but rather the end of a world, which I was faithful to until it caved in on me. The Greek philosophy of human brotherhood has been proved a lie, humanism has been laughed to scorn as the Utopian illusion of dreamers. He who builds the bigger bomb is right, and has the right to seize all other good things for himself, just as having a larger cudgel enabled the cave-dweller to win by virtue of being the stronger! Woe to the conquered! Before long the whole of mankind will have been conquered by the ape-man who stirs so vigorously in all of us. Make the best you can of your life, and find yourself a monastic cell where you can paint, like St Luke.

All best wishes,   yours, OK

To Hans Meyboden

[London,] 24. Dec. 45

Dear Hans Meyboden,

Just a few hasty lines to let you know that I've not forgotten. I see you there and am with you, as I am with all innocent sufferers. [. . .]

The whole thing is a blanket catastrophe, which will drag every country in eventually, one after another. It's a new 'Völkerwanderung', because the dam or framework of society has been broken. An unstoppable flood of people is streaming from east to west, but they do not know what drives them. The two so-called 'world wars' were nothing more than the breakdown of a purely technological, materialistic civilization. The only thing on which people could agree was destruction. 'The greatest happiness of the greatest number', proclaimed by the political economist Jeremy Bentham at the dawn of the technological age, has turned into 'the greatest unhappiness of the greatest number'. Austria is hermetically closed from here. But thank you for your kind intentions, which show that only people who are themselves in great spiritual distress can make the comparisons that permit them to sympathize with others. What you tell me, writing from your camp, is an epitome of the situation here in general, and throughout the entire world. The conscience can't be

175

organized, or rented by any political party. Parties themselves are a manifestation of the merely mechanistic, mathematical way in which the human family is thought of today. Either the white man and his European culture will be destroyed this time or . . . When the Roman Empire fell, for similar reasons, the situation was similar. But then the neighbouring cultures were not so handicapped, primitive democratic society had not ceased to exist, and was able to convey some of its own vitality to the sorely afflicted social body. Written Roman law had lost some of its authority, but the living moral law of the primitive order of society still held good, whereby the individual is part of one community made up of the dead, the living and the as yet unborn. That moral law is everyone's responsibility towards everything that can be called culture. Today that is an empty concept, and so the responsibility does not exist. The individual believes he is free to do everything that the police do not actively prevent him from doing. When the police are no longer in charge of traffic, the law has no more value than the piece of paper it's written on. Our generation has destroyed – and persists in destroying, mindlessly – more than all previous generations since mankind first formed the notion of history. We think the world is our personal and sole possession, or that it's an objective for which it's quite in order for us to fight other people with physical force. As long as the purely technological, materialistic doctrine continues to recruit pupils – as now in the East – there is no light to be seen, even coming from the East.

Arm yourself with the strength of one walking to meet disaster with his eyes open. We can't escape. All we can do is help, help others undauntedly, by trying to open their eyes. The light must come from within. What shines in the East is the sun.

With my best wishes, and the cordial hope that your health does not suffer too greatly, yours very sincerely,   Oskar Kokoschka

To Alfred Neumeyer

London, I. III. 46

My dear Alfred Neumeyer,

I was so touched by your splendid essay and the fine understanding with which you laid my work before the readers of the *Magazine of Art*. It was the more surprising for me as here one seems, after eight years of life, so out of touch with the rest of the world.

Of course the kind of world I would like to return to, my world in which I travelled as a happy tramp, does not exist any longer. Big towns have disappeared from the surface of the earth, great countries left as deserts. There is no end yet even of the murdering, which now goes on in a cold systematic way, no less inhuman than the murdering with weapons and machinery. Power politics extended the hunger-blockade after the 'cease-fire'. To the destruction of cultural documents (of my home town, Vienna, only shabby remains tell of its former glory) the annihilation of humanistic values is connected in a way that makes seem normal today the callous views towards human life which we despised in Fascism. 10,000 children in some liberated countries are exposed to starvation, cold, and mental despair in detention-camps because they belong to undesirable minorities. Their only fault is that they belong to a linguistic group which is not that of the ruling one. What Hitler sowed is ripening. His insane mind conceived the idea of the collective guilt, and, unfortunately, the postwar world sticks to this delusion of a madman, dispensing justice on such conceptions. I cannot live in such a world! I feel individually responsible for the crimes of a society of which I am a member.

Modern society absolutely ignores that the world is not the property of one generation. We squander the spiritual and earthly heritage we got from our fathers; our children will have all reasons to curse us for having condemned them to pauperism and savage conceptions of social life. It all must end in an unreparable catastrophe. But to shout is to shout into empty space, for the power is impersonal which leads us deeper into the quicksand with every additional hour we live. The inhuman force driving us all is the technical, materialistic civilization of ours which lets us plan society on blueprints, which is hostile to the creative man, and kills imagination, compassion and happiness. I see no future for the artist. What today we call art is shallow 'Kunstgewerbe'. Without philosophy there is only applied science in the pay of the state; calories feed a robot who may be kept alive or can be starved according to the necessities of production for production's sake. This is not a world with any future, hope, or faith. Civilized man is dying without being conscious of it, like the rocket bomb kills before its approach is heard. I am working still, but I know it is a lost battle. What keeps me still alive is a growing compassion for the misery of the innocent children. The money I earn I mostly give away for charity. I gave £1,000 for the Stalingrad Hospital with the demand that the wounded enemy should equally be treated and educated to a better understanding.

Another £1,000 I gave last year for the war orphans of the Czechoslovakian Republic. I did not expect the political changes happening there which led to the elimination of $3\frac{1}{2}$ millions of citizens, most of whom had been loyal to the constitution. Now I wish to get another £1,000 for the Viennese children who are starving. Austria was the first and utterly ignored victim of Hitler. The 'Anschluss' was officially recognized by the great powers, but the Austrian people had no say in this. They still have not.

Those £1,000 I want to find in the States for a political painting I did in 1943, with the title: *What We Are Fighting For*. It is a large and striking work. If you know somebody or some institution interested in it I would like to send you a photograph of it. [. . .]   Oskar Kokoschka

To Augustus John (original English)

[London,] 24th April 1946

My dear Augustus John,

Instead of bothering you with my personal apparition, although I do not look ghostly yet, not so much older than in the days of the Paris of the past when you showed me the drawings of Joyce and were heavenly drunk! I shall state my case by letter. The fact is that I am badly in need of a British Passport.

As you know, in Czechoslovakia one must speak correctly the Czech language, or one is bound to land in a Detention-camp. Austria is occupied by the four Big Powers, even Vienna is divided into four zones. You can be kidnapped if you are an Austrian and wish to visit a relative in another zone. So what can I do in this world, born a Viennese and a bearer of a Czech passport?

I want to paint until I die. I cannot do that in the U.S.A. because I would go crazy from the noise, business and advertising in the States. The last fight in the last ditch of the battle must be fought here in your good old England, the battle for the Peace of the Mind, Humanist Tradition and Private Life in a circle of intimate friends.

I have been living in London during the whole war, and now, if I had to leave it, I would probably become more homesick for London than I ever was for Vienna, which lies more or less in ruins. Anyway, the Austrian world that I loved had vanished already with the first world war. Now it seems to me that England resembles my old Austria more than any other country in the whole world, since music, theatre and arts have had such a tremendous revival here.

You and Iris Tree are the two English people who know me longest, you can judge my character and know that I do not bother anybody with my existence. Will you please be so nice and sign this form? You do not accept any responsibility except for assuring the authorities that I am no murderer, thief, drug addict, afflicted with an incurable disease, physically or mentally. Painting – not even bad painting, which you kindly credited me with – is not an insane occupation in this chaotic world of ours, otherwise you would not do it yourself. [. . .]

[Yours, O. Kokoschka]

To Sir Kenneth Clark (original English)

[London,] 29th April 1946

Dear Sir Kenneth,

In England it is polite to start a speech with an apology and I have a
reason to do so, because I intend to ask you a favour. The fact is that I am
badly in need of an English passport. [. . .]

Dear Sir Kenneth, you know my work long enough and myself fairly well
to be able to judge the merits of my case. Would you therefore be so kind
and sign the enclosed form? You do not accept any responsibility except
assuring the authorities that I am no murderer, thief or afflicted with an
incurable disease, mental or physical, and that I do not bother anyone
with my existence. In seven years I have not even had an exhibition in
England. I should indeed be very grateful for your support in this serious
case.   [Yours sincerely, O. Kokoschka]

To Arnold Schoenberg

[London,] 26 June 1946

My dear Herr Schoenberg,

I've wanted to write to you a hundred times, to thank you for the
happiness listening to your music has given me, before the war in
Dresden, Paris and Vienna, and now in London, where I've spent nearly
nine years waiting for freedom, on the (alas) rare occasions when
something of yours is performed. Tomorrow, however, is to be one such,
during the musical festival!

I had the pleasure recently, at Dartington Hall, of hearing your most
recent compositions played from the piano score by one of the few
musicians who are completely immersed in your music. He was a pupil of
Anton von Webern for six years (as you will already know, that great and
unforgettable pioneer was killed after the 'liberation' of Austria!!!). In the
indolent and brutal world of today the people who really understand, as
this young man Emil Spira does, are increasingly exceptional. At the
moment he's at a progressive school (Dartington Hall College, Totnes,
England), throwing all his enthusiasm and ability into preaching the
gospel of your art. His dearest wish, however, is to visit you and complete
his study of formal theory as your pupil. Until just before his death,
Webern was teaching him here in England by correspondence, since
Spira, a Jew, was forced to leave Vienna. If you attach any value to my
request, and my ability to recognize a worthy aspirant when I see one,
please extend your hand to this dedicated musician, for old times' sake.
He says he has written to you but had no reply.

I hope with all my heart that you are fit and well! To judge by what I
heard, you must be at the height of your powers. Being here is like being

at a historical distance, it makes it easier to understand how facile all other contemporary music sounds, because one can be impartial here, since art has absolutely no soil or roots in England. Do read a private letter I wrote about the total spiritual and intellectual barrenness of the present time, which, to my malicious delight, I found was published by the American Federation of Arts, in the *Magazine of Art*, Washington. Instead of a lot of boring personal information about my life, the letter says everything that everybody concerned for the spirit and the intellect would want to say at the present time. If you ever spare me a thought, please send me a snapshot of yourself, so that I can see your eyes sparkling and your brain working behind your brows.

Please give my warmest regards to your wife, and Kolisch, to whom I was so greatly attached. Bring a great work into the world, to be the joy of future generations (and me). May God bless you! (That wretch Egon Wellesz is a scabby Beckmesser!)

Ever yours in admiration and gratitude,   Oskar Kokoschka

To a German Prisoner-of-War (Fritz Schahlecker)

[London,] 4 July 1946

A close friend showed me the drawings you made in the *camp* in England. He told me of your prospects of soon regaining your freedom and returning home to Tübingen. Like many of your fellow-Germans, you were abused in your early youth by a criminal demagogy and thrown into a war of aggression, during which the authority of human precepts was thoroughly and totally suspended, and which appears even now to threaten the future validity of those same precepts.

As an older man, I am in a position to make comparisons which shed light on the changes that have taken place in the moral sphere. That gives me a right to offer a younger man some advice that may come in useful when you are home again. After every great disappointment – in your case, when one has been the victim of a betrayal – one's insight is clouded, because one is always overcome by weariness at the same time. The tendency to feel sorry for oneself is only a natural consequence of that weariness. You are honest in your drawings, but it seems to me that you tend towards the kind of idealized view which comes from being in the centre of a world that one is trying to rebuild. In your drawings you are trying to give shape to a new world with the artistic expressive media available to you, after the reduction of your old world to ruins. You want it to be a human world, in contrast to the physical, materialistic world where naked force ruled, and in my view that is the hopeful and promising aspect of your experiment.

But the advice I would like to give you, however great your present need

180

and poverty may be, is this: stop surrendering to a tendency to study yourself alone and to forget that a sentimental outlook is just as sure to lead to waste and failure as the entire order that is collapsing before our eyes today. That order sprang from individual egoism, and was helped to ripen by nationalistic narrowmindedness. Humanism was believed dispensable. This materialistic attitude found its complete embodiment in Fascism. Bear in mind that your personal need and poverty, both physical and spiritual, are nevertheless infinitesimal compared to the need and poverty of the children abandoned to savagery in today's world. If your heart turns in hope to the work of rebuilding, because you are young and want to do good, you must help to make a better world for these children. You saw for yourself that what was achieved by the sword came to nothing in the end, therefore take up your pencil in the hope of doing better. You do not succeed in expressing anything about the pain throbbing in mankind today, because you are not yet able to give shape to *genuine* emotions. It will be like that for as long as you idealize yourself as a man of sorrows, instead of looking for the redeemer in every innocent child. The child can truly be the redeemer, if we genuinely believe in the possibility of a better world. Sentimentality does not help us to discover new worlds, it makes us cling to the past in fascination. The new world can only be given shape if we love our neighbour. If we are warmed by love, the sight of our neighbour, other people, a foreign nation, another race, will enable us to shape a new image of the world, in the contemplation of which the isolation of the individual and his nameless torment in a ruined world will give way to the splendour in which the embrace of love will illumine the choice, form and shape of a new order of humanity. All art, that of the great epochs as well as that of primitive cultures, that of coloured races as well as our own folk art, is rooted in this soil, in which the moral man has vanquished dust, decay and force. Man overthrows the dictates of physical laws and the dominion of blind elements, and by that means fights his way up from the subjection of blind obedience to human freedom.

Art is a means of feeling our way forwards in the moral sphere, and it is neither a luxury of the rich nor the rigid formalism that comes out of the theories of the academies. The modern art of the present time also tends towards arid formalism. Art is like grass sprouting from the frozen earth at the end of winter, like growing corn, and like the spiritual bread in which the human inheritance is passed on to future generations.

In the hope that you will find the inner strength to practise the spiritual office of artist in the future, I leave you with my best wishes,

yours, Oskar Kokoschka

P.S. I have no objection whatever to your making use of this private letter in your communications with the authorities and those sympathetic friends who are trying to assist you in your task.

To Jack Carney (original English)

Elrig, 7th Sept. 46

My beloved Jack,

Your last letter must not be the last one. You must continue to be my friend under any circumstances, however I may have hurt your feelings. Please, first of all, keep in your mind that I, being a human creature, am liable to errors, mistakes, doubts and depressive moods. I stand truly and honestly for socialism, i.e. a social order out to restore: firstly the human values mankind had lost, at least since the Industrial Revolution, a period covering what we call the Capitalist rule. Secondly, to create in the true meaning of the word, a state of the world, where the cultural traditions of individual nations (or better groups of settled people which one used to call nations) must be encouraged but where the criminal chauvinism, as a consequence of the idea of National State, is abolished and humanity is cured through the means of international humanist education. Socialism means an international order.

As I said before, I am victim of depressions, because I naturally feel for the people of the country I come from a deep affection in their suffering, growing in proportion to the state of the misery there. Grumbling is, as you know, an Austrian habit. Criticism, on the other hand, is a sign of intellectual activity! I may be unjust and open to correction when grumbling but, relying on the limited information to which I have access, I cannot shut out my curious intellect to learn what is behind the curtain of Real Politics, manifest in what is represented as facts in the press and reports from people coming from Austria, Czechoslovakia and Germany, or in letters from these countries.

The idea of Transfer, for example, to which I wholeheartedly object, has become such a fact of Real Politics, supported by the Communist Parties of those countries, as I know from their speakers. I disagree with it for ethical reasons although I wholeheartedly embrace the principles of Socialism.

To illustrate my point I may mention in this context the Idea of Christianity, whose socialist philosophy has degenerated into you know what thanks to the Real Politics of the responsible ones, although people by no means stopped believing in Christianity. Nevertheless its idea changed into its contrary. Why did it happen? For the good reason that the Church ordered Faith in the Dogma of Infallibility in a human person or persons, while banning the functioning of the critical mind. Consequently it will not save the Idea of Communism, if we are made TO

BELIEVE without cold objective scepticism added to the Faith, in order to create the best possible results we all are longing for.

Believe me, I have no vested interests to defend in this capitalist world of ours, no worldly possessions worth mentioning, and I was never tempted to acquire them, even when I was young. When I feel so alarmed by the growing suffering, since the Peace set in, of peoples everywhere that I sometimes want to run amok, it is not to amuse myself or to gain something by it. I only run myself down as well. That I know!

One thing I ask of you as a token of true friendship: to believe that by arguing with you I am the last to accuse you or make you responsible for a silly or wrong policy, in which you play a part just as little as I do. If argument and counter-argument should not be permitted between friends, where else?

I know Mina and you well, with your good hearts and your kindness, and I would never like to have to damp down my natural attitude towards you. Instead, allow me to behave genuinely and ask you when in need of an answer that helps me. For the material support which you gave me, you never will accept thanks. That is between us.

I wish you a very good journey to Switzerland, good weather and recreation which you deserve more than anybody. I hope this reaches you before you leave. We both, Olda and I, accompany you with our best love.

Both yours sincerely   Oskar

To Viktor Matejka

[London,] 15 January 1948

My dear Dr Matejka,

[. . .] You must issue an invitation, at once, in the name of the Burgomaster and the City of Vienna, to Michael Tippett, Morley College Concerts Society, 61 Westminster Bridge Road, S.E.1, to perform his 'Oratorio' in Vienna, on his way to Budapest, where he is to conduct it in March. He is the best conductor and teacher, a fine composer, and caused a stir with the very successful concerts he gave here during the war. [. . .] I should dearly love to see Austria acquire him for good, to make the country's musical life mean something in the world again, as in Schubert's day, when every family, in the city and the country alike, nurtured a musical tradition. All we have today is blether about the 'City of Song'. He ought to be appointed as a kind of national musical adviser, with a particular duty to remind the people of Austria of their older musical heritage. Furthermore, you and Tippett should arrange to get Anton von Webern's cantata performed in Austria at long last. It is a disgrace and a scandal that no one there knows anything about the greatest work of the twentieth century, whereas three great performances were heard in London two years ago, under Rankl, the Viennese conductor, who is also unknown in Vienna. Loos would turn in his grave if he heard that Vienna has yet to show any interest in the cantata, because only the little cliques are listened to, who are just as busy today as they ever were, scratching each others' backs in the cause of their own genius and their own world renown!

I am making real progress in the matter of the artificial limbs. All I need now is additional technical information giving details and the purpose of the prostheses, a provisional estimate of how many more cases there are likely to be in the country, how many patients there are in hospitals waiting for amputations, and how many of those returning to the country, on average, will need these kinds of prostheses. Start a campaign in the press, to attract the attention of all the sufferers who have given up hope and not even notified the authorities. Use my name!

The people in Amsterdam simply sent off the pictures belonging to Vienna City Council and the state, without letting me know, on the grounds that an exhibition is being put on in Vienna in the spring. But I told you, my dear friend, that I give a higher priority to the need to use my pictures to support my publicity campaign abroad, and I have no wish to be represented by a few canvases, as A. N. OTHER, in the town where only a few years ago they were tearing my paintings from the walls and jeering at me as a 'degenerate artist'. Nor do I wish to be shown there at all, until such time as I can arrange a retrospective exhibition and make the selection myself. As a painter, I am not just any Austrian Tom, Dick or Harry, and it is not for me to serve as the cream in the coffee of other painters, dead or alive, who happen to be Austrians. That's the game Nierenstein (now of New York) has always played, trying to inject some red blood-cells into the veins of his stable of native geniuses – Schiele and the like – so as to boost their commercial value. To this day, people are still inventing fairy stories to link me with all those cliques, and have succeeded, perhaps intentionally, in falsifying the course of historical events. That's why I hate those plummy voices mooing 'He's one of our own, after all', I'm fed up with it, and I will not show my paintings in Vienna until the initiative is mine. [. . .]

In sum, I need my paintings, including the ones that belong to the city and the state, for the Venice Biennale this spring, where I am to have a retrospective, together with Van Gogh. From there the collection, which consists entirely of borrowed works – apart from the political ones, which belong to me – goes to the States, to the six best galleries in North America. If my paintings are denied me, I know what conclusions to draw.   [Oskar Kokoschka]

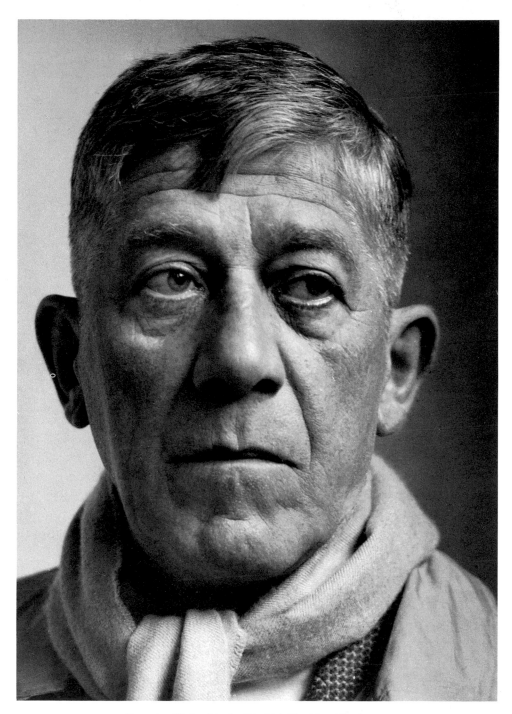

14 Portrait of Kokoschka by Friedrich Hewicker, Hamburg 1951.

15, 16 Kokoschka in London:
(left) at the home of Antoine,
Count Seilern while working on
the *Prometheus* triptych, 1950/51;
(below) at the major Tate Gallery
retrospective in September 1962,
with *The Mandrill* (1926), one of
his few paintings with an animal as
its subject.

Opposite
17, 18 Giving advice to students
at the 'School of Seeing' in
Salzburg, at which Kokoschka
taught regularly each summer from
1953 to 1963.

19   Strolling with Chancellor Adenauer in April 1966, when the West German leader sat for a portrait while on holiday at the lakeside resort of Cadenabbia in northern Italy.

20, 21 (opposite) Cityscapes of London: Kokoschka beside the last of his twelve panoramic views of the capital, *London View with St Paul's Cathedral* (1970), and at work on *London View with the Houses of Parliament* (1967), seen from the Shell Centre on the South Bank.

22–24 Oskar and Olda Kokoschka taking tea at home in the Villa Delphin, Villeneuve, where they lived from 1953, the year in which they made Switzerland their permanent domicile; (above) the artist in his studio, *c.* 1960, with the unfinished painting *Penthesilea*.

25 In Hyde Park, September 1962, while in London for the opening of the Tate Gallery retrospective exhibition.

London N.W.8, 13th May 1948

My dear Mr Plaut,

It is very kind of you to invite me to write a few words which can be used as a preface to the catalogue of the first representative exhibition of my paintings to be held in your country.

First of all, let me sincerely thank you for taking the initiative in this exhibition, and for devoting your time and energy to the task of making American art-lovers acquainted with what is more or less my life's work. Up to now, owing to two world wars, it has been practically inaccessible to them.

Of course, visitors to Germany between the two wars became aware of the fact that Paris was not the only Mecca of modern art. But already before the outbreak of the second world war, unfortunately, modern art was driven underground in a Germany overrun by Hitler. Thus the last time, for ten years or more, that my pictures could be shown was at the infamous Exhibition of Degenerate Art in Munich in 1937; this exhibition was visited by two and a half million sad Germans and foreigners who came to say good-bye – as they must have thought then, for ever – to my fellow artists and me.

It is true that many a brave museum custodian did his best to protect my work by hiding it at great personal risk. Nevertheless a good third of it was lost later on, owing to the devastation of the war in Europe, and the upheaval of the liberation.

It was indeed a great effort on your part to have traced enough important paintings of mine to furnish characteristic examples of more or less all periods of my development.

Some visitors, well acquainted with modern art movements, may be puzzled to find that in my work there is none of the experimenting with all the different phases, from impressionism, pointillism, cubism to non-objective art, which they are used to. The explanation is simple enough: I never intended to entertain my contemporaries with the tricks of a juggler, in the hope of being recognized as an original. I simply wanted to create around me a world of my own in which I could survive the progressive disruption going on all over the world. If this my world will survive me, so much the better. But I cannot *corriger la fortune*.

After forty years of work, however, it saddens me to have to listen to certain pronunciamentos of this, that or the other fashionable artist of today, abjuring his own work and denouncing modern art altogether, just because he finds himself in a blind alley. Unfortunately, such confessions of failure are bound to come just at a time when committee-controlled art makes news. I myself see no cause to retrace my steps. I shall not weary of testifying by the means given to me by nature and

193

expressed in my art, in which only vision is fundamental, not theories. I consider myself responsible, not to society, which dictates fashion and taste suited to its environment and its period, but to youth, to the coming generations, which are left stranded in a blitzed world, unaware of the Soul trembling in awe before the mystery of life. I dread the future, when the growth of the inner life will be more and more hampered by a too speedy adaptation to a mechanically conceived environment, when all human industry is to be directed to fit in with the blue-prints.

Individually, no one will see his way before him. The individual will have to rely on hearsay for his knowledge, on second-hand experience, on information inspired by scientific inquiry only. None will have a vision of the continuity of life, because of the lack of spiritual means to acquire it. For the growth of the inner life can never be brought into any scientific formula, whatever the technician and the scientist of the soul may try. The life of the soul is expressed by man in his art. (Do we not already need experts to lecture us on how to see a modern work of art?) The mystery of the soul is like that of a closed door. When you open it, you see something which was not there before.

Do not fear that I intend to lead you right off into metaphysics, whereas you only asked me for an introduction to the exhibition of my work. But if I were not a painter I could explain it all fully in words. So there we are. Very sincerely yours,   Oskar Kokoschka

To Marcel Ray

Hotel Berchielli, Lungarno, Firenze until 15. xii,
and then the London address which our dear 'Nylon' knows
5. xii. 1948

My dear, dear Marcel Ray,
Your letter lifted my heart, and I've been carrying it about with me in my breast pocket for nearly six months, so that now I can hardly read it. But before it becomes completely illegible, and because it is still impossible for me to come to Vienna (which was my firm intention and wish), in order to say to you personally all the things that I can scarcely put in a letter, I will write quickly, after all, to assure you of my unswerving friendship. I was overjoyed to learn, my dear friend, that you are as loyal as ever to all the good spirits we both knew, that you and Ludwig Ficker and Matejka think of me, and think so highly of my work at a time when artists are dying out because they're not needed, and the *misère* has become too general for anyone to waste thought on their work. But what made me rejoice most of all was the fact that you survived the whole *canaillerie*, because I had grown very anxious, hearing over and over again after the 'Peace' that no one knew anything of your fate. [. . .]

All my pictures, or at least all that have been found and rescued, or were safe in countries not invaded by Hitler, have been sent to America by their owners on a tour of museums. It's the first time that I've been worthily shown in *God's own country*. Up until now I was not worth discovering, because I produce too little for the international art trade to look on my work as a *business proposition*. Now, I suppose, they think 'he's over sixty, how much longer will he keep going?', and reckon it's time to draw up the balance-sheet. I can afford to grin at that, under my somewhat wrinkled skin, and I take care not to waste my breath gasping at the strange ways of the big world. Tears came into my eyes yesterday when I unexpectedly found myself standing beside Michelangelo's tomb in the church of Santa Croce. It was the first time that the fact was borne in on me that this god of an artist is dead, because I simply do not know the dates of birth and death of the artists I honour.

The Italians are droll people, and always choose the right moment for a grand gesture. It said in the papers this week that they had sent the David to Washington on loan, as an expression of their gratitude for Marshall Aid. I was horrified, and in a rage for several days over the barbarism of it. To think that, after the destruction of so much irreplaceable cultural wealth during the two wars, people were now, in peacetime, prepared to systematize the very same cold indifference towards works of art, and swathe it in fine phrases! Why hadn't they sent the copy that stands in the Piazza della Signoria, I demanded of the Soprintendente, the Americans would have liked the copy just as much, and who would have known the difference? Today I went into the Accademia with the Soprintendente, Dr Poggi, and – there was the David, god-like, just like the hundred times that I've seen it before. He gave a sly smile as he explained that they'd shipped the little David, which is not entirely by Michelangelo and is not irreplaceable. In spite of the cold I grew quite warm with joy that there is still such a thing as a cultural conscience.

Italy is still immeasurably rich, in spite of everything that the victors in all the 'just wars' have hacked to bits, burnt, stolen and carted off! It strikes me as peculiarly horrible that victors always fall upon works of art, instead of leaving them where they were made, as part of a people's spiritual and intellectual inheritance, because once it has been robbed of that inheritance the impoverished nation necessarilly sinks into barbarism. History is full of examples. You yourself, dear friend, know enough Austrian history to seek the explanation for the fate of Schoenberg, Loos, Trakl, Altenberg etc. in Vienna's spiritual and intellectual impoverishment and decline into moral barbarism. It began with the sale of the spirit and the intellect to the highest bidder, and Waldmüller, Grillparzer, Nestroy and Karl Kraus all kept their eyes open and spoke out against it in their time. To speak of my own case at a modest distance:

195

a third of my work has disappeared without trace, despite a great deal of official and backdoor enquiries in the two Germanies of today. My œuvre is not so great in numbers, but perhaps it was and is more important to the young people of many countries than all the fine theories of art that have been in and out of fashion in my lifetime. Those theories came increasingly to remind me of the theological disputations of Byzantine monks, but far from doing any good, the various sects did not rise above the chaotic mental condition of society. In an age when you hear so much talk about human rights, the human being disappears entirely from art, which has gone abstract! It's enough to make a cat laugh! There, now my fingers are blue with cold, but my heart is warm with the pleasure of having had a long overdue conversation with you. Please commend me very warmly to your wife, who I remember very well from that time in Paris. Many regards to my dear Ludwig Ficker, and to all our few friends, and I will see you in the spring. Look after yourself. Embracing you, your devoted   OK

Those remarks about Corbusier at the Loos ceremony in Vienna were hilarious!

In memoriam Karl Kraus

Vienna, 25. IV. 49

In commemoration of the 75th anniversary of the birth of Karl Kraus. The ability to speak and write our mother tongue properly is a means of salvation and teaches us to think properly – which means to live as reasonable beings.

Karl Kraus preached this message in Vienna. With what success?

Oskar Kokoschka

To Olda Kokoschka

Berkshire Museum School, Pittsfield [Mass.]

Sunday, 30. 7. 49

My dear Hold,

I'm getting worried because I still haven't heard from you, although I've been here since Monday. Did you write the address down wrong?

I'm glad you're not here, because it is so dreary, in spite of Tanglewood being nearby and *all of it*. There's no life, more like ghosts, the grown-ups at least all look like fat frogs, and in the evenings, at dinner parties, when they're all in their best clothes, the men in white *dinner jackets* and the fat, elderly women half-naked in gaudy print *evening dresses*, they all sweat as much as if they were in a Turkish bath, but try, nevertheless, to make sparkling conversation and behave as if this is living. Everything is very clean, *Georgian*, hygienic, *chapel*, *library*, *museum* (with *natural history, modern art by third-rate artists and annual members' night mixed into one*), but it's airless, stifling. I don't know how I shall stick it out until 25 August. The exhibition in New York runs till 25 September, and the reviews are long but appallingly uncomprehending. They think they're making me a compliment if they say I'm nearly on a par with Modigliani or Soutine. And everything is so frightfully *joyful* and self-confident, perhaps due to the strong admixture of Brünn and Proßnitz.

It cooled a little overnight, thanks to a thunderstorm, which chose its moment to send the audience of 14,000 at a Koussevitsky concert running for cover from the grass where they had been lying, rapturously kissing, sweating and smoking, to the music of Gounod's *Faust*. I had to wait until each of the *car-owners* had extricated their vehicle from 100,000 others in the parking lot, and got it on to the road, for I simply couldn't go on listening any longer, I felt ill from the heat, and perhaps from the rich food, which seems to come out of a machine, whether it's meat, fruit or dessert. Feigl was here yesterday, apparently on his way to sell the Florence to the Minneapolis Museum, for which 3,000 comes to the artist (as agreed on his first visit to New York). Henry was here too, with his family, the night before last, and wanted me to go to Croton for a weekend, but I'm too tired to travel long distances in an *air-conditioned train*, where you feel as if you're in a tomb, because the windows are hermetically sealed, and the air feels icy, although it's kept only 10 degrees below the temperature outside. Everything is very heavy going, but especially so in a place like Pittsfield. I hope you're all right. Don't forget Plesch and, much more important, don't forget me.

Missing you dreadfully,   always your OK

To Olda Kokoschka

                                             [Pittsfield,] 16. Aug. 49

My dear Hold,

I'm just reading the letter you wrote in the sleeper. You are such a nice girl, everything you do is enormously interesting, the way you tackle Jane Austen and so on on your own. Spare Rome a thought too, now and then, because it won't be long before we're there again, seeing the churches and museums. Here the world is made of oil tanks, *drugstores* and banks, like a kid's toy, fitted out with a clockwork railway and too many signals. I'm at a loss to understand why the young people are so 'sympathisch', in spite of all; they're so softhearted that they're already beginning to get tearful because I'm leaving in about ten days and shall probably never see any of them again. Unlike England, not one of them is *highbrow*, unteachable or in a shell. At twenty-five they are still as affectionate as children, and even

197

the Jews (who make up the majority) are first and foremost children of a new world, with none of the complexes they would have in Europe. There are also two blacks here, who get on as easily with the others as if they were out of the same *litter*. They're as gentle as kittens. I suppose it's different in the South, but this is New England, where a new kind of social existence has developed, especially among the young who experienced the war, and it's an example worth following. Obviously, with Tanglewood nearby, music is the dominant factor. They live frugally, six or ten together in the little summer bungalows, several to a room, which scarcely allows individuality, is probably never cleaned properly, and yet is never dirty. They dress like tramps, often half-naked, in spite of rain and extremes of temperature. They share everything, money is more like a bus ticket that has to be shown to the conductor. What I have not yet been able to discover is why they change so much when they grow up and get a *job*, start families and *push*. The *colleges* have given the great majority of them a good education, at all events. These young people are independent, lead a separate life from the grown-ups, and are happy. [. . .]
Good night, drink your milk, and give me a kiss,   your OK

To Arnold Schoenberg

[Pittsfield,] 19. Aug. 49

My dear Schoenberg,
I only want to say a profound 'thank you' for the experience, a milestone, of hearing your Third and Fourth Quartets played by Mann, Kopf, Hillyer and Winograd.
In Paris once, thanks to the old Kolisch Quartet, I suddenly grasped the family relationship of Austrian music, from Haydn to you. It made an impact on me as if on someone going through life like a tramp who all at once discovers a world of the spirit and the mind that he can call his home.
But I wept as I listened to the Fourth Quartet. Now I know for certain that you are the last Classical composer: your cradle was Beethoven's Grosse Fuge, where there is none of that Russian, French or English folklore, and the barbarism of presenting a symbol instead of a direct experience (giving a *leitmotiv* a meaning which convention is then expected to convert into a musical value which is a fiction, like the face value of paper money) was halted in its tracks by the immense necessity of expression. Bach, Beethoven and Schoenberg are the last composers capable of erecting a musical structure that can – must – be regarded as an organic world, such as nature creates in crystals, plants and living beings. All music but theirs is either galvanized, artificially stimulated

198

folkweave (which will never be creatively original again, since the steamroller of technical advance levelled out one country after the other, and one continent after the other) or purely abstract aural geometry with *queer sounds* and *odd effects* touting for the listener's custom. The Russians have done their sums, admit their guilt, and hope to please Papa Stalin by writing local versions of *White Horse Inn*, or making the ghosts of sounds long dead walk again.

I would so much like to see you, but I don't know if I shall have the chance to make the long journey this year. My wish for your birthday is that you enjoy the great inward happiness of one who is isolated and not understood, and in spirit I kiss you on both cheeks.

Yours gratefully,   O Kokoschka

To Olda Kokoschka

Minneapolis, 15. 9. 49

My dear Hold,

Your letters are probably with Pearlman, who is taking an eternity to forward them. I've been here three nights already, and am well away with the painting. As usual, I don't know what will come out, but the start was good. It's not easy to do two nearly lifesize figures in so large a format, and then alter what has already been well done (and would satisfy a Frenchman!), with the risk of losing everything that has already been achieved. But then, I want substance, not just a purely decorative plane with lines and planes distributed across it. The surface must become a three-dimensional space, in which body, depth, expression and movement are composed from the paint. John, the good fellow, sits for me on his own for three or four hours every afternoon, because Mrs Cowles had to fly to New York this morning to see her children, and will not return until Tuesday. He keeps on asking me which is the better painter, Matisse (they own a huge odalisque by him with a few blots and brush-strokes) or Derain (there is a very good self-portrait by him, from the same period as the one in the Moscow collection). All I can do is repeat the same answer: Derain, because he made paintings. In saying that, I forgo my chance of making my own task easier and being content with throwing together a decorative sketch. I should be very glad of your encouragement, like the way you wrote to me in New York, when the reviews made me angry. Incidentally, even Wheeler and Rockefeller said that the only thing that matters in New York criticism is the length of the article. What it says is of no importance. And the articles were long enough in all conscience. [. . .]

Good night, bolt the door, don't catch cold.

Auf Wiedersehen   Your OK

[Minneapolis,] 20. 9. 49

My dear Hold,

You're quite right about the soffitto, middle panel, and Wastl must hold out for 25,000. I will make the middle panel large, with lots of figures. I will do it – or at least begin it – next winter. He will need to provide a studio for me. The side panels will come in due course, as I work on it. Why should I be *cross* with you, you little nitwit? Ask Wastl what he thinks of 25, or if he thinks he wouldn't get more than 20. The painting would be bigger, and I'd enjoy it more.

Think of me, and good night and sweet dreams about, tonight, the weary painter   OK

Give my love to Fred and his wife!

To Olda Kokoschka

[Minneapolis,] Monday 2 Oct.? [1949]

My dearest Hold,

I painted for eight hours today, and am ready to drop, but I've done it and need have no doubts about it. So, even if they pull faces when they see it, I at least am sure of myself. I scrubbed the whole thing yesterday for the third time, and painted it all over again, and then of course I was appalled at having wasted the work of forty long sittings (or however many it was), and I had no time to restore order in the chaos of something half-finished. But I had no choice, because the painting wasn't dense enough, and the individual elements were not painted enough – I mean, created in paint. Even a nose, or the corner of an eye, an arm, a body, the space, must be created by the painter, as if such a thing had not existed before. [...] You have to spend the whole day painting in the company of two people of mature years, who had too much whisky the night before, bass voices, smiling at each other, and light-heartedly miming the roles of a harmonious married couple (badly). So imagine how glad you feel when the whole day is at last more or less over, and you can look down with a sudden rush of benevolence at the Adam and Eve you have created; and it is for you to tell this couple to rise up and go forth according to my word. For I have made them, essentially, haven't I, Hold? I haven't touched whisky for a week, myself, so as to be fresher the next morning, although I badly need a drink when I've finished work. I'm looking forward enormously to the chance of a rest with you. I couldn't live in America in the long term. Besides, life is not always as rosy, even here, as people think it is. I'm sorry to say that I see the cracks in the wall again here, as elsewhere in the past. Good night, my darling.

Olda Kokoschka, lithograph, 1957.

Give my love to all our friends, especially Fred and Wastl, and take care of yourself.
Always with you   your OK

To an American student (original English)

London, 24th Nov. 1949

Dear Mr Kania,

I answer your letter from London, to where I returned from America. Your thesis interests me very much as it seems that you are not happy with the statement that takes the influence of El Greco's art on my painting for granted, although it has been repeated again and again in books and essays dealing with my art. To my knowledge so far, nobody has ever made the attempt to justify such a view or correct the prejudice. To state the facts as they are: El Greco's work has only been rediscovered and propagated throughout the world when my earlier work has already been made known to the public in Vienna, Berlin, etc. Why the work of this great Baroque Master impresses society so much at present, the reason is perhaps that everybody thinks to find in the Baroque art a way out of this blind alley into which society has been led by science. It is only too obvious at present that the individual has either to re-cast his way of life or expire. The main motive of rational approach to life – selfsupport – lacking values of biological survival, is no longer so potent a drive as it was in the era of the progress of technical civilization. In view of the frustration everyone is feeling after the two world wars we see, especially in the Protestant countries, that the process of the annihilation of the Ego has been accomplished. Even the leading teachers of physics today are participating in this sad opinion. They cling to mystic philosophy in search of a way out from a myopic mental field of a surfacial, superficial and merely functional perception of a world. The universal worship of the so-called physical laws has resulted in a fatalistic belief in mechanics ruling Life.

El Greco's appeal to modern man was at first not due to the fact that the modern man can again participate in Baroque culture, which was the last cultural effort to create a social pattern based on a static social order. Greco's work has been rediscovered for aesthetic reasons which form a link between classic painting and Cézanne's effort to reinstate the validity of illusion in painting, i.e. three dimenstional perception of space or static order. As you know, Cézanne's work was intended as a protest against the impressionistic, scientific painting of his time, in which the motives of movement, speed and scientific exactness of observation confused application of optical laws with the artistic composition. Actually Cézanne's protest against dynamism made modern man aware

202

of the danger of his own civilization. It is purely accidental that precisely Spanish art has been taken out of its general setting that is Baroque culture. And already Manet's art, under the influence of the neighbouring Spanish painting, has received a strong stimulus, badly needed in France at that time, where the genuine tradition has been interrupted since the Enlightenment and the Revolution.

Generally it is not known well enough that the Baroque era had created a cultural pattern which had been accepted in a short time of 80 years all over the Catholic countries and spread from the Empire under the Habsburg Crown, after the defeat of the Turks near Vienna, even as far as to the recently discovered New World. In the Catholic society, spiritually reformed in the Thirty Years religious wars, the Baroque style had become the universal perception according to the faith of the Ecclesia Triumphans, its main feature being the relativity in space and time, the immortal soul of man as a solid rock.

In this Catholic commonwealth, the Habsburg Empire, the impact of the beginning industrial revolution had been softened due to the resilience of this cultural pattern, notwithstanding the division of the Empire under Charles V into the Austrian 'Erblande' and Spain. As a specific style Baroque art was still active in both parts, while in more progressive Protestant countries the period of unsuccessful experiments began, leading ultimately to the quick succession of imitations of foreign imported styles and 'isms', dictated by the commercialized and commercializing art trade. In the same way, the fallacies of the mode of thought professing rationalization could mislead man to exchange the faith in his immortal soul, participating in creation, for a notion of a machine-minded world, in which his Ego has no right of existence. Riding on the crest of the wave of the nationalist movement, he more and more lost contact with humanity and will end as a number in the statistics of a totalitarian state.

Returning to your query, El Greco had his origins in the Byzantine culture, but circumstances enabled him to merge the glory of Venetian painting with the mystic vein of austere Spain where, though the mediaeval state order had outlived its day as well (Cervantes), the dynamism of modern thought had always been viewed with distrust, producing an ascetic mood, tending to escape the changes of our world, and rather to accept the annihilation of individuality in a monastic order. Therefore I assume that it is not the Baroque background of El Greco as a cultural pattern, the postulate for modern Catholicity, I assume that it is the mystic vein, the desire to glorify Creation in spite of all suffering, destruction and waste on earth in which reason ultimately must recognise its true expression. In this way El Greco must be considered an expressionist painter. Expressionist art has inspired the pre-war generation in Germany, Italy and now, finally, France. My own work is closely linked up with its present success, as you may judge for yourself in your country. Out of the deeper strata of the mind of a frustrated generation, Expressionism has become a popular movement even in the Protestant countries in protest against time-bound fashionable theories on art, advocated by the official schools which cage the artist in an Ivory Tower.

As you may know my own origin is in Austria, where the Baroque culture was still a tradition alive in my boyhood. Baroque art impressed me deeply because it was typical for my country. Maulbertsch, the great master of murals, although unknown to you, but who equals Greco as a personality, Daniel Gran, Kremser Schmidt, the sculptor Matthias Braun, whom I would compare to Giovanni di Bologna, considering his inventiveness and daring, the great architects Fischer von Erlach and Hildebrandt, – all these men instilled into me the sadness of Memento Mori as soon as the first wonders of modern Technology appeared, advertised by Neon Lights. In harmony with the visual arts, the galaxy of the great Austrian composers, culminating in Haydn, Mozart, Beethoven and Schubert, encircled the heavens of my youth. This Baroque culture, of which still thousands of humble votives, shrines and crucifixes on the crossroads are witnesses, has saturated me with the same mystic vein as you and your friends find in El Greco: the desire to survive the running-out of time and the disappearance of space into a world catastrophe.

These few lines may help you to find a direction in which your research may be recompensed with success. Please let me know when you think to have done a good job of your thesis.

Yours sincerely   [Oskar Kokoschka]

To Antoine, Count Seilern

[London,] 14. 1. 50

Dear Count Seilern,

I write to confirm the agreement we reached today, on the basis of which I undertake to paint the central panel of the ceiling for 17,500 francs. Payment on completion.

In the hope that you will be satisfied, my dear friend, I am

yours sincerely, O Kokoschka

204

[London,] 15. 7. 50

My dear Magister Hodinus,

I put the last brush-stroke (I feel like saying axe-stroke) to my ceiling painting yesterday, and now I feel more despondent than I have for many a long year. The thought of having finished something on which it will be impossible to change the minutest detail has poleaxed me. I was as little prepared for it as for death. I'm profoundly sad, and in a rage with the entire world. I try to find reasons for my rage, such as that this epic, this saga, will belong from now onwards to a despicable contemporary world and an even more stunted posterity, and become a property of the spiritually and intellectually destitute, who will be free to dispose of it as they please. They're like flies, all preferring the two-dimensional plane, at which I wove like all three Fates in one person, in the cosmos I myself created, day after day, for six months, for as long as my two legs would support me. The last of the three panels, with Demeter, Persephone and Hades, is the one I care about most, naturally, because it was the last, the one which completed my statement's great arc into the void, and rounds off the composition too, an organic whole in terms of both myth and form, as if it had been lying ready since the beginning of the world for anyone gifted with the eyes to see. My only comfort is that Uccello, too, was no better understood when his own spiritual and intellectual need led him to invent perspective for the renaissance world. Ignoring the spiritual adventure (as daring as Columbus's search for the two Indies), all that his successors made of it was an academic formula of linear perspective, for the use of the journeymen employed by the magnates of the time to make 'modern' art. Until Michelangelo once more shook the pillars of this temple that had been turned into a shop.

Please make arrangements through Dr Blunt, who you've met, to study my work in peace and quiet at Count Seilern's house, 56 Exhibition Road, and to get hold of a set of the superb pictures taken by Mr Bell, the Courtauld Institute's photographer, which show both the whole and details. This is perhaps my last big painting, and perhaps it's my best, and Seilern doesn't entirely know what he's got.

He won't make it accessible, and he'll hear it criticized by stupid society people who pay him personal calls, until in the end he may put it in an attic. [. . .]

All the best,   yours ever, OK

To Will Grohmann   Hotel St Peter, Zurich,
                                                            7. XII. 51

Dear Herr Grohmann,
Your letter caught up with me only today, thanks to my ceaseless gipsy
roving.
I would indeed by very interested in designing the opera *Wozzeck* by
Alban Berg, who was a friend of my youth. I was with him at the première
in Vienna in the twenties, and I saw it again in Salzburg last summer.
The work is as powerful now as it was then. Of course it will be necessary
to fix the date of my invitation to Berlin quite a long time in advance,
because I am likely to be moving around just as much in the next twelve
months as in the last few years, and consequently my post reaches me only
after a great delay.
Why has *Orpheus* never yet been performed in Berlin? The American
Institutes do my plays in some twelve cities, young people are doing them
in Frankfurt (University) and Hamburg (at the Brücke), the Sezession
theatre in Vienna is on the point of staging me, and there will be
something at the Biennale in Venice next year, in a translation by Benno
Geiger – only the 'adult' theatres in Germany won't take the plunge. Is it
absolutely essential to be French to get performances in Berlin? Won't the
directors allow themselves to be persuaded even by the recommendation
of Thornton Wilder? At a lecture he gave at Frankfurt University two
years ago he said my plays provide models for the American experimental theatre. At all events, I was pleased to hear from you, and your review
of my exhibition in Berlin did my heart good, restoring the city's honour
after the Nazi years. My journey through Germany made an excellent
impression on me this time. I should have liked to go to Berlin as well, had
not my wife given me her 'flu.
All best wishes,   yours, O Kokoschka

To Alfred and Senta Marnau
                                                  [Zurich,] 22. XII. 51

Dear Fred and Senta,
Here's a fine state of affairs! You will already have left London when I fly
back on Wednesday and (*cross the bones!*) arrive in London! I was so
looking forward to us all being together again, after spending the last nine
months on the move among strangers. I cannot even come home for
Christmas, because my painting (portrait of a big industrialist, *fi donc!*)
still needs a little more work to finish it. Olda will be sad, too. I'm
whacked, and almost blind from the constant thick fog here. I've been
working non-stop on this portrait for the last six weeks, mornings and
afternoons to start with, but recently from 9 till 2, quite long enough to

get bad-tempered. I really can't listen to Swiss German any longer, and I'm positively looking forward to hearing English again, with its slack vowels!

Your pen painted the landscape as beautifully as if you'd used a brush. I'm very curious to see your new home, when we come to Innsbruck and sing the Andreas Hofer song together. A memorial to Emperor Maximilian, the Last of the Knights, should have been hewn out of the Martinswand long ago by a sculptor – not Thurek, or whatever that Salzburg Nazi is called, or Wotruba, but one of those who cast the iron kings and queens. I shall think of you a lot on Christmas Eve, which I shall spend alone in my little hotel room, because the people here are getting on my nerves. I try to imagine your *Melancolia*, and will be very happy if you will send me a copy of the poem. You must have a whole world of unforgettable impressions from your journeys in your head now, inside your beautiful skull, like a little box made of seashells brought from some distant land by a sailor. Treat them very carefully, don't break them, keep them dusted and put them under a glass cover, they might be made of wax. My salutations go also to Prince Eugen's steed Fridolin Kajetan, who bears his master's name. Of course I will do the drawing for the dust-jacket of *Der Gast*, I'm looking forward to reading it.

Is Senta glad to get her breath back at last, after all the 'holidaying' with the tourists? Is the 'cello with you, and is Senta playing it beautifully? I'm very, very sad to think of you being so far away now. But at least good old Ficker will be pleased. I wish him a very happy Christmas! Make sure you winkle out his address at last. We rang every newspaper, in vain, that time.

Now, my very best of wishes to you, my Fred and my Senta, and a warm hug. A very good New Year to you both, the poet and Senta the musician, from your   OK

To Ruth and Adolf Arndt

From Monday: Hotel St Peter, Zurich
3. 6. 52

Dearest Arndts,

I had a long conversation yesterday with an intelligent Frenchman, called something like Dr Rabatet, who has what sounds like an influential job with the Council of Europe in Strasbourg, and is due to move to Bonn shortly for a year or two. We were both guests at the country house of my old friend Major Beddington-Behrens, the financial specialist in Strasbourg (for the Conservative Party here). Unlike our host and the English in general, who, whether Labour or Conservative, look on Germany exclusively as an industrial rival – which is why English policies will never favour European union and will scarcely tolerate it – this Frenchman was very open-minded. I very much hope that Avo will get to know him and that both, being younger men, will play a part in making this idea of European union a fact instead of merely something the young dream about, and push back the frontiers of nationalist prejudice. It's a job for younger people, who have tasted something of the bitter lessons of a Europe rending its own flesh. M. Rabatet also called the Saar question a shameful error of French policy, and above all he knows full well that there is no time to spare for foolish games and prejudices, or *invested interests* [*sic*], when the thin varnish of an illusory prosperity (thanks to the current boom in the armaments trade) can crack open at any moment, making the un-European ideology of a state without humanity the beneficiary of despair and a sense of impending doom. It did my heart good to talk to this Frenchman, because he thinks as a European and not as a nationalist.

Please dear Avo, get in touch with him as soon as he reaches Bonn. [. . .] I would so like to see you, and also to hear more of Avo's views on the future. The young people of Europe must not be allowed to become cynical.

Much love, and I hope to see you soon!
Best wishes,   yours, Oskar

To Walter Feilchenfeldt

[Pontresina,] Sunday, 24. 8. 52

Dear Feilchen,

This is the worst day we've had for a week, cloud, rain, cold, and Olda and I are sad, too, because poor, dear Grete no longer rides around on her broomstick. I'm stunned by the thought that it had to happen, and that she now lies six feet under, instead of pottering about in that old house in London, secretly slipping me a whisky, smuggled through Customs under her skirt. I always claimed to have my doubts about her petticoats, and she would insist that they were clean and came from the very finest lingerie stores, darling Gretchen. I'm so glad that I was reconciled with her by the time the war ended, otherwise I would never have found out what a noble personality was hidden under that rough shell. I will study her book about the French Middle Ages now, because I didn't know before what an authority she was in that field. But I would much rather she was still alive! Was it bad, the funeral? Ending up is cruel, although we are reminded every day that we're only dirt, once the ether of the soul is no longer present to make us spirit. Will good old Grete's spirit be somewhere, do you think? Perhaps she knows that we don't want her to quit our lives yet.

208

Look after yourself, my dear Feilchen. Wonderful Marianne, who was such a tower of strength to our good witch, will take even better care that you stay young for your old friend, who has the prospect of going to America in the winter,   OK
Give my best wishes to my two bad boys.

To Alfred Marnau

[Minneapolis,] 27. XI. 52

Dearest Fred,

Many thanks for your letter. How I wish I was there and all the rumpus here was already over and done with. It is a dreadful strain to have to play the successful, famous man every day, who doesn't know the meaning of the word tired, and simply 'electrifies' the town. I've had enough of it. The programme at the college and the round of public speaking are almost over. Yesterday I kept 500 old *ladies* in a lunch club on the edge of their seats for two hours, after a three-hour teaching session in the college in the morning, followed by a concert in the evening somewhere out of town in snowdrifts. I've had enough!!!

But I have another two to three weeks to spend painting a portrait at a house in the country, where we are to be guests, so we won't have a single hour to ourselves, and if there's a blizzard like today we shall just be frozen in. I hope we shall get home before the end of January, but I don't like the idea of flying in winter. The Salzburg thing may be possible, if I can talk round some people here in Washington. But I have little desire to do a lot of travelling in this weather [. . .]

I'm very much looking forward to your book, and as soon as I get it I will show it or leave it with someone in New York on our return journey, if you are looking for a publisher there. I'm also curious to see how the drawing came out, and am touched by the fuss you're making about it! Take care of yourselves, my two darlings, and try and have a rest, to gather your strength for the year to come! Fred, you must not start looking for a subject for a new book straightaway, and you must not get worked up if you don't find one at once. You have such an inexhaustible nature that you must not get restless. Look after your nature: when you are older you may use a stick from time to time, but for the present even a gentle tap with a riding crop may startle the nature of the fiery Kajetan you ride. *I would like to be with you both, and so would Olda, whether it be Heidelberg or elsewhere, Sentalein. I kiss your lovely forehead, the scented one, and embrace you both*

yours, Oskar

To Ludwig von Ficker

London, 10. I. 53

Dear Herr von Ficker,
I am sending you my Munch essay at Fred's urging, as he says you would like to read it. I should of course appreciate having this copy back in due course, as soon as you've read it; it's the only one I have, because the magazine sold out at once, there was such a demand for it.
It wasn't only for Edvard Munch that I wrote the article. I regard him as a great, possibly the last great artist, but I also wanted to remind people once again of the connection between a work of art and the thinking of an era. Visual art has become too commercialized nowadays, while society brings nothing to art out of its own resources and has become too dependent on experts to help it form its opinions – as in every other aspect of life, for which state control of education may well be to blame. I thought it was important, therefore, to draw attention once again to the interrelationship of spiritual and intellectual processes in any one particular age. As an optimist I'm sorry to have to make our short period on earth such a black-on-black one, and yet I don't have a fatalistic belief in the Decline of the West, so long as it is possible to cite an example like the Holy Father in Rome, who preserves in his reverend person the spiritual and intellectual inheritance of the West since the days of the Greeks. To be so close to him two years ago made me very happy.
I hope you are as well as I would wish you to be, my dear friend. The fact that you like my dear Fred so much pleases me not only on his account, but also on yours, because the number of people one can like is not that large.
I'm very unhappy at the present time, because my poor beloved sister in Prague is lying without hope in a hospital, gravely ill, and this merciless world does not allow me the smallest possibility of giving her help or comfort.
With all best wishes for the New Year and warmest regards,

gratefully yours, Oskar Kokoschka

To Josef P. Hodin

Villa Delphin, Quartier Byron, Villeneuve, Canton Vaud,
10. 10. 53

My dear Magister Hodinus,
We're fully fitted out at last. We've bought furniture, curtains, light fittings and lampshades, even a lawnmower and pruning shears. The only thing we're waiting for, for ever and ever, amen, is the telephone. So we feel rather isolated, not seeing a soul for days on end, after all the hurly-burly, first in the USA and then in London and Salzburg. The

School was exhausting but stimulating, with really dedicated students, who achieved miracles because I wanted them to. Even the general public and the city fathers were roused to enthusiasm, and I contrived to involve the latter in two splendid free lectures, for which a lot of people, who had only 'come to see Kokoschka', couldn't get tickets. Seeing and hearing both failed them, in the event, when I got serious about my 'School of Seeing'. I had to summon up all my magic powers, because it was far harder for me than in the States, where no one harbours resentment against me. I don't know yet if I'll be able to do it again next year. It would take a lot of money from an American foundation to set up dormitories, kitchens, studios, lecture rooms for the European students, most of whom are penniless; the old barracks up at the castle only served as a temporary measure. I don't see why my students should starve. But it's out of the question for me to raise help of that kind in the USA, because I can only build things spontaneously, I'm not methodical or logical. My life is too short for that, and organization bores me. Unless by some miracle it drops down the chimney, there will be no 'School of Seeing' next year, where the young people of Europe can grapple in earnest with an education worth more than any of the botched, piecemeal schemes of politicians. Learning to see, and learning to know what they see, was always the first essential. Every dispute, every quarrel, every division in the history of Europe started with someone theorizing instead of seeing what is there under the sun, which is the same sun, even if it rises in the east and sets in the west. Let their elders chase after Picasso, who dresses beautiful windows giving on to a future paradise as only a window-dresser can. Someone with the adroitness of a ringmaster in a flea-circus can go far in a society which lets itself be persuaded that all men are the same, good enough to give blood and pay an entrance fee for the privilege, in order to watch the gnomes at work. How I hate these politicians, who chase after the masses, and deny all the glory, majesty, magnificence, exaltation and divinity of the human spirit!
My thanks to Beautiful for the lovely postcard she sent from Belgium, I wish she was here now, so that I could draw her! You said recently that Pamela wanted to visit our area this autumn. What about now? She could take home with her that watercolour you want. I can't put it in the post, because making up a parcel and filling in all the forms is beyond me. How are you? Write to me again, please, I miss you just as much!
All best wishes,   yours, O Kokoschka

To Theodor Heuss

[Villeneuve,] 20. XII. 53

My dear Herr Bundespräsident,

Now I have to thank you very sincerely for two copies of your *Vorspiele des Lebens*. It's magnificently written and so vivid. I gave no one any peace until the first copy turned up finally, in England. I could not let it be lost, because your kind inscription was in it. Now for my impressions. Our dear friend Dr Gubler, who is here quite often now, and always for a week or two at a time, read the book aloud to me; it was almost painfully moving, day by day, to watch these people ripening to citizenhood before our very eyes, with no tragic foreknowledge of the future. The world they lived in must have seemed permanent to them, but we could see that it was built on sand, and could be rubbed out in an instant by an invisible, mighty hand, like a sum on a blackboard with the wrong answer. It calls for great inner serenity to be able to draw such a line, arching back to ancestors who are like characters from Gustav Freytag, but I think such serenity must have been inborn in you, and you developed it instinctively in the course of your eventful life, so that it has been the dominant element in your spiritual existence. I was often reminded of Jane Austen, whose style Lord David Cecil (a great essayist, and I'm sure you find him 'sympathisch') holds up as a model to present-day authors, and I could wish that all young German writers were made to read your memoirs. But it's also a European book, if the word still means anything, if the mechanistic age we live in still allows the voice of organic European culture to be heard on the lips of its representatives: a citizenry stamped by the heritage of Greece and Rome. I am always pleased to see the Protestant Church in Germany standing up so bravely for the cause of humanity, under Hitler and now in the East. It is because German Protestantism has not altogether forgotten the Catholic ideal under the influence of nationalism, as must be abundantly evident to any reader of your book. I wish the English Archbishop, Dr Fisher, would follow the German example, instead of choosing this moment, when the Catholic Church is being so diabolically persecuted, to sneer at the martyrs and fawn on the tyrants, wagging his tail the while. No doubt he did it in a moment of panic at the total failure of the version of Protestantism forced on the English under Henry VIII. The outcome is that today they have virtually forgotten that their fate is inseparable from that of Europe. That kind of parochialism is, however, completely incompatible with the concept of a citizenry steeped in the joint Roman and Catholic heritage. So it is your duty, my dear citizen, Herr Theodor Heuss, to stay young until such time as the breach is sealed and the next generation but one is mature enough to take the torch from your hand in order to keep the flame alight.

212

Allow me to close by sending you my very best wishes for a merry Christmas and many heartfelt hopes for the coming year, and the same to your friends, and on behalf of my wife as well.

Auf Wiedersehen, yours gratefully and sincerely,   O. Kokoschka

To Henriette von Motesiczky

Villeneuve, 2. v. 54

My dear friend Henriette,

Olda and I were both very sorry to hear your news, but it's for the best for poor Marie. She had been ill for years, after all, and I often thought to myself that there was no hope of recovery. The fact that she lived as long as she did is entirely to the credit of you and Florizl, for the two of you had a relationship with her of a kind that one hardly dares to look for any more, since the masses rose to power, and completely transformed human relationships – so that the interests of the machine are served instead of those of the human being. Marie came with you when you left your homeland, and it was thanks to her that you did not have to live in a strange country, because you found that the word 'homeland' has more dimensions than the purely local one. For both of you, your homeland was reflected in good Marie's soul. There might be a danger that you will feel uprooted now that this piece of your homeland has been returned to the earth. But – to come back to the soul – there is no risk of being abandoned, for a human being's soul doesn't have a machine's heart and is therefore immortal. The masses believe the doctrine of man's descent from apes, but they overrate themselves: animals have instincts, but progressive man, modern man has nothing of that kind, nothing whatever, as the history of our time demonstrates only too abundantly every day. [. . .]

Don't weep for good Marie, she is at rest. Make your cherry strudel, your Salzburg dumplings and your rice pudding as good and tasty as she used to. May we perhaps invite ourselves to come and call on the two of you in the autumn? Or shall we perhaps see you here in our house in Villeneuve before that?

With love as ever,   yours, OK

Villeneuve, 26. XI. 54

My dear friend, dear Dr Furtwängler,

There is no one else I can talk to as I can to you. Your last visit here is now longer ago than I can endure, and I can't accept your absence as if it was a concert tour, or some other arrangement that you're obliged to honour. I would so terribly like to paint you, because the world will not know the like of you again. The mysterious musical spirit which fills you inspires everyone who has the luck to hear you, and he is left desolate until you make that spirit resound in his soul once more, and then again and again. You are the only musician still alive. You are about to enter a new phase in your life, but with the aid of a benign providence you will survive this harshest of trials. Your will, all your knowledge and experience, all the physical inessentials, even the weak and fearful body will recede into the background in the face of the sudden happiness of spontaneous creation after the catharsis that you will have to undergo, just as Beethoven had to in his loneliness, as no one knows better than you. Think of it as a fire consuming everything that we have carried around with us without noticing how the age, the general situation and the particular circumstances of our individual lives have heaped it on us – and stopped you bursting into song like a lark spiralling up into the sky over a field on a spring morning. You are unhappy because you haven't yet done what you were created to do. You experience it as a fear of something that you can't define, you think and persuade yourself that this or that is behind it. Even your illness and weakness are a way of escape, or rather, of hiding like a child from the wonder that is waiting for you behind the curtain of your soul. You must not be so ungrateful to providence. You must not think of throwing your life away like an empty sack! The only thing we ought to fear is not having made good use of all the potential that was in us. Don't weaken even by half! Life is so unfathomable that we have to survive the test with patience, like Job. I was shot in the head, a day later I had a bayonet through my lungs, and was alone for a day and a night. Only my dying horse, kicking me in its death throes from time to time, woke me from the lethargy that could have ended in my death. And so I learned that we only have this one time to live as the person we entered the world as. Without a doctor, without provisions, without a régime, without help, in the swampy forests of the Ukraine I made up my mind to live, and I survived. Do the same, my dear friend, and then you will have experienced the wonder and will never forget it. Everything else is unimportant by comparison. Your temporary problems with your hearing will get better if you're patient. Let *Zauberflöte* give you catharsis, with my loving help, put off the American tour, let that old tomcat Toscanini put himself about for one more year as undisputed king, just as

I let my pal Picasso carry on with his little jokes until I'm ready to sort him out. Then we'll go to Greece together, and kneel down on the Acropolis in the morning light to give thanks for our human existence, for being alive and able to leave a record of our life's work, praising providence for your recovery!

Will you, my very dear friend?!   With love, yours, O Kokoschka

I look into the human heart, that's why I'm right. As a painter I am distinct from portraitists in the same way as you are from 'modern' musicians.

To Alice Rosenlew
[Villeneuve,] 28. XII. 54

My dear Colibri,

What a lovely letter, a sign that you remember me, after all this time. Why didn't you enclose some photographs of the two daughters, who you claim to be so pretty, and just the right age to be introduced to life by an experienced man? I too am still very pretty, but then, I always was. When are you coming here? Olda says you cut a very good figure, so come straight after New Year.

With regard to Aalto, the two million kilometres he has under construction matter less than what he could give to the young people I expect to collect about me in Salzburg, 19 July to 15 August, half of them from America; there were 120 students last time. Someone has got to do something to stop all the imagination in the world being ground down to nothing. There is a campaign afoot to make people lose the habit of seeing – hearing too, to judge by the latest UNESCO session, where physicists, sound-engineers and 'composers' are experimenting partly with real old music, interwoven with atonal and natural sounds, partly with every conceivable kind of machinery and noise-producing instruments. God-less time-wasters, all of them living off the 'dumb' American taxpayer who has no opinion of his own and believes in 'progress' as devoutly as I believe that the stork brings babies. I'm afraid I can't move my summer school to the winter for the sake of your Finnish summer holidays: it must coincide with the festival. An American architect like Johnson or Mies van der Rohe, who build for millionaires (only there aren't any any more), is precisely what I don't want, nor do I want Corbusier, who builds nothing but giant cages for the bureaucracy through whom the workers of the world will be governed from a world centre in the régime of the future. I would like a Finnish or a Danish master-builder who understands how to use the indigenous building materials to create places for country people to live in: houses that belong organically to the soil, and at the same time benefit from all the recent technical innovations, so that people's brains don't turn to pulp in the country, and make them move into the cities to add to the proletarian masses. What is needed to stop the flight from the land is a farming collective, in a modern, humane sense. The Scandinavian countries have been gaining practical experience in just that for the past hundred years, with the result that Scandinavian culture is *de facto* a modern farming culture, and that's why I'd like to have a master-builder from up there. But he is not to flirt with 'the art of our time', as they call the 'abstract' muck of those designers of fabrics for American neckties, who've escaped from their cage. Everyone in Germany is wild about it at the moment, just as under Hitler they believed the visual arts ought to allow you to count the hairs on the thighs of nude female models in your sleep. They woke up from that dream to find darkness all around them, but then they promptly fell asleep again to dream the 'abstract' dream, in which they all wish to express or share in an inner life. Impossible, unfortunately, because Germans eat too much sausage. Now, however, it's just the same in France, England and America, and so I want to amuse myself by scattering a few grains of sand in Salzburg Castle, to disturb the merry, frictionless running of the modern mass brain-pulper.

There's no literature, because I've neither the time nor the desire to start a reform 'movement'. All I want around me are young people who are desperate because, now that there are no more artists, but only hydrocephalics and barbers, no one gives them the things to listen to, and above all see, that went with culture, humanity and individual achievement to create a civilized society in centuries past.

Please write to Aalto for me, and ask him if he values his contracts more than young people. If he doesn't want to do as I do, and give up a month in the summer for this project, perhaps you know another architect from one of your rustic countries who has not been spoiled in Paris, and is an individualist. I owe it to these young people who idolize me (and there are always some very pretty little dolly-birds amongst them!), and therefore expect me to recruit the right person for every department – architecture in your case – so that the 'School of Seeing' founded by me sets an example for similar efforts which are in the air. It's only the terrorism of the genie of 'abstraction', together with the art trade, the world press and the political background (it's no mystery to me why that should promote mass brain-pulping so vigorously), which stands in the way of a humanitarian and humanist education of society, such as art always nurtured in the past.

Please let me have a practical answer soon, because the prospectuses should have been ready in Salzburg long before this, and they are waiting for my decision. I think it would do Aalto good, incidentally, to have a bit

216

of fun with me in Salzburg. It's so sad that my dear, brilliant friend Furtwängler has died. I was to have done *Die Zauberflöte* with him there, and join him in enraging the abstract and atonal hydrocephalics. We loved and understood each other very well. Now there is nobody of my calibre left in the world, brrrh. Bring the Russian ballerina with you, if you come with Niels, Ennehjelm has gone too, and Damaris is God knows where, and unfaithful to boot. Are there any beautiful girls at the dance school? Most Russian girls are fat and *swarthy*, aren't they?

If Aalto comes this summer, I'll visit Finland afterwards and paint something extraordinary there, because there have always been strong roots binding me to Finland since my earliest youth. I will get you priority for him, because I'm virtually co-regent of Austria! I hope you're still pretty! Come soon, both of you, auf Wiedersehen and *Happy New Year* 1955,   your OK

Wilhelm Furtwängler in memoriam

Villeneuve, 28 January 1955

It is hard for those who did not attend the burial of Wilhelm Furtwängler's mortal remains to believe that this artist of genius is dead; yet there are others who will never know their loss, because they had no direct experience of his art. He was a messenger from another world which held him in thrall, and from which he broke out with elemental force simply because he had to make his message known. It may be that with him the world loses the last man never to know what it is that the time-servers in our society recognize each other by: the style expressed in the art of our time, with its lawlessness and transient effects achieved at no matter what price. Here I think in particular of Germany, whose government paid the artist no mark of respect at his funeral. And yet this was the man, surrendering his life to art, rather than his art to the age, whom pre-eminently we have to thank for the fact that in those days of spiritual perplexity some sense remained alive that there is a world of the spirit, founded on an existence which is independent of fashion, ideology or terror, and abides in the inner vision.

Now it has come to pass that a potential world, such as Furtwängler's interpretation revealed in Beethoven's symphonies, has been extinguished with the human brain where it found its natural form. We must ask ourselves, then, what killed Wilhelm Furtwängler, if not this same self which alone was able to preserve that inner world. Or is it not the case that he made himself ready for the last journey with such lucidity and determination that all would have thought it presumptuous to hold him back? The only thing we could even attempt was to console him for the failings of the present time. Socrates' friends also pleaded with him in vain to turn his back on ungrateful Athens – live in another city! But no one can live in another time, and for that reason Wilhelm Furtwängler, kindly as ever, pointed the way into the kingdom of the shades as the only escape.

A rare human being, imperturbable in an age like ours, in which a human bearing threatens to become as unfamiliar as the spirit of classical antiquity already seems to the people of today, and as incomprehensible. It is said: 'A man must live!' No, there's no compulsion! The prayers of our nearest and dearest, the skill of the doctors, are of no avail when there is no will to live. He may have thought so. Do not the preachers already tell their congregations to cease listening to the bells, and hear the sirens of the temples of technology instead, because that is where the pulse of the future beats?

Even in the obituaries, it continued to be a reproach against this German that he did not seek safety in a foreign country while the spiritual plague raged in Germany. He remained misunderstood in his unceasing struggle against the obscurantists, those to whom 'the language of their fate no longer speaks in art' – a circumstance which 'has made art redundant from within'. The obscurantists today set up a 'modern' music, suiting the fashion of the time, in opposition to a 'classical' art of the past, which the historians have isolated from the living organism of music. He must have feared that victory would not be his, having suffered as no other artist did from the fact that his opponents, knowingly or not, strove to serve the mechanistic idea of progress by subjugating that realm which is God's, not Caesar's.

I find it very hard, now, to write a last farewell to the friend I revered so greatly – the friend whose visit to our house, only a few days before he entered the sanatorium in the Black Forest where he was to die, gave us no reason to fear that we would never meet again. I would have been the last person to imagine that his sudden illness might end in his death. It so happened that the youthful spring in his step as he came across the lawn towards us caught my eye, and I looked very closely at his legs, which showed no sign of the unsightliness of age. And each hand was a separate, individual entity, with a refined organization of its own. The large, wide, radiant eyes beneath that mighty forehead! Those brows should have worn laurel, and it is beyond my comprehension that they were so soon to wear the glass panel with which we cover the face of death!

He was a seer. We were standing in front of my painting *Thermopylae*, when he started to speak, or rather think aloud, quite clearly and distinctly, and yet in a manner that was not of this world. All of a sudden I was convinced that my guest was passing a mysterious commission on to me. And yet he had watched the making of this picture from start to finish. As if I had to speak of a vision, all I can say in my amazement is

218

that, isolated as he seemed in the eyes of all men, he looked across to us from the spiritual world.

Our contemporaries have nothing in common with that spiritual world, and have run aground in those leaky conceptions of 'the art of our time' which are now widespread. Just as it was given to initiates in the age of barbarism to read the written word, so it was given to the tone-poet Wilhelm Furtwängler to see directly with his eyes, because he was one who knew. I already regret having betrayed so much. For we should also remember that he said that those who know can say as little about Beethoven as the Christian can of belief. Oskar Kokoschka

To Carl Jacob Burckhardt

Villeneuve, 24. III. 55

Dear Dr Burckhardt,

I would very much have liked to thank you in person for your gifts, first Charles V, and now this wonderfully drawn portrait of Maria Theresia. Once I have Prince Eugene from you as well, these three stars in my old Austrian heaven shall be encased in the noblest binding a Florentine bookbinder can make, and stand on my bedside table for as long as I live. Unlike the romantic historians to be found in France, for example, your inspiration is not that of an epigone who, like ivy, sucks life from the stem and weakens the tree. Your inspiration is the much rarer one of someone who knows, a new shoot sprouting from the tree, from the same roots, even when time – or perhaps lighting, or the stupid haste of little men who must always see everything levelled – has already destroyed the majestic plant itself. The English will never understand either our heroes or your depiction of them, because they cannot afford to admit the truth of it all without abandoning their claim to the rights of a master race. I'm still waiting for an answer to the reviewer in the *Times Literary Supplement*, and I'll ask Stephen Spender to read your books. Would it be a good idea to send them to him, and say it was done at my request? I've had 'flu, and couldn't shake it off, and that's why I couldn't accept your kind invitation. I would have greatly enjoyed talking to our friend Gubler about your books, they are so full of ideas and so well-written.

With the very best wishes to your family from both of us,

yours gratefully, O. Kokoschka

Villeneuve, Vaud, 28. III. 55

Dear Dr de Wilde,

I want to congratulate you on the acquisition of my picture *The Power of Music*, which I painted in 1919 after recovering my health against all expectation. It was bought from Paul Cassirer of Berlin for the once world-famous Dresden Gallery in 1920 by its then director, the far-sighted Dr Hans Posse, who rated it a major example of Expressionist art. The artist was outlawed under Hitler, and his painting pilloried in that disgraceful show in Munich – like everything produced in the artistic renaissance which was just beginning to stir in every country in Europe – but it was auctioned in Lucerne and thence made its way to America.

Expressionism – it is perhaps not too much to call it Europe's last artistic statement – may seem to be finished from the standpoint of today's fashion in art. If that is the case, it is rightly so, for the spirit of uniformity and collectivism was as alien to the pronounced individualism of that age, as the rules, theories and ideologies of the present would have been to Expressionist artists. People hope that a global artistic style will spring from these rules, theories and ideologies in the future, benefiting from the popularization of a formal repertory which is for the most part non-European in origin, but unless this last is convincingly assimilated in organic creative processes, the synthesis they seek is not likely to happen of its own accord.

A spiritual confusion similar to that of the present day reigned once before in Europe and England. The individual's understanding of life, the social order, the world view, were displaced by a new rationalism, but the speculative philosophy of the Reformation lacked the depth of ideas and the formal genius which would have enabled it to arrive at a new understanding capable of establishing a new world view in the place of the old one, with its reliance on tradition, magic and religion.

Then a new artistic age dawned in the Netherlands as the creative expression of the new middle class, and it dominated until the pre-war period, revealing in naturalism an understanding of life which did not contradict rational ways of thinking. It was a cultural achievement of outstanding importance and every European owes your nation a profound debt of gratitude. It has long been my wish, therefore, that my work should find a permanent home in your country.

It is impossible for me to give you any explanation of my painting, it would require an ability to analyse the creative process which comes naturally to the present age, but not to me. For me, as for the painters of the Dutch School, light and colour alone make visible a world which has become invisible to the garrulous apologists of non-objective art, inasmuch as it is incomprehensible.

I beg you to excuse my delay in replying, I mislaid these notes. I hope you will send me a copy on publication.

With the very kindest regards,   yours sincerely, Oskar Kokoschka

To Elisabeth Furtwängler
Hotel König von Ungarn, Schulerstraße, Vienna I
7. 6. 56

Dear Elisabeth,

I was dumbfounded to get a letter from you, and such a nice one too, after having been such poor company throughout the whole trip, or most of it, leaving everything to you two, not lifting a finger to help (I opened the petrol tank once, and afterwards I wasn't sure if I'd screwed the cap back on properly or not). I just let you drive me about and lead me everywhere. Shame on my grey hairs! But you were so lively and receptive, and now at last I realize how glorious everything was! The sculpture at Khalkis was the most beautiful I've ever seen, how can a mere mortal be such a great artist – and Titian was another.

I shall see young Roman tomorrow and give him your stamps – very many thanks! I like the kid so much. I've nearly finished my painting. They rigged up the lights again especially for me, and the opera house will be floodlit until the 24th of this month. I paint from 5 in the afternoon until 10.30 at night, with an hour's break, because I want to get home to Olda and you again soon. I've had a wooden cage built for me on the seventh floor of the Heinrichshof, which is still covered in scaffolding, and at night I'm sure I can hear ghosts in the vast empty building.

In Bonn I shall listen to what Dr Tiburtius (is that his name? the man from Berlin) has to say about the spiritual health of the nation, and make up my mind afterwards. The leading personalities, with the exception of François Poncet and perhaps Ambassador Conant, about whom I know nothing, are second-raters, every man jack of them. And a 'reading' of one of my plays would be like hearing a symphony played on the piano. But perhaps I'll go to it after all, since you, my dear friend, recommend it. Olda is to eat properly and not take too much on herself.

With my best wishes to your Maréchal Niel roses, and yourself, and Kathrin and all the children,   yours sincerely OK

To Carl Jacob Burckhardt
[Villeneuve,] 5. 11. 56

Dear friend, dear Dr Burckhardt,

We don't know if you had already returned home from your travels before the slaughter of a defenceless, heroic people, who wanted nothing but their freedom, was allowed to go ahead without civilized humanity bestirring itself to more than 'sharp' protest. It was of course the right moment for a new hammer-blow, and it will be followed by others, for they could be certain that the West itself, pursuing its own shortsighted and lawless policies, would disavow the moral consensus, established by the Nuremberg hearings, that war criminals ought to be put on trial. The warrant for this is the appeal to the human conscience as the authority which even sovereign states, if they call themselves civilized, have undertaken to submit to or at least acknowledge.

Listening to the radio in Switzerland this week, we could follow the course of the Hungarian tragedy as told by eyewitnesses, up to the last SOS, and the last breath drawn in truth.

We came to the conclusion that the only explanation for the fifteen abstentions at the plenary session of UNO (the eight Noes from the Eastern bloc don't surprise anyone!) is that the delegates in question had only a vague idea of the character of this uprising by a nation in torment. It is hard to imagine that those people could have abstained like that if they could have listened, as we could, to the direct reports from the lips of the insurgents themselves and on-the-spot observers, from start to finish of the tragedy. The immeasurably important contribution made to Switzerland's humane work by the gentlemen of the Red Cross, Swiss reporters, and the Swiss French- and German-language radio must not be allowed to be forgotten. The radio stations also gave instantaneous translations of Hungarian speakers, such as the Hungarian professor who admitted that his students paid no attention to his Communist lectures, which had made him stop and search his heart, and the wounded peasant who was asked if he trusted President [sic] Imre Nagy, and answered, Yes, if it could be proved that Nagy had not called in the Soviet troops, and a great deal more very impressive stuff!

My dear friend, I'm writing to ask you to use your influence with your friends in the Red Cross and UNO in order to arrange a plenary UNO session in memory of the Hungarian people, at which a tape of the most important of those eyewitnesses could be played, because it makes all the difference if an experience is heard at first hand rather than summarized by a second person.

The Soviet delegate to UNO lied when he claimed that the entire national uprising was nothing more than a putsch by anti-Communist reactionaries, for which the West is to blame. It could be refuted if the Red Cross presented UNO with a list of the refugees who reached Vienna, including the statistics of their backgrounds, occupations, class and age-group.

I hope that this request is not a nuisance, and also beg you to excuse this letter which I have written much too quickly and excitedly.

222

Perhaps you will find a chance to have a word in the appropriate Swiss quarters, and lend your authority to our idea, if you think such a move would serve a useful purpose.

With the most affectionate and cordial greetings to your family and yourself from both of us,   Oskar Kokoschka

To Theodor Heuss

                                           Villeneuve, 24. xi. 56

Dear Herr Bundespräsident,

I'm afraid you must submit to a tidal wave of delayed expressions of thanks. I have been completely immersed in designing a *Midsummer Night's Dream* for England, but at last I have my head above water, and can begin by thanking you for the invitation to meet Raab. I would have been very glad to meet that courageous man, who has demonstrated once again, during the bloody tragedy of Hungary, the difference between the old Catholic humanist culture and the cultural twaddle of time-servers: namely that one does not bury one's head in the sand or adopt 'leave me in peace' as the basic principle of co-existence, and that the idea of a fellow human being is not an abstract concept, whatever the Communist fellow-travellers among the cultural apostles may proclaim. Today Austria is shielding 50,000 more refugees from the butchers, in addition to the 50,000 who were already there, in spite of the fact that those butchers are no more than a half-hour tram-ride away from Vienna, and the Austrians know very well that nobody in the West would lift a finger if their country joined the seven other nations along the Russian frontier and disappeared for ever. There is an inner sense of freedom that has nothing to do with the 'abstract idea', or else nations like the wonderful Hungarians could live in 'abstract' freedom. It was for people like them that I painted my *Thermopylae* two years ago. [. . .] We have fine words to utter, and tears to shed for our brothers on the other side of the frontier of *Realpolitik*, may the devil take it! I wrote a little book of stories last winter which is out now, called *Spur im Treibsand*, published by Atlantis in Zurich. I recommend it to readers in Germany in particular, for the above and other reasons.

To proceed with my thanksgiving: my sincere thanks for the little portfolio of your drawings, proof that healthy eyes are always ready to do their job, if only one keeps them open. Thank you also for the kind accompanying message. Finally, in order not to subject the eyes of the father of his country to unnecessary strain with my handwriting, which I know looks as if a hen has dipped its claws in the inkpot, thank you for the speeches on cultural topics. I want to read them again, however, in a more relaxed frame of mind, before daring to say anything about them.

At the present moment I am too upset by the concrete fact of genocide proceeding without a single technical hitch, and with no prospect of a Nuremberg trial to follow, to have any emotions left over for what anyone – even so eminent an authority as yourself – has to say about the 'abstractions' of cultural fashions.

May I also thank you, dear Herr Bundespräsident, for conveying my best wishes to our worthy Bott.

That really is the end. With the warmest regards from us both, as ever

yours, O Kokoschka

To Edith Hoffmann-Yapou

Villeneuve, Vaud, Suisse, 7. XI. 57

Darling,

I saw your article about the Welz book in Florence and was very touched by it. How cleverly you adduced the solid evidence for Wingler's claim that I dropped straight from heaven as a painter, without fathering me on influences from left, right and centre, as art-historians invariably do. Breughel, yes, I'll admit to him, and Maulbertsch too, whose name now begins to mean something even in the USA, since my pupils have been telling the people there about him. I just get hot under the collar when people wish on me godfathers like Soutine, for example, as they keep on doing in the USA, although Soutine himself writes in his diary of how excited he was by my exhibition at [the Galerie] Georges Petit, when he had only been painting in Paris a short time himself. Not that I have anything against him. He and Chagall were and remain the best of the younger painters who were there then. It's a great shame that he died before he could develop properly [. . .] You are sweet and lovely, and to think that I used to take you round the Dresden Gallery when you were a little girl! And your book is still the most human, even if the Americans have given up reading and watch television instead.

We were supposed to fly to Minneapolis on 15 November, where I was to do some teaching and painting, but they suddenly started making difficulties about visas. As if I'd invented the Sputnik, or some other evil-smelling thing that will now take people to the moon. Wasn't it fun flying kites on Hampstead Heath, in spite of the ack-ack guns! And how lovely you were, and how jealous I was of Yapou, who was always sleepy! How old is your daughter now?

All my love and auf Wiedersehen, your OK

In Salzburg this year I had 182 students from 22 countries, including Chile, Brazil, Finland, Egypt, Turkey and Israel, all enormously enthusiastic.

To Max Brauer

Villeneuve, 19. 3. 58

Dear Herr Burgomaster,

Your plenipotentiary, my dear friend Carl Georg Heise, has accomplished his mission, and has charmed me into selling my best painting, *Thermopylae*, to the University of Hamburg after all. Had you not been re-elected Burgomaster, I could not have brought myself to do it, because a great deal more water will have flowed down the Elbe before this painting is really understood. It certainly won't happen before the humbug of so-called 'non-objectivism' in the visual arts is finally recognized for what it has been all along, in the background: the complete destruction of German roots. The Germans have buried their heads in the sand for the time being, and think history will overlook their fault in turning their backs on the facts of life. They take a romantic line, go overboard about rehashed Arts and Crafts – with African seasonings à la Guernica, or Bushman art – and think they can go back to Stone Age naturalism, but the fact remains they're Europeans: the European soup has been long in the cooking, and they've got to drink it. Being European means keeping up a constant fight against the barbarian inside oneself. 'To be a human being, it is not enough to be born: each of us has to become one', a Greek philosopher said. That is what my painting says. The figure of Freedom faces everyone who passes in front of the picture, holding out her hand to him. Freedom can only be gained individually, never collectively! I invented a perspective construction especially for this symbol, it has never been used before. Let's hope the students will take it as an example instead of believing what they hear from the art critics, who don't understand art because they never learned to see and don't want to!

Dear Herr Brauer, please go to Munich and take a look at my life's work! It will never be collected together from the four corners of the earth like this again. Fifty-three years of painting. Thank you most sincerely for your faith in me, and I wish every success to your years in office.

With love, as ever,   yours, O Kokoschka

To Josef P. Hodin

[Villeneuve,] 12. 5. 58

Dear Magister,

I'm curious to see what the Eindhoven painting will look like in large-scale colour reproduction, and what my dear Hodinus will say about it. Do please go to Vienna to see the exhibition. In our 'non-objective' epoch, especially now that they have the *action painters* from the USA to add to the chimpanzee shows at the Institute of Contemporary Art, it is the last to breathe the spirit of Western art. It may even mark the completion – i.e. the end – of the European mission in art, because no new life is going to grow from technological civilization, that's for sure!

The Power of Music and *Strength and Weakness* were both titles I gave the painting. 'Strength and Weakness' referred to the colours, yellow, red, orange, hot, blue-cold, fading, feminine colours. 'The Power of Music' to the subject, because a trombone fanfare, yellow, shoots out of the painting, and the immense, radiant mass of colour (radiant as stained glass, Rouault never managed to do anything like it, Van Gogh is matt and whitish-grey by comparison!) begins to tremble like a living organism set in action. This is '*action painting*' in the true sense of the word, and there are no other examples of it in the entire history of art, except for Grünewald in Colmar, Dürer's Apostles in Munich, Titian's *Pietà* in the Venice Accademia. The painting is in fact the outcome of the whole series of my Dresden experiments to draw heat and cold from colour. You ought to see it in the original, I had the chance to do so recently for the first time in thirty years, and I was speechless, because I had just been to a giant Van Gogh exhibition in New York, and it was fresh in my memory. It was the actual power of the music of colour, of which a Russian philosophaster and romantic babbler like Kandinsky can only dream, while never having managed to produce more than a homunculus from a test-tube. But that's good enough for the abstract Sputniks!

My best love to Pam and yourself,   yours, O Kokoschka

To Helene Kempff

Villeneuve, 26. 6. 58

Dear Madame Kempff,

Thank you for your beautiful letter, I can scarcely recall when I last had the pleasure of receiving such kind words and praise from a kindred spirit. Now I can revel in the double joy, not only of having heard Wilhelm Kempff play but also of being able to count him, and through him you, his lovely and love-inspiring wife, among my very few true friends. Olda, too, was very touched by your spontaneity and the gift, which is so rare nowadays, of understanding with both the heart and the mind simultaneously. It is moving to find it again in your letter, and we are both looking forward to September. For the present, we wish you the best of weather for your holidays, and say a sincere 'thank you' to your husband for the Bach recital, which he remembered to send without delay. It must have been very moving when he played it in that unhappy city in the cause of good.

All best wishes to both of you and all the girls,

yours gratefully, Oskar Kokoschka

226

To Alfred Marnau

[Würzburg,] 26. 8. 58

Dearest Fred,

We've been to see your wonderful Riemenschneider and the imperial Tiepolo. What a miraculous accident that those airborne Zulu Kaffirs managed to miss this wonder of imagination and (God-given!) fantasy. Let the *tachistes* mourn, for us 'monks' it is a benison in a barbaric age. Much love to Corinna, Senta and yourself, ever yours, OK

To Helene Kempff

[London.] 18 October 1958

My dearest belle Hélène,

He sat on a star, and we all came to marvel at his playing! It was a taste of eternal bliss. Much love and thanks, yours, OK

To Alfred Marnau

[Villeneuve, December 1958]

My dearest Fred,

You spur boldly across the Lake Constance of our existence, always seeing beneath its frozen surface the beauty that you seem never to have enough time to write about. For life is your game, and your steed's hoofs strike sparks from things that appear to have no surface but only depths and even greater depths. I'm so relieved to have your book again, and I shall never lend it to anyone again, because the you I find in it fully fleshed is someone who keeps himself well hidden the rest of the time. Senta, your dear wife, and Corinna, your elf, do God's work in seeing to it that you have a home where you can settle down again when you return to it after cavorting and galloping about from one year's end to the next. You are a travelling minstrel, a direct descendant of Walther von der Vogelweide, who has laid his hands upon you. The Red Cardinal was the lobster to whom you have written, glory be, the most beautiful ballad ever addressed to a submarine creature – the white shark included. Somebody gave me a bottle of Heidsieck, and Olda and I have just drunk it to the health of you three Marnaus, as a way of warding off the foul fiend who sometimes tries to blunt your courage. What you ought to do is write down everything that happens to you on bits of paper, and then at the end of next year pull one or other of them out of the hat, like the little boy drawing the lottery, and lo and behold, the Prince of Darkness will be unmasked as a pedantic member of a present-day society which has had the nerve to set itself up for the purpose of exploiting even poetry, the most elementary of our playful urges, for some utilitarian purpose.

227

And now, a very happy New Year 1959 to my three dear people, and all my and Olda's love and thanks for your existence.

Your *Commander of the whole British Empire*,   OK

[Villeneuve,] Christmas 1958

Dear Dr Angelus,

Because it is Christmas and because Sweden, in spite of her neutrality and without taking out political reinsurance, has awarded the Nobel Prize to a humanist for once, for a book which reminds us that man is a noble being, you shall have the autograph you asked for.

Christmas is a time for meditation. And it is certainly food for thought that a regime which adopted the policy of enlightening human society, and taught hundreds of millions of illiterates to read and write, has been so badly frightened by *Dr Zhivago* that it has forbidden the hundreds of millions to read it – and branded the man who wrote it a traitor.

It may be that the capitalist West was thinking primarily of the Christmas market in turning out hastily manufactured translations of this new gospel of neighbourly love, but that's only to be expected. The difference is that we in the West are not forbidden to read either the Gospels or Pasternak's book.

There is a necessity about what happens in 'the best of all possible worlds', as Voltaire reasoned.

Gold, frankincense and myrrh were the gifts brought to the Son of Man in the cradle by those who followed the star from the east; but the Nobel Prize is carried off by the people who have invented the Sputnik to be star and light for those who stayed at home.   Oskar Kokoschka

To Ernst Gombrich (original partly in English)

[Villeneuve,] 8. 1. 59

My dear friend Gombrich,

Many thanks for your kind telegram. I believe I have to congratulate you, too, on similar grounds. Of course I was pleased with the award bestowed on me by our most gracious Queen without being able to judge for myself whether my artistic efforts so far deserve such a shining triumph in the country where I had been received as a foreigner and where the nonobjective 'art' rules the day. I feel a little frightened between Sir Alfred Munnings and the action painters on the other side and still do not believe Botticelli and Burne-Jones to be *the* only way of escape.

Joking aside, would you come to Salzburg again next summer? Last year

I had 213 students in my class, including Indians, blacks and one Chinese. Unless I am run over by the proverbial bus, I shall take part in the School of Seeing just once more. My wife doesn't want me to, but this will be the very last time (as I say every year).

With warmest regards and best wishes for the New Year to you and your family from both of us,   yours, O Kokoschka

To Paul Westheim

Villeneuve, 29. 6. 59

My dear Paul,

First of all, I'm very sorry to be so late (it's because I've no sense of time), but let me wish you both very many years of happiness together. Ernst Rathenau has told me repeatedly how well suited you are to the lovely woman who is now united with you in the bonds of matrimony. You're such a marvellous chap that it does my heart good to know you have someone to look after you, so that you will be able to give your fellow human beings even more from your abundant storehouse of experience, enriched by your absolute spiritual and intellectual integrity.

You need only look about you – here in Germany, for example – to see these artistic dictators at their game. [. . .] In Russia the visual arts are used to serve political propaganda, but in West Germany a succession of scoundrels have succeeded in making such fools of people that they forget the heritage of Greece and Rome, and look for spiritual qualities in the daubs that not only the painters but also the monkeys in the zoo are forced to paint. Our society is ripe for Armageddon, and the atomic bomb is the tool of destiny. I'm re-reading Euripides' *Bacchae*, as it happens. You should do the same, my dear friend. All best wishes,

yours, OK

To Alice Rosenlew

[Salzburg,] 14. 7. 59

My dearest Colibri,

So, you and my elk-child have forgotten all about me, because I spent too long on my hands and knees in spoil-heaps piled up above the remains of Greeks, Arabs and Hohenstaufens. Do not punish me, even for what must look to you like the thoughtlessness of taking nearly a year to return Isolt von Marsanyi's very appreciative article about your nest. I'm afraid it's a bit crumpled, too, because I kept it on me, together with your and Marion's letters and pictures.

We got back scarcely a week ago, and today I'm already in Salzburg surrounded by my pupils and Olda will follow in two weeks' time. Then another eternity will ensue before she sends your letters back to you – but you have probably already realized that, since, as you are aware, we have no sense of time. She has a great deal to do, but has every intention of making copies of them. You're right, somebody ought to publish them, and there is a Dr Hodin in London who would be glad to do it, only first certain outbursts, indiscretions and names must be removed, which were meant innocently at the time but might cause unnecessary trouble now. I suppose you are already in your Glahn-land, watching the sun fall blood-red from the stormy sky into the sea, because the reeds cannot support such a burden of happiness. Spare me a thought, and I don't want the elk-child to run raging into the forests to escape me, either. Give our dear Niels a hug, and come and see us soon,   Ko

To Paul Westheim

Villeneuve, 8. 8. 6o

Dear Paul Westheim,
I've just heard from Dr Rathenau that there are some misunderstandings about Wingler's book. It doesn't clash with yours at all, it's to be a catalogue of the graphic works, something that's long overdue, and has been planned for years by Welz in Salzburg. [. . .]
Viewpoints for my drawings? I used as many vantage points as there are drawings – in some years I preferred drawing to painting. Love, or the urge to get on the trail of a lovely woman, make up a story about it, words to go with the paintings, and sometimes a kind of diary entry to help me remember something for ever, only very rarely a sketch for a painting, more like a shorthand character. But never an experiment or technical jiggery-pokery or any other of those tricks which are *de rigueur* in Paris. Always, first and foremost in importance, the purely human angle, the most personal and intimate of all. I can't think of anything to add to that, it was not for nothing that my first album of graphics was called *Der gefesselte Columbus*, the discovery of a predominantly feminine world, relating only to myself. Dear Paul, I hope you and yours are as well as may be, perhaps the two of us will come and visit you after all. [. . .]
With a loving hug,   yours, OK

To Wilhelm and Helene Kempff

Villeneuve, 23. 9. 6o

My dear Wilhelm and Helene,
I have nothing to say except I'm glad that you exist, and that my Wilhelm must indeed take a little rest until his hand is better. Helene has sent me several sweet letters, but I've been up to my ears in work, and surrounded by hordes of people, and moreover I have no sense of time. I

230

always meant to write back at once to thank you for being such dear, good friends, and so damned gifted.

You have been sad, my dear Wilhelm, but sometimes we have to be if we are not to forget that all love and dedication is within the bounds of human existence. Only the art of the demigods – Beethoven, Bach, Mozart, Michelangelo, Titian, the Greeks and Shakespeare – these transform even our span of life into an eternity, often in the twinkling of an eye. When it happens to me it's as if angels have appeared, a gentle draught from beating wings sends a shiver down my spine. You have made me feel that more than once. A warm, tender kiss to you and to my belle Hélène, and Olda too says I must give you her love, and auf Wiedersehen! Ever yours, Oskar

To Paul Westheim   London, 8. xii. 60
We hope to spend a few weeks at home,
from 16. 12 onwards!

My dear Paul,

I've been painting a portrait here, which is almost finished at last, but has taken more than six weeks. I have to have a *check-up* at the *hospital* on Friday, and hope to be finished with old Sieff (of world-famous Marks & Spencer) on Monday or Tuesday, but he is loath to let me go because he finds me so entertaining. I too am very much looking forward to the Rathenau book, and your preface in particular. I need something to cheer me up, because my beloved sister has died in Prague, alone, after long and very painful suffering. [. . .] For me it's like a knife in the heart, exactly like it was when my mother died. Tell Rathenau about it when you write to him. He's not to mention it when he writes to me, but he ought to know about it, and why I've not written a single line to him, or anyone else, for the past three weeks. I've dried my tears now, but I have awful dreams, probably from my bad conscience, because I could never bring myself to go to that god-forsaken land of Red Nazis to give her moral support and comfort. Nobody dared to associate with her, for fear of being denounced, I had to pay on the nail through devious, furtive channels for every brief visit – and still they let her die alone there. The Czechs are a degenerate lot, good enough to lick the Russians' boots, and they did the Nazis' dirty work for money, too – and afterwards protested that their hands were clean! I know well enough that comfort can't come from words, we must wait for the pain to burn itself out within us.

I'm not sure if I'm not too old to travel such a long way, dearly as I'd love to see you! Your plans for an exhibition in Mexico show how young you are – a month ago I'd have leapt for joy at your suggestion! Now I even intend to give up my summer school, in spite of all the joy and love and

231

recognition it brings me. I've run it for eight years, this year there were 254 in my class, literally from all over the world, but now nothing gives me any pleasure. Please ask Rathenau not to take offence if I still can't write to him. I don't want to talk about the thing that fills my heart, and the other matter is less important now. I wanted to write to you about it, but no one else. My very best wishes to you both for the New Year. Write, but don't say anything about this.

In love, yours, OK

To Walter Neurath

[Villeneuve,] 17. 5. 61

My dear Walter,

Your book, what a wonderful surprise! There's just one mistake on the jacket, which touches my cavalryman's honour: I was an Imperial and Royal dragoon, not an 'uhlan' or whatever. The colour and the printing of your two new pictures, *London* and *Logan*, are wonderful, much better than in the case of the *Davis Children*, for example, because that was a bad photograph to start with. Now I'm looking forward more than ever to *Spur im Treibsand*, and can't wait to see the *proofs*. I may obscure some names and places that are too obvious at present, to avoid hurting people's feelings. I'm sure you must have had good reasons for the title you've invented for the English readership? It's all right by me, because you know best, I only thought that a lot of my friends already know the German title, and are looking out for the book, and won't recognize it under the new title. Of course I bow to your superior judgment. I have one more suggestion: Harry Fischer of the Marlborough Gallery has two or three beautiful photos of a portrait bust of me that my poor dead sister and I made together last year, which is now being reproduced for sale by the Berlin Porzellan-Manufaktur. The head is enormously expressive, better than any death-mask will be when that day comes. I would so much like to have that photo somewhere in the volume of stories, if you agree.

Come over and see us soon, we'll be at home until the end of June.

A thousand thanks and much love to all of you, all the very best,

yours, Oskar

To Walter Neurath (final paragraph in English)

[Villeneuve,] 8. 6. 61

My dear Walter,
I write at once in reply to your letter, so as not to hold up the printing. You know very well that I'm looking forward to this book enormously. The only thing I have to say about our English friends' advice is that there were just a few things in the translation that I didn't think were in my sort of language, e.g. the frequent repetition of *'actually'* (I try to avoid using words like that, which don't say anything), and at the end of the Jessica story: *'even an old woman with a shopping bag'* – which doesn't convey the situation people were in in Berlin in those days at all well. Olda and I are in agreement on all the other suggestions, once she had read the stories aloud to me, so that our ears could test whether my text and the translation chimed together. For the most part it's fabulous. Don't lose heart, accept as many of my suggestions as possible after studying them objectively. We want the critics to praise the translation, at least, without any reservations. Of course not every suggestion is right, I'm not an Englishman, after all. The *jacket* is excellent. The colours you've chosen are just right, and I've long been completely satisfied with Eva's title, but please do put the German title and the place and date of the original publication somewhere inside. And perhaps the dedication to Olda could be something like: 'Stories told to my beloved wife Olda'.
What about a title like *'Steps in the Sand'*. Would it be any good? But no Blake please! I like my own cabbage grown in my own little garden better than any other, may it be as beautiful as possible. [. . .]   yours, Oskar

To Alice Rosenlew

[Villeneuve,] 25. XI. 61

My dear Colibri,
What a sad letter, and what a wonderful picture of the elk-child. Whatever has got into you? Of course Khrushchev is a mass-murderer, like every other ruler Russia has ever had, but at the same time he's as cunning as every other peasant, and won't push the Finns so far as to make them take up arms again. That would mean the end for those heavy boots of clay, which are just part of the political bogey. The bogey doesn't really frighten the West very much, but their primary concern is with business and trading with Russia. Both sides have an equal interest in that, so they won't let the worst come to the worst! Besides, don't you think that if the Finns lost patience, the Estonians, the Livonians, the Lithuanians and the Karelians wouldn't also come alive? And then the Hungarians, the East Germans, and even the Balkans in the end? Only the Czechs would shilly-shally, wondering if it would be in order for them

to pull down the 150-metre-high Stalin in Prague, or if it wouldn't be wiser to wait and see if a Stalinist-Molotovite group brings down Khrushchev. Don't worry, and don't worry about radiation fallout either. I'm convinced that the stench of low-grade petrol in the cities and the exhaust from the thousands of planes in the sky do far more to poison the atmosphere than megaton bombs – and yet the human race goes on living cheerfully in spite of it.

I'm not at my wit's end over the elk-child's future, only over ways and means of having her about me here, because I will not suffer any other man to have this divine child, least of all that sailor she has never mentioned to me. I'm jealous now, and no longer regard myself as bound by my promise never to write to her enchanting cousin in England. Tell her so, please! I don't even know Marion's address. I shall be here until 14 January, and then I have to go to Vienna. It would be splendid if you dropped by.

With a warm kiss for his Colibri, your Lover

To Walter Neurath

[Villeneuve,] 18. XII. 61

My dear, dear Walter,

It's nearly Christmas, and a New Year is upon us, for which we send our warmest greetings and sincerest good wishes to all of you. You have realized my dearest wish this year in preparing the English edition of my stories. I shall always be grateful to you for that, and I hope I shall get Mr Nobel's literature prize for it as well, once the poets of all the free and unfree small nations have been awarded this distinction for political reasons. The Kremlin's bootlicking scribblers have withheld the distinction from Pasternak, the greatest writer of our time, which is all that can be expected from slaves, although no one in Cambridge dared tell the spokesman for those riffraff so to his face.

Please use your authority in your publishing house at this final stage, to ensure that the book comes out as I want it to be for English readers. [. . .] I enclose the list of queries. [. . .] And the very last, but complete, misunderstanding, *Page 270: But that cry was* for *the dying Glasberg. – Doch dieser Schrei gehörte noch dem sterbenden Glasberg: 'The cry came* from *the dying Glasberg.'* It must be so. I'm no adherent of naturalism, and I can allow myself to take a liberty. Mimi and the heroine of *La Traviata* sing lengthy arias while coughing up their heart's blood, and Pavlov's decapitated dog's head forms saliva in its mouth because someone holds a sausage under its nose. Please permit me to do as much as experimental scientists! Let Glasberg's decapitated head utter its last scream, there's nothing else for him in this world, while Ann Eliza will go on living quite merrily. So

234

much for the text. The dedication less like something on a gravestone, but very simple, as follows: 'Stories told to Olda'.
And will the bust of me, done jointly by my sister Berta and me, come on the title page, as on the proof you sent? Please do this! Now give your eyes a rest.
With a big hug to all of you,   yours gratefully, OK

To Elisabeth Furtwängler

[Hamburg,] 23. 2. 62

Dear Elisabeth,
I was so glad to hear from you, your letter reached me before the two from Olda, after I likewise had been without news from Villeneuve since Sunday, and had worked myself up into imagining there must have been an avalanche there or something of the kind. Emergency services and official business had priority for telegrams, and I came a long way down the list. But there was nothing I could do about it. The telephone's working again today for the first time, I tried to call at 3 o'clock, as soon as I got back to the hotel, and again during the afternoon, and now (8 o'clock) I'm giving up.
Olda spoils her parents, if you ask me! It will only make it all the more difficult for all concerned when the time comes to break the habit. I've finished twenty-four lithographs, including tracing all of them – one or two I had virtually to draw again from scratch. Now it will be about ten days before I can see and approve the proofs. I'm going to pass the time painting fish, at a fish wholesaler's down by the Elbe. Today was the first day anyone could get there in a taxi rather than a boat. It will be rather cold, because everything's kept on ice, and there's a lot of stuff rotting on the wet floor. But I've taken it into my head to paint fish, they're rotting here anyway, and I wouldn't get the wide range of sea-monsters anywhere else. I shall be all alone in the storeroom on Saturday and Sunday, they've given me the key to their treasury.
Your quotation from *Pan* is the best, most moving and most heartless passage in the whole book. It's winter, alas, grey, frosty, wet and – I'm a fish – born that way; but at least I don't have to drink water while I still have whisky, which helps a bit.
Always thinking of you tenderly,   yours, OK

To Anna Kallin

My dear Mirli,

You've suddenly remembered me after all this time, and you're in for a disappointment when you see the grey-haired codger who was blond when you first knew him. I spent a whole month in Hamburg, working, eating absolutely nothing, because of the risk of typhoid, keeping body and soul together on whisky. The two of us are coming to London on Easter Sunday or thereabouts, staying at the Hyde Park Hotel, where I've already booked rooms. I will never do television in London again, those people are incompetent, but of course I'll do radio for you, my dear. Only on tape, however, so that I can make corrections, because my English is now very bad, from lack of practice. Even so, Deutsche Grammophon has made a very nice recording, 'Oskar Kokoschka speaks on his life and work – a self-portrait', which I did in both German and English. It's due in the shops at Easter. Also at Easter, Thames and Hudson are bringing out a first-rate translation of my stories under the title *A Sea Ringed with Visions*. You will recognize things from Dresden in it, but for the sake of the invented story – a nightmare which I find too beautiful to be able to bring myself to omit it (*Ostern auf Zypern*) – everything is fantasy, rather than exactly as it really was. I know you will enjoy reading it, no one else today writes or tells stories as I do!!! We must have your drawing, I'll write to the Marlborough Gallery. There is a photo of me in the book, very handsome, but also a bust of me on the title page, done by my poor dear sister, not long before she died in Prague, from where they wouldn't allow her to leave. It's an amazing likeness, me myself as on my gravestone.

Tempestuously embracing you, your Un

To a school-leaver

Villeneuve, 18. Nov. 1962

It appears from your letter that you are about to take your school-leaving exams. Your question shows me that you have formed an idea that I think is worth a little preliminary discussion. I have never claimed to be able to show anyone the right path to art. Even at my 'School of Seeing', I only promise to open the eyes of those who come to me. The sole purpose of the school is to make them aware of what 'seeing' really means. For most people it's nothing more than what the camera can do, taking in a moment in a purely mechanical way, functioning just like the retina of the eye. This never leads to the perception that conditions a spiritual and intellectual process – the first step, on the never-ending path to art, visual art.

Because most visual artists of the present day find that path too laborious, they let themselves be dazzled by society's fear of life, and close their eyes to the view of the world that should be nature and reality. The slogan 'abstract art' is used to conceal that fact. Now, all art is abstract in any case, but visual art has never been non-objective at any time in human history. Art without an object is art without form, chaos. Every creative human being is committed to the spiritual and intellectual process of perceiving unknown possibilities for human development. We do not have access to any other possible kinds of development, but the human ones are infinitely accessible to us. Every age also finds a form of its own in which to present previously unexplored possibilities objectively, so that they can be understood as part of nature. The alternative is defeatist drifting, as at the present time, which seems to lack a sense of direction, even in respect of yesterday and tomorrow.

Now for your question. I feel more affinity to the work of Anton von Webern than that of contemporary composers, because I have an especially clear perception of his creative sense of direction, as defined above. It so happens that yesterday I heard the Italian Quartet playing Webern's op. 28, followed by Beethoven's Quartet no. 11, op. 95. In both the late Beethoven and the Webern, who died too soon for his life's work to be called completed, the artist perceived a thing in nature such as had never previously been given a shape, and formed it to make an object in the work of art. Now, all of a sudden, the natural forms in human emotional life – dreams, fears, humility, the tenderness and the ravings of love, grief and mourning, even presumptuous curiosity, sounds which want to be regarded as having meaning in themselves, perhaps based on mathematical theories or dependent on the random output of electronic machines, or on the noise of the human race crammed together in a mechanized civilization, even folklore in the end – have been wiped as if with a duster from the blackboard of what human beings are capable of experiencing. Elemental natural forces such as lightning, thunder, or the roar of the sea, are disregarded altogether, or apparently not related to human beings. It's as if man has abandoned nature, and with it himself. And now, my dear friend, you will see the essential difference between the work of those two composers and the spiritual and intellectual attitude of society today, for which existence is non-objective. It is the difference between snow and ashes. Both cast a blanket of whiteness, but new green things are growing beneath the snow, while beneath the ashes something lies dead. I'm no musician, but from the language of old, deaf Beethoven and from that of murdered Webern alike I can hear things breathing in an air laden with ozone, the notes played when blades of grass and the stems of reeds brush together, harmonies like the ones heavy masses strike as they fall through the layers of air offering them proportional resistance, sounds like those of birdsong expressing things that only birds can understand, perceptions falling from my nakedness like veil after veil, when nothing utilitarian is left being done, or known, or seen, or heard. I repeat, I'm a layman, a musician would not need to turn lyric poet – as I have – in order to answer your question, but this is the way I must put it in words. Klee does the same, in the poetic titles he gives his paintings, lyric poetry has everything to do with words, and nothing with music, and it has to do at most marginally with visual art, as in the case of Klee, who you mentioned in this connection in your letter.

I hope you can be satisfied with this purely personal interpretation of where I stand with regard to the work of Anton von Webern, and I hope it will entertain you.

Best wishes,

yours, Oskar Kokoschka

To Marion Rosenlew

[Villeneuve,] 8. IV. 63

My dearly beloved Elk-maiden,

Here is a picture of me, taken last summer in Salzburg. I hope you won't be too disappointed, and look forward to hanging above your bed, so that you do not forget me altogether. I'm very sorry that the School is finished now, and also that you could not pass this way after leaving Gstaad to show me how fat you'd got and prove you hadn't broken your lovely long elk-legs. Next time you read *King Lear*, think of me with all the drawings, which you will see here one day, and with the stories I wrote about my life, which you must read to the very end (oh, please, for God's sake!), and then perhaps you'll believe that Lear's story is mine too. I can only draw and paint what I have lived myself, which is why I wear the visible scars on my skin, in order to prove it to those who won't take my word for it now. The present is a time, after all, when most people don't experience their lives any more, because they're not proud enough, and would rather approximate to the average than go at existence full-tilt, like an adventurous ride through time. Lear was a proud man, and measured people by his own yardstick. Finding them too small, he flew into a rage, and tried to force them to be like him, but they only laughed, mocked him, and drove him away. Still he believed that they only misunderstood him, until finally it dawned on him that they did not want to understand him, because it was not given to them to do so by destiny. Then he was alone and old, and the jewels in his crown were replaced by thorns. What you wrote and told me of your ideas about this tragedy was very beautiful. I was surprised that a young girl should understand so much so soon, but then I reflected that an elk-child is not like other children. Your home is not among the traffic in the streets, in houses with television and telephones, but out in the tundra among the endless lakes. I would like another picture of you, swimming or walking on the sand, under birches, eating red berries.

I love you, my elk-maiden, for as long as I live,   ever yours, OK

To Carl Georg Heise

Naples, 17. 5. 63

My dear Pasha,

Your Serene Highness's address on the subject of my triptych was so wonderful, warm and astute that I am truly filled with admiration for you, dear Pasha. A young person can understand it and still sense that something yet greater lies behind what you say. It is even more persuasive than your beautiful essay in the little Reclam book, especially for young people, which is the most important thing now, for my picture is in their keeping.

Hardly anything of what we older folk inherited has been passed on to the present generation – unadulterated materialism and brutish existentialism is all these poor kids get, the roots have withered, and a single generation can't invent a world to equal the one we had from the Greek tradition, where the gods were human and the men divine.

We're travelling about more or less aimlessly at the moment, more in the hope of experiencing that direct spiritual contact again – perhaps for the last time – thanks to the strength still radiating from a few great works. And tears spring to my eyes every time, because this most primitive and intimate experience of genius revealing itself may never again be manifested in Europe – not as an immediate human concern, at least, for the many generations who now live in the gigantic beehives that European cities have become.

I'm very much looking forward to seeing you again, my dear Pasha, after Salzburg. It rains every day here, and everywhere else we go. Take care of yourselves, both of you. Embracing you both warmly,   yours, OK

To Otto Klemperer

[Hyde Park Hotel, Knightsbridge, London,]
28. x. 63

Dear Otto Klemperer,

We were at the *Missa solamnis* – miraculous, the way you bring Beethoven to life in the midst of all the noise and racket of the present day. Thank God that you are there to wield your baton, so that instruments and voices could again lift human hearts towards the divine. The choir this evening was like a human race from some earlier time, perhaps from

classical Greece, resurrected in our day and age. How strange to be able to produce such an intensity in a few hundred people, so that they all sing as if with one voice. And what a blessing that you have this English orchestra, now that you no longer wish to travel so much: it obeys you as if you had cast a spell over it. A thousand sincere thanks to you, you wonderful, stubborn man, and equal thanks to your daughter who watches over you. I hope you will come to Lucerne one day, where there is a musical community – quite different from the abstract Zurichers.
I look forward to meeting you again one day,

yours sincerely, Oskar Kokoschka

To Paul Westheim

[Villeneuve,] 17. xii. 63

Dear Paul

You must be very happy to be in Berlin, and your wife too! It can't be too bad, either, to feast at Kempinski's after all those years of Mexican food! But don't catch a cold, the Berlin wind is bitter. I would have come and given you a big hug long ago, but I don't want to leave my little shack, where I paint and paint. Being at home again at last is such a joy, after the strenuous year I've had. Rathenau and I write to each other frequently, mostly about you. In spite of his eye-trouble he travels a lot, and will certainly see you before I do. Kinkel wrote and told me how eager you are to see and do everything, and how extraordinarily receptive your response to it all is. Bravo!

Why should you have changed? You have always been like this, and now you have the good Berlin air to boot! There's not much of Berlin itself left! I was there a few years ago, and a small avant-garde theatre did the third act of my *Comenius*, I was very moved. Perhaps you recall it: the visit to Rembrandt, who has just painted *The Night Watch* and had a vision. Perhaps Dr Reidemeister has a copy. You can see a plaster-cast of one of my reliefs, a potter, at the Berlin Porzellan-Manufaktur. The director's name is Franke: ask him to show it to you. Porcelain is not really the right medium for it, but I want it cast there in lead by Noack. Take a look at it, and also at the bust of me by my poor sister, who died in Prague. It is the best portrait of me. She was alone and isolated, and neither the Nazis nor the Communists would allow her to leave Prague. I suffered a great deal on her account!

Now both of you take good care of yourselves. A merry Christmas and a happy New Year from   your sincere friend OK

To Mariana Frenk-Westheim

[Villeneuve,] 22. 12. 1963

Dear Frau Westheim,

I have just received your news, and I am so very sad. Paul was one of the few people in the past, and almost the last one left today, who gave me a sense of security in my life, and made me believe in my work, regardless of all the rapid changes of fashion in art, especially in this century. He was a pillar of rock in an age when everything shifted like sand yielding to pressure. He was a man of vision. I don't speak of myself alone, but it is due to him that almost every second book published today is a picture book, not just in Germany but everywhere, in London for example, where forty years ago, before his series of art books, *Orbis pictus*, you did not see a single book about the art either of Europe or of other continents. Today there are more illustrated art books in Germany than dry treatises about art. He taught the world how to see in pictures, true to the precept of Amos Comenius. People still don't realize the importance of Westheim's part in this, and he won't be properly appreciated until it has been fully grasped. The secret is: as soon as people learn to see what they are doing, then it simply becomes impossible to commit mass crimes.

What a good thing he was able to see Berlin again, and have a foretaste of recognition in the country which drove him into exile. I heard from Herr Kinkel how lively he was in Berlin, full of curiosity and receptive to all he discovered. It must have given him a lot of pleasure and satisfaction. Returning to his country of exile after a time would have been sad for him.

Dear Frau Westheim, you looked after him and protected him, and he loved you very much. Bear your loss bravely. There is much that you will do for his work yet. Please let me have news of yourself from time to time. All my very best wishes,   yours, Oskar Kokoschka

To Friedrich T. Gubler

Villeneuve, 21. 1. 64

My dear Fritz,

Now you really must come and see us more often, even if it makes you seethe because I had a young lady here during your visit. I can't cut myself off from young people altogether, after having had to give up my 'School of Seeing' on the advice of Olda, who thinks you should quit while you're winning. But the ladies and gentlemen of the Abstract School will be relieved to have this thorn out of their flesh. You must read Dorothea Christ's article about Tobey in the latest *Werkheft* (with a large coloured illustration, all dots): she says it beats Altdorfer's *Alexander's Victory*. The *Frankfurter Zeitung* published a piece about Pollock recently (another dotty painter), saying that his work could be compared only to Michelangelo's frescoes in the Sistine Chapel. Long live negritude, from Mau Mau to the Nirvana of non-objectivity, before long we shall be able to set down the white man's burden on the moon, and no one will give a damn about it.

It was lovely to see you again, and so kind of Ella to regale us with quince jelly (incidentally, when are we going to see anything of Regula again?) and *Prinz Eugen* is a consolation in this democratic age. Thank you very much indeed for it, and for the Homer, the poor vagabond. When will the other three volumes of the *Prinz Eugen* come out, if ever? Life is too short. The author will never manage it.

Please call the architect, Spoerli, and ask him to get a move on with sending the plans etc. to our builder. He's had to put off building our room for the second time, until the spring now, because he hasn't heard a single word from Spoerli. Presumably he's taken on another contract, and we shall have to live in a wilderness of dust, with an army trampling all over the garden, until the middle of the summer. I haven't got that much longer to live!

I'm doing 'Odysseus's Return', but it looks to me as if I'm the one who will have to leave home. Let us hear from you again soon, take care of yourselves, both of you, and the willowy Regula, come and see us again, and be embraced by your true friend,   OK

To Wolfgang Fischer

[Villeneuve,] 12. 3. 64

My dear Dr Wolfgang,

We've just received the graphics catalogue with your conversations, and we're both delighted, it's beautifully produced and so simple, clear, just what was called for. The way you conducted the conversations, and present them to a public which nowadays knows nothing at all about art, is a real achievement, even if it may not be understood for some time to come. You have made me very happy, dear Dr Wolfgang. One day soon we will make a book aimed at an even darker, even more barbaric future, so as to leave a few visible traces of a more human past. The American devastation in the physical and moral spheres: Hiroshima, pornography, art reduced to dribbling [. . .] has bitten too deeply into the flesh of European society, and grinning Asia waits to pop the European missionary, or what's left of him worth eating, into the cooking pot. But we shouldn't be afraid of it and take refuge on the moon, I don't see any point in that, either. You're both enjoying it, now the birds are singing again, for as long as any remain to sing. Voltaire recommended cultivating the garden, instead of trying to change the world, and that's

242

what we intend to do. Give Harry a big hug from me, for having defied the non-objectivity of our life and times and produced such a beautiful piece of work as our graphics editions and this catalogue!!! Please embrace my favourite red-head, and let her embrace you from me, and tell Elfriede (my Isotta) not to forget me. My thanks, a hundred times, for everything,   your loving OK

To Elisabeth Furtwängler

[Freiburg,] 7. v. 64

My dear Elisabeth,
Very many thanks for your letter. I'm longing to be home, because it's been an exhausting time here. But if it turns out that once again you allow yourself to be seen only once a month (even if you are wearing your Polish hussar's boots and that flirtatious petticoat), then I shall have to turn hermit and procure myself a lion (maybe a stuffed one, because a living one would need too much attention, and might bite to boot) and live like St Luke or whichever saint it was.
Let us see you soon, on Saturday if possible, although then you will only be there for your precious Kempff and not for my sake at all.
Hearty congratulations on your newly acquired *Columbus*, although you ought not to throw all your money away!
I'm looking forward to seeing you soon, dear Frau Elisabeth,

ever yours, OK

Thank you for all your kindness to my Olda!

To Carl Georg Heise

[Villeneuve,] 23. 8. 64

My dear Pasha,
What better, I ask you, can a man do with his short life in this 20th century, then spin himself into a cocoon and shut the 20th century out? If a good friend then comes to his rescue and encourages him in his work, then it is no longer a matter of fleeing from the outside world, which drove him to despair and made him 'spin' (as we say in Vienna), far from it: believing the encouraging words he hears, he realizes that what he has done is create his own world. And he takes comfort. Thank you, dear Pasha, many, many thanks for your words of comfort. Your essay on the drawings was clear, a masterpiece of form, and so rich in its content. How you managed to write it in scarcely two days is simply astonishing!
At the moment we are fighting over our one copy of your biography of Warburg. The language, the presentation of a rich intellectual life in a style close to narrative, thrilling from start to finish, and thus 'history' as

story – it's masterly! I would have written to you straightaway, but I had bad bronchial catarrh, and it made me very tired. I'm all right again now, and hope that you two dear people are too. Please come and see us again very soon. Rathenau is looking for someone to write the preface for the third volume of OK's drawings . . .

All best wishes from both of us, and very warm regards, ever yours, OK

To Gotthard de Beauclair

[Villeneuve,] 11. 5. 65

Dear Herr de Beauclair,

I am glad the Ezra Pound meets with your approval. Please send the fee directly to him, through his publisher if need be, as payment for *his* poem. I don't want my name mentioned, it might embarrass him, and me too. You see, my dear friend, that persistence brings results in the end, even with me. I suppose you have a press agency. You should get them to send you the reviews from Munich, where I gave an impromptu speech on Bavarian Radio to more than 500 invited guests on 23 April, and from Hamburg, where I opened the exhibition of my graphics and theatre work at the Museum für Kunst und Gewerbe with another speech, on 29 April. Perhaps you would ask them to send me the cuttings too. [. . .]

I think your idea for a recording is excellent (I'd like a copy of that, too, please!), but for God's sake never mention this impending birthday again, or any future ones, if there are any. To the abstract non-objectivites it would be nothing more than the skirt of my robe, a chance to attack me, as breezy David did King Saul when he was answering the call of nature.

All best wishes,

yours, O Kokoschka

To Alice Rosenlew

[Villeneuve,] 23. XII. 65

My beloved little Colibri bird,

Alas, another New Year is upon us, and I'm getting older and older, and there's nothing I can do about it. I don't look any different, maybe I drink more whisky than I used to, but the leaves fall off the calendar faster and faster. It's because people don't have time any more, but rush about in supersonic aircraft and locust-swarms of motorcars, killing themselves in greater numbers than in both world wars, and on top of that they want to congratulate me on my birthday. I would gladly murder every single person who is going to remind me of that accursed anniversary, because I thought I still had plenty of time to be idle in, and take my ease. There's no lack of girls, they spring up like snowdrops in the winter of my *discontent.* Only my elk-child is careering about with a young man in the beloved Finland of my *Dreaming Youths*, without even reading it, because sheer young married bliss makes her too busy, although it's the most beautiful book of the 20th century. I wish her every happiness with her young man, even though he is merely a human and not an old elk stag like me. But you must not fret, my faithful little Colibri-humming bird. You still have me, and neither of us will ever forget the good old days we shared in Dresden. It won't be long before the spring flowers pop up again, and you will see the sunshine before we do. We scarcely caught a glimpse of it this year, with all the rain we had. Take care of yourself, think of me as fondly as ever, and let me embrace you,   your OK

To Konrad Adenauer

[Villeneuve,] 21. IV. 66
Please don't trouble to answer!

My very dear Herr Bundeskanzler,
Just a few words, so that you don't squander any more of your time on us – your valuable time must be given to your next political task alone. On behalf of my wife and myself, I want to tell you that our hearts fly out to you, and that we took our leave from you feeling enriched by the knowledge that a human being like you still exists! One further plea, concerning your visit to Israel: please excuse yourself on doctor's orders, white lies are perfectly in order, as soon as you detect the slightest sign that it's getting too much for you. After all, you have still to carry out the more important task which we talked about.
My warm thanks, once more, to kind, clever Fräulein Poppinga for everything, and also for undertaking to read to you from my story book in the evenings, so as to amuse you with the things I like to laugh at in myself – and a very warm embrace, and the most fervent wishes for the success of your journey.
Yours gratefully and very sincerely   Oskar Kokoschka

To Fritz Schmalenbach

[Villeneuve,] 12. XI. 67

My dear Dr Schmalenbach,
Thanks to your scientifically scrupulous analysis of my work, anyone who wants to write about art will follow your example, until such time as our hectic attitude to art gives way to a historically more lucid one. There is too much superficial writing about art at present – one might call it impressionist journalism – for the simple reason that people nowadays are more interested in technology, physics and space-exploration, and

that will continue for as long as the present wave of 'Völkerwanderung' lasts. Appreciating art is the preserve of periods where people are able to reflect; one such is bound to come along soon, just as surely as one followed the cultural chaos and the barbarian tide that inundated the Greco-Roman world when the Roman Empire came to an end. A few monks saved and translated the books of Ovid and Virgil, kept the classical spirit alive for future generations, while the manifestos, declamation, rhetoric of the age of iconoclasm faltered and faded. It is to the classical vision that mankind owes that particular species of the human spirit which enquires into causes and effects, and which we could perhaps regard as the thing that distinguishes Europe from the rest of mankind. The rest of mankind lacks the farsightedness, the historical consciousness which contrasts, I would say, with the capricious, magical world of the non-Greek universe. It's easy enough nowadays to show the credulous a canvas painted black, tell them it's the latest avant-garde art-form from Eastern Europe, and read a series of learned papers explaining its content, but teaching people to see, to use their eyes, will remain a pipe-dream for as long as the world and existence continue to be regarded as non-objective, like refugees. I have devoted more than sixty years to my trade of seeing the world with my eyes open. In the same curiosity about the associations of cause and effect, my dear friend, you have found my modest œuvre worthy of a study that I would like to describe by the simple word classical. Great as my gratitude must be, the future will have even more reason to thank you, for you demonstrate by example how to think about the visual arts. My thanks are late in coming. I read your book from cover to cover on the first evening, but I wanted to wait until I had a quiet day in which to tell you how delighted I am, dear Dr Schmalenbach. Is there any chance that you and your wife will be coming this way before long? It is time that we saw each other again. All best wishes to both of you, from my wife and from yours sincerely,

O Kokoschka

To Alfred Marnau

[Villeneuve,] 13. 1. 68

Dearest Fred,

What a delightful letter, full of 'Weltschmerz', far exceeding even my own profound antipathy, winter, Wilson, a reforming Pope, and the worldwide dream of Communist redemption in the paradise of the *peace marchers*. I just hope frost-bite doesn't get their toes. Herbert Read writes, idealistic chappie that he is, enclosing letters by Graham Greene for me to sign, as a protest against American terrorism; he himself has flown to the conference organized in Cuba by the bearded Fidel Castro. While students are being locked up in the USSR and the Czech SSR, German students are smashing windows in Berlin and elsewhere in the Federal Republic, and chucking rotten eggs at those who support Johnson and his peace-feelers – but they live off American grants! And the Pope never stops kissing the long-bearded representatives of apostate religions. All we need is another Makarios, to apply himself to finishing off the poor *Kümmeltürken*! Olda wants to go to Turkey, so that I can paint Constantinople again, because the Czechs will neither show my old painting nor let it be reproduced. The Nazis stole it from Mr Abacus, and now the Czechs say it is the property of the Czech people and have hidden it in the office of the Communist Commissar in Bratislava. I am even more afraid of the snow in Turkey than of the war, I feel for you in your troubles, dear Fred, but as a fellow Austro-Britisher I hope it will all pass and we shall survive. Things are bound to get worse, as they used to say in Maria Theresia's Austria.

Fondest love,   yours, OK

To Heinz Spielmann

[Villeneuve,] 10. 3. 68

My very dear Dr Spielmann,

We were very pleased to see the two of you here, and delighted to know the fans are in safe hands. [. . .] Since you were here, we have had a visit from Herr de Beauclair, who brought the first proofs of *The Frogs*, which have come out amazingly well. I gave him your letter with the warmest commendation – he will be writing to you.

I am giving thought to the interpretation of the fans. It is safe to say that I was influenced at the time by Flemish Books of Hours, and more especially by Irish illuminated manuscripts, particularly in the ornaments of the earliest fans, which are not decorative in intent but organic interwoven constructions of humans, animals, plants, spirits and winged beasts, as in the *Book of Kells*. On my mother's side I am remotely descended from Irish monks who christianized the Austrian Alps, and perhaps that justifies the thought that an atavistic throwback may have played a part here. When I was very young, I was always more excited by the imaginative monstrosities of Romanesque, Lombard, Celtic and Gothic ecclesiastical sculpture than by great art, of which I was still rather in awe, while the narrative style, with its wealth of associations, was a pictorial language that spoke to me directly, as do letters and diaries. My fans are love-letters expressed in pictures, as are my early plays and essays such as *Bewußtsein der Gesichte*. I knew nothing of modern art in those days (I'm talking about the time when I was studying at the Kunstgewerbeschule) and I would have been far too humble for high classical art to make any impression on me. I dwelt long in that state of spiritual arrest, all the while that I was writing and drawing *Die träumenden Knaben*, until a woman woke me and drew me into the realm of 'I' and 'Thou' and man and woman. The real reason why these fans are so important to me is that previously I had known only a timeless, vegetative existence, and thereafter I was confronted with 'life-time', and experienced the drama of being, becoming and ceasing to be; I became conscious of being actively one with life, which meant, in my case, seeking an artistic expression for my existence. I suppose that's what the term 'Expressionism' means, which was given to a period of change when suddenly young people expressed themselves in every area of European art.

All my love to you [. . .] for the fans,   yours gratefully, O Kokoschka

To Wolfgang Fischer

[Villeneuve,] 10. IV. 69

My dear Wolfgang,

Many thanks once more for your very welcome visit, marred only by the fact that it was over so quickly, as always, it's a shame. We're delighted that your exhibition is a success, and actually drawing a lot of young visitors, that's amazing! The catalogue is one of the most handsome I've ever had! Bravo! It's very sad that the British press gives the show too little space, or none at all. But there's nothing we can do about that. What has happened to the painting of Constantinople? It would have made a good pair with the New York one, to give an overview of my work in the last two years. But the exhibition is wonderfully well displayed in any case, and we two and Frau Furtwängler are looking forward to coming to London on 28 April to see it.

Please be kind enough to explain to Mrs Agatha Christie that I can't possibly paint a picture in three days. Lord Snowdon takes that long over a photo, and perhaps Graham Sutherland doesn't need many days more, but he usually arrives armed with two photographers, or so Adenauer told me. If she can't take the painting seriously, then it would be better to drop the whole idea, because once I start something I take it very seriously. Furthermore, it would cost her a pretty penny. Penrose's four Picassos, for example, are worth more than 700,000 marks today, more than a good Rembrandt, and Henry Moore's casts cost the same, why should I sell myself cheaply? But while I may be expensive, I don't turn out rubbish. Dear Wolfgang, please make sure she understands all that. Thank dear Jutta for the murder stories. I send you all a big hug until we see you in London! Spring has suddenly arrived here, it's glorious.

All the very best,   yours, OK

248

To Carl Georg Heise

[Villeneuve,] 22. IV. 69

My dearest Dr Pasha,

We have to fly to London on Monday, for a preview of new rooms in the British Museum, Rembrandt, proofs, one or two plays for Olda, so I'm very glad to have had the chance to read your letter and the witty (far too flattering) article in the *Zürcher Zeitung* first. I'd already had a letter about the article, from Herr de Beauclair, a touching creature, mad about books and also a printer who honours the work under his hands, which is rare in these filthy days of *sex* and *pop*. A master-printer like our equally exceptional Mardersteig in Verona. They are mountain-peaks in an age of morass, deceit and quicksand. The master presses the engravings with the balls of his hands and takes the skin off them: that's unbelievable these days, when in Paris, for example, painters no longer draw their own lithographs but only sign them for the market. Yet they cost hundreds in Germany, and Herr de Beauclair is certainly not making a fortune. But he's mad about books, and his heart is in it. I've just engraved another ten or eleven plates for my beloved *Penthesilea* for him, and hope he won't completely ruin his hands on them. Sooner or later a publisher will turn up to do a cheap offset edition for the mass market, but I'm not 'modern' enough for Germany, and elsewhere my work is not well enough known. In any case, I have no faith in the masses, my memories are too unhappy. All I have faith in is the chance to do something of my own and the understanding of the few friends I have in the world, of whom you, my dear Pasha, are one.

All best wishes to you both, yours gratefully, OK

To Heinz Spielmann

[London,] 12. V. 69

My dear Dr Spielmann,

[. . .] I have painted a not at all bad portrait of Agatha Christie, who was enchantingly entertaining, while her husband, the great archaeologist Mallowan, is simply splendid! As soon as he set eyes on it he cried out: 'It's her! I've known her thirty-two years, and I should know.' Yesterday he gave us a ceremonial lunch, with champagne, and we are firm friends. Quite by chance we had read books by both of them independently, without knowing that they were married.

Come again soon. I will probably have to go to Scotland in June, to paint the Duke of Hamilton. His pretty wife (in spite of having five sons!) has sought me out, and they are both great admirers, and have paid frequent visits to my – really beautiful – exhibition here. Please embrace your lady wife from me, and yourself too, from yours gratefully, OK

To Fritz Schmalenbach

[Villeneuve,] 7. III. 70

My dear, amazing Dr Schmalenbach,
I was so impressed by the lecture on 'the young O K', which you kindly sent me, that I simply couldn't grasp how another person could see into my inner being, into my process of creation! The way you dismiss all the misinterpretations which have circulated in the art periodicals for getting on for ninety years now, and set about explaining my contribution to the art of our time is astonishing. I have already shown the essay to several friends, and should be very grateful if I could have more copies.
I would have liked to be at your lecture in Basle, but I was the first victim of a 'flu epidemic which then spread like wildfire locally.
I'm in the middle of writing an autobiography, which I was talked into doing, alas, and which will contain nothing but incidents and anecdotes, some true, some imaginary, because I've no sense of the past, no memory, nor any notion of a future. I'm a man of the moment. I hope there will be many more of them, however brief they may be.
Is it likely that you could come to a party in Hamburg in June? It's not so far for you. The Museum für Kunst und Gewerbe is celebrating the completion of a big tapestry by me. I like the director, Frau Dr Möller, and her co-director, Dr Spielmann, very much, and so we're going to it. I kiss your wife's hand, and am, with very warm thanks and cordial regards, yours sincerely, O Kokoschka

To Elisabeth Furtwängler

[Villeneuve,] 23. IV. 70

Dear Elisabeth,
Little Ninny, I would have broken my journey, gone to bed with a bottle of whisky, and slept till the chill was gone. We won't scold – you've enough to put up with – we only hope that you'll stay in hospital long enough to get completely better. Seeing a skinny pair of pins as recently, instead of your lovely legs, takes away my very pleasure in life itself. Even so, you were all rather clever, especially, I suspect, Banni who, I would guess, whisked you into hospital at once, so that you didn't wear yourself out coping with it at home, but . . .
You must take things easy now, fewer antibiotics, more food, more peace of mind, everything will calm down and be good. You are all we have, dearest Elisabeth, and you must see to it that before long you look as pretty as before your departure from here, when really you looked like a poppet of a schoolgirl, proof of just how quickly you can get better if you take a few days' rest and allow the trusty Oberkiefer to take over the driving seat.

250

Olda is sending you some spring flowers, she was deeply shocked when she read your letter. We had already become worried and wondered what was wrong, having had no news from you. Well, *God bless you to and fro*, as ever. Look forward to your garden, where spring has now sprung, as soon as you get home. But don't be impatient, stay in the clinic as long as is necessary.

All our best wishes, to Kathrin and Banni and the children too, and a tempestuous embrace at long distance from your devoted

Olda and OK

To Gottfried von Einem

[Villeneuve,] 15. 8. 71

Dear Gottfried,

I was very moved to learn of your decision to set my *Träumende Knaben*. I would never have dreamed of such a thing when I wrote it more than fifty years ago, as a love-letter to Lilith. Lilith never saw the book, because we fell out, and you, my dear friend, were still plucking a heavenly harp, up above the clouds. I hope you get great pleasure from the enterprise. What you have selected is a proper whole, in my opinion. We're all very excited to see what ideas the love-letter will give you, and wish you every kind of luck and joy.

Your opera was an experience. I hope the two of you will visit this part of the world again before long.

With very best wishes,   yours sincerely, OK

To Heinz Spielmann

Villeneuve, 3. Nov. 71

My dear friend, Dr Spielmann,

Yesterday's letter from you made me laugh. You really are incorrigible, playing one trick after another on your opponents [. . .] and something for good always comes out of it. Wimmer's head is good, regardless of who the subject may be, and it deserves to be in a museum in an age when so much trash is on offer, and there is no sign that things will get any better, not for the visual arts in Germany, at all events [. . .]

People simply don't want to see, and they make thinking hard for young people, who are beginning to worry about the present spiritual state of Germany. Commercial travellers have turned to journalism because they can't find any other employment, and pour scorn on the things that some of us still value. They're obviously preparing themselves for a future of slavery in the Russian jail of nations, so long as they earn good money in the interim. Wimmer will be proud and happy, and you, my dear friend,

251

did well to advise your financial benefactor to insist on his right to say how his money should be spent. Why do none of the papers mention the political development my book describes, in spite of my efforts to make reading it and thinking about it easier by inserting anecdotes? [. . .]
We're still enjoying good weather, and hope it's the same with you in Hamburg and that all three of you are well and in good spirits. With all our love and hoping to see you again soon,   yours sincerely, OK

To Hans M. Wingler

Villeneuve, 23 Dec. 71

My dear Herr Wingler,
I interpret your long letter of 3 December as a blunt reproof, because I took the liberty of drawing your attention to the fact that your preface to the catalogue of my graphic œuvre misses the most important point. You say I should be the last person not to acknowledge the integrity of another person's serious intellectual work, and that encounters in the intellectual realm are only possible in sovereignty, if we are in favour of intellectual freedom!
Long live intellectual freedom, but it never entered my head to criticize your scientific integrity in the field of psychiatry, in which I am not an expert. On the other hand, I am only too well aware, especially given that sexual complexes are all the rage in Germany at the moment, that it is very easy to lose one's way in the uncharted realms of psychology, from which there is perhaps no means of egress. You invoke a right (unknown to me, I must say), guaranteed by the general consensus of educated people and by law, to interpret the personality of the subject in a portrait. You warn me against 'scribbling' on your scientific portrait of me.
My dear friend, we are at cross-purposes here. You can write a scientific paper, representing Karl Kraus, Adolf Loos and even me as men afflicted with mother-complexes if you want to, though my hair stands on end when I think what Kraus would have had to say about it. But there are still quite a few people in the world who have a very thorough knowledge of the work of those two great men. They would be unanimous in protesting against the scientific interpretation that you, dear Dr Wingler, lay before the reader.
     In this particular case, however, we are not even talking about the interpretation of sexual problems, but about the introduction to the long overdue, and now very urgently needed, catalogue of my graphic œuvre. The purpose of the catalogue is to provide the general public with objective information about original graphics by me, and about the forgeries which unfortunately are encountered all too frequently these days. My corrections to the galley proofs relate to technical matters, for

252

example, the assertion that in my early life I was not interested in the craft side of lithography, and left it to some craftsman to copy my drawings by photolithographic means. On the contrary, I did not attend an academy of fine arts, I went to the school of arts and crafts, the Kunstgewerbeschule, in order to learn crafts. With the exception of *Die chinesische Mauer*, when I was absent from Vienna, and a few of the relatively primitive postcards, I have to date drawn every one of my lithographs on the stone, or corrected it on the stone after the drawing was transferred from paper. Every lithographic printer will tell you that lithographic crayon transfers equally well from any kind of paper, it doesn't have to be transfer paper. Finally you refer to a proof-copy of a drawing for the Bach Cantata, where a Dante quotation is in mirror-writing, as conclusive evidence that the drawing was not lithographed by me. In fact, you have proved exactly the opposite, as you can see for yourself if you turn a letter face down on your blotting paper while the ink is still wet. Let us confine ourselves to factual information in an œuvre catalogue, and not stray into the byways of either psychiatry or technology. It's what I expected from your preface.

With sincere good wishes for a happy new year in 1972,

yours, Oskar Kokoschka

To Heinz Spielmann

[Villeneuve,] 27. XII. 71

My dear friend Dr Spielmann,

I'm all behind with my letter-writing, it would suit me to have a year without a New Year. Your letters cheer me up enormously, especially as it's so dark and foggy here now that we can hardly get anything done at all. And I must not be idle, my years are numbered, I must say what I have to say now, because I won't get the chance in purgatory. But your lovely Casals card was just the ticket, he's ninety-five this week, I find that very encouraging.

The Wimmer head does stick in the mind, you made a good choice there. [. . .] I'm eager to see the books by Leach and especially Sauerlandt, who is like you, my friend, in regarding art as a social matter, not a science for specialists. Take your time over your history of art, it will be a very important book for the younger generation, which doesn't know anything beyond itself because it's been cut off from the past. The collapse of Greco-Roman civilization as a consequence of Platonic illusionism and oriental ideologies; the 'Völkerwanderung', which infected the Christian faith with recondite beliefs, especially Celtic ones; the French Revolution, which put paid to the individual and preached *égalité* in a mechanistic age – a faith which Marx set his seal on, when God was pensioned off: those are the stops on the tram-route of progress. These critical periods in European history are all documented in the visual arts, and Western youth must be made aware of them, if Europe is not to decline again into an oriental slave society. Art shows what human history is, visual art that is, because in music there are already composers who can't read music any more, electronic music makes it redundant, and radio no longer aims at listeners who concentrate, but broadcasts noises to stir the sensorium sent to sleep by chaos. I'm not a pessimist, and you, my dear friend, are even less of one, because you are young! The battle is lost in Germany, since Brandt, but we must remember Thermopylae!

In love,   your old friend OK

Happy 1972! I hope you'll help me open the door soon, I've had an idea!

To Fritz Schmalenbach

[Villeneuve,] 7. x. 72

Dear Dr Schmalenbach (and Frau Schmalenbach)

We were very sorry indeed not to have visited you in Gstaad. It simply wasn't possible, and we very much hope that there will be another chance to see you soon, dear friends. We're leaving home the day after tomorrow, just going across the border into Burgundy for about ten days. Olda needs a break from the monotony of housework, and it will do me good, too, to refresh my spirit with the sight of some churches and museums, now that the sun is at last revealing its presence after nearly a year of grey, rain and cold.

I was very pleased with your article. At last! someone who can distinguish me in my work from the decorative style of 'Expressionism'. You are the first person to say it, my dear friend. The article as a whole is written with so much warmth and understanding of the essentials of my contribution to present-day art that I can only be thankful to you from the bottom of my heart, because word will get about, even if the people who write about painting at the moment still rely on catch-phrases, and can't distinguish the essential from the fashionable. We live in an age when people don't see, the clearest proof of which lies in the exhibitions they put on nowadays. I was really sorry that we hadn't more time to see each other and talk, I feel so lonely, and life is too short to hope for the rise of a generation better equipped spiritually and intellectually. Two world wars have devastated Germany in that respect. You are the only person, dear friend, who can salvage something for the young. Long may you remain in office!

With heartfelt thanks and very cordial greetings to you both,

yours sincerely, O Kokoschka

254

To Wilhelm Kempff

Villeneuve, 15. 1. 73

My dear Meister Wilhelm,
You played under a bright star the night before last, truly. To my knowledge, the word 'blessed' rarely passes my lips. We played your recording yesterday evening to make a comparison, but the concert in Paris with Rostropovich was different!! You rarely allow your inmost self to venture out so freely, mysteriously and shyly, all at the same time, into the cynical reality of today, but Beethoven's Archduke Trio gave you wings and you triumphed over human transience. I certainly have no right to talk like this, as a non-musician, but I believe that the whole audience in Paris had the same experience, as if earthly eyes saw the light for the first time, instead of the murderous heat which dries the soul and scorches us, yet is mistaken for 'spiritual' light in our foggy world. We, your contemporaries, accept a fate which seems to doom us to transience, and then unexpectedly, like a ghost-moth, you open your wings, and show us a path leading from death towards eternal light, like a guardian angel.
Thank you, blessed Meister Wilhelm, I kiss your hands. May you be eternally newborn, and may you often play with your Russian friends. Perhaps you may do so in Vevey one day, so that we can say, we were there.
Warmly embracing you and and your belle Hélène,

always, yours sincerely, OK

To Josef P. Hodin

[Villeneuve,] 25. 3. 73

My dearest Magister Pepi,
We got back yesterday from Israel, where I drew wonderful Golda Meir, General Dayan, the Chief Justice, the Greek Patriarch and sundry others, all in the course of a single week, for an album which is to be sold in the USA and elsewhere in aid of Israel. Tomorrow I have to paint a Canadian, who has flown over here specially. Quite an undertaking at my advanced age. I'd no idea you were in Gibraltar, too far from Jerusalem. The photos are of drawings I dashed off in 1906, in my evening classes at the Kunstgewerbeschule, to show my students the movements you can capture in a matter of seconds, if only you use your eyes. Those evening classes at the Kunstgewerbeschule, with about a hundred students, eventually had a seminal influence all over Europe, where the academies had for so long taught by means of sterile nude classes – with an old man in a loin-cloth having to pose stiffly for a week at a time.

I never talked to Bernal about atomic bombs, I didn't understand physics even in secondary school, and as a result nearly failed to matriculate. What Bernal did for me was devote weeks to helping me translate my Comenius paper into English for Oxford University Press. So far as I remember, I didn't draw him, unfortunately, because he was suddenly called away on some military mission.

I wish your son and his fiancée every happiness. The young lady eating cherries in her dressing gown looks good enough to nibble herself. Will the two of you, my *beautiful one and you*, come here again soon? We're going to Sicily for three weeks at the end of April. In spite of the many protestations of devotion that pour in from friends all over the world, I feel lonely. But my two paintings, *Leo Kestenberg* in Jerusalem and *Saul and David* in the Tel Aviv Museum, are the best in Israel [. . .].

Embracing you both tenderly,   yours, OK

To Gilbert Lloyd (original English)

[Villeneuve,] 26. x. 73

My dearest Gilbert,

I got your colours today but not the bill, so I am more in your debt till we meet again – soon I hope, because there is so much we could talk about and writing letters is not my forte, as you know. For example the Tokyo exhibition. It would be very good to show a complete graphics show there in order to introduce me. The Japanese know better about graphics than about painting, spoiled now by the 'modern' European output in oils, and the time also would be too short for arranging a show worthy of my life's work. And there is, on the other hand, less risk sending a collection [of graphics] over to Japan at the [present] time. [. . .]

Do come and love to you, my only friend,   yours devoted OK

To Heinz Spielmann

Villeneuve, 13. Nov. 73

My dear Dr Spielmann,

[. . .] I'm afraid the Jews face disaster this time, and they'll have to scatter across the face of the earth again. Military victories don't solve problems, Hitler could have taught them that. I hope you're not freezing yet in Hamburg, but prepare yourselves for the worst. Brandt can kiss the Russians' boots for all he's worth, but they won't give him enough fuel to light his cigarettes with, even if he tells Golda Meir that it breaks his heart to join all the others in the boycott against Israel. Look after yourselves, all of you, and let's hope at least for an end to this senseless war, which is decimating the youth of Israel without having any effect on the fate due

to befall all modern civilization and its mechanization, which is destroying humanism. [. . .]
All best wishes and auf Wiedersehen   yours, OK

To Heinz Spielmann
                                          Villeneuvre, 24. XII. 73
My dear friend Dr Spielmann,
First let me wish you a very merry Christmas, especially to Claudia, who can still enjoy a Christmas tree, and next a very good new year in 1974 to all three of you. May the Arab goat-herds not leave you to freeze, and instead of building better atomic bombs, may we soon learn how to milk the sun. After all, that's the reason why the computer is being introduced everywhere to replace the usual primary school education common to all nation states. Since people no longer know how to think, the computer will think for them in future. That is the future of our technological civilization.
There used to be creative individuals in the visual arts, but that's all finished. The arts put up no resistance, nor do the spiritual and intellectual movements of our time, which isn't even good enough to have descended from apes. The poor gorillas are dying out and the guerrillas are multiplying!! But you mustn't let yourself be upset by my jeremiad, my dear friend! Just make sure you get your book on to the Ark before the deluge comes! I'm very impatient to see it! [. . .]
Think of life as being as short as a match, which is struck, burns your finger and goes out before the finger starts hurting. What you said about the theatre and *Comenius* would be wonderful, if I survive long enough! I embrace the bishop warmly, good luck to him, because he still believes in a god. After all, God was really one of the most progressive ideas mankind ever had!
I eagerly await Volume 2, in everlasting gratitude, yours sincerely, OK

To Willy Hahn
                                          [Villeneuve,] 7 April 75
My dear Golden Cockerel,
Please don't worry about me, they say I'll be able to see again in four to five weeks (with glasses), which is not the worst thing that could happen to a painter in his ninetieth year. Only it can't last long, because of the calendar, invented by that damn' fool of a saint to bring us nearer to the next world. I'd be perfectly content with this world, if there was any hope of its lasting a good long time. I'm in no hurry! There's still a lot I could do. The ever-patient Olda is now copying the third volume of my art

articles, which you will see in print after Whitsun, and will entertain you, I hope. Painting might do the world more good – or the art-dealers, at any rate – but it looks as if they will have to go over to the abstract junk, because painting is dying out. Poor Utopians, born too late, but how can art and love of life survive in this rotten climate, with an ice age impending?

Take care of yourselves, my two dear friends, and come over again soon to comfort   your melancholy OK

To Heinz Spielmann

Villeneuve, 27. XII. 75

My dearest Dr Spielmann,

I'm very much afraid that with the amount of things you do for me you are forgetting yourself and your own work! It is some consolation to remember that Claudia has a level head and will stop you overdoing things. She is going to be an exemplary human being one day, and I already begrudge letting her go to some man who will come running after her one day. She is easily disappointed, because she thinks originally and acts accordingly. Thinking is a second-hand activity today, and she can't grasp that!

Let's hope she's lucky!

We're very much looking forward to your visit, if it's not a waste of your own precious time. My time is limited, so I can't have enough of you, and I wish I was young enough to have you living nearby, and see you more often. Letters are like music for a deaf man who could once hear. This is not a very cheery Christmas letter, but it will soon be the new year, and I have a parcel of drawings for *Pan*, which I shall ask you to look at or take with you for an eventual publisher, and I have other plans, if my calendar allows. Only I'm afraid that you are taking on too much for my sake, which gets in the way of your own creative work, and that fear cautions me against being a nuisance to you.

I wish you everything you wish yourself for the New Year, and expect you all with open hands (likewise Olda). Don't catch 'flu or anything of that sort!   Ever yours gratefully, OK

The article was very impressive!

To Alfred Marnau

[Villeneuve, autumn 1976]

Dear Fred,

It is up to us to reform the Vatican, or Catholicism will die out before the end of the century. The Pope urgently needs the spiritual influence of a young person who is not attached to any clique. You possess the charm to convince him in the faith. The Pope isn't a believer at the moment, you see, but has to pretend he is and he's a bad actor.

Come soon, so that we can talk about it, you eternally young soul. With love, always, your old, blind OK

To Heinz Spielmann

Villeneuve [*c*.1975

Afterword

[. . .]

Like the great ironist of the eighteenth century, I still believe, even as I approach ninety, that our planet is the best of all possible worlds, so long as it is inhabited by human beings, for without them life would have no meaning. There have been two world wars this century, and a third – an atomic war – might yet follow them, and during this period our world has shrunk to a dirty, foggy speck in the universe.

Not being a Utopian, I do not look through the same glass as the progressives! Without prejudice: what a wonderful world we live in, if only we would open our eyes! Unfortunately, it is given to most people only to hear what others say. Most of the friends I have had in my long life were not given enough time to experience the spellbinding reality of existence, which far outstrips all fairy tales, all follies and superstitions of the past. They went to heaven – or hell: soon there will not be much to choose between the two, once no one feels curiosity any more about what becomes of us, once there is nothing left to wonder at, once our world is the world-state of amoebae and infusoria: only sceptics can no longer be surprised!

I think especially of the young people of Germany, who may perhaps gather from my fleeting steps in the quicksand of time that all of this is to be found in the newspapers every day, if one only stops to read, for I am neither a romantic nor a psychopath. Oskar Kokoschka

Notes on the Letters

The following editions of Kokoschka's written works and catalogues of his œuvre are cited in the annotations to individual letters:

Oskar Kokoschka, Das schriftliche Werk, 4 volumes, ed. Heinz Spielmann, Hamburg, 1973–6 (I: Dichtungen und Dramen; II: Erzählungen; III: Aufsätze, Vorträge, Essays zur Kunst; IV: Politische Äusserungen).

Oskar Kokoschka, My Life, translated by David Britt, London and New York, 1974 (German original edition, *Mein Leben*, Munich, 1971).

Oskar Kokoschka, Handzeichnungen, 5 volumes, ed. (and published by) Ernst Rathenau. I (to 1931/2), Berlin, n.d. [1934]; II (to 1959), Berlin and London, 1962; III (1906–65), New York and Berlin, 1966; IV (1906–69), New York and Berlin, 1971; V (to 1976), Berlin, 1977. Cited as 'Rathenau'.

Wingler, Hans Maria, *Oskar Kokoschka, das Werk des Malers*, Salzburg, 1956; English edition, *Oskar Kokoschka, the Work of the Painter*, London, 1958. Cited as 'Wingler'.

Wingler, Hans Maria, and Welz, Friedrich, *Oskar Kokoschka, das druckgraphische Werk*, Salzburg, 1975. Cited as 'Wingler-Welz'.

Present ownership or the source of the text of each letter included in this selection is given in the heading to the relevant note. Grateful thanks are extended to private owners and to institutions which have provided details of original documents, both for the German-language edition and for this translation based on it. A small number of letters not available for inclusion in the original German edition have been inserted and are identified in the notes.

To Leon Kellner, Vienna, December 1905, ms., present owner unknown. From a photocopy (auction catalogue, Dorotheum, Vienna).

To Erwin Lang, late 1907, text as printed in *Agathon, Almanach auf das Jahr 1948*, Vienna, 1948, pp. 290f.

Lilith Lang: Erwin Lang's sister and, like Kokoschka, a student at the Kunstgewerbeschule in Vienna. She was the model for the 'girl Li' in Kokoschka's poem 'Die träumenden Knaben' (cf. *My Life*, p. 20).

Wiesenthal: the dancer Grete Wiesenthal (cf. below, the two following letters to Erwin Lang and the letter of 28 October 1912).

in Löffler's crammer: at the Kunstgewerbeschule, Kokoschka was originally in the graphics and printmaking class of Carl Otto Czeschka, who left to take up a post in Hamburg in the spring of 1907. He then enrolled in the class of Bertold Löffler, from the summer term of 1907 onwards.

Delward, the old rattlebag: Marya Delvard sang songs by Frank Wedekind at the Fledermaus cabaret; one of these is printed in the programme of the second show put on at the cabaret. (With the word 'Kindmordlieder', a pun seems to be intended on 'Wede*kind*' and Mahler's *Die Kindertotenlieder*, which were first performed in Vienna in January 1905.)

Carl 'Ollitzer ('Refined Artist'): i.e. the painter Carl Hollitzer, who was responsible for four musical ensemble items in the second Fledermaus show, in which he sang, in addition to directing and designing the sets and costumes.

sung meltingly by 3 Jews: the cabaret artists R. Koppe, T. Kraft and K. Bernhardt.

bitten the lavatory attendant: Karl Kraus had written in *Die Fackel* of 18 November 1907: 'There was a long argument as to whether they [i.e. the cabaret's lavatories] are better served by the paper, on which the art reviews of [Bertha] Zuckerkandl are printed, or by a costume for the attendant, which Professor [Josef] Hoffmann was said to be designing. In the end, however, it was agreed to paint the facilities white and overlay that with the popular chequerboard motif . . .' ('Eine Kulturtat' – a review of the Fledermaus cabaret).

my book of fairy tales: Kokoschka's poem 'Die träumenden Knaben', printed by the Wiener Werkstätte in March 1908 (as is proved by an unpublished letter from Fritz Waerndorfer to Carl Otto Czeschka, 4 March 1908).

Janke: Urban Janke, a fellow-student at the Kunstgewerbeschule, represented by a tapestry and other items at the 1908 Kunstschau.

To Erwin Lang, winter 1907–8 and February/March 1908, ms., private ownership, Vienna.

Winter 1907–8:

Isepp: the painter and picture-restorer Sebastian Isepp, who was a friend of Kokoschka and Loos, and went to Paris with them in 1924. He was also one of Kokoschka's circle of friends during the years of exile in England. In London, in 1951, Kokoschka painted his portrait, which was first shown in public at the 1952 Venice Biennale (cf. Wingler, no. 368).

February/March 1908:

in the white Beethoven: the passage refers to numbers danced by the Wiesenthal sisters in the third show at the Fledermaus cabaret, which opened in January 1908. In his review of the show in the *Wiener Allgemeine Zeitung*, Peter Altenberg mentioned 'the Beethoven face of the dancer Grete, whose grave depths are more credible than her smiling . . .'.

In my earliest childhood, by a ghastly chance: presumably refers either to the birth of his sister in 1889, or of his brother in 1892.

To Max Mell, Vienna, March 1908, text as printed in the auction catalogue of Hartung und Karl, Munich, 11–13 May 1977, lot no. 1,951. (The lot also included six sheets of proofs with the text of 'Die träumenden Knaben'.) In the original ms. commas and full stops are rendered by oblique strokes, as in the printed edition of 'Die träumenden Knaben'.

To Arnold Schoenberg, September(?) 1909 and 13 October 1909, ms., Library of Congress, Washington, D.C.

The 'play' referred to in the first note and hinted at in the second might be Kokoschka's *Der brennende Dornbusch* or an early draft of Schoenberg's *Die glückliche Hand*.

To Lotte Franzos, 28. 1. 1910, typed copy in the Kokoschka Archive, Villeneuve.

cosmopolitan stylists: the word is garbled in the copy, and the reading ('Cosmopolitstilisten') is therefore uncertain.

Your portrait: portrait of Lotte Franzos, painted in Vienna, in the autumn of 1909 at the latest (Wingler, no. 11).

To Richard Dehmel, 10 October 1910, ms., Staats- und Universitätsbibliothek, Hamburg.

It will be difficult to draw you: Kokoschka drew Dehmel for *Der Sturm*, probably not long after this letter was written. The drawing was published in the periodical and also in the portfolio *Zwanzig Zeichnungen*, published by Verlag 'Der Sturm' in 1913.

To Adolf Loos, 23 December 1910, ms. in private ownership, text from Ernst Rathenau, 'Ein Kokoschkabuch', in J. P. Hodin, *Bekenntnis zu Kokoschka*, Berlin and Mainz, 1963, p. 118.

Schlieper: Kokoschka painted Hans Schlieper's portrait in Berlin late in 1910. The whereabouts of the picture is currently unknown; see Wingler, no. 47.

four pictures: in addition to that of Schlieper, these were probably the portraits of Peter Baum, Hugo Caro, Rudolf Blümner and Tilla Durieux (Wingler, nos. 43, 44, 45, 46).

K.K.: Karl Kraus.

To Lotte Franzos, 24 December 1910, typed copy in the Kokoschka Archive, Villeneuve.

To Alma Mahler, Vienna, letters of April 1912, typed copies in the University of Pennsylvania Library, Philadelphia.

Many of the letters to Alma Mahler are undated, which makes it hard to determine the order in which they were written. Alma Mahler numbered the sheets of the typed copies, but it often proved necessary to emend the order she put them in, for it does not match certain facts referred to in the letters themselves (such as the dates or extent of journeys). In all probability the letter of 15 April is the first letter Kokoschka wrote to Alma Mahler, immediately after their first meeting. The following day, 16 April, both attended the

Schoenberg concert promoted by the Academic Society for Literature and Music in Vienna.

The letters of 25, 26 and 29 April 1912 are from a group about which Alma Mahler noted that Kokoschka sent them to her in Paris, where she went at the end of April with Frau Lilly Lieser.

25 April 1912:

our Guckerl: Anna, the seven-year-old daughter of Alma and Gustav Mahler, known by the pet-name 'Guckerl' or 'Gucki'.

the three of us: presumably himself, Guckerl and Alma Mahler's mother, Anna Moll.

29 April 1912:

Frau Sanders: The portrait of Emma Veronika Sanders (Wingler, no. 26) has hitherto been dated to the autumn of 1909, on reliable evidence. For the present it must remain undecided whether the portrait should be given a later date.

To Alma Mahler, Vienna, 1 or 2 May, 3 May and 8 May 1912, typed copies in the University of Pennsylvania Library, Philadelphia.

Alma Mahler notes that these letters were sent to her in Scheveningen.

To Alma Mahler, letters of May and June, not more precisely dated, typed copies in the University of Pennsylvania Library, Philadelphia.

May 1912:

the text and the picture: possibly the text of *Der gefesselte Columbus* and a drawing relating to it; the text already existed, as *Der weiße Tiertöter*, but, under the impact of his meeting with Alma Mahler, Kokoschka gave it a new interpretation for her and for himself.

June 1912 [1]:

Concerning the date, an ms. note by Alma Mahler reads: '. . . after the first run-through of the 9th Symphony of Gustav Mahler.' As the first performance of the symphony, under Bruno Walter, was given in Vienna, on 26 June 1912, rehearsals must have taken place in the preceding weeks.

To Alma Mahler, letters of 12, 14, 15 and *c.*17/18 July 1912, typed copies in the University of Pennsylvania Library, Philadelphia.

Alma Mahler notes that these were sent to her in Scheveningen.

14 July 1912:

a lot of portraits of children: this might refer to *Jacques de Menasse* (Wingler, no. 57), *Girl seated* (sketch, lost; Wingler, no. 73) and *Girl with Pekinese* (Wingler, no. 74).

Three illegible words omitted.

a lithograph for [Karl Kraus]: this became a series of lithographs, illustrating Kraus's *Die chinesische Mauer* (Wingler-Welz, nos. 35–42), published in the spring of 1914.

Kammerer: Dr Paul Kammerer, biologist. After Gustav Mahler's death, Alma Mahler worked for him as an assistant for a time.

Kraus tried to tempt me with a Malayan snake-dancer: Kokoschka relates this incident in a different context in *My Life* (pp. 54–5).

*c.*17/18 July 1912:

small portrait for 200 fl.: This might refer to the *Lady in Red* (Wingler, no. 58), the only portrait in a small format dating from *c.*1912. The subject is thought to have been the wife of the Viennese representative of a champagne importer: that too would fit

Kokoschka's remark that 'I'm doing everything that will enable me to come to you, including things I would otherwise have refused.'

To Alma Mahler, 25 and 27 July 1912, typed copies in the University of Pennsylvania Library, Philadelphia.
According to a note by Alma Mahler, Kokoschka sent these letters to Munich, where she stopped on her way back from Scheveningen. He met her there (probably leaving Vienna immediately after 27 July), and travelled with her to Mürren in Switzerland.
27 July 1912:
a Jewish word for a succubus: According to Alma Mahler, this refers to 'the girl Li' in 'Die träumenden Knaben', Lilith Lang.

To Erwin Lang and Grete Wiesenthal, Vienna, 28 October 1912, ms., Österreichische Nationalbibliothek, Vienna. Date in another hand.

To Alma Mahler, mid-November, 1912, 3 January 1913, early February 1913, typed copies in the University of Pennsylvania Library, Philadelphia.
Mid-November, 1912:
I will have so much strength that your whole life will be like a rebirth: The passage corresponds to the first picture on the second of Kokoschka's fans for Alma Mahler (Kokoschka and Alma Mahler in 'Rebirth through Flames'; cf. H. Spielmann, *Oskar Kokoschka, Die Fächer für Alma Mahler*, Hamburg, 1969).
Early February 1913:
This is one of several letters which, Alma Mahler notes, were sent to her in Nice where she was staying at the end of January and early February.
this picture: there is a girl's portrait of about this time, for which Kokoschka may have expected to be paid.
The picture will . . . make an impression: probably refers to the double portrait of Alma Mahler and Kokoschka (Wingler, no. 71).

To Alma Mahler, Vienna, March 1913, typed copy in the University of Pennsylvania Library, Philadelphia.
One of four letters of the same period, datable only by the references they make to the journey the couple were about to make to Italy (probably 20 March–9 April 1913), and by references (here: 'only a year for me') to the length of time they had known each other.

To Alma Mahler, April 1913, typed copy in the University of Pennsylvania Library, Philadelphia.
One of four letters of the same period, which can be dated only by the allusions to Kokoschka and Alma Mahler having first met a year previously. The mood is also consistent with their having recently returned from Italy, which makes a dating in the weeks following 10 April 1913 reasonable.
my class: Kokoschka taught at the Kunstgewerbeschule in Vienna. He left at the end of the summer term, 1913.
The picture: Kokoschka is evidently describing his painting *The Tempest* (Wingler, no. 96) in its first version, which he may have started earlier than has hitherto been supposed in

all the literature about him (see also note to letter of December 1913). The passage 'In the midst of the confusions of nature . . .' also recalls Alma Mahler's description, in her memoirs, of a storm they saw in the Bay of Naples.

In the book: a reference to drawings for *Der gefesselte Columbus*, which Kokoschka would have traced on to transparent paper, for transference to the stone in the lithographic process.

what you said about that bad night: probably the night following the operation Alma Mahler underwent at the end of February 1913.

my self-portrait: almost certainly the *Self-portrait (The painter at the age of 26*, 1912: Wingler, no. 62); its small format (51 × 40 cm.) would make it easily portable.

Maud: the nursery-maid.

the text: perhaps the revised version of the text of *Der weiße Tiertöter* for *Der gefesselte Columbus.*

To Alma Mahler, letters of May 1913, typed copies in the University of Pennsylvania Library, Philadelphia.

There are thirteen of these altogether, assigned by notes in Alma Mahler's handwriting to the time of her stay in Paris in May 1913. The exact order remains hypothetical, except in the case of those dated by Kokoschka.

[II]:

the Russians in the Debussy 'Nocturnes': Kokoschka may have confused what he read in the Paris newspapers about 'the Russians' and 'Debussy's Nocturnes'. The Ballets Russes were at the Théâtre des Champs Elysées in the second half of May 1913 (their performances included the world première of Stravinsky's *Le Sacre du printemps*); in the first half of May another company performed in the same theatre, dancing two of Debussy's Nocturnes.

[III]:

The exhibition at the Salon d'Automne: nothing came of this plan.

a little surprise: possibly the third of the seven fans for Alma Mahler, representing the idea executed in *The Tempest.*

Dr Fleischmann: possibly the writer Bruno Fleischmann.

[IV]:

Reinhold: the actor Ernst Reinhold, who was involved in the rehearsals for *Der brennende Dornbusch*. The play was scheduled for June 1913, but the performance was banned by the censor.

To Alma Mahler, June 1913, typed copy in the University of Pennsylvania Library, Philadelphia.

One of a group of three letters which cannot be more precisely dated, though the content suggests that this is the second.

To Alma Mahler, July 1913, typed copies in the University of Pennsylvania Library, Philadelphia.

Two letters from a group of thirteen which are mostly undated, but are known to have been written 5–26 July 1913. Alma Mahler notes that they were sent to her in the spa town of Franzensbad (now Františkovy Lázně, Czechoslovakia), where she spent most of that month. According to her memoirs, Kokoschka visited her unannounced and they quarrelled because his self-portrait was not hanging in her room.

July 1913 [II]:
Justi: Justine Rosé, Gustav Mahler's sister.

To Alma Mahler, 21 August 1913, typed copy in the University of Pennsylvania Library,
Philadelphia.
After her return from Franzensbad, Alma Mahler spent only a short time in Vienna before
setting off again, probably to the Dolomites, where Kokoschka joined her after 22
August.

To Alma Mahler, autumn 1913, typed copy in the University of Pennsylvania Library,
Philadelphia.

To Herwarth Walden, December 1913, 3 and 27 January 1914, ms., *Der Sturm*-Archiv,
Berlin.
December 1913:
sad child, cat chasing mouse, burnt-out building, faint signs of spring: the allegorical *Still-Life with
Putto and Rabbit* (Wingler, no. 95), the completion of which can be dated to the turn of
the year 1913–14, on the strength of this letter. It is very probable that the 'putto'
represents the idea of an unborn child of Kokoschka and Alma Mahler; 'signs of spring'
should be understood as a premonition of spring 1914, rather than a memory of spring
1913.
The contribution to the book by Herr Neitzel (Alsace, Saverne): this project cannot be identified.
the [drawing] with the boy pointing: one of the drawings for the edition of *Mörder Hoffnung der
Frauen*, probably Rathenau, I, pl. 19.
Tristan and Isolde: i.e. *The Tempest*, which received its definitive title *Die Windsbraut* only
when Georg Trakl visited Kokoschka's black-painted studio in the Hardtgasse.
Kokoschka had a very high regard all his life for the music of Wagner's *Tristan*, and saw
in the work a reflection of his relationship with Alma Mahler. The claim to have been
working on it 'since last January' is an exaggeration, as are the dimensions – the painting
measures 181 × 220 cm.
I need to raise 10,000 kr. . . . a bond!: The need to raise what was at that date a very large sum of
money, in order to secure the bond for his future brother-in-law, placed Kokoschka in
great financial embarrassment for a considerable period, lasting until after he
volunteered for military service, even though he was able to command steadily
increasing fees.
commissar: Emil Patočka was an official in the Austrian Admiralty.
I am already working on something else on the same scale: unclear. It perhaps refers to a work on
canvas which was never started, but certainly not to the murals for the crematorium in
Breslau (for which Kokoschka had received a commission arranged by Walden in April/
May 1912), which in the end were not executed.
3 January 1914:
The picture: Still-Life with Putto and Rabbit (Wingler, no. 95).
the big picture: The Tempest (Wingler, no. 96).
the 10,000 kr.: the receipts survive. Kokoschka corresponded on the matter with the bank
manager, Dr Prager, and Herr Lajos Kriser, both of Vienna, on 4 and 5 January 1914.
The contract for the loan of 10,000 kr., for the purchase of an annuity for Fräulein Berta
Kokoschka, was signed on 9 January. (All documents in private ownership, Vienna.)

27 January 1914:
the picture I promised: Still-Life with Putto and Rabbit.
a characterful portrait of an old man: perhaps *The Prisoner* (Wingler, no. 91).

To Alma Mahler, Vienna, 3, 7 and 11 March 1914, typed copies in the University of
 Pennsylvania Library, Philadelphia.
Alma Mahler went to Paris on 3 March, where she stayed for at least two weeks.
11 March 1914:
Wolfi: perhaps a dog.

To Herwarth Walden, 28 April 1914, ms., *Der Sturm*-Archiv, Berlin.
a gallery: Halle?: as the result of a dispute between the director of galleries in Halle, Max
 Sauerlandt, and his counterpart in Berlin, Wilhelm von Bode, word had got round that
 Sauerlandt was a champion of modern painting.

To Alma Mahler, Vienna, 10 May 1914, typed copy in the University of Pennsylvania
 Library, Philadelphia.
In May 1914 Alma Mahler went to her newly-built house in Breitenstein on the
 Semmering Pass between Lower Austria and Carinthia.
take three ferocious devils on myself . . .: the image is reminiscent of the design on the sixth of the
 fans Kokoschka made for Alma Mahler (see note to letter of February 1915 below).
'my maternal genius': suggests an association with the middle panel of the fan, a young
 woman with a newborn lamb.
fully finished examples in the world: the words following these are illegible in the copy.

To Alma Mahler, letters of late July 1914, typed copies in the University of Pennsylvania
 Library, Philadelphia.
[1] Monday:
the Ochses: a reference to Siegfried Ochs, German conductor, then aged fifty-six. He visited
 Alma Mahler at her house on the Semmering, in spite of her reluctance to receive him.
Berliners: probably Arnold Berliner, a musician.

To Alma Mahler, 30 August 1914, typed copy in the University of Pennsylvania Library,
 Philadelphia.
The absence of the usual signature suggests that the text is incomplete. A passage may have
 been deliberately suppressed by Alma Mahler.

To Albert Ehrenstein, Vienna, October 1914, ms., University Library, Jerusalem.
the picture: The Tempest.
the Princess: Princess Mechthild Lichnowsky.
the red picture: cannot be identified.

To Ludwig von Ficker, 17 November and 6 December 1914, ms., *Der Brenner*-Archiv,
 University of Innsbruck.
17 November 1914:
this unhappy news: Georg Trakl died after taking an overdose of cocaine. It is uncertain
 whether he did so deliberately with the intention of committing suicide.

268

6 December 1914:

this generous assistance: Ficker had arranged for the Wittgenstein Foundation to give
   Kokoschka a grant of 5,000 kr. The artist's receipt, dated 6 November 1914, is also in the
   Der Brenner-Archiv.

To Alma Mahler, letters of January 1915, typed copies in the University of Pennsylvania
   Library, Philadelphia.
Immediately following New Year 1915, Kokoschka went to Wiener Neustadt, to start his
   training as a dragoon in a cavalry regiment. The 'days of exile' can be dated precisely,
   because two unimportant letters dated 7 and 8 January 1915 (not included in this
   selection) clearly follow the one dated '4th day in exile'.
Letter of mid-January, 1915:

my future horse: With help from Loos, Kokoschka used the proceeds from the sale of *The
   Tempest* to purchase a half-breed mare called Minden Ló ('All horses'). See *My Life*,
   p. 85.
Bittners [etc.]: refers to various musical luminaries, including the composers Julius Bittner
   and Hans Pfitzner, the critic Ludwig Karpath, Karl Wiener, director of the Vienna
   Conservatory, and the conductors Siegfried Ochs and Bruno Walter (whose family
   name was Schlesinger).
Liesingers: Lilly Lieser.
Late January 1915:

What . . . made you so incensed with me?: perhaps a reference to Alma Mahler's reaction to
   Kokoschka's grumbles about her circle of friends, or could be a sign of their growing
   estrangement since she had met Walter Gropius.
when you go to Berlin: Walter Gropius had gone to Berlin, and Alma Mahler followed in
   February 1915. She travelled with Gropius from Berlin to Hanover, and then went back
   to Berlin to see Schoenberg.

To Ludwig von Ficker, 6 February 1915, ms., *Der Brenner*-Archiv, University of
   Innsbruck.

To Alma Mahler, first half of February 1915, typed copy in the University of Pennsylvania
   Library, Philadelphia.
lest a branch should seize us: Alma Mahler noted at this point in the original letter there was a
   drawing, which must have been a caricature of Kokoschka on horseback.
Pfitzerich: Hans Pfitzner.
where I am charging three dragons: a reference to the middle panel of the sixth of the seven fans
   Kokoschka painted for Alma Mahler (the fifth to survive: Walter Gropius burned one).
   It shows Kokoschka, as 'Red Cross Knight', fighting a three-headed monster: one of the
   heads is that of Gustav Mahler, and, on the evidence of this letter, the other two may
   represent Pfitzner and Siegfried Ochs.

To Ludwig von Ficker, 21 February 1915, ms., *Der Brenner*-Archiv, University of
   Innsbruck.
another 700 kr. from the Foundation: in response to Kokoschka's letter of 6 February 1915,
   Ficker had succeeded in getting him another grant from the Wittgenstein Foundation.
   Kokoschka did not know the identity of the donor.

269

To Alma Mahler, late February 1915, typed copy in the University of Pennsylvania Library, Philadelphia.

my poor brother: Bohuslav Kokoschka was a conscript serving in the Austrian navy.

For personal reasons, the penultimate sentence has been omitted.

To Alma Mahler, 2 and 5 March 1915, typed copies in the University of Pennsylvania Library, Philadelphia.

5 March 1915:

I only pray: the criticism of modern culture and society that Kokoschka voices here foreshadows his writings of four or five decades later, even in the very language he uses.

the Great Wall of China: an allusion to Karl Kraus's book of essays of that name (*Die chinesische Mauer*), which Kokoschka had illustrated with eight lithographs that paraphrased his relationship with Alma Mahler.

To Albert Ehrenstein, *c.* 8 March 1915, ms., University Library, Jerusalem.

thank you for your generous eulogy: an article on Kokoschka by Ehrenstein, which was published in *Zeitecho* in 1915.

To Alma Mahler, 16 and 18 March and early April 1915, typed copies in the University of Pennsylvania Library, Philadelphia.

16 March 1915:

your protégé's theatrical activities: Hans Pfitzner was Alma Mahler's guest during the rehearsals for the première of his opera *Der arme Heinrich*.

Early April 1915:

old money-bags L. L.: Lilly Lieser, who financed a concert at which Arnold Schoenberg conducted Beethoven's Ninth Symphony with Mahler's revisions. The performance proved so lacklustre, however, that it was not a success and incurred Alma Mahler's wrath.

To Alma Mahler, letter of May or early June 1915, typed copy in the University of Pennsylvania Library, Philadelphia.

The end of the letter has not survived.

To Alma Mahler, letters of late June 1915, typed copies in the University of Pennsylvania Library, Philadelphia.

Late June 1915 [II]:

They wrote . . . the pictures: perhaps the news that *The Tempest* was not, after all, going to an exhibition of his work in San Francisco.

To Adolf Loos, 22 July and 6 August 1915, ms., in private ownership, texts from Ernst Rathenau, 'Ein Kokoschkabuch', in J. P. Hodin, *Bekenntnis zu Kokoschka*, Berlin and Mainz 1963, pp. 120f.

In 1913 Lemberg (now Lvóv, Poland) was capital of the Austrian province of Galicia.

To Herwarth Walden, 12 August 1915, ms., *Der Sturm*-Archiv, Staatsbibliothek, Berlin.

To Albert Ehrenstein, Galicia, 24 August 1915, ms., University Library, Jerusalem.

On 29 August 1915 Kokoschka was seriously wounded, shot in the head and stabbed in the chest with a bayonet (see *My Life*, pp. 93ff.). After a few days in a field hospital, he was transferred to Brünn (Brno, now in Czechoslovakia) for several weeks. During the second half of October he was moved to the Palffy Hospital in Vienna, where he probably remained until February 1916.

To Herwarth Walden, 27 October 1915, ms., *Der Sturm*-Archiv, Staatsbibliothek, Berlin. Ehrenstein and Loos added their own messages when visiting Kokoschka in hospital.

To Albert Ehrenstein, Vienna, 25 March, 31 May and 10 July 1915, ms., University Library, Jerusalem.
25 March 1916:
the Hentschel woman: Grethe Hentschel. Loos had worked on a house and studio for her in 1914.
I've revised . . . the 'Drama': this was the third version of *Mörder Hoffnung der Frauen*, published in 1916 by 'Der Sturm' Verlag.
the Zeitecho poem: 'Allos Makar', a group of poems Kokoschka began writing for Alma Mahler in the spring of 1914. The title is (almost) an anagram of Alma-Oskar and means 'another is happy' in Greek.
31 May 1916:
Bennoplatz 8: the Kokoschka family home.
Ehrentafelstein: literally 'Stone Plaque of Honour'.
10 July 1915:
Kurt Wolff: literary historian and publisher. During the First World War he bought the remaining stock of Kokoschka's first literary work, 'Die träumenden Knaben', and published his early plays.
K.K.: Karl Kraus.
set out with those painters: Kokoschka was sent to the Italian Front as a liaison officer, and had to escort a group of journalists and war artists to Ljubljana.
Kestenberg: Leo Kestenberg, a partner of Kokoschka's dealer, Paul Cassirer. He had political connections and was later a section head in the Prussian civil service. Kokoschka painted his portrait in the winter of 1926–7 (Wingler, no. 223).
Bode: Wilhelm von Bode, director-general of art galleries in Berlin.

To Ludwig von Ficker, 21 August 1916. ms., *Der Brenner*-Archiv, University of Innsbruck.
On the following day, as Kokoschka ventured into no-man's-land, a grenade exploded very close to him. He was severely shell-shocked and it was the end of his active service. He spent a long period in a military convalescent home, the Weißer Hirsch, Dresden.

To Adolf Loos, 25 April 1918, ms., copy in the Kokoschka Archive, Villeneuve.
This letter was not included in the German edition; it is published here by kind permission of the heirs of Dr Ernst Rathenau.
Dirsztay: Victor von Dirsztay, Hungarian man of letters. Kokoschka painted his portrait in 1911, and illustrated two of his books: *Lob des hohen Verstandes* (1917, 6 lithographs) and *Der Unentrinnbare* (1923).
Penthesilea: by Heinrich von Kleist.
my idol: Alma Mahler-Gropius.

To Alma Mahler-Gropius, Dresden, undated telegrams and letter of 20 June 1919, telegram forms and typed copies in the University of Pennsylvania Library, Philadelphia.

The second of the telegrams bears only the text given here and the addresses of the recipient and sender ('alma gropius / elisabethstrasse 22 / wien / weißerhirsch'), on Form no. 769, (printed 1918). Kokoschka may have sent the first of the two telegrams in connection with his completion of *Orpheus und Eurydike*, or with his sending of a copy of the book *Vier Dramen*. The date on the typed copy, '7 February 1917', cannot be right, as *Orpheus und Eurydike* did not appear until 1919.

Kokoschka's appointment to the teaching staff of the Dresden Academy was arranged in the summer of 1919. The contract of employment is dated 18 August 1919, with effect from 1 October. On 22 October Kokoschka took the oath to uphold the German constitution and to honour the conditions of his employment, and on 23 October he presented his identity papers.

To Ludwig von Ficker, 8 December 1919, ms., *Der Brenner*-Archiv, University of Innsbruck.
the sad story of his sister: Grete Trakl had taken her own life in 1917, in Berlin; Kokoschka was convalescing at the time and had not been informed.

Open letter to the inhabitants of Dresden, March 1920. After first publication (as a poster), this was later included in the edition of Kokoschka's writings (*Das schriftliche Werk*, vol. IV, pp. 334 and 31f.).
a masterwork by Rubens: later research suggests that it was a work of the School of Rubens.
Kokoschka's piece provoked two hostile responses in the Berlin journal *Der Gegner*. 'Der Kunstlump' (The Art Blackguard), by George Grosz and John Heartfield, appeared in no. 10–12 of vol. 1 (1919), pp. 48ff., and Kurt Hiller's 'Zum Fall Kokoschka' (The Kokoschka Affair) in no. 1–2 of vol. 2 (1919–20), p. 45. See *My Life*, p. 111.

To Alice Graf, 18 August 1920, ms., private ownership, Helsinki.
Colibri: 'humming-bird', the pet-name that Kokoschka always used for Alice Graf in his letters to her and to Anna Kallin. In this letter, 'she' also refers to Alice.
Reindeer sleigh: Alice Graf grew up in St Petersburg, but spent some time in Finland after the Russian Revolution; for that reason references to Finland and reindeer occur frequently in Kokoschka's letters to her.
Edwarda . . . Lieutenant: Edwarda and Lieutenant Glahn are leading characters in Knut Hamsun's novel *Pan*.

To Lotte Mandl, October 1920, ms., private ownership, New York.
Inscription in a copy of Paul Westheim, *Oskar Kokoschka*, Potsdam–Berlin, n.d. [1918].
You were ten years old . . . five years later: references to the age of Lotte Mandl, whom Kokoschka first met at her parents' house when she was ten. She was fifteen when they next met and he drew his first portraits of her, of which there were to be many more.

To Lotte Mandl, January 1921?, ms., private ownership, New York.
The date of the letter is not certain, but the wording of the inscription on the photo (a

portrait of Kokoschka) suggests that he gave it to her when about to leave Vienna after quite a long stay.

To Alma Mahler-Gropius, 27 May 1921, typed copy in the University of Pennsylvania Library, Philadelphia.

an exhibition here of my most important works: the exhibition mounted by the Künstler-Vereinigung Dresden, June–September 1921. Kokoschka designed the poster himself (*Artist and Muse*, Wingler-Welz, no. 148). The picture to which he refers in the letter is the *Double Portrait with Alma Mahler* (Wingler, no. 71).

the owner: Herbert Garvens-Garvenburg, of Hanover.

my green pavilion: during the time he spent teaching at the Dresden Academy, Kokoschka lived in one of the old lodges in the Großer Garten park.

your ring, your red necklace, your coat: Alma Mahler's engagement ring, a necklace that was concealed in a flower-pot while Kokoschka was in the army, and a red housecoat, which he often wore in his studio during Alma Mahler's frequent absences, up to 1915.

our experiences: a reference to the play *Orpheus und Eurydike*.

Ever the happiness of the one in the other: a reference to Kokoschka's poem 'Allos Makar'.

To Anna Kallin, letters of September 1921, ms., Kokoschka Archive, Villeneuve, and National Archives, Helsinki.

First half of September 1921:

I loved a woman: Alma Mahler. Most of the letter refers to the end of Kokoschka's relationship with her, her marriage to Walter Gropius, and Kokoschka's war wounds in August 1915. In *My Life* (pp. 93–5) he describes how, already wounded by a bullet, he was bayoneted by a Russian soldier.

Theseus is always there: obscure. Perhaps an allusion to Theseus's death at the hands of Lycomedes, after surviving so many earlier perils.

like simple Edith: Edith Rosenheim.

Hulda: Kokoschka's servant in Dresden (whom he sometimes called Reserl).

Mid-September 1921:

my two little flower-sisters: Kokoschka addressed Anna Kallin by a number of pet-names (see the biographical note), and liked to pretend that they referred to separate people, as here: Niuta and Malina.

Late September 1921:

[I]:

*that * * * Italian:* quite possibly Kokoschka invented this rival.

Hilde Goldschmidt: one of Kokoschka's students at the Dresden Academy, and also an amateur dancer.

Mary Wigman: the dancer, an exponent of modern dance.

I'm writing a play: probably a play called *Saul*, which was never completed, and was eventually lost.

[II]:

Fareweller: Kokoschka peppered his letters to Anna Kallin (and, later, to others) with English expressions, sometimes invented, as here.

tula metal: Russian niello, an alloy of silver, copper and lead.

[III]:

almost as long ago as 1907: Kokoschka here equates the end of his minority in 1907 with the exhibition of his works at the Kunstschau shows in Vienna in 1908 and 1909, and the public outcry that greeted them.

To Anna Kallin, letters of January 1922, ms., Kokoschka Archive, Villeneuve, and National Archives, Helsinki.
Venice . . . exhibition: the thirteenth Venice Biennale, at which Kokoschka showed twelve paintings.

To Adolf Loos, January(?) 1922, ms., copy in the Kokoschka Archive, Villeneuve.
This letter was not included in the German edition; it is published here by kind permission of the heirs of Dr Ernst Rathenau.

To Alice Lahmann, second half of January 1922. ms., Kokoschka Archive, Villeneuve.
Dage: Alice Lahmann's son.

To Anna Kallin, *c.* 5 May 1922, ms., Kokoschka Archive, Villeneuve.
you are now nothing more than a picture: a reference to the painting *Lot and his Daughters* (Wingler, no. 147), in which Kokoschka gave one of the daughters Anna Kallin's features; he gave his own to Lot.

To Alice Lahmann, two letters of May 1922, ms., private ownership, Helsinki, and Kokoschka Archive, Villeneuve.

To Alma Mahler-Gropius, 9 October 1922, typescript copy in the University of Pennsylvania Library, Philadelphia.
in Venice: Kokoschka had met Alma Gropius briefly during the Biennale in Venice (see *My Life*, p. 75).
Mörder Hoffnung der Frauen: Paul Hindemith set Kokoschka's early play to music in 1919. The première took place in the Landestheater, Stuttgart, in 1921, and it was next staged in Frankfurt am Main. The production at the Dresden Staatsoper was thus the third.
I foresee Orpheus: it was actually set by Ernst Křenek in 1922 (see letter of 19 November 1925 to Anna Kallin).

Anna Kallin spent the vacation, from July until the end of October 1922, in London with her parents; a large number of letters which Kokoschka wrote to her during that period are preserved in the Kokoschka Archive and in the National Archives in Helsinki.

To Anna Kallin, letters of October 1922, ms., Kokoschka Archive, Villeneuve.
[III]:
the theatre, where I was up on the grid: presumably Kokoschka had the entrée backstage at the Opera House because the production of *Mörder Hoffnung der Frauen* was then in preparation.
one of Lahmann's potions: Alice Lahmann's husband was director of the Weißer Hirsch sanatorium in Dresden, where Kokoschka had been a patient in 1916–17.
[IV]:
The Bustelli figurines: modern reproductions from the Nymphenburg porcelain factory in Munich.

To Anna Kallin, dated and undated letters of March 1923, ms., Kokoschka Archive, Villeneuve, and National Archives, Helsinki.

Once again, the series of frequent letters to Anna Kallin dates from a period she spent in London with her parents during a vacation.

Early March 1923:

the eighteen-year battle: Kokoschka reckons his artistic career from October 1904, when he entered the Kunstgewerbeschule in Vienna.

the painting: Jacob, Rachel and Leah (Wingler, no. 152).

Late March 1923:

Reserl: Hulda, Kokoschka's servant.

The cut in the postscript is of one sentence concerning an errand on behalf of Anna Kallin's parents.

29 March 1923:

my letter about your helplessness: dated 28 March 1928 (not included in this selection). In it Kokoschka compares his working to support his family with the pampering of Anna Kallin by her parents.

my painting: Jacob, Rachel and Leah.

Fritsche: head porter at the Dresden Academy.

End of March 1923:

syolnushka: Russian, 'little sun'.

To Alice Lahmann, 25 August 1923, ms., Kokoschka Archive, Villeneuve.

Böhler: the Munich art-dealer Julius Wilhelm Böhler, who opened a branch in Lucerne after the First World War.

To Anna Kallin, early November 1923, ms., Kokoschka Archive, Villeneuve.

The passages omitted consist of self-reproaches for not having visited his parents at Christmas 1922, and a reference to remarks made by Anna Kallin in a letter to Kokoschka's brother Bohuslav.

let me have the painting: perhaps refers to a view of Lake Geneva, left behind in Blonay, where Kokoschka and Anna Kallin had spent the month of September, until he had to depart in a hurry on hearing of the deterioration in his father's health.

To Alice Lahmann, early and mid-November 1924, ms., Kokoschka Archive, Villeneuve, and National Archives, Helsinki.

Mid-November 1924:

Niuta only stuck to me: after the death of Kokoschka's father and an interruption in their correspondence perhaps out of consideration for his mother's anxiety that they might form closer ties – Kokoschka and Anna Kallin became estranged for a period of several years.

The passage omitted is illegible.

To Alexandrine, Countess Khuenburg, 18 April 1924, ms., Zentralbibliothek, Zurich.

I am travelling with a German: the art-dealer Jakob Goldschmidt, an associate of the Berlin dealer Paul Cassirer (with whom Kokoschka had a contractual arrangement). Goldschmidt accompanied Kokoschka on his travels through Italy, France, Spain and

Portugal in 1925, taking care 'not only of the travel tickets and hotels, but of painting supplies and the packing and shipping of completed pictures' (*My Life*, p. 127).

I wanted to finish my picture in the Castle: Kokoschka had started to paint in the Castelo de São Jorge which overlooks Lisbon, but the events he describes prevented him from finishing the picture (Wingler, no. 197).

since the earthquake: much of Lisbon was devastated in 1755.

The Braganza Chapel: the pantheon containing the tombs of the royal house of Portugal, in the refectory of the Augustinian convent of São Vicente de Fora.

To Alice Lahmann, 23 and 24 April 1925, ms., Kokoschka Archive, Villeneuve, and private ownership, Helsinki.

24 April 1925:

the shadow of someone else: i.e. Philip II of Spain.

P.C.: Paul Cassirer.

give me a reindeer too: a reference to Damaris Brunow, a cousin of Alice Lahmann, often alluded to by Kokoschka as 'reindeer' (see biographical note on Alice Lahmann).

a little sweetheart . . . from Biarritz: Marguerite Loeb, whom Kokoschka had met on or around 8 April 1925.

To Marguerite Loeb, 11/12 May and late May/early June 1925. ms., private ownership, Tangier.

To Anna Kallin, late May/early June 1925, ms., Kokoschka Archive, Villeneuve.

Friedländer: Max J. Friedländer, from 1929 director of the Berlin Print Room and Art Gallery; he had entered the museum service in 1896.

To Marguerite Loeb, dated and undated letters of June, July and August 1925, ms., private ownership, Tangier.

19 July 1925:

On Wednesday I leave here for Amsterdam, . . . I've almost finished my second painting here: Kokoschka's first painting in London was of Tower Bridge (Wingler, no. 198). The next cannot be identified with complete certainty. He arrived in Holland on 24 July. In a letter to his brother, sent from Amsterdam on 30 July 1925, Kokoschka told him that he was going to Switzerland on 5 August. It is not known how long he stayed in Pontresina, nor where he spent the next two months. He was in Berlin in November for Cassirer's exhibition of his work, and then went to Vienna to see his family.

To Anna Kallin, 19 November 1925 to 11 January 1927, ms., Kokoschka Archive, Villeneuve

19 November 1925:

Dukes: perhaps Ashley Dukes, the English dramatist, critic and theatre manager, husband of the dancer Marie Rambert.

the 'Hymn to the Sun': probably the 'big number' from Rimsky-Korsakov's *Golden Cockerel*.

the 'Indra' song: 'Indra' was a name Kokoschka used for Anna Kallin in the caption to a drawing (Rathenau, I, no. 106).

the news about the Wartmann exhibition: Wartmann was the director of the Kunsthaus in Zurich, where a major exhibition of Kokoschka's work was held in the summer of 1927.

I wrote that particular play once before: Kokoschka is drawing a parallel with his relationship to Alma Mahler, as depicted in his *Orpheus und Eurydike*, where 'misfortune' chiefly befalls the despairing poet, i.e. himself, not the woman.

the divorced son-in-law of the victim: Ernst Křenek was married for a time to Anna Mahler, daughter of Alma and Gustav Mahler. The phrase 'victim and principal character in the opera' refers to Alma Mahler.

world première . . . in Kassel in October 1927: in fact it took place earlier, on 26 November 1926.

I have started something somewhere else: an allusion either to an exhibition that Kokoschka hoped would be mounted in the USA but which came to nothing, or to his relationship with Marguerite Loeb.

that English book by a lady anthropoligist: Katherine Routledge, *The Mystery of Easter Island*, London, 1919.

11 January 1927:

the head from Dresden: head of the Athena of Myron, a marble copy from the bronze group *Athena and Marsyas*. There is a copy of the Athena with head in the Liebig-Haus Museum, Frankfurt. The museum in Dresden has a copy of the head alone, which is regarded as the best of the known copies.

the old turtle: Giant Turtles (Wingler, no. 224), painted in the Berlin Aquarium.

not counting the ring: Kokoschka bought a solitaire for his mother as a security; it was later sold at a loss.

Marek: Anna Kallin's brother. During the Second World War he served as an officer in the Royal Navy and was killed in action while escorting one of the Russian convoys.

In the autumn of 1927 Kokoschka set off on travels that took him to Italy, southern France and North Africa.

To Anna Kallin, October and November 1927, ms., National Archives, Helsinki.
Mid-November 1927:

Ovington Gardens: Kokoschka had rented a house in Kensington for several months, from March to September 1926.

my Saul: an unfinished play, now lost.

To Anna Kallin, 15 January 1928, ms., Kokoschka Archive, Villeneuve.

the whole world and its centre . . . : alongside these words Kokoschka drew a dotted circle, with a dot at the centre.

Alaoui: now part of the Bardo Museum in Tunis.

my petroleum-find: in the desert Kokoschka had found fossil remains of snails with a left-hand helix, and was convinced they were a sign of oil below the sand. Oil was, in fact, found there later.

Lütjens: Kokoschka's travelling companion, an employee of Paul Cassirer, who joined him in Venice and accompanied him as far as Algeria.

Halpern: a banker, Russian emigrant, married to a friend of Anna Kallin.

To Anna Kallin, 22 January and 3 March 1928, ms., National Archives, Helsinki.
The letter of 22 January has a passage missing.
3 March 1928:

an Arab monastery: the monastic complex of Temacine, 7 km. from Touggourt.

277

My Col de Sfa landscape: the painting *Exodus (Col de Sfa near Biskra)* (Wingler, no. 236).

To Anna Kallin, letters of 17 April and 4 May 1928, ms., Kokoschka Archive, Villeneuve.
17 April 1928:
feast of fools: probably a reference to the many processions held in Seville during Holy
   Week.
Joanna the Mad: Kokoschka expounded his ideas about Joanna and her son Charles V in
   Shylock's monologue in his play about Comenius, written during the 1930s.
Franz I and my grandmother: allusion to a family story, told to Kokoschka by his father
   Gustav. After his abdication, Franz I once visited the workshop of Kokoschka's
   grandfather in Prague; Gustav Kokoschka must have been between three and five years
   old at the time, however; there is no foundation in fact to support the fanciful
   speculations set out here.
Your Habsburg: unexplained allusion to an acquaintance of Anna Kallin.
The woman who says she's the Tsar's daughter: rumours about Anastasia, youngest daughter of
   Nicholas II, who was said to have survived the massacre of the Romanovs at
   Ekaterinburg, continued to flourish in the popular press till well into the second half of
   the century.
that museum in London: Madame Tussaud's waxworks.
The Chinese lady: the actress Anna May Wong.
4 May 1928:
Titian . . . Adam and Eve: throughout his life, up to his last visit in 1975, Titian's paintings
   and the Rubens copies of them were the pictures that most interested Kokoschka in the
   Prado.
the Athena by the potter Antenor: Antenor's Kore in the Acropolis Museum in Athens, which
   Kokoschka knew only from casts in Dresden. His referring to a sculptor as a potter is not
   unusual for him. His relief of 1963 and the accompanying lithographs (Wingler-Welz,
   no. 273) depict a sculptor working on a bust, but they bear the title *Der Töpfer* (The
   Potter).

Kokoschka's further travels in the late spring and early summer of 1928 are not altogether
   clear. He probably went to Vienna, but he also visited Garmisch-Partenkirchen at some
   point at the end of May or beginning of June, as he sent his family a postcard of the
   Zugspitze. The collector Marcel von Nemes lived in the vicinity, and Kokoschka
   painted his portrait (Wingler, no. 245). A letter to Nemes of 29 May 1929 (not included
   here) demonstrates that the portrait was painted at an earlier date than has previously
   been thought. In June and July he travelled to Ireland and England, but not to
   Scotland, as previously supposed; he first went there in August and September 1929.

To Anna Kallin, 24 June 1928, ms. (postcard), National Archives, Helsinki.

To Alice Lahmann, 29 July 1929, ms., Kokoschka Archive, Villeneuve.
our tall Miss: Damaris Brunow (see biographical note on Alice Lahmann, her cousin).
   Kokoschka gave poetic form to his encounter with her in his story 'Ostern auf Zypern'
   (*Das schriftliche Werk*, II, pp. 322ff.)
the gentleman who . . . on his own forelock: a reference to one of the tall tales of Baron
   Münchhausen.

278

a tax prosecution . . . a financier's complaint: Kokoschka's letters to his brother frequently refer to tax problems which arose after he re-registered as a resident of Vienna. The identity of the financier and the nature of his complaint have not been established.

Feilchenfeldt & Ringelnatter: on Paul Cassirer's death in 1926, the direction of his art-dealing and publishing business passed to Walter Feilchenfeldt and Grete Ring ('Ringelnatter' means 'grass snake').

During August and September 1929 Kokoschka visited Scotland to paint, then appears to have spent most of the winter in Vienna; in March 1930 he returned to Tunisia. He sent his family and Alice Lahmann various short letters and postcards in the course of these journeys.

To Anna Kallin, 22 June 1930, ms., Kokoschka Archive, Villeneuve.

I want to write an English play: the ambition was not realized until the English version of *Comenius*, written during the Second World War, but that cannot be regarded as finished.

Poor Heinrich: a nobleman in medieval Christian legend who becomes a leper, but is miraculously healed when he learns selflessness from the example of a good woman who loves him. The story is the subject of a poem by Hartman von Aue (*c.*1195) and a play by Gerhart Hauptmann (1902).

a nemchik: Slavonic diminutive meaning 'little German'. Its use here may be a personal allusion understood only by Kokoschka and Anna Kallin.

Djerba: island off the coast of Tunisia. The story 'Djerba' (*Das schriftliche Werk*, II, pp. 227ff.) is a wholly fantastic version of events that have a basis in reality, though the account in this letter is already highly coloured. Kokoschka's attempt to make the acquaintance of a young Jewish girl turned the whole community against him, and, apparently with the hope of placating them, he donated a new chandelier to the synagogue. When he returned to Djerba in 1971, he was unable to tell which of the chandeliers still hanging there was his gift.

To Alice Lahmann, 11 June 1931, ms., Kokoschka Archive, Villeneuve.

Kokoschka had moved into a small house previously occupied by his friend Jules Pascin, who had died. It no longer exists.

drawings of the 'Holy Mass': the idea occurred to Kokoschka again in 1968, in support of the campaign to retain the Latin Mass after the Second Vatican Council. On neither occasion was the plan carried out.

the young woman: Damaris Brunow.

To Albert Ehrenstein, 18 January 1933, ms., University Library, Jerusalem.

George Grosz, the well-known International Communist: 'Euer George Großkommunist'. Having denigrated Kokoschka as a 'whore' at the time of the latter's Open Letter to the inhabitants of Dresden of March 1920, and spent the 1920s actively promoting Marxist views in his satires, Grosz had by now gone to the United States and completely changed his convictions as well as the style and subject-matter of his work.

Open letter on behalf of Max Liebermann, published in the *Frankfurter Zeitung* of 8 June 1933. The text of the letter appeared with the following preamble from the paper's editors: 'It gives us great pleasure to publish this open letter from the painter Kokoschka, the more so because it is rare nowadays for a "German" to speak out so warmly on behalf of a "foreigner".'

later Emperor Friedrich: Friedrich III (1831–88) held liberal views, unlike his father (Wilhelm I) or his son (Wilhelm II). He died only a few months after his accession in 1888.

Gründerjahre: strictly speaking the term applies to the German economic boom of 1871–3, but like many people Kokoschka uses it loosely to refer to the early part of the Wilhelmine Empire.

the possession even of a forged Florentine Madonna: probably a reference to Wilhelm von Bode's purchase, for one of the Berlin galleries in his charge, of a forgery passed off as a work by Leonardo da Vinci.

the Aryan Paragraph: anti-Semitic legislation introduced by the National Socialist government.

After the appearance of this letter, it was risky for any newspaper to publish any letter from Kokoschka, especially if it was critical of the government. The *Frankfurter Zeitung* was published by Jews, and was soon closed down by the National Socialists.

To Albert Ehrenstein, 22 September 1934, ms., University Library, Jerusalem.

Tubutsch: the name of the hero of a story by Ehrenstein, which Kokoschka illustrated in 1911.

M.: Moscow.

Robert Briffault: English anthropologist. See the biographical note on Helen Briffault, p. 298.

a preface: this could be the essay 'Totem und Tabu', written in 1933 (*Das schriftliche Werk*, IV, pp. 43ff.).

Gorky: the Russian writer Maxim Gorky, whom Ehrenstein had evidently met in Moscow.

To Anna Kallin, 5 October 1934, Kokoschka Archive, Villeneuve.

The passage omitted at the beginning of the letter is of no interest.

blue-blooded gigolos: the Austrian Foreign Minister Count Starhemberg and the right-wing government, which enjoyed Fascist support. In April 1934 Austria had become a one-party, corporatist state under the chancellorship of Engelbert Dollfuss, who was assassinated the following July.

toadying cardinals: Cardinal Theodor Innitzer (1875–1955), Archbishop of Vienna since 1932, was known to sign his letters 'Heil Hitler!'.

my lectures and essays: see *Das schriftliche Werk*, IV, pp. 43ff.

To Albert Ehrenstein, autumn 1934, ms., University Library, Jerusalem.

the Vienna Nirenstein: the art-dealer Dr Otto Nirenstein-Kallir. The reference, a few lines later, to 'gallstones or kidneystones' ('Nierensteine') is a pun on his name.

Federer: managing director of the Witkowitz steelworks in Mährisch-Ostrau, and a collector of paintings; among other works by Kokoschka, he bought the early view of Istanbul (Wingler, no. 243).

the famous Prague landscape: the identification is uncertain – Kokoschka painted at least three views of Prague in 1934.

the 'Martyr-Chancellor': Dollfuss, the recently assassinated Austrian Chancellor.

280

Edith Sachsl: she accompanied Kokoschka to Prague, but their relationship was short-lived. He later attempted to provide the financial security she would have needed to be permitted to enter the United States by making over to her the fees for his portrait of Thomas G. Masaryk, the President of Czechoslovakia.

Rowohlt: the publisher Ernst Rowohlt, whom Kokoschka knew, and drew, in Berlin during the First World War.

my poor mother: Romana Kokoschka had died earlier in the year.

To Helen Briffault, 8 February 1935, typed copy in the Kokoschka Archive, Villeneuve.

young lady: Edith Sachsl.

lactic acid-amidogen: it is not at all clear what Kokoschka meant by this.

To Albert Ehrenstein, June or July 1935, ms., University Library, Jerusalem.

Ehrenstein had left Moscow, and was living in Switzerland.

M: Thomas Masaryk.

Prager Tagblatt: one of the two mass-circulation, German-language daily newspapers published in Prague.

a little call to arms: Kokoschka's response to a reader's letter to the newspaper, published on 6 July 1935 under the title 'Humanity through the elementary school' (see *Das schriftliche Werk*, IV, p. 351).

Habsburgers: the right wing in Austrian politics.

To Anna Kallin, 11 July 1935 and February 1936, ms., National Archives, Helsinki.

11 July 1935:

the enclosed article: see above, the note on 'a little call to arms' in the letter to Ehrenstein, June or July 1935.

the little Czech girl: this allusion has not been identified.

February 1936:

the late king: King George V had died shortly before, 20 January.

the cartridge manufacturer Mandl: not a reference to Kokoschka's Viennese friend, the industrialist Erich Mandl.

He got the idea from Streicher: from *Schwarze Korps*, one of the cultural-political propaganda magazines of National Socialism, edited by Julius Streicher.

To Anna Kallin, 22 November 1936, ms., Kokoschka Archive, Villeneuve.

Arbeiterzeitung: daily newspaper of the Social Democratic party.

'gleichgeschaltet': 'gleichschalten' (past participle 'gleichgeschaltet'; noun 'Gleichschaltung'), meaning 'co-ordinate' or 'make conform', was unlucky enough to be adopted as National Socialist jargon. In his letters of the 1930s and '40s Kokoschka often alluded directly to that usage, even when he wrote in English, therefore to translate the term in his German-language letters would lose the point.

Völkischer Beobachter: newspaper of the German National Socialist party.

Gringoire: French right-wing newspaper.

London News: Illustrated London News, London weekly of a conservative slant.

In the summer of 1937 Kokoschka went to Mährisch-Ostrau (Ostrava) to paint, but was taken ill and admitted to the hospital of the Witkowitz steelworks.

To Alma Mahler-Werfel, undated letter of summer 1937, and 30 July 1937, ms., Kokoschka Archive, Villeneuve.

These two letters were not included in the German edition of Kokoschka's letters.

30 July 1937:

another woman: Edith Sachsl.

Sch.: Kurt von Schuschnigg, Chancellor of Austria. See below, Kokoschka's letter to him, dated 3 August 1937.

Innitzer: Cardinal Innitzer, Archbishop of Vienna.

To Kurt von Schuschnigg, 3 August 1937, typescript, carbon copy in the Kokoschka Archive, Villeneuve.

The copy bears the following ms. note by Kokoschka: 'No answer received, even though delivered by hand to three separate offices.'

To Alma Mahler-Werfel, 16 December 1937, ms., Kokoschka Archive, Villeneuve.

This letter does not appear in the German edition of Kokoschka's letters.

Carl: Carl Moll, Alma Mahler-Werfel's stepfather.

To Anna Kallin, 28 February 1938, ms., National Archives, Helsinki.

A passage about a book given to Kokoschka by Olda Palkovská – *The Gentle Savage* by Richard Wyndham – has been omitted.

To Homer Saint Gaudens, 15 April 1938, typescript, carbon copy in the Kokoschka Archive, Villeneuve.

Führer-Neid: the Führer's hatred and envy (of me).

Gleichschaltungs-Nudelwalker: a machine for mixing noodle or pasta dough; for 'Gleichschaltung' see above, note on the letter to Anna Kallin, 22 November 1936.

Freie Deutsche Kulturbund: the Free German League of Culture.

Modezeichner: fashion artist.

the occupation of Austria: the 'Anschluß' or annexation of Austria into Greater Germany in March 1938.

Trostpreis: consolation prize.

To Herbert Read, 17 May 1938, ms., collection of Professor Oto Bihalji-Merin, Belgrade.

'Modern German Art' exhibition: this was originally planned for London, as a counterblast to the 'Degenerate Art' show in Munich, but after diplomatic pressure from the German government its scope was enlarged to include the work of other German artists, who had not been vilified by the National Socialists.

our friend W.: Paul Westheim.

Hore-Belisha: Sir Leslie Hore-Belisha, Minister of Transport, 1934–7, and Secretary of State for War, 1937–40.

To Augustus John, 26 May 1938, typescript, carbon copy in the Kokoschka Archive, Villeneuve.

Some minor corrections have been made to the English.

Fincham: D. C. Fincham, assistant curator at the Tate Gallery, London.

Ossietzky: the German writer and pacifist Carl von Ossietzky (1889–1938) was interned in a concentration camp 1934–6 for his opinions. He was awarded the Nobel Peace Prize in 1935. He died of the effects of his detention.

Pranger: 'pillory', i.e. the 'Degenerate Art' exhibition.

To Carl Moll, summer 1938, ms., copy (draft version?) in the Kokoschka Archive, Villeneuve.

Moll had made an accommodation with the National Socialists, and in the course of explaining himself to Kokoschka had made reproaches which demanded a circumstantial reply. A cut is indicated in a sentence in the third paragraph because the German, although grammatically coherent, is clearly incomplete.

an old portrait: Portrait of Robert Freund, I, 1909 (Wingler, no. 89). It was restored after the Second World War.

the Frankfurter Zeitung *leader, 1929:* on 31 December 1931 (not 1929), the *Frankfurter Zeitung* had published an Open Letter from Kokoschka, setting out his side of his dispute with the proprietors of Paul Cassirer. (The letter is published in volume II of the German edition of his letters.)

To Ruth and Adolf Arndt, 20 October 1938, ms., Frau Ruth Arndt, Kassel.

The letter was sent unsigned, for reasons of security.

'Girls Bathing': Summer II (Zráni) (Wingler, no. 321).

The cases stayed behind in Prague: they reached London eventually, but were empty.

Lord Cecil: Viscount Cecil of Chelwood, who was President of the League of Nations Union, 1923–45.

Holda: i.e. Olda Palkovská.

The big painting is with Kuoni: The Fountain, the current (and final) version of a painting Kokoschka had started in Dresden in 1923, when its title was *Jacob, Rachel and Leah;* he revised it in Prague; in 1937 he referred to it by the title *Nymph* (see Wingler, nos. 152 and 313). Kuoni is a shipper (and travel-agent), based in Zurich.

Herr Fleischmann: a Berlin art-dealer, who had emigrated to Switzerland.

To Albert Ehrenstein, September 1939, ms., University Library, Jerusalem.

Genia . . . Hemme: Dr Eugenie and Dr Hermann Schwarzwald, in whose house in Vienna Kokoschka was a frequent guest in 1911–12, and again in 1932–4. Hermann Schwarzwald had died shortly after the couple had escaped from Austria.

To Anna Kallin, 1 October 1939, ms., Kokoschka Archive, Villeneuve.

A few sentences giving the same information about Bohuslav Kokoschka's plans as in the preceding letter to Ehrenstein, have been omitted.

Olda's father joined the Polish army: Dr Palkovsky went to Poland shortly before Prague was occupied, and from there he reached Paris via Yugoslavia. A long trek took him via Bordeaux to Portugal, and he eventually reached England in the autumn of 1940.

To Joseph Needham, 4 November 1941, typescript, Cambridge University Library.

Overton: Richard Overton (fl. 1640s), leader of the Levellers, printer and pamphleteer.

T. More's Utopia: Sir Thomas More's *Utopia* (1516 in Latin; English translation 1551) was an attack on conditions in England as compared with the communistic society he described in his vision of the island of Utopia, created by him.

Hartlib: Samuel Hartlib (d. 1662), printer, publisher of Comenius; interested in educational and social reforms.

To Anna Kallin, 5 November 1941, ms., Kokoschka Archive, Villeneuve.
Three minor corrections have been made to the English.

To Paul Westheim, early 1942(?), Mariana Frenk-Westheim, Mexico City.
Fred: Fred Uhlmann, secretary of the Free German League of Culture in Great Britain.

To Joseph Needham, spring 1942, ms., Cambridge University Library.
Two minor corrections have been made to the English.
your book: The Teacher of Nations. Addresses and essays in commemoration of John Amos Comenius, ed. J. Needham, Cambridge 1942.
Winstanley: Gerrard Winstanley (1609–76), English political visionary, leader of the Diggers.

To the editors of several daily newspapers, 1942(?), typescript, carbon copy in the Kokoschka Archive, Villeneuve.
None of the papers published it.

To Joseph Lauwerys, 27 June 1943, typescript, carbon copy in the Kokoschka Archive, Villeneuve.
A few minor corrections have been made to the English.
my essay: either 'The War as Seen by Children' or 'The Fifth Anniversary of the Free German League of Culture' (*Das schriftliche Werk*, IV, pp. 246ff. and pp. 261ff.).
an Irish friend: Jack Carney (see note to letter of 7 September 1946).
proskynesis: prostration in religious ritual.

During the war years Oskar and Olda Kokoschka lived in a borrowed eighth-floor flat in Park Lane in London. Between 1941 and 1946 they were also able to spend a month or so at a time with friends in Wales, southern Scotland or near Ullapool in northwest Scotland.

To Ivan Maisky, 1 January 1944, typescript, carbon copy in the Kokoschka Archive, Villeneuve.
One minor change has been made to the English.
Beddington-Behrens: Major Edward Beddington-Behrens (1897–1968), English banker who formed a close friendship with Olda and Oskar Kokoschka during the Second World War. He was instrumental in arranging for Kokoschka's portrait of Maisky (Wingler, no. 328) to be presented to the Tate Gallery.

To Donald Wolfit, 4 May 1944, typescript, carbon copy in the Kokoschka Archive, Villeneuve.
A few lines have been cut because they are illegible.

To Jack and Mina Carney, 18 August 1944, Zentralbibliothek, Zurich.
the Stursas: Jan R. Stursa, nephew of the Czech sculptor, and his wife.

Korner: Professor Emil Korner had been financial director of the Witkowitz steelworks in Mährisch-Ostrau (see above, note on Kokoschka's letters to Alma Mahler-Werfel in the summer of 1937). He and his family moved to London in 1938 and in 1941 bought The House of Elrig, Portwilliam, in southern Scotland.

Morrison & Bevin: Herbert Morrison and Ernest Bevin, respectively Home Secretary and Minister of Labour and National Service in Britain's wartime coalition government.

The Machiavellians: the book by James Burnham, published in 1943, was subtitled *Defenders of Freedom.*

To Edith Hoffmann-Yapou, 24 December 1944, ms., property of the addressee, Jerusalem.

this book . . . : Edith Hoffmann's monograph, *Kokoschka, Life and Work,* published in 1947.

To Herbert Read, 27 June and 6 September 1945, typescript, University of Victoria, British Columbia.

Some minor corrections have been made to the English.

In the letter of 27 June, opening remarks about publishing projects have been cut. Kokoschka had written a polemical essay which he wanted to be included as an appendix in Edith Hoffmann's monograph about him. There was a possibility that T. S. Eliot (a director of Faber and Faber, who were to publish it) might write a preface for the monograph.

27 June 1945:

Kennerley: Morley Kennerley, a director of Faber and Faber.

5 September 1945:

Fierlinger: Zdeněk Fierlinger, a member of the Czechoslovak provisional government in London, where Kokoschka had some contact with him. Fierlinger returned to Prague with Beneš and became Prime Minister of Czechoslovakia.

Céline: Kokoschka had known Céline (Louis Ferdinand Destouches) during his residence in Paris in the early 1930s.

To Josef P. Hodin, September 1945, ms., the addressee, London.

Democracy today and tomorrow: originally a group of lectures that Beneš gave at the University of Chicago in 1939.

Košice: town in Slovakia, which was nominally an independent state under the German occupation of Czechoslovakia.

blood [and] soil: Nazi slogan ('Blut und Boden').

Salut! Nazdar! Živio!: the French, Czech and Serbo-Croat equivalents of 'Heil'.

To Hans Meyboden, 4 October and 24 December 1945, ms., Frau Grete Meyboden, Fischerhude, near Bremen.

4 October 1945:

ways of helping you: towards the end of the war, Meyboden was ill in Switzerland. He was interned there, and did not return to his home in Fischerhude until the spring of 1946. The passage omitted describes Kokoschka's attempts to help him through the agency of the British Embassy in Berne.

24 December 1945:

Some matters of no great importance, referred to near the beginning, have been omitted.

the greatest happiness of the greatest number: Kokoschka's study of Bentham went back to the
1930s; see the essay 'Jeremy Bentham contra souveräner Staat' (*c.*1935), *Das schriftliche
Werk*, IV, pp. 137–51.

To Alfred Neumeyer, 1 March 1946, as published in *Magazine of Art*, Washington, D.C.,
May 1946, vol. 39, no. 5, p. 196.
your splendid essay: an article by Neumeyer had appeared in the November 1945 issue of
Magazine of Art, pp. 261–5.
'Kunstgewerbe': arts and crafts.

To Augustus John, 24 April 1946, typescript, carbon copy in the Kokoschka Archive,
Villeneuve.
Iris Tree: English actress, whom Kokoschka had got to know in Paris between the wars.

To Sir Kenneth Clark, 29 April 1946, typescript, carbon copy in the Kokoschka Archive,
Villeneuve.
The second paragraph, here omitted, repeats in similar words Kokoschka's sentiments
expressed in his letter to Augustus John.

To Arnold Schoenberg, 26 June 1946, ms., Library of Congress, Washington, D.C.
musical festival: the 18th festival of the International Society for Contemporary Music was
held in London, 7–14 July 1946. It included a performance of Schoenberg's *Ode to
Napoleon* on 10 July.
Egon Wellesz: the Viennese-born composer and musicologist was a lifelong supporter of
Schoenberg, but capable of critical comment. This remark probably refers to a storm in
a teacup.
Schoenberg's cordial reply to Kokoschka's letter, dated 3 July 1946, is printed (with some
cuts) in *Letters*, selected and edited by Erwin Stein, translated by Eithne Wilkins and
Ernst Kaiser (London, 1964).

To Fritz Schahlecker, 4 July 1946, typescript, carbon copy in the Kokoschka Archive,
Villeneuve.
Other than what emerges from the letter, nothing is known of the circumstances or life of
the addressee. Kokoschka responded without knowing Schahlecker personally.

To Jack Carney, 7 September 1946, typescript, copy in the Kokoschka Archive,
Villeneuve.
One correction has been made to the English.
Your last letter: Jack Carney, an idealistic Communist, refused to see the criminality of acts
perpetuated by Stalin and the Soviet Union. This led to violent arguments between him
and Kokoschka. His 'last letter' – a reply to one from Kokoschka dated 18 August 1946 –
remained his last.
Real Politics: i.e. *Realpolitik.*
Transfer: the policy adopted by postwar governments in Eastern European countries of
expelling established minorities who differed in language and/or race from the majority
of the population in their respective countries (cf. above, the letters written by
Kokoschka in September 1945 to Herbert Read and Josef P. Hodin).

To Victor Matejka, 15 January 1948, ms., the addressee, Vienna.
Some passages concerning less important questions of only passing interest have been
  omitted.
[Tippett's] 'Oratorio': A Child of Our Time.
Webern's Cantata: the world première of Webern's First Cantata, op. 29, was given in
  London on 12 July 1946, at the 18th ISCM festival (cf. the letter to Arnold Schoenberg,
  26 June 1946).
the artificial limbs: Kokoschka had visited Vienna in November 1947, to see his brother. He
  was moved by the sight of the many ex-servicemen who had lost limbs, and had
  suggested painting a portrait of the Burgomaster, Dr Theodor Körner, in order to raise
  money for artificial limbs.
Nierenstein: see above, the note relating to the letter to Albert Ehrenstein, autumn 1934.
fairy stories: Kokoschka was angered by claims made by Nirenstein-Kallir, putting an
  earlier date on some of Egon Schiele's early works than they had previously been given.
  Most of the evidence, which proved unfounded, had been circulated in cyclostyled form
  during the war and the immediate postwar period.

To James S. Plaut, 13 May 1948, published in the catalogue of the retrospective exhibition
  of Kokoschka's work shown at the Institute of Contemporary Art, Boston, Mass., in
  1948, and then in a number of other American cities.
corriger la fortune: a quotation from Lessing's play *Minna von Barnhelm.*
artist of today, abjuring his own work: possibly Kokoschka had Giorgio de Chirico in mind.

To Marcel Ray, 5 December 1948, typescript, copy in the archive of Frau Wissmann-
  Ficker, Innsbruck.
A passage in which Kokoschka speaks of his concern for his brother Bohuslav has been
  omitted.
remarks about Corbusier: at a ceremony commemorating Adolf Loos, Ray had enumerated
  the features in Le Corbusier's work that derived from Loos.

In memoriam Karl Kraus, 25 April 1949, Dr Viktor Matejka, Vienna.
The poet and writer Karl Kraus (1874–1936) had been editor of the outspoken journal *Die
  Fackel.* Matejka may have asked Kokoschka for a contribution to his own publication,
  the weekly *Österreichisches Tagebuch.*

To Olda Kokoschka, 30 July and 16 August 1949, ms., Kokoschka Archive, Villeneuve.
30 July:
Tanglewood: a reference to the annual summer music festival held nearby, directed by the
  Russian-American conductor Serge Koussevitsky.
Brünn and Proßnitz: an allusion to the large number of people of German-Jewish origin
  living in the Pittsfield area.
Feigl: Hugo Feigl, art-dealer, originally of Prague, who had emigrated to the USA.
  Kokoschka had met him in the 1930s.
Florence: view of Florence Cathedral (Wingler 1956, no. 352).
Henry: Henry Pearlman, Kokoschka's host in New York in January 1949, whose portrait
  he had painted in London in 1948.
Plesch: the Kokoschkas' doctor in London.

287

To Arnold Schoenberg, 19 August 1949, ms., Library of Congress, Washington, D.C.

Mann, Kopf, Hillyer and Winograd: Robert Mann, Robert Kopf, Raphael Hillyer and Arthur Winograd, the original members of the Juilliard String Quartet, founded in 1946.

your birthday: Schoenberg was seventy-five on 13 September 1949.

From Pittsfield, Kokoschka went to New York for a few days and then to Minneapolis, where he was to paint the double portrait of John and Betty Cowles (Wingler, no. 361). The series of letters he wrote his wife from there is exceptional in their depiction of the artist during the creation of a painting.

To Olda Kokoschka, 15 and 20 September and 2 October 1949, ms., Kokoschka Archive, Villeneuve.

15 September 1949:

Wheeler and Rockefeller: Monroe Wheeler and David J. Rockefeller, trustees of the Museum of Modern Art, New York.

20 September 1949:

soffitto: the ceiling painting *Prometheus*, which Kokoschka was to execute in the London house of Antoine, Count Seilern, beginning in the spring of 1950. (The triptych is now in the possession of the Courtauld Institute, London; Wingler, nos. 362–4.) See also letter of 14 January 1950.

Wastl: Sebastian Isepp, painter and restorer, a friend of Kokoschka since his student days.

Fred: Alfred Marnau.

Remarks in the letter of 2 October about some of the paintings in the Cowles collection have been omitted.

To an American student, 24 November 1949, typescript, carbon copy in the Kokoschka Archive, Villeneuve.

Two corrections have been made to the English.

Erblande: the hereditary Habsburg domains in central Europe.

To Antoine, Count Seilern, 14 January 1950, ms., Courtauld Institute, London.

To Josef P. Hodin, 15 July 1950, ms., the addressee, London.

Dr Blunt: Anthony Blunt, who since 1947 had been Professor of the History of Art, University of London, and Director of the Courtauld Institute.

To Will Grohmann, 7 December 1951, ms., Grohmann Archive in the Staatsgalerie, Stuttgart.

Wozzeck: nothing came of this proposal, and there are no known preliminary studies.

To Alfred and Senta Marnau, 22 December 1951, ms., Alfred Marnau, London.

portrait of a big industrialist: Emil Bührle (Wingler, no. 374).

Andreas Hofer: champion of Tyrolean independence (1767–1810), shot by the Austrians.

Thurek: Josef Thorak, a protégé of Hitler, who was returning to favour in Salzburg in the early 1950s.

Wotruba: Fritz Wotruba, Austrian sculptor.

iron kings and queens: twenty-eight magnificent over-lifesize bronze figures surrounding the tomb of Maximilian I in the Hofkirche in Innsbruck (the work of several artists, 1509–50).

To Ruth and Adolf Arndt, 3 June 1952, ms., Frau Ruth Arndt, Kassel.
The passage omitted consists of details of Kokoschka's travel plans.

To Walter Feilchenfeldt, 24 August 1952, ms., Frau Marianne Feilchenfeldt, Zurich.
Feilchenfeldt and Grete Ring took over the management of the art-dealing business of Paul Cassirer after the latter's death in 1926. Kokoschka's relationship with the firm deteriorated, due to disagreements about the terms of his contract, and he eventually severed the connection in 1931, after which his personal relationships with Ring (especially) and Feilchenfeldt were also bad for a number of years.

To Alfred Marnau, 27 November 1952, ms., Alfred Marnau, London.
the college: The Minneapolis Art Institute.
a portrait: Pete Gale (Wingler, no. 378).
The Salzburg thing: Kokoschka was planning his 'School of Seeing' at Salzburg, which started in 1953.
The passage omitted concerns the finances of Kokoschka's brother.

To Ludwig von Ficker, 10 January 1953, *Der Brenner*-Archiv, University of Innsbruck.
my Munch essay: 'Der Expressionismus Edvard Munchs', *Das schriftliche Werk*, III, pp. 162ff.
To be so close to [the Pope]: Kokoschka was allowed to draw sketches during a canonization ceremony in St Peter's.

To Josef P. Hodin, 10 October 1953, ms., the addressee, London.
Beautiful: Kokoschka's pet-name for Pamela Hodin, Josef's wife.

To Theodor Heuss, 20 December 1953, ms., Deutsches Literaturarchiv, Marbach.

To Henriette von Motesiczky, 2 May 1954, ms., Marie Louise von Motesiczky, London.
poor Marie: family cook, and former nanny of the addressee's daughter, the painter Marie Louise von Motesiczky (Florizl).
The passage omitted continues the theme of modern degeneracy, with reference to the popularity of Picasso.

To Wilhelm Furtwängler, 26 November 1954, ms., Elisabeth Furtwängler, Clarens.
This letter does not appear in the German edition of Kokoschka's letters. Furtwängler died on 30 November 1954. See also below, under 28 January 1955.

To Alice Rosenlew, 28 December 1954, ms., Kokoschka Archive, Villeneuve.
I was to have done Die Zauberflöte: Kokoschka's designs, originally done at Furtwängler's invitation, were used in the production of the opera at the Salzburg Festival in 1955 and 1956, conducted by Georg Solti. It was his first work for the theatre, apart from designs for his own plays.

Ennehjelm: the Finnish operatic singer Hjalmar Ennehjelm, whose portrait Kokoschka painted in 1912 (Wingler, no. 68).
strong roots binding me to Finland: Kokoschka had never been there, and the predilection was entirely imaginary.

Wilhelm Furtwängler *in memoriam,* 28 January 1955. Originally published in *Wilhelm Furtwängler im Urteil seiner Zeit,* ed. Martin Hürlimann, Zurich and Freiburg, 1955, pp. 41–4.
Thermopylae: Kokoschka's triptych (Wingler, nos. 384–6).

To Carl Jacob Burckhardt, 24 March 1955, ms., Frau Burckhardt, Vinzel.

To Edy de Wilde, 28 March 1955, typescript, from the copy in the Kokoschka Archive, Villeneuve.
The Power of Music: the painting which Dr de Wilde had recently acquired for the Stedelijk-Van Abbe Museum in Eindhoven (Wingler, no. 130).
send me a copy: i.e. of the museum's Bulletin, which was to publish Kokoschka's comments on the painting.

To Elisabeth Furtwängler, 7 June 1956, ms., the addressee, Clarens.
This letter does not appear in the German edition of Kokoschka's letters.
the whole trip: the Kokoschkas and Elisabeth Furtwängler had been visiting Greece together.
young Roman: Kokoschka's nephew, the son of his brother Bohuslav.
my painting: a picture of the Vienna Opera House by night.
In Bonn: a reference to a Round Table conference on cultural affairs. Those attending included Dr J. B. Conant and M. François Poncet, respectively the American and French ambassadors to the Federal German Republic, and Dr Tiburtius, Senator for Cultural Affairs in Berlin.

To Carl Jacob Burckhardt, 5 November 1956, Frau Burckhardt, Vinzel.
the slaughter of a defenceless, heroic people: the suppression by Soviet troops of the Hungarian uprising in November 1956.

Kokoschka's protest also took the characteristic form of two lithographs (Wingler-Welz, nos. 209–10).
To Theodor Heuss, 24 November 1956, ms., German Federal Archives, Koblenz.
a Midsummer Night's Dream *for England:* Kokoschka drew designs for two stage sets, and a series of costumes, intended for a production at Stratford-on-Avon, but they were damaged while on the way to England, which led to a disagreement with the producer, Glen Byam Shaw.
Raab: Julius Raab, Federal Chancellor of Austria, 1953–61.
Bott: Hans Bott, Heuss's personal assistant.

To Edith Hoffmann-Yapou, 7 November 1957, ms., the addressee, Jerusalem.
the Welz book: Hans Wingler's *Oskar Kokoschka, das Werk des Malers,* published in Salzburg in 1956 by the art-dealer Friedrich Welz.

290

Soutine: in spite of all the evidence to the contrary, the Russian painter Chaim Soutine (1894–1943) is still regarded in France as an influence on Kokoschka, most recently in commentaries on the Kokoschka retrospective held in Bordeaux in 1983. Soutine arrived in Paris penniless in 1913, and there met Chagall.

To Max Brauer, 19 March 1958, ms., from a photograph supplied by Dr Hans Harder; the location of the original is unknown.
selling my best painting: the triptych was presented to the University by Philipp F. Reemtsma.
my life's work: a reference to the Kokoschka retrospective held at the Haus der Kunst, Munich.

To Josef P. Hodin, 12 May 1958, ms., the addressee.

To Helene Kempff, 26 June 1958, ms., Kempff family, Ammerland.
September: Wilhelm Kempff regularly played at the 'Septembre Musical' festival in Montreux.

To Alfred Marnau, 26 August 1958, ms. (on the back of a picture postcard of Riemenschneider's 'Kneeling Angel'), the addressee.
Riemenschneider and . . . Tiepolo: a reference to Würzburg's great art treasures. The Kokoschkas had stopped in Würzburg on their way to Lübeck and Hamburg, where Kokoschka painted some city views.

To Helene Kempff, 18 October 1958, ms., Kempff family, Ammerland.

To Alfred Marnau, December 1958, the addressee.
You spur boldly: a reference to the ballad *Der Reiter überm Bodensee*, a motive used by Marnau in a novel.
The Red Cardinal: 'Der rote Cardinal,' a poem by Marnau.
the white shark: rather, the white whale, Herman Melville's Moby Dick.
Commander of the whole British Empire: an allusion to Kokoschka's appointment as a Commander of the Order of the British Empire (CBE) in the New Year's Honours List, the details of which had not yet been announced.

To Oskar Angelus, Christmas 1958, from a handwritten draft in the Kokoschka Archive, Villeneuve.
Nothing is known about the addressee or why he approached Kokoschka, or about the final form this letter took.
Gold, frankincense and myrrh: in one of his stories Kokoschka called three Oriental delegates to the 1917 Socialist peace congress in Stockholm 'the Three Kings' (*Das schriftliche Werk*, II, pp. 145ff.).

To Ernst Gombrich, 8 January 1959, the addressee.
With the exception of the opening sentence, the first paragraph was written in English.
Sir Alfred Munnings: Munnings (1878–1959) was elected President of the Royal Academy in 1944. He was noted as a painter of horses and for his strong anti-modernist views.

To Paul Westheim, 29 June 1959, Mariana Frenk-Westheim, Mexico City.
Ernst Rathenau: publisher of the five-volume edition (Euphorion Verlag) of Kokoschka's
   drawings.

To Alice Rosenlew, 14 July 1959, ms., Kokoschka Archive, Villeneuve.
elk-child . . . Marion: Alice and Niels Rosenlew's daughter.
on my hands and knees in spoil-heaps: Olda and Oskar Kokoschka had spent six weeks in
   Southern Italy and Sicily, and had seen a lot of archaeological remains.
Glahn-land: Scandinavia, a reference to Knut Hamsun's *Pan.*

To Paul Westheim, 8 August 1960, ms., Mariana Frenk-Westheim, Mexico City.
A passage describing differences of opinion about the planned catalogue of the graphic
   works has been omitted.

To Wilhelm and Helene Kempff, 23 September 1960, ms., Kempff family, Ammerland.

To Paul Westheim, 8 December 1960, ms., Mariana Frenk-Westheim, Mexico City.
the Rathenau book: the second volume of Kokoschka's drawings, published by Rathenau's
   Euphorion Verlag.
old Sieff: Israel Sieff, later Lord Sieff of Brimpton.

To Walter Neurath, 17 May and 8 June 1961, ms., Eva Neurath, London.
Your book: Oskar Kokoschka, *Watercolours, Drawings, Writings,* with an introduction by
   John Russell, published by Thames and Hudson in 1962.
the title . . . for the English readership: A Sea Ringed with Visions, translated by Eithne Wilkins
   and Ernst Kaiser, and published by Thames and Hudson in 1962.
a portrait bust of me: it was begun by Berta Patočka-Kokoschka, but considerably altered by
   Kokoschka himself. The Berlin company produced a limited edition of it.

To Alice Rosenlew, 25 November 1961, ms., Kokoschka Archive, Villeneuve.

To Walter Neurath, 18 December 1961, ms., Eva Neurath, London.

To Elisabeth Furtwängler, 23 February 1962, ms., the addressee, Clarens.
emergency services: storms in February 1962 caused widespread flooding in Hamburg.
twenty-four lithographs: the series *Homage to Hellas,* printed by Fritz Lindau.
painting fish: the outcome was a still-life, *Storm Tide in Hamburg,* which was commissioned by
   the collector Wilhelm Reinold; he later presented the painting to the Hamburg
   Kunsthalle.

To Anna Kallin, 13 March 1962, ms., Kokoschka Archive, Villeneuve.
'Oskar Kokoschka speaks': the English version of the record (DG 33–9113) was issued in
   Britain in September 1962, in connection with the Tate Gallery's exhibition of
   Kokoschka's paintings.

To an unknown school-leaver, 18 November 1962, typescript, carbon copy in the
   Kokoschka Archive, Villeneuve.

To Marion Rosenlew, 8 April 1963, ms., the addressee, Helsinki.

all the drawings: Kokoschka had just completed a set of lithographs illustrating Shakespeare's play for the Ganymede Press, London.

To Carl Georg Heise, 17 May 1963, ms., Kokoschka Archive, Villeneuve.

[your] address . . . essay in the little Reclam book: Heise had spoken at the unveiling of *Thermopylae* at Hamburg University, and his essay was included in the book on the triptych (to which Kokoschka and Bruno Snell also contributed) published by Reclam as one of the titles in a series of monographs on individual works of art, *Werkmonographien zur Bildenden Kunst.*

To Otto Klemperer, 28 October 1963, ms., Lotte Klemperer, Zollikon.

this English orchestra: the Philharmonia, with which Klemperer had been associated since 1954.

To Paul Westheim, 17 December 1963, ms., Mariane Frenk-Westheim, Mexico City.

Kinkel: Hans Kinkel, art critic living in Berlin, author of numerous articles on Kokoschka's work, sometimes illustrated with his own photographs. See in particular the collection *14 Berichte – Begegnungen mit Malern und Bildhauern*, Stuttgart, 1967.

Dr Reidemeister: Leopold Reidemeister (1900–87), art-historian, at that time director-general of municipal museums in Berlin. Ten years earlier, as director-general of museums in Cologne, he had been instrumental in making the arrangements for Kokoschka to paint a portrait of Theodor Heuss, first President of the Federal German Republic.

To Mariana Frenk-Westheim, 22 December 1963, ms., the addressee, Mexico City.

To Friedrich T. Gubler, 21 January 1964, ms., Ella Gubler, Winterthur.

Tobey . . . Pollock: Mark Tobey and Jackson Pollock.

Prinz Eugen: by Max Braubach, Munich, 1963.

'Odysseus's Return': the first of the lithographs Kokoschka executed in his series of forty-four illustrations of the *Odyssey.*

To Wolfgang Fischer, 12 March 1964, ms., the addressee.

the graphics catalogue with your conversations: the Marlborough Gallery's catalogue of Kokoschka's recent series of graphics, which also contained the text of an interview in which the artist discussed them with Wolfgang Fischer.

Harry . . . my favourite red-head . . . Elfriede: respectively Wolfgang Fischer's father, wife Jutta, and stepmother.

To Elisabeth Furtwängler, 7 May 1964, ms., the addressee, Clarens.

Columbus: a copy of *Der gefesselte Columbus*, Kokoschka's series of twelve lithographs of 1912, published 1916.

To Carl Georg Heise, 23 August 1964, ms., Kokoschka Archive, Villeneuve.

'spin' (as we say in Vienna): not only in Vienna. In German the verb 'spinnen' means not only 'to spin' (as in the previous sentence), but is also slang, 'to be crazy'.

your biography of Warburg: Heise's *Persönliche Erinnerungen an Aby Warburg* first appeared in New York in 1947, and was reissued in Hamburg in 1959. Aby Warburg (1866–1927), the Hamburg art-historian, established the iconological school in art-history.

To Gotthard de Beauclair, 11 May 1965, ms., the addressee.
Ezra Pound: Kokoschka had done a portrait drawing in December 1964, which was included in the edition of *The Seafarer* published by de Beauclair on the occasion of Pound's eightieth birthday in 1965.
David ... Saul: Kokoschka illustrated the incident (I Samuel, 24) in his series *Saul and David* (1968).

To Alice Rosenlew, 23 December 1965, ms., Kokoschka Archive, Villeneuve.
young married bliss: Marion Rosenlew had married in 1964.

To Konrad Adenauer, 21 April 1966, ms., Stiftung Bundeskanzler-Adenauer-Haus, Rhöndorf.

To Fritz Schmalenbach, 12 November 1967, ms., Frau Schmalenbach, Lübeck.
your ... analysis of my work: Schmalenbach's monograph on Kokoschka appeared in the series 'Die blauen Bücher', Königstein, n.d. (1967).

To Alfred Marnau, 13 January 1968, ms., the addressee.
my old painting: the painting *Istanbul*, June 1929 (Wingler, no. 243). It was in fact in Ostrava, not Bratislava.
Abacus: 'Zifferer', an invented name meaning 'enumerator'.
Kokoschka added a drawing at the end of the letter, *Cricket Playing the Violin.*

To Heinz Spielmann, 10 March 1968, ms., the addressee.
A few personal references have been omitted.
The letter was first published in Heinz Spielmann, *Die Fächer für Alma Mahler*, Hamburg, 1969 (2nd ed., Dortmund, 1985).
the fans are in safe hands: a grant from the Hamburg Art Collections Foundation had enabled the Hamburg Museum für Kunst und Gewerbe to purchase the six surviving fans (out of seven made for Alma Mahler).
the first proofs of The Frogs*:* a series of engravings illustrating Aristophanes.

To Wolfgang Fischer, 10 April 1969, the addressee, London.
Some remarks about the time of the Kokoschkas' arrival in London have been omitted.
your exhibition: the exhibition at the Marlborough Gallery in London, March–May 1969, at which Kokoschka's most recent series of graphics, paintings and watercolours were shown.
murder stories: probably a volume of Agatha Christie.

To Carl Georg Heise, 22 April 1969, ms., Kokoschka Archive, Villeneuve.
The master ... takes the skin off [his hands]: de Beauclair sent Kokoschka's engravings to Hermann Steidle of Essen for printing; he used his bare hands to press the paper on to the steel plates, with their sharp grooves and edges.

my beloved Penthesilea: the second series of engravings, illustrating Kleist's play, published by Edition de Beauclair.

To Heinz Spielmann, 12 May 1969, ms., the addressee.
A personal passage at the start of the letter has been omitted.
the Duke of Hamilton: Kokoschka painted a double portrait of the 14th Duke and his wife in July 1969.

To Fritz Schmalenbach, 7 March 1970, ms., Frau Schmalenbach, Lübeck.
A passage at the end, criticizing another museum director, has been omitted.
an autobiography: Mein Leben, published 1971 (English translation, *My Life,* published in 1974).

To Elisabeth Furtwängler, 23 April 1970, ms., the addressee, Clarens.
Elisabeth Furtwängler had developed pneumonia during a trip to Munich.
Oberkiefer: literally 'upper jaw'; a reference to Dina Kiefer, Elisabeth Furtwängler's housekeeper.

To Gottfried von Einem, 15 August 1971, ms., the addressee.
Your opera: Der Besuch d. alten Dame, a performance of which the Kokoschkas saw at the Vienna Opera.

To Heinz Spielmann, 3 November 1971, ms., the addressee.
Wimmer's head: the portrait bust of Kokoschka by Hans Wimmer, which had been acquired for the Hamburg Museum für Kunst und Gewerbe.

To Hans M. Wingler, 23 December 1971, ms., Frau Hedwig Wingler, Berlin.
your preface to the catalogue of my graphic œuvre: the catalogue of Kokoschka's graphic works, compiled by Hans M. Wingler and Friedrich Welz, was published in 1975.
a drawing for the Bach Cantata: one of the series illustrating 'O Ewigkeit, du Donnerwort', published in 1916.

To Heinz Spielmann, 27 December 1971, ms., the addressee.
your lovely Casals card: a Christmas and New Year greetings card with a reproduction of Kokoschka's portrait of the 'cellist Pablo Casals, published in aid of a musical charity with Kokoschka's consent.
the books by Leach and especially Sauerlandt: a German translation of Bernard Leach's *A Potter's Book,* with an introduction by Heinz Spielmann, was published in 1970. Leach and Kokoschka knew each other. Max Sauerlandt, director of the Museum für Kunst und Gewerbe in Hamburg, 1919–33, was a champion of Expressionist art. His book *Reiseberichte 1925–32: Aufsätze und Referate* was published in 1971.
your history of art: Heinz Spielmann, *Spektrum der Kunst,* Gütersloh, 1975, and later editions.

To Fritz Schmalenbach, 7 October 1972, ms., Frau Schmalenbach, Lübeck.
your article: 'Der junge Kokoschka', in *Argo, Festschrift für Kurt Badt,* Cologne, 1970.

To Wilhelm Kempff, 15 January 1973, ms., Kempff family, Ammerland.

To Josef P. Hodin, 25 March 1973, the addressee.
a Canadian: J. G. McConnell.
Bernal: J. D. Bernal, Professor of Physics, Birkbeck College, University of London, 1937–
   63, thereafter Professor of Crystallography. He was acquainted with the Kokoschkas
   during their time in England.
The young lady eating cherries: the daughter of Josef and Pamela Hodin.

To Gilbert Lloyd, 26 October 1973, ms., Marlborough Fine Art Ltd, London.
A few minor corrections have been made to the English. The passage omitted concerns
   contractual problems.

To Heinz Spielmann, 13 November and 24 December 1973, the addressee.
the Jews face disaster this time: a reference to the aftermath of the Yom Kippur war, in which
   Egyptian and Syrian forces launched a surprise attack across the Suez Canal on 6
   October 1973, so demonstrating to the Arab world that Israel was not an invincible
   military force in the area.
Claudia: the daughter of Heinz and Angelika Spielmann.
the bishop: Dr Hans-Otto Wölber, Evangelical-Lutheran bishop of Hamburg.

To Willy Hahn, 7 April 1975, ms., estate of the addressee.
Cockerel: 'Hahn' in German.
I'll be able to see again: Kokoschka had had an operation to cure a cataract in one eye.
Olda is now copying the third volume of my art articles: Kokoschka's writings on art were
   published in *Das schriftliche Werk*, III, 1975. He used his convalescence in April 1975 to
   review his political writings, with Olda's help. They were published in 1976, in vol. IV.

To Heinz Spielmann, 27 December 1975, ms., the addressee.
a parcel of drawings for Pan: 17 lithographs illustrating Knut Hamsun's *Pan*, published by
   Hoffmann & Campe, Hamburg, 1976.
The article: an article by Spielmann, 'Kokoschkas *Comenius*', was published in *Das
   Fernsehspiel im ZDF*, Mainz, 1975, when a programme about the artist was shown on
   West German television.

To Alfred Marnau, autumn 1976, ms, the addressee.
reform the Vatican: Marnau was for some years English chairman of the Latin Mass Society.
   Kokoschka was strongly opposed to the reforms requiring Mass to be celebrated in the
   vernacular following the Second Vatican Council in 1968 (see also note to letter of 11
   June 1931).

To Heinz Spielmann, c.1975, the addressee.
Written as an afterword to the final volume of *Das schriftliche Werk* before its publication in
   1976. The opening expressions of thanks to the publisher and editor (Heinz Spielmann)
   have been omitted. The piece was not used, after all, because the collection of 'political
   writings' making up the fourth volume only went up to 1946, and the text is more in the
   form of a letter than an essay.
steps in the quicksand: an allusion to the title of his autobiographical volume *Spur im Treibsand*
   (English translation published as *A Sea Ringed with Visions*).

Biographical notes
on recipients of letters from Oskar Kokoschka

Adenauer, Konrad (1876–1967)

A lawyer from Cologne, he was first elected to the German Reichstag (parliament) in 1906. From 1917 to 1933 he was Oberbürgermeister (lord mayor) of the city of Cologne, but was ousted by the National Socialists. Following the unsuccessful plot to assassinate Hitler in 1944, he was arrested and imprisoned for a while. Although restored to his former mayoral office after hostilities ended in 1945, he was dismissed shortly afterwards by the British military government. With the creation of the Federal Republic of Germany, he became leader of the Christian Democratic Union in the British zone of occupation and, after the CDU had established itself as a political force nationwide, he was elected its chairman. As leader of the ruling majority in the Bundestag (parliament), he became the first Chancellor of the Federal Republic. His friendship with Kokoschka dated from 1966, when Adenauer sat for his portrait while on holiday at Cadenabbia, a resort on Lake Como.

Arndt, Adolf (1904–74) and Ruth (b. 1901)

Their acquaintance with Kokoschka dated from before the Second World War, and they helped his brother when Austria came under National Socialist rule. Adolf Arndt was elected to the Federal German parliament (Bundestag) after 1948 and became Social Democratic spokesman on legal questions. He was Senator for Arts and Sciences in the *Land* government of Berlin in 1963–4.

Beauclair, Gotthard de (b. 1907)

After thirty years with Insel-Verlag as production supervisor and artistic director, he set up his own company, Verlag Ars Librorum, which published four titles with illustrations by Kokoschka: Ezra Pound, *The Seafarer* (1965); Aristophanes, *Die Frösche* (The Frogs, 1968); Heinrich von Kleist, *Penthesilea* (1970); Kokoschka, *Bild Sprache und Schrift* (1971, with a self-portrait). Beauclair also published the etching 'Ich und meine Kritiker' and the lithograph 'Pan mit Panflöte'.

Brauer, Max (1887–1973)

A glass-blower by trade, he was elected mayor of the Hamburg borough of Altona in 1924. He escaped to the United States during the years of National Socialist rule, returning to Hamburg after the Second World War, he became mayor of Hamburg and threw his energies into the rebuilding and regeneration of the city. Thanks to the initiative of Carl Georg Heise (q.v.), Kokoschka painted his portrait for the collection of the Hamburg Kunsthalle in 1951.

The wife of the English scholar Robert Briffault (1876–1948), who probably met Kokoschka in Vienna in 1933–4, at the house of Eugenie and Hermann Schwarzwald. Robert Briffault had studied with the Swiss anthropologist Johann Jakob Bachofen (1815–87), and discussed the latter's theory of matriarchy with Kokoschka. His major book was *The Mothers* (London, 1927).

Burckhardt, Carl Jacob (1909–74)

Historian and diplomat, member of an old Basle family. He was a member of the International Committee of the Red Cross from 1939, and its president, 1944–8. He was Swiss Ambassador in Paris, 1945–9. From 1953, the year in which he made Kokoschka's acquaintance, he lived in Vinzel on Lake Geneva. His writings include a three-volume life of Richelieu and shorter biographical essays (on Charles V, Maria Theresia and others).

Carney, Jack (d. 1955) and Mina (c. 1899–1974)

Mina Carney was American by birth and a friend of the Mexican painter Diego Rivera. She married the Irish journalist Jack Carney, who held strong left-wing opinions. They were among the Kokoschkas' circle of friends in London during the Second World War, thanks to an introduction from Viktor Matejka. Jack Carney's continuing support for Stalin after the war led to the breach in the friendship; disillusionment during the 1950s contributed to a deterioration in his health and to his death from a heart condition.

Clark, Sir Kenneth (1903–83)

English art-historian, who was director of the National Gallery, London, 1934–45. Because of security regulations, Kokoschka needed an official permit to paint out of doors during the war years, and Clark was instrumental in arranging this. He was chairman of the Arts Council of Great Britain, 1953–60. He received many honours, and was made a life peer in 1969.

Dehmel, Richard (1863–1920)

One of the most influential poets in the German language at the turn of the century. In addition to naturalistic and impressionistic elements, his work is marked by a confessional expressivity and an ecstatic rhetoric which owes much to Nietzsche. These features made him attractive to the younger, Expressionist poets fostered by Herwarth Walden in *Der Sturm*, and his connection with the periodical also led to the portrait drawing by Kokoschka. Dehmel was a friend of a number of contemporary painters, including members of the Hamburg Secession and Max Liebermann (who painted his portrait).

Ehrenstein, Albert (1886–1950)

Viennese poet of Jewish descent, born in the same year as Kokoschka, whose lifelong friend he was from 1910. He made his mark with the story 'Tubutsch', the illustrations for which constituted one of the most important of Kokoschka's early series of drawings. A portrait in oils and several drawings testify to the close relationship between the two men, and this is also evident from the letters, which Ehrenstein preserved throughout all the vicissitudes of his life. Ehrenstein had no money, but his selfless and practical support led to him being regarded by Kokoschka as one of his few reliable friends. Although they planned many journeys together, only one of their often highly fanciful projects was carried out, when they went to the Eastern Mediterranean, Egypt and Palestine in the spring of 1929. The depiction of a travelling companion in Kokoschka's story 'Ostern auf Zypern' is based on Ehrenstein, but it is consciously a caricature, not a portrait. In 1931 Kokoschka illustrated Ehrenstein's volume of poems *Mein Lied*. Shortly after that, Ehrenstein moved to Moscow, and during 1934 Kokoschka came close to joining him there. They planned to travel across the Soviet Union together by train, continuing as far as Shanghai, but nothing came of it. Eventually Ehrenstein emigrated to New York, where he was helped by the publisher Robert Freund; Kokoschka saw him there for the last time in 1949.

Einem, Gottfried von (b. 1918)

The Austrian composer met Kokoschka in 1950 while a member of the board of the Salzburg Festival. He set Kokoschka's early poem *Die träumenden Knaben* for chorus, clarinet and bassoon in 1971.

Feilchenfeldt, Walter (1894–1953)

On the death of Paul Cassirer in 1926, the management of his publishing company and art gallery passed to Walter Feilchenfeldt and Grete Ring. Kokoschka's contract with Cassirer went back to before the First World War and had been renewed several times. In the wake of the world economic recession, serious disagreements arose between the artist and the company in the early 1930s and the contract lapsed. Feilchenfeldt emigrated to England in 1933 and he and Grete Ring refounded Paul Cassirer in 1938. The outbreak of the Second World War found him in Switzerland, where he remained, operating as an art-dealer, until his death.

Ficker, Ludwig von (1880–1967)

Editor of *Der Brenner*, a literary and art journal. He probably met Kokoschka through Adolf Loos (q.v.); another mutual friend was the poet Georg Trakl. Kokoschka painted his portrait in January 1915 (Wingler, no. 104). Ficker was the administrator of the foundation set up by Ludwig Wittgenstein as a means of renouncing his inherited fortune; he was thus able to help Kokoschka when he was in great financial need in 1914 and again in 1915. Except for the period between October 1938, when Kokoschka fled from Prague, and the end of the Second World War, the two remained in touch until Ficker's death, and a photograph taken before his funeral shows that Kokoschka's portrait of him was displayed above his open coffin.

Fischer, Wolfgang Georg (b. 1933)

In 1963 he joined the Marlborough Gallery, London, of which his father, Harry Fischer, was co-founder. He has been in charge of exhibitions of Kokoschka's work, and has supervised editions of his graphics, including the cycles *King Lear*, *The Apulian Journey* and *Homage to Hellas*. He has written novels, as well as essays on Kokoschka's work.

Franzos, Lotte (née Rapp; 1881–1957)

Born in Erfurt in eastern Germany, Elisabeth Lotte Rapp travelled extensively in France and Italy as a girl. She married Emil Franzos, a lawyer, in 1904. Their house in Vienna became a meeting-place for people engaged in the arts, literature and politics. Lotte Franzos was especially interested in seeking out young people of talent; she was one of the first patrons of Kokoschka, who painted her portrait probably towards the end of 1909. The letters he wrote her in the following months are among the first in which he bared his soul to a sympathetic woman. He met her again in Washington, D.C., in 1952.

Furtwängler, Wilhelm (1886–1954) and Elisabeth (b. 1910)

The German conductor and his wife first met Olda and Oskar Kokoschka in Rome in 1949, and formed a close friendship when the Kokoschkas moved to Villeneuve in 1953. Wilhelm Furtwängler's death in November 1954 prevented the realization both of his plan to work with Kokoschka on a new production of *Die Zauberflöte* at Salzburg, and of Kokoschka's plan to paint a portrait of him. In later years Elisabeth Furtwängler often accompanied the Kokoschkas on travels in the Mediterranean area. Kokoschka painted her portrait in 1970.

Gombrich, Ernst (b. 1909)

The Vienna-born art-historian moved to London in 1936, and began work on Aby Warburg's papers in the Warburg Library, which had also been moved there. He was Director of the Warburg Institute, 1959–76, and Professor of the History of the Classical Tradition, University of London. Kokoschka got to know him when living in London, and later persuaded him to give lectures at the 'School of Seeing' in Salzburg. He gave the address in commemoration of Kokoschka in 1980, at a session of the Federal Republic of Germany's Order of Merit (of which Kokoschka had been a member since 1956). He was knighted in 1972 and awarded the British Order of Merit in 1988.

Graf, Alice, see Lahmann, Alice

Grohmann, Will (1887–1968)

German critic and writer on art, who was personally acquainted with many modern artists in the years between the two World Wars. He held a leading position in the cultural life of Berlin, and published a large number of books about contemporary art.

Gubler, Friedrich T. (1900–65)

Zurich-born journalist, arts editor of the *Frankfurter Zeitung*, 1929–32. After being expelled from Germany in 1934 for his political views, he returned to Zurich to study law, which he practised from 1940 until his death in a motoring accident in New York. His acquaintance with Kokoschka dated from their time in Dresden, when he was a student at the Technical University and the painter was teaching at the Academy. He acted for the Kokoschkas when they built and moved to their house in Villeneuve. He was also active in public life in Switzerland, especially in cultural affairs in his home town, Winterthur.

Hahn, Willy (1896–1988)

Pianist, composer and operatic conductor who assembled, from 1919 onwards, one of the most important collections of Kokoschka's drawings, a group of his paintings and a substantial number of his graphic works. The collection has formed the basis for a series of exhibitions.

Heise, Carl Georg (1890–1979)

Kokoschka's friendship with the Hamburg-born art-historian dated from the period immediately following the First World War, when Heise and Hans Mardersteig published the periodical *Genius*; Kokoschka painted a double portrait of the two friends. Heise was director of the art museum in Lübeck from 1920 until 1933, when his championship of modernism led to his dismissal. He spent the years of the Second World War editing a series of monographs on European art. He was director of the Hamburg Kunsthalle, 1945–55, and was instrumental in the commissioning of Kokoschka's portrait of Max Brauer in 1951 and in the acquisition of his triptych *Thermopylae* for Hamburg University. It was shortly after painting Brauer that Kokoschka painted the first of his views of the port of Hamburg, and *The Magic Form*, a self-portrait intended at first to be inserted as the middle section of the Heise-Mardersteig double portrait, but that idea was abandoned. Kokoschka drew a portrait of Heise in 1964. They met for the last time in 1974. Heise burned most of the letters Kokoschka sent him.

Heuss, Theodor (1884–1963)

In 1949 he was elected the first President of the Federal German Republic. Kokoschka painted his portrait in 1950 and a friendship grew up between the two men. This continued after the end of Heuss's term of office in 1959. Kokoschka contributed to the *Festschrift* published to celebrate Heuss's seventieth birthday.

Hodin, Josef P. (b. 1905)

He met Kokoschka for the first time after moving to London in 1944, but their correspondence had begun earlier, when Hodin was living in Stockholm. He has written monographs on Edvard Munch and Hilde Goldschmidt, as well as several books about Kokoschka, which reflect his very personal approach to him, and include discussions of the artist's often critical attitude to his time.

Hoffmann-Yapou, Edith (b. 1907)

Art-historian, born in Vienna. She moved to England in 1934, and worked at the British Museum and for the *Burlington Magazine*. She started her monograph on Kokoschka during the Second World War, although the circumstances were extremely difficult for such a work. She had the artist's support, and the book, *Kokoschka, Life and Work*, is still regarded as one of the essential texts on him. It was published by Faber and Faber in 1947, with a preface by Kokoschka, 'Petition from a Foreign Artist . . . for a secure and present Peace', one of the artist's most important political essays. Edith Hoffmann-Yapou and her husband have lived in Jerusalem since 1951.

John, Augustus (1879–1961)

The celebrated portrait-painter met Kokoschka in Paris *c.* 1930, and again later in London.

Kallin, Anna (1896–1984)

The daughter of a Jewish-Russian merchant family, she arrived in Germany, with her parents, in 1912. She was studying singing in Dresden when she first met Kokoschka in the spring of 1921. After staying with her friend Alice Lahmann at the Weißer Hirsch nursing home for some time, she moved in to live with Kokoschka in his lodge in the Großer Garten park in Dresden. She regularly spent her vacations with her parents, in Berlin in 1922, and later in London, but always returned to Dresden to study. She accompanied Kokoschka to Switzerland in 1923. The death of his father meant that Kokoschka had to spend a long period in Vienna, and this led to an estrangement which was not healed until 1925, when a long period began in which Kokoschka travelled to paint. In the intimate letters he sent her, cast as a rule in a light-hearted tone, he employed a wide variety of nicknames, often playing on them as if they represented different people. 'Niuta' is a common Russian diminutive for 'Anna'; the others that he used most frequently are:
'Ben', 'Benin': Kokoschka claimed that the shape of Anna Kallin's head reminded him of Benin bronzes.
'Malina' (Russian, 'raspberry'): Anna Kallin often sang the scene from Tchaikovsky's *Eugene Onegin* in which the characters are preparing raspberries; she was also fond of eating them.
'Mirli': possibly an adaptation, of the kind Kokoschka liked to make, of 'Annamirl', an Austrian diminutive form of 'Anna'.
'Rahel': the German form of Rachel, the favourite wife of Jacob.
'Rhamnis': no certain explanation can be given.
Kokoschka often referred to himself in the letters as 'Flèche' (French, 'arrow') and 'Un', which originated in Anna Kallin's practice of calling him 'unmöglich' (impossible).
From the mid-1920s onwards, Anna Kallin lived in London, teaching. In 1940 she went to work for the BBC overseas service as a radio presenter, at first of German-language programmes and then in the Russian service. From 1946 to 1964 she worked on the Third Programme.

Kellner, Leon (1859–1928)

Austrian teacher of English, president of the Austrian Shakespeare Society. He taught Kokoschka while the latter was a pupil at the state secondary school in the XVIIIth district of Vienna, and the artist retained grateful memories of him throughout his life (see *My Life*, pp. 15–16). In 1906 Kellner moved to the University of Czernowitz (Chernovtsy) in his home province of Galicia.

Kempff, Wilhelm (1895–1991) and Helene (1908–86)

It was the pianist's regular appearances at the Montreux Festival during the 1950s that led to the friendship between the Kempffs and the Kokoschkas. In 1959 the Kokoschkas were invited to Italy as guests at the Kempffs' summer home in Positano, where Wilhelm Kempff gave master-classes on the interpretation of Beethoven.

Khuenburg, Alexandrine (Countess, née Mensdorff-Dietrichstein; 1894–?)

In the early summer of 1916, while Kokoschka was still convalescing from his war wounds, he painted an (unfinished) group portrait of Prince Alexander Dietrichstein-Nikolsberg and his sisters, the Countesses Alexandrine, Olga and Marie. Alexandrine, then twenty-two years old, was one of his nurses, and played an important role in restoring his spirits, then desperately low (see *My Life*, pp. 97–8). In gratitude he dedicated to her the series of lithographs on Bach's 'O Ewigkeit, du Donnerwort'. He continued to write to her at intervals.

Klemperer, Otto (1885–1973)

The conductor first met Kokoschka in 1963, and subsequently in London and Zurich.

Lahmann, Alice (née Graf, later Rosenlew; 1899–1986)

The daughter of a German engineer from Riga and his wife (by birth Baroness Cedercreuz), Alice Graf grew up in St Petersburg. Her father was banished to Siberia during the First World War, but released at the time of the Russian Revolution, and while her parents were still in Russia, Alice Graf fled to Finland. Her father brought her to Germany in 1919. At his wish, she went to study at the Conservatory in Dresden, where she soon made the acquaintance of people in artistic circles, including Kokoschka. She formed lifelong friendships with him and with Anna Kallin (q.v.). In 1921 she married the director of the Weißer Hirsch nursing home in Dresden; they had a son, but were divorced in 1930. Through Alice, Kokoschka also got to know her cousin Damaris Brunow; unfortunately his letters to her are lost, and it is now impossible to separate fact from fiction in his sometimes poetic representation of their relationship (see, especially, the story 'Ostern auf Zypern', *Das schriftliche Werk*, II, pp. 271ff.). In 1932 Alice Lahmann married an engineer, Nils Rosenlew; they lived successively in Sweden, London, Germany and Finland, and frequently visited the Kokoschkas. Nils Rosenlew died in 1982.
In his letters to her, Kokoschka always called her 'Colibri'. He frequently refers to her daughter Marion.

Lang, Erwin (1886–1962)

A fellow-student of Kokoschka's at the Kunstgewerbeschule in Vienna, in the classes of both Carl Otto Czeschka (1907–8) and Berthold Löffler (1908–9). He later married the dancer Grete Wiesenthal (q.v.), who performed at the Fledermaus cabaret with her sisters.

Lauwerys, Joseph Albert (1902–81)

After studying chemistry and physics, he turned to the theory of education and became Professor of Comparative Education at London University. After the Second World War he was an adviser to UNESCO.

Liebermann, Max (1847–1935)

Starting out from the realist tradition in German art, in his maturity Liebermann produced an œuvre worthy to be regarded as a German answer to French Impressionism. His distinction can be measured by the fact that the French government made him a Chevalier de la Légion d'Honneur in 1896. He was one of the artists handled by Cassirer, and it was through that connection that Kokoschka got to know him personally. They maintained a friendly relationship through the 1920s, expressed not only in exchanges of *bons mots* but also in the portrait-lithograph of Liebermann that Kokoschka executed in 1923 and dedicated to his mother as a token of the great personal esteem in which he held the older artist. Kokoschka held him in higher regard, possibly, than any other living painter.

At a time when Kokoschka was in great financial difficulties himself, living in Paris in the early 1930s, he joined with Romain Rolland and others in an (unsuccessful) attempt to mount a large-scale retrospective exhibition of Liebermann's work to mark his eighty-fifth birthday. Kokoschka's open letter, published in the *Frankfurter Zeitung* in June 1933, was a last public demonstration of friendship and lifelong respect.

Lloyd, Gilbert (b. 1940)

The son of the co-founder of the Marlborough Gallery in London, he became its director in 1968. He had organized the Kokoschka retrospective at the Marlborough-Gerson Gallery in New York in 1966, and has subsequently been closely associated with the public showing of the artist's work. He has presented a series of exhibitions at the Marlborough Gallery and contributed to the retrospectives held in Madrid (1975) and in London, New York and Zurich (1986). He has also published a series of catalogues of the œuvre and has worked on the question of Kokoschka forgeries.

Loeb, Marguerite (Mrs McBey; b. 1905)

Born in Philadelphia, and educated there and in Switzerland. In 1925, while continuing her studies at the Sorbonne in Paris, she met Kokoschka; they formed a close relationship which lasted a good year. In the latter part of the 1920s she took up bookbinding and had a studio in New York. In 1931 she married the Scottish painter and engraver James McBey, and the couple travelled extensively. Marguerite McBey took up photography and, in the

304

1960s, watercolour. In 1980 she opened a gallery in Tangier, which primarily promotes the work of artists resident in, or inspired by, Morocco.

Loos, Adolf (1870–1933)

The Austrian architect spoke of himself as a 'master builder' and reacted vigorously against the ornamental excess of the late nineteenth century, in which he included the work of the Wiener Werkstätte. When Kokoschka's work was first put before the general public in the Vienna Kunstschau of 1908, Loos immediately recognized that here was a painter with something new to say that would lead beyond the *Jugendstil* (Art Nouveau) formalism of the Werkstätte. He became an active patron, buying many of Kokoschka's early paintings, and helped him to make his first major journey abroad to paint, in Switzerland. The work resulting from this journey includes the portrait of Dr Forel, the view of Les Dents du Midi, the portrait of Loos's wife (the cabaret artist Bessie Bruce, who was being treated for tuberculosis in Les Avants), and an unfinished portrait of the companion of Dr Beer, who had commissioned Loos's early work, the Villa Karma, near Montreux. There was a close affinity between Loos and Karl Kraus, who supported Loos's artistic aims and aspirations. Both were among Kokoschka's closest friends, and jointly introduced him to Herwarth Walden (q.v.), but he regarded Loos, in particular, as a mentor. The relationship seems to have been less close during the period of Kokoschka's passionate love-affair with Alma Mahler from 1912, but Loos was very helpful when Kokoschka volunteered for military service in 1914, and was instrumental in his joining the cavalry. The friendship endured until the architect's death. The last visit Kokoschka paid the ailing Loos was deeply distressing (see *My Life*, p. 48).

The correspondence between Loos and Kokoschka was voluminous; although only a small part of it is available at present, it shows that Kokoschka was always completely frank and unsparing of himself with Loos.

Mahler, Alma (née Schindler, later Gropius, later Werfel; 1879–1964)

The daughter of the painter Emil Jakob Schindler married the composer and conductor Gustav Mahler in 1902; they had two daughters, but one died as a child. Through Mahler, especially while he held the post of director of the Vienna Court Opera (until 1907), Alma moved in the highest artistic and musical circles in Vienna and other European cities, and continued to do so after his death in 1911. Her stepfather, Carl Moll (q.v.), commissioned Kokoschka to paint her portrait in 1912: the passionate relationship they immediately formed was burdened from the first by Alma's involvement in a social milieu which Kokoschka repudiated. The stages of the relationship are recorded in an important series of paintings. Between April 1912 and the time when Kokoschka was sent to the Russian Front in the summer of 1915, he sent Alma Mahler nearly four hundred letters, which are among his most direct and personal written documents. In 1915 she married the architect Walter Gropius. After a divorce, in 1929 she married the writer Franz Werfel, with whom she emigrated to the USA in 1940. She spent the 1940s in California, where there was a circle of German or German-speaking exiles; Franz Werfel died in 1945. From 1952 Alma Werfel lived in New York.

After 1915 Kokoschka wrote to her only very infrequently. They met by chance at the Venice Biennale in 1922.

Maisky, Ivan Mikhailovich (1884–1975)

Soviet ambassador to Great Britain, 1932–44. The portrait of him (now in the Tate Gallery) which Kokoschka painted after the Battle of Stalingrad was used to raise money to buy X-ray equipment with which to treat the Russian and German injured.

Mandl, Lotte (Mrs Friedländer; b. 1905)

The industrialist Erich Mandl and his wife Anna belonged to the circle of Kokoschka's friends and acquaintances in Vienna. Their daughter Lotte was eleven when the artist first met her, and her lively personality cheered him during his subsequent visits to Vienna, which were often occasions for despair. She frequently sat for him, above all in the winter of 1923–4, after the death of Kokoschka's father, when he produced a large number of drawings and watercolour portraits of her. She and her husband Walter Friedländer emigrated to the United States, and she now lives in New York.

Marnau, Alfred (b. 1918)

Poet, novelist and translator, born in Preßburg (now Bratislava). Marnau and his wife Senta formed a close friendship with Oskar and Olda Kokoschka in London during the Second World War. Kokoschka designed the jacket for one of his earliest books.

Matejka, Viktor (b. 1901)

An adviser on educational affairs to the Socialist city government of Vienna in the 1930s, and one of those who promoted the giving of a commission to Kokoschka to paint a view of the city. He was interned 1938–45. After the war he was a member of the central committee of the Austrian Communist Party until 1957, and head of Vienna's department of education 1945–9.

Mell, Max (1882–1971)

Austrian writer of lyric and dramatic poetry and short fiction (much of it on Christian themes, especially in middle life), a member of Hugo von Hofmannsthal's circle. Mell's interest in Kokoschka's early poem 'Die träumenden Knaben' may have been influenced by his own early work (*Die drei Grazien des Traumes*, 1906); they may have met in connection with the performance of a mime-work by Mell at the Kunstgewerbeschule in 1907. Mell's review of 'Die träumenden Knaben' was published in the journal *Die Zukunft* in 1908, and is one of the first and most appreciative essays on Kokoschka's early poetry.

Meyboden, Hans (1901–65)

One of Kokoschka's students at the Dresden Academy, 1920–23. He served in the German Army during the Second World War.

Moll, Carl (1861–1945)

Austrian painter. He studied under Emil Jakob Schindler and became a friend of the family. In 1895 he married Schindler's widow, and thus became stepfather to Alma Schindler, the future wife of Gustav Mahler. He joined the Viennese Secession in 1897 and was the group's president in 1900–01, but in 1905 he was one of the Klimt faction which seceded from the Secession. He acted as adviser to the Miethke gallery, and was able to put work in Kokoschka's way from 1911 onwards, including the commission, in 1912, for a portrait of Alma Mahler, by then widowed.

After his separation from Alma Mahler, Kokoschka remained friendly with Moll until a short time before the outbreak of the Second World War. In 1937 Moll organized a major exhibition of Kokoschka's painting in Vienna, which coincided with the 'Degenerate Art' exhibition in Munich. Following Kokoschka's flight from Prague to England, further contact was impossible. Moll died shortly before the end of hostilities in Europe.

Motesiczky, Henriette von (1882–1978)

Mother of the painter Marie-Luise von Motesiczky, whom Kokoschka first met during the period he spent in Vienna in the early 1930s. The father of the family died young, and the only son died in Auschwitz. Mother and daughter and their servant Marie moved to London in 1938, and renewed the acquaintance with Kokoschka, which lasted until his death.

Needham, Joseph (b. 1900)

Originally a biochemist, he was a lecturer and from 1933 to 1966 Reader in Biochemistry at Cambridge University; he was sent to China in 1942 as head of a British scientific mission, and the four years he spent there led to a lifelong study of the history of Chinese science. He was Master of Gonville and Caius College, 1966–76, and subsequently has been director of the Needham Research Institute in Cambridge.

Neumeyer, Alfred (1901–73)

Art-historian of German birth, who emigrated to the USA in the 1930s. His article on Kokoschka, published in the *Magazine of Art*, November 1945, pp. 261–5, was the first on Kokoschka's work, on an international level, since the outbreak of the Second World War.

Neurath, Walter (1903–67)

Born in Vienna, he moved to London in 1938, and with his wife Eva founded the publishing company Thames and Hudson in 1949. The lasting friendship with Olda and Oskar Kokoschka began in London during the Second World War, when Kokoschka sought Walter Neurath's support for the Free German League of Culture.

Plaut, James S. (b. 1912)

As director of the Institute of Contemporary Art in Boston, he edited the catalogue of the first major exhibition of Kokoschka's work to be seen in the United States, in 1948.

Ray, Marcel (d. 1951)

French writer and Germanist. He translated some of the writings of Adolf Loos in 1912, and Kokoschka made his acquaintance around that time in Vienna, at the house of Eugenie and Hermann Schwarzwald. Ray taught at the University of Montpellier and was French Plenipotentiary in Siam. He also wrote a monograph on George Grosz.

Read, Herbert (1893–1968)

A champion of contemporary art, he was friendly with many leading artists of his time. He wrote an introduction for the book on Kokoschka by Edith Hoffmann-Yapou (q.v.), and it may have been through her, when she was on the staff of the *Burlington Magazine*, that he had first met the Kokoschkas. The relationship led to visits to the Read family home. He received a knighthood in 1953.

Rosenlew, Alice, see Lahmann, Alice

Rosenlew-Krogius, Marion (b. 1945?)

Daughter of Alice Rosenlew, known to Kokoschka since childhood. She lives in Helsinki.

Saint Gaudens, Homer (1880–1958)

Director of the Carnegie Institute in Pittsburgh from 1922. His frequent journeys to Europe brought him into contact with many artists whose work he showed. He acquired Kokoschka's portrait of Thomas Masaryk for the Carnegie Institute.

Schmalenbach, Fritz (1909–84)

German art-historian who spent the 1930s and '40s in Switzerland. Director of Museums in Lübeck 1956–74, and honorary professor at Kiel University from 1971. His published work includes several essays on Kokoschka.

Schoenberg, Arnold (1874–1951)

The intensely expressive *Verklärte Nacht* (1899) and *Erwartung* (1909) treat subject-matter close to Kokoschka's early dramas, *Mörder Hoffnung der Frauen* and *Der brennende Dornbusch*. It cannot be said with any great certainty what the influence of Kokoschka's plays may have been, on *Erwartung* in particular; the two were already on sufficiently friendly terms by around 1909 for the composer to seek the younger man's opinion and advice. Kokoschka publicly supported Schoenberg throughout his life, not least when he began to develop the ideas that led to twelve-note composition (based on a theme using all twelve notes of the chromatic scale). Remarks made by Kokoschka about Schoenberg in a letter to Alma Mahler (5 March 1915) may mean that Kokoschka knew about it, long before any compositions in the new manner were completed or performed. Kokoschka went to performances of Schoenberg's works whenever possible. The surviving letters, some from the last years of the composer's life, reveal the uninterrupted regard and esteem Kokoschka felt for the friend of his youth. In 1934, at a time when the Nazis were confiscating his paintings, he was unaware that Schoenberg wrote to an American collector asking him to use his influence to bring about an exhibition of Kokoschka's work in the United States, in order 'to procure him his right as one of the most important painters of our time: to have his paintings in every art gallery of any importance'.

Schuschnigg, Kurt von (1897–1967)

Following the assassination of Dollfuss in 1934, Schuschnigg became Austrian Chancellor and Minister of War; from 1936 he was also 'Leader' of the Patriotic Front party. He failed to preserve Austrian independence, and he was kept under arrest from 1938 to 1945, latterly in a concentration camp. He taught at the University of St Louis, Missouri, 1948–67.

Seilern, Antoine, Count (1901–78)

Of aristocratic, Austrian descent, he was born in Frensham, Surrey. He collected both old and new European art during the 1930s, and published catalogues and essays by himself about his collection. He commissioned Kokoschka's triptych *Prometheus* for his house in London in 1950. He bequeathed his collection to the Courtauld Institute in London.

Spielmann, Heinz (b. 1930)

German art-historian who became in 1960 director of the modern section of the Hamburg Museum of Arts and Crafts, which he regenerated after its closure and dispersal under the National Socialists. A major Kokoschka retrospective in 1965, featuring work done in the service of specific causes, led to a close relationship with the artist. In addition to organizing exhibitions in Germany, Spain and Japan, and publishing essays on Kokoschka, Spielmann has overseen editions of his graphic work, and the realization of his tapestry *Die Zauberflöte*, his mosaics *Ecce homo* and *Ecce homines*, and his film on Comenius. He edited the four-volume edition of Kokoschka's prose, drama and poetry (*Das schriftliche Werk*, 1972–6), and was co-editor, with Olda Kokoschka, of the four-volume German edition of his letters (1984–8). Since 1986 he has been director of the Landesmuseum of Schleswig-Holstein.

Walden, Herwarth (pseudonym of Georg Levin; 1878–1941)

The pseudonym was adopted c.1900, when a promising career as a concert pianist seemed to beckon; he had studied with Conrad Ansorge and also composed. In 1901 he married the poet Else Lasker-Schüler. In 1903 he founded an 'Association for Art', a forum for the discussion and practice of contemporary literature and visual art. After working on the editorial staff of a number of periodicals, Walden founded his own journal in 1910, with the title *Der Sturm* (The Tempest). From an early date, Walden promoted Kokoschka: *Mörder Hoffnung der Frauen* and the drawings that accompany it were first published in *Der Sturm*. In 1912 Walden opened a gallery, also called Der Sturm, where he mounted a series of exhibitions in which Kokoschka was well represented from the start. The 'First German Autumn Salon' in 1913 was the first show in Germany to give a general survey of modernism. In 1914 Walden began publishing books, in 1916 he founded a school for almost all the visual art disciplines, followed in 1917 by a bookshop and a theatre, all bearing the name 'Der Sturm'. The hundredth 'Sturm' exhibition in 1921 denoted a last zenith of these activities. While he continued to seek out younger artists, Walden became increasingly active as a communist. After financial difficulties had caused *Der Sturm* to cease publication in 1932, Walden emigrated to the Soviet Union. He settled in Moscow, but fell victim to Stalinist persecution, and was arrested in 1941. There is no information about his fate later than 13 March 1941, but his daughter Sina was later told that he died that year in a transfer camp.

Westheim, Paul (1886–1963) and Mariana Frenk-Westheim

Paul Westheim's acquaintance with Kokoschka began around 1918. He published two editions of a monograph on Kokoschka, which remains a standard work, especially on account of his interpretation of the œuvre. He also wrote a series of essays on the graphics and paintings. He escaped to Mexico after the Fall of France, and remained there for the rest of his life, becoming an authority on Mexican art. In 1959 he married Mariana Frenk, the widow of a friend, who worked with him at the Mexico City Museum.

Wiesenthal, Grete (Frau Lang; 1885–1970)

She first became known to Kokoschka as a dancer, performing with her sisters at the Fledermaus cabaret in Vienna. She was the friend and later wife of Erwin Lang (q.v.), Kokoschka's class-mate at the Kunstgewerbeschule. His friendship with the couple continued for some time after their move to Berlin. Wiesenthal later appeared occasionally in productions directed by Max Reinhardt.

Wilde, Edy de (b. 1919)

After studying law, he became responsible in 1945 for recovering looted Dutch art treasures from Germany and Austria. In 1946 he became director of the Stedelijk Van Abbe Museum in Eindhoven, and increased its collections of Cubist and other twentieth-century art. As director of the Stedelijk Museum, Amsterdam, 1963–84, he brought his term of office to a close with the 'grande parade' exhibition of art since 1940.

Wingler, Hans M. (1920–84)

Art-historian and museum director, who made a special study of Kokoschka's œuvre, and compiled the catalogue of his paintings (1956, English edition 1958), and, with Friedrich Welz, the catalogue of the graphic works (1975). He also organized exhibitions of the works, and published a number of essays. He was associated with the establishment of the

Bauhaus-Archiv, and was its director from the time it was moved from Darmstadt to Berlin in 1972 until his death.

Wolfit, Donald (1902–68)

The English actor-manager toured with his own company, performing Shakespeare, Jonson and other classics. Oskar and Olda Kokoschka saw them in London when the opportunity arose. He was knighted in 1957.

Chronology of Kokoschka's Life

1886   Kokoschka born on 1 March, the second son of Gustav and Romana Kokoschka, at Pöchlarn in Lower Austria.

1905–9   After leaving school, he studies at the Kunstgewerbeschule (School of Arts and Crafts) in Vienna. During these years he designs postcards, fans etc. for the Wiener Werkstätte; his poem 'Die träumenden Knaben' is published in 1908 and the play *Mörder Hoffnung der Frauen* first performed in 1909.

1909–10   Visits Switzerland for the first time, in the company of Adolf Loos; paints portraits.

1910   Travels to Berlin, where his drawings appear in *Der Sturm*, a well-known periodical edited by Herwarth Walden. Kokoschka's work is exhibited at the gallery of the Berlin dealer Paul Cassirer, with whom he subsequently enters into a contractual arrangement.

1911–12   Returns to Vienna and teaches briefly at the Kunstgewerbeschule.

1912   Meets Alma Mahler, widow of the composer Gustav Mahler, who had died in 1911.

1913   Travels with Alma Mahler to Italy. He writes the poem 'Allos Makar'. Lithographs for Karl Kraus's volume of essays *Die chinesische Mauer* (published in 1914) and for his own *Der gefesselte Columbus*.

1914   Parts from Alma Mahler. Paints *Die Windsbraut* (*The Tempest*). Volunteers for the army and becomes an officer cadet in the cavalry.

1915   After a period of military training near Vienna, he is sent to the Russian front in Galicia, where he is seriously wounded in action.

1916   After recovering in hospital, he is sent to the Italian front as a liaison officer, but is subsequently invalided out of the army in September. Publication of lithographs (executed in 1914) illustrating the Bach Cantata 'O Ewigkeit, du Donnerwort' and *Der gefesselte Columbus*. Exhibitions at Der Sturm Gallery, Berlin. Contract with Cassirer in Berlin commences.

1917   Spends several months convalescing in the Weißer Hirsch nursing home in Dresden and visits Stockholm in the autumn for further medical tests.

1918	Etchings for the play *Orpheus und Eurydike*. Paul Westheim publishes a monograph on Kokoschka in *Die Zeitschrift für bildende Kunst*.
1919	Becomes a professor at the Dresden Academy, where he teaches until 1923. *Mörder Hoffnung der Frauen* is set to music by Paul Hindemith (performed in 1921 first in Stuttgart, then at the Frankfurt opera house).
1922	Participates in the Venice Biennale and there briefly meets Alma Mahler (now married to Walter Gropius).
1923	Illustrations for Victor von Dirsztay's *Das Unentrinnbare*. The play *Orpheus und Eurydike* is set to music by Ernst Křenek (first performed in Kassel in 1926). Gustav Kokoschka dies on 23 October.
1924–5	Beginning of a period involving travels, including a visit to Paris with Adolf Loos and Sebastian Isepp. With Paris as a base, he makes journeys to various countries, including Spain and Portugal, followed by the Netherlands and England.
1926	Further travels to London and Berlin.
1927	From Paris he makes trips to Venice and Switzerland. Preparations for a one-man show at the Zurich Kunsthaus.
1928–9	Travels in North Africa followed by visits to Spain, then Ireland and Scotland. Travels to Egypt, with visits to Jerusalem, Istanbul and Venice.
1930	Visits Algeria, Italy and Annecy in France.
1931	Contract with Cassirer in Berlin terminated. Returns to Vienna at a time of financial crisis.
1932	Returns to Paris. Exhibits work at the Venice Biennale.
1933	After spending several months in Rapallo, decides to leave Paris and return to live in Vienna.
1934	Sinister political developments in Germany and Austria cause him to move to Prague following his mother's death on 4 July.
1935	Paints portrait of Thomas Masaryk, President of Czechoslovakia. Meets Olda Palkovská, his future wife. The publication by Ernst Rathenau of the first volume of Kokoschka's drawings leads to problems with the official censor in Germany.
1936	Works on the play *Comenius* (begun the previous year).

1937	One-man show at the Museum für Kunst und Industrie, Vienna. In Germany over 400 works by Kokoschka are removed from public collections and nine of his paintings are featured in the officially sponsored exhibition of 'degenerate art' held in Munich. The painting *Self-portrait of a Degenerate Artist* is Kokoschka's response.
1938	Kokoschka and Olda Palkovská flee from Prague as the German army invades Czechoslovakia. They reach London with no resources.
1939–45	Living in London, with occasional visits to Scotland. In 1942 he paints the portrait of the Russian ambassador, Ivan Maisky, which is sold in aid of Russian and German troops wounded in the battle for Stalingrad. In 1945 he sends money to help war orphans in Czechoslovakia.
1947	Takes British citizenship. Major exhibitions in Basle and Zurich. *Kokoschka, Life and Work* by Edith Hoffmann published in London by Faber and Faber.
1948	Makes an extended visit to Italy, and exhibits paintings at the Venice Biennale.
1949	Visits Vienna and Rome, and travels to the USA for the first time.
1950	Travels from London to Salzburg, Munich (where a major exhibition is held at the Kunsthaus), and later Italy. In Germany he visits Frankfurt and Bonn (where he paints a portrait of the President, Theodor Heuss).
1951	Travels to Hamburg, then visits Switzerland and Italy.
1952	Makes an extended visit to Switzerland, then travels to Hamburg, London and Minneapolis (as visiting professor at the School of Art).
1953	Inaugurates the 'School of Seeing' at Salzburg, which becomes a regular event each summer until 1963. Acquires the Villa Delphin at Villeneuve on Lake Geneva, and takes up residence in Switzerland.
1954	Begins work on the triptych *Thermopylae*. At the suggestion of Wilhelm Furtwängler he designs stage sets for a production of Mozart's *The Magic Flute* planned for the Salzburg Festival of 1955.
1955	One-man show at the Vienna Secession.
1956	Receives the Order of Merit of the Federal Republic of Germany. Makes his first visit to Greece. Publication of the monograph by H. M. Wingler, *Oskar Kokoschka: Das Werk des Malers* (English edition, 1958) and of *Oskar Kokoscha: Lithographien*, with introduction by Remigius Netzer.
1958	Major retrospective exhibitions in Munich and Vienna.

1959   Appointed a Commander of the Order of the British Empire.

1960   Receives honorary doctorate (D.Litt.) from Oxford University. Death of
            Kokoschka's sister Berta (b. 1889).

1961   Second visit to Greece.

1962   Paints *Storm Tide at Hamburg* following flooding in the city. Retrospective at the
            Tate Gallery, London (September–November).

1964   Prepares lithographs for the *Odyssey* cycle.

1966   Special 80th birthday exhibitions: major retrospective at the Zurich Kunst-
            haus, one-man shows in Salzburg, Stuttgart, New York and Karlsruhe. Begins
            illustrations for *Saul and David* (portfolio published 1969).

1967   Begins work on the cycle *The Frogs*, based on Aristophanes, as a political
            allegory (military dictatorship in Greece).

1968   Oil painting *The Frogs* executed in response to Soviet military intervention in
            Czechoslovakia.

1969   Exhibition of graphic works at Marlborough Fine Art, London. Paints portrait
            of Agatha Christie.

1970   Exhibition of recent work at the Museum für Kunst und Gewerbe, Hamburg.

1971   Special 85th birthday exhibitions: Salzburg, Vienna (Belvedere), Rome,
            Heidelberg, Prague, Munich and London. Autobiography *Mein Leben* pub-
            lished (English translation, 1974).

1972   Revision of the play *Comenius* and other writings.

1973   Opening of the Oskar Kokoschka Archive at Pöchlarn on 14 July. Publication
            of the first volume of *Das schriftliche Werk* (ed. Heinz Spielmann, 4 vols., 1973–
            76). Filming of *Comenius* begins (completed in 1974).

1974   Serious problems with eyesight (cataracts) necessitate an operation in
            Lausanne early in 1975. Major exhibition at the Musée de l'Art Moderne de la
            Ville de Paris.

1975   Major retrospective in Hamburg and Madrid. Resumes Austrian citizenship.
            Publication of *Das druckgraphische Werk* (ed. H. M. Wingler and F. Welz).

1976   Death of Kokoschka's brother Bohuslav (b. 1892) in Vienna. Many special
            exhibitions to mark the artist's 90th birthday and, later, 'Homage to
            Kokoschka' at the Victoria and Albert Museum, London.

1977   Publication of the fifth and final volume of drawings (series begun by Rathenau in 1935).

1978   Major exhibition (450 works) in Japan. Travelling exhibition 'Homage to Kokoschka' (100 works) shown in the USA and Canada.

1980   Kokoschka dies at Montreux on 22 February and is buried in the nearby cemetery at Clarens.

List of Illustrations

Sources of illustrations
Photographs were kindly supplied by the following:
Olda Kokoschka, Villeneuve: pages 21, 86; plates 1, 5, 6, 10, 13, 15, 16, 17, 18, 19, 20, 21, 22, 23, 24, 25;
the Kokoschka Archive, Pöchlarn: plates 3, 4, 7, 8, 9, 11, 12;
Alfred Marnau, London: page 201

Index

McConnell, J. G. 296n.
Magazine of Art (Washington) 176, 180, 286n.
Mahler, Alma (later Gropius and Werfel) 8, 9, **20, 22, 23, 24, 25, 26, 27, 28, 29, 30, 31, 32, 33, 36, 37,** *38,* **40, 41, 43, 44, 45, 46, 47, 50, 51, 52, 53, 54, 56, 57, 59, 60, 62, 63, 65, 66, 67, 68, 74, 76, 85, 145, 146, 150,** 294n., **305,** 312, 313, *pl. 2*
Mahler, Anna (Guckerl, Gucki etc.) 22, 28, 40, 41, 42, 47, 51, 57, 264n., 277n.
Mahler, Gustav 62, 63, 264n.
Maisky, Ivan Mikhailovich 161, **166,** 284n., **306,** 314
Mallowan, Sir Max 249
Manchester Guardian 141
Mandl, Erich 281n., 306
Mandl, Lotte **76, 306**
Marc, Franz 71
Mardersteig, Hans 249
Maria Theresia (Empress) 119, 219
Marnau, Alfred (Fred) 10, 202, **206, 209,** 210, **227, 246, 259,** 288n., **306**
Marnau, Senta 206, 227, 306
Marx, Karl 143, 253
Masaryk, Thomas G. 9, 140, 142, 158, 161, 313
Matejka, Viktor **183,** 194, 298, **306**
Matisse, Henri 199
Maulbertsch, Franz Anton 204, 224
Meir, Golda 255, 256
Mell, Max **18, 306**
Metternich, Klemens, Prince 165
Meyboden, Hans **174, 175, 306**
Michelangelo Buonarroti 10, 195, 231, 242
Mies van der Rohe, Ludwig 215
Modigliani, Amedeo 197
Moll, Anna (formerly Schindler) 40, 45, 51, 264n.
Moll, Carl 9, 150, **155,** 282n., **307**
Möller, Lise-Lotte 250
Moore, Henry 248
More, Sir Thomas 160, 283n.
Morrison, Herbert 168, 285n.
Motesiczky, Henriette von 9, **213, 307**
Mozart, Wolfgang Amadeus 10, 231, 314
Munch, Edvard 210, 289n.
Munich: 'degenerate art' exhibition 148f., 193, 282n., 314
Munnings, Sir Alfred 228, 291n.
Mussolini, Benito 143, 163

Nagy, Imre 222
Needham, Joseph **160,** 161, **162, 307**
Nemes, Marcel von 278n.
Nestroy, Johann 195
Neue Freie Presse (newspaper) 156
Neumeyer, Alfred 9, **176, 307**
Neurath, Walter **232, 233, 234, 307**
News Chronicle 165
Newton, Isaac 10
New York: Metropolitan Opera 87
Nicholas II (Tsar) 278n.

Nirenstein-Kallir, Otto 136, 184, 280n., 287n.

Ochs, Siegfried 53, 58, 61, 63, 268n., 269n.
Ossietsky, Carl von 154, 282n.
Overton, Richard 160, 283n.

Palkovská, Olda, *see* Kokoschka, Olda
Palkovsky, Dr 168, 283n.
Parma, Prince of 60
Pascin, Jules 279n.
Pasternak, Boris 228, 234
Patočka, Emil 267n.
Paul VI (Pope) 246, 247
Pearlman, Henry 197, 199, 287n.
Penrose, Roland 248
Pfitzner, Hans 58, 61, 65, 269n., 270n.
Picasso, Pablo 211, 215, 248
Piper Verlag (publisher) 36
Plaut, James S. 10, **193, 308**
Plesch, Dr 197, 287n.
Pollock, Jackson 241f., 293n.
Poncet, François 221, 290n.
Posse, Hans 88, 220
Pound, Ezra 244, 294n.
Prager Tagblatt (newspaper) 140, 141, 142, 144, 281n.
Prussian Academy of Arts 133, 141

Raab, Julius 223, 290n.
Rabatet, Dr 207, 208
Rankl, Karl 184
Rathenau, Ernst 229, 230, 231f., 240, 244, 292n., 313
Ray, Marcel **194, 308**
Read, Herbert 9, **153, 170, 171,** 246, **308**
Reidemeister, Leopold 240, 293n.
Reinach, Salomon 138
Reinhold, Ernst 44, 266n.
Reinold, Wilhelm 292n.
Rilke, Rainer Maria 71
Ring, Grete 128, 208, 279n., 289n., 299
Rockefeller, David J. 199, 288n.
Rosé, Justine 46, 267n.
Rosenheim, Edith 78, 82, 83, 142, 273n.
Rosenlew, Alice, *see* Lahmann, Alice
Rosenlew, Marion **238,** 294n., 303, **308**
Rosenlew, Nils 217, 303
Rostropovich, Mstislav 255
Rothenstein, Sir John 157
Rouault, Georges 226
Routledge, Katherine 277n.
Rowohlt, Ernst 36, 137, 281n.

Sachsl, Edith 137, 281n.
Saint Gaudens, Homer **151, 308**
Salzburg: School of Seeing 10, 209, 210f., 216, 228f., 229f., 236, 238, 241, 289n., 314, *pls. 17, 18*
Sanders, Emma Veronika 23, 264n.
Sauerlandt, Max 253, 268n., 295n.
Schahlecker, Fritz **180,** 286n.
Schiele, Egon 287n.

319